THE ORIGINS OF
SELF-CONSCIOUSNESS

IN *THE SECRET DOCTRINE*

Other Theosophy Trust Books

Wisdom in Action
Essays on the Spiritual Life
by Raghavan Iyer

The Dawning of Wisdom
Essays on Walking the Path
by Raghavan Iyer

Teachers of the Eternal Doctrine
From Tsong-Ka-Pa to Nostradamus
by Elton Hall

Symbols of the Eternal Doctrine
From Shamballa to Paradise
by Helen Valborg

The Key to Theosophy
An Exposition of the
Ethics, Science, and Philosophy
by H. P. Blavatsky

Evolution and Intelligent Design
in *The Secret Doctrine*
The Synthesis of Science, Religion and Philosophy
by H.P. Blavatsky
compiled by The Editorial Board of Theosophy Trust

The Origins of Self-Consciousness

in *The Secret Doctrine*

By

H. P. Blavatsky

Compiled by
The Editorial Board of Theosophy Trust

Theosophy Trust Books
Washington, D.C.

The Origins of Self-Consciousness
in *The Secret Doctrine*

Theosophy Trust books may be ordered through Amazon.com and other booksellers, or by visiting:

http://www.theosophytrust.org/online_books.php

ISBN 978-0-9793205-4-5
ISBN 0-9793205-4-2

Library of Congress Control Number 2008942725

Printed in the United States of America

Dedicated to

all those students of Theosophy who find

The Secret Doctrine daunting

but whose desire to learn from it

yet remains undaunted

CONTENTS

INTRODUCTION

Theosophy is the English name given to the current expression of the Eternal Teaching; in Sanskrit, it is called the *sanatana dharma*; in Greek, it is *theosophia*. In any language, it is the knowledge and wisdom that underlie the universe, which has always existed but which becomes manifest as human awareness is prepared for it. All the great religious traditions, past and present, have drawn this wisdom from the same well, and all mirror more or less its vast content. Like ocean waves breaking upon a shore, some of this Teaching is as apparent as it is true, but, like the ocean whose depths even now have not been fully explored, much is hidden—occult—beyond the shore's watery horizon. A more public awareness of Theosophy—the expression we have today—emerged in the latter quarter of the Nineteenth Century because human understanding was ready to give it fair consideration, and because it was needed to counter tendencies in human thought that threatened to bury it in misunderstanding, confusion and delusion.

In the West, and then across the world as imperial civilization intruded into Africa, the Americas and Asia, the rise of theoretical and empirical science opened the doors of understanding human beings and the universe in which they live. Though Copernicus challenged the absolute authority of religious institutions to decree the nature of the world, the rise of experimental and theoretical science in the Seventeenth Century launched a tidal wave of discovery that has continued down to the present and promises to continue without end. This breakthrough liberated human consciousness to reconsider everything humans thought they knew about themselves and the world. As with all new opportunities, the possibility of creating new forms of ignorance arose with that of gaining new understanding.

Both theoretical and empirical science flourished in the Nineteenth Century, helping to make possible the emergence of Theosophy as we know it. But a shadow also emerged—lifeless materialism—from two different sources. Titanic thinkers like Sir Isaac Newton showed that it was possible to learn a great deal about the physical world without having to invoke some idea of God as part of the explanation. Curiously though, Newton himself thought that he was showing how God operated the universe, but his *Principia* explained gravity without including Deity in the equations.

The second source was an analytic empirical method that provided stunning results, reducing complex matters—objects, for example, and later, energies—to their simplest components to understand how they are built up out of them. The discovery of elements, and then atoms, and the joining of electrical phenomena and magnetic phenomena into one set of equations, were triumphs of human understanding that would have boggled earlier minds. But the dark shadow of this method was a reductionism that was soon converted into a metaphysical view of the nature of reality. The success in understanding the material world became an ontological commitment to the view that the material world, alone, exists. Had the profound exploration of consciousness found in ancient Hindu and Buddhist texts been better understood in the West, this unjustified leap from method to worldview might not have occurred. But it did, and it obscured any deeper understanding of consciousness itself, in part through not considering it at all for some time, and then by addressing it only by reducing conscious states to brain states. From another standpoint, this view held that subjectivity could be reduced to objectivity, a philosophical blunder that only in the last few decades has been tentatively explored by philosophers.

Theosophy, the Wisdom Religion, teaches that the Eternal Doctrine is never completely lost in the world. There are those who, having gone deep into the ocean of wisdom, maintain that knowledge, which, indeed, is writ into the very nature of the cosmos. Called Masters and Mahatmas ("Great Souls"), they share that wisdom as it is possible to do so—given the conditions that humans make for themselves—sometimes by inspiring a lone voice, sometimes by affecting the mind set of an age, sometimes through movements, communities and cultures open to spiritual understanding.

By the latter part of the Nineteenth Century, a Maha-Yogin of such extraordinary wisdom and insight that he is known simply as the Maha Chohan (and of whom another Mahatma once wrote), ". . . to whom the past, present and future lie like an open book," declared in 1881: "It is time that theosophy should enter the arena."

Guided by these great beings, Helena P. Blavatsky founded the Theosophical Society in 1875 and published *The Secret Doctrine* in two volumes in 1888. The selections that comprise this book, *The Origins of Self-Consciousness*, are drawn from that great work. Using ancient texts as well as works by then-contemporary scientists and thinkers, she sought to counter the dark and destructive shadow of materialism by explaining the vast range and depth of Theosophy in a contemporary idiom. As she herself states, there are presently limitations of language and thought that prevent saying everything, but much can be said that can be understood by the earnest student of the subject.

As she makes clear early in *The Secret Doctrine*, the foundation of all Theosophical Teaching consists of two fundamental ideas: karma and reincarnation. And the whole of the two volumes seeks to show how spirit and matter lie on a continuum. They are not two different substances, as Descartes thought, but necessarily intermingle at every point and on every level of the cosmos. Spirit manifests as consciousness in matter, but how it manifests depends upon the nature of the matter present. It is only in the human being that consciousness can emerge as self-consciousness, and so the human being is the pivot between unconscious nature and divine spiritual reality. Given the two fundamental ideas of karma and reincarnation, the whole of existence is evolving toward this state of self-consciousness and beyond it to those states never fully characterized though pointed to by honoring the Mahatmas and by using terms like 'Enlightenment.' And beyond that? As the Buddha said, some questions do not tend towards edification. Our answers to this question will always be woefully inadequate to the point of simply being wrong.

The cosmos is presented as a vast hierarchy of unfoldment as matter evolves into support for more explicit and higher degrees of consciousness, and spirit moves into, indeed impels, that evolution. The whole of cosmic history, going back much further than current estimates of the age of the universe (which is only the age of the material universe as we presently understand it), is one long involution into consciousness and matter, variously manifested over time, and a gradual evolution of consciousness into ultimate realization.

Such ideas were stunning to many people in the late Nineteenth Century. In contemporary language, Helena Blavatsky was "pushing the envelope" as far as possible. To a reductionistic and materialistic way of thinking, such ideas were just too far-fetched to be taken seriously by the scientific and philosophic thinkers of her time. At the time, the atom was hardly understood, subatomic particles had not proliferated in cloud chambers and mighty accelerators, and quarks could not have been conceptualized, much less other dimensions or the relativity of space and time. But as the Twentieth Century drew to a close, a view such as that presented by Helena Blavatsky seems less contrary to the discoveries of empirical science. We have watched the concept of matter be reduced to a quark-infested sea and the vacuum of supposedly empty space become rife with virtual particles. Perhaps today we are in a better position to ask, "Just what is matter?" for it certainly is not the hard stuff of earlier materialistic conceptions. Indeed, "common sense," which is often little more than traditional prejudices, has abandoned us as we struggle to absorb the views of contemporary scientific cosmologists, including Einstein's theories, which are already a century old.

Consciousness, declared in the last hundred years to be a mere subjective experience of matter, has not become any more pliable to reductionist materialists. The empirical studies of subjective human experiences that led William James to assert that experiences of the transcendental are real to consciousness and to refrain from judging their ontological merit, gave way to Sigmund Freud's psychological theories, now seen to be grounded on rather thin evidence. The failure to get to the heart of the nature of consciousness is reflected in the ramification of schools of thought in the Twentieth Century. With the reaffirmed realization that subjective states do not provide objective data, and that objective experiments do not capture their reality, we are only now beginning to explore anew the nature of consciousness, and of consciousness in matter. His Holiness The Dalai Lama, spiritual leader of Tibetan Buddhism, has led the way in bringing spiritual practitioners together with forward-thinking scientists to see how subjective conscious states, including meditation, might be explored in ways comprehensible to good science. His keen appreciation of Theosophical Teachings is widely known.

If the nature of matter has turned out to be elusive, the nature of consciousness is even more subtle and complex. As Helena Blavatsky made clear, as the universe unfolds, matter becomes increasingly dense, until we reach the present degree of materiality. Similarly, as spirit involves itself in matter (recall that both lie on a continuum), its manifestations also become more articulate, until their evolution and involution meet in the human being. ('Human being' refers, of course, to the members of present humanity but does not exclude parallel manifestations of self-consciousness elsewhere in the cosmos; 'human being' is not defined by a particular bodily form but by self-consciousness itself. Whatever has self-consciousness is 'human' in this sense.) Given the fundamental principles of karma and reincarnation, actions result in precise reactions—cause and effect—on every level, from the physical to the spiritual. In a self-conscious being, those actions and reactions become subject to choices regarding how we respond to circumstances that we have generated in the past, perhaps many lives ago, and how we direct our awareness into the future. At the human level, consciousness begins to directly participate in self-guided evolution. Our semi-conscious awareness of this fact is reflected in the now common view that humanity holds its future growth or destruction in its own hands.

Any attempt to explain the mysterious connections between consciousness and matter, and self-consciousness in particular, becomes increasingly complex. Because all levels of relative reality are ever-present, each human being embodies the entire cosmic hierarchy: a microcosm of the macrocosm, to use an insightful Renaissance expression. Besides the physical human body, there are the dynamic structural plan of that body (called the 'astral body'), the desire nature, the life-force that permeates all living creatures, consciousness involved in sense perception and practical operations, consciousness capable of universal thought and awareness, and pure consciousness manifest in pristine spiritual intuition. Above these six principles of human nature broods the luminous spirit called the Atman. Many people are seldom aware of anything more in themselves than the first five of these principles, although many do have fleeting intuitive glimpses of universal understanding, often as transcendent experiences which cannot be sustained. Because understanding cannot be separated from experience, and experience cannot be divorced from the way we live, think, feel and have our being, various spiritual traditions have offered practices to nurture these inner awakenings to our higher natures, to a greater awareness of spiritual reality. Theosophy connects together how we live our lives, what we think and how we focus our attention, the bold exploration of our inner natures, how we react to what comes to us (karma), and how we can build depth of awareness across lifetimes, with Enlightenment.

Spirit and matter are mutually involved at every level of manifest existence; therefore, value is as much a part of the cosmos as so-called objective reality. Theosophy, therefore, connects ethics and action, which, Theosophically, includes not only bodily acts on the physical plane, but even more causally, the occurrence of thoughts and feelings. Where we are ignorant of all the dimensions of our circumstances— and hence are short of Enlightenment — our motive for 'action' is limited to the attempt to alter our individual karmic trajectory and future incarnations.

The selections from *The Secret Doctrine* in this book are gathered with a focus on the consciousness exhibited in Nature, its origin and destiny, and, in particular, on human self-consciousness. This book therefore explores one vital current in the Ocean of Wisdom that is Theosophy. A careful reading will expand and alter one's understanding of consciousness and of one's place in the greater scheme of things.

Raghavan Iyer, the great spiritual Teacher who gave the Teachings of Theosophy to many thousands of students around the world in the second half of the Twentieth Century through the incomparable *HERMES* Lead articles, explained the origin and nature of human consciousness in the following luminous words:

The *Voice of the Silence* teaches: "Shun ignorance, and likewise shun illusion. Avert thy face from world deceptions: mistrust thy senses; they are false. But within thy body—the shrine of thy sensations, seek in the Impersonal for the 'Eternal Man'; and having sought him out, look inward: thou art Buddha." Tragically, the divine origin of human consciousness is all too often forgotten by individuals who permit themselves to become entrapped in "world deceptions". Just as people in a room with artificial light forget the light of the sun, consciousness, when it is focused through a lucid zone that points in the realm of externals in one direction, is in the very activity of awareness shutting off a larger consciousness. Human beings reinforce each other in assigning reality to the visible tip of the whole of life, to that which is maintained and activated by words, names and desires which have public criteria of recognition that can be fulfilled on the plane of external events. On the other hand, an individual who senses the rays of the Spiritual Sun, enfolded in the blackness of the midnight sky, comes closer to wisdom. Participating in the reflections of lesser lights, while retaining an inward reverence for the cosmic ocean of light, is living within the moment with a calm awareness of eternity. *The Secret Doctrine* suggests that what is called light is a shadowy illusion and that beyond what are normally called light and darkness there is noumenal Darkness which is eternally radiant. (From Raghavan Iyer's article, "The Eye of Self-Existence," HERMES, 1989)

Elton Hall, Professor Emeritus
Boise, Idaho
October 2008

Editor's Note

The idea for this book came from Raghavan Iyer. During his long years spent as the primary inspiration for the Theosophical Movement in the last century, Professor Iyer gave many discourses – both public and private – upon the many themes treated in *The Secret Doctrine* (referred to by him as "the textbook of the 21st Century"). These discourses were delivered through Sunday evening lectures on Theosophy in Santa Barbara; during Wednesday evening Study Classes at the United Lodge of Theosophists in Santa Barbara, California; in private meetings with members of the Pythagorean Sangha; and through the many "Lead" articles he authored and published in the golden journal, *Hermes*.

Professor Iyer spoke on many occasions about the need to make *The Secret Doctrine* by Helena P. Blavatsky (HPB) more accessible to students of the Wisdom Religion, as the abstruse nature of its thought was a deterrent for many students because of the systematic study needed to piece together a coherent and comprehansive picture of cosmic and human evolution. Added to the difficulty of the ideas was the presence of many terms – of Sanskrit, Greek, Hebrew and Tibetan origins (to mention just a few) – that were either unfamiliar to or simply misunderstood by most Western students. On top of these difficulties was the somewhat forbidding construction of the book, which Prof. Iyer attempted to mitigate by creating pamphlets that extracted passages relevant to particular themes in *The Secret Doctrine*. These pamphlets comprised the "Secret Doctrine Series" and bore titles such as Space, Motion, Meta-Geometry, Meta-Chemistry, and the like. They were used in Study Classes in the Santa Barbara ULT through the 1970's and 1980's, and many students found them particularly helpful in their efforts to isolate and focus upon particular themes.

It is in this sense that this volume and its predecessor – *Evolution and Intelligent Design in The Secret Doctrine* – continue Prof. Iyer's original effort to make *The Secret Doctrine* more accessible to students of the Theosophical Philosophy by selecting from that work the passages that are most pertinent to the subject of the book, presenting them in a condensed, sequential order, and linking them through a dedicated Glossary and Index. The end result is, we hope, a useful workbook that will enable the student to get to the heart of the subject with minimum hindrance and maximum focus.

The passages in this book are taken directly from the original work of 1887 without changing any of HPB's words. What is different about this volume from the original are the treatment of variations in spelling of common terms, the uses of italics, and the correction of some obvious punctuation errors. HPB remarked in several letters to her colleagues about the inconsistencies of spelling, punctuation, and formatting in the original printed version as it came from the typesetter/printer and how she wished she could correct the many errors that had crept into the book but was unable to do so because of constraints of time and other duties. One will find through a close examination of *The Secret Doctrine* that there are many instances of what can only be called inconsistencies in spelling. These variations are to be distinguished from her way of signifying universal principles by the use of all caps – e.g., 'MONAD', as distinguished from the individualized 'Monad', used when referring to the "human Monad," and 'monad', in the case of the "mineral monad." One notices inconsistencies in the spelling of many common terms in the original. For example, one will find *Ahankara* and *Ahankâra*; *Avalokitâswara*, *Avalokiteswara*, and *Avalôkitêswara*; *Kabeiri* and *Kabiri*; *Sastra* and *Shastra*; etc. Some of these variations can be explained as simply the differences between various English transliterations and in original spellings, but in most cases, there is no good reason to retain these variations, as there is simply no need to perpetuate another level of complexity that may stimulate confusion rather than enhance clarity. Needless variations in spelling also give bad headaches to an indexer who attempts to bring order and systematic treatment to the work and to provide a usable and logically structured index.

To rectify this problem of spelling, we have elected to use the most common form of spelling of the term and change the other usages to that one form. For example, we elected to use Avalôkitêswara as the preferred spelling for that term, as it comes closest to the original Sanskrit. For those who desire to see nothing changed from the original work, it would be best if they continue to use the original 1887 work or its photographic reproduction, which remains in print.

While retaining the fairly obvious uses of italics by HPB for emphasis of certain terms or ideas or passages, we have sought to simplify the formatting rule by applying italics to the following: 1) non-English terms that are not personal names of beings; and 2) that have not yet been adopted into common usage. For example, Brahma and Brahmâ both are non-English names of Hindu deities and are therefore not italicized; but

Parabrahm denotes – according to the *Theosophical Glossary* - " 'Beyond Brahmâ', literally. . . .The impersonal and nameless universal Principle." The key to this is that *Parabrahm* refers to an "impersonal" principle and not a personal deity; therefore, it is italicized. Another more complex illustration of this rule is the treatment of the "*Kumâras*", a "class" of divine beings involved with the origins of Humanity, and which is therefore italicized. But particular members of this class – such as Skanda-Kumâra and Sanat-Kumâra – are NOT italicized because those are personifications denoting particular beings, so to speak. However, when Sanat-Sujâta – the chief of the *Kumâras* – is called *Ambhamsi*, that word *is* italicized, because it refers to the impersonal "Waters", another name of the "Great Deep," the primordial Waters of space or Chaos.

The names of texts or books – like the *Vishnu Purâna* or the *Rig Veda* or the *Bhagavad Gîtâ* – are also italicized. The book known as *Genesis* is also italicized, even though it is included in the Christian *Bible*. Terms denoting abstract conceptions – such as *Manvantaras* or *Maha-Pralaya* – are also italicized. Non-English words that have become common in English – e.g. karma – are not italicized, nor are English adjective forms, such as Puranic or manvantaric.

We have done our best to consistently apply these rules for italics throughout this work; however, there are sure to be mistakes and inconsistencies. We would be most grateful if the reader would send a note to editor@theosophytrust.org alerting us to errors when found.

Lastly, the Glossary and the Index to this book deserve special mention. The Glossary was developed around the terms listed in the Index, itself developed by a very careful analysis of the terms used in the selections chosen for the book. Every term thought to be of special importance for the serious student to know and analyze was chosen for listing in the Index; all of the terms thus found in the Index were then matched to HPB's original *Theosophical Glossary*. Every term found to occur in both the Index to this book and in HPB's *Glossary* was included in this book's Glossary. Thus, the student has an extraordinarily valuable research tool at his/her disposal to aid in the comprehension of that most mysterious of topics, the origins of self-consciousness in man. If this book serves that purpose for students, it will have been worth the effort.

Editor, Theosophy Trust Books

THE FUNDAMENTAL IDENTITY
OF MAN WITH BEING

The Secret Doctrine teaches:

The fundamental identity of all Souls with the Universal Over-Soul, the latter being itself an aspect of the Unknown Root, and the obligatory pilgrimage for every Soul – a spark of the former – through the Cycle of Incarnation (or "Necessity") in accordance with Cyclic and Karmic law, during the whole term. In other words, no purely spiritual *Buddhi* (divine Soul) can have an independent (conscious) existence before the spark which issued from the pure Essence of the Universal Sixth principle – or the OVER-SOUL – has (a) passed through every elemental form of the phenomenal world of that *Manvantara*, and (b) acquired individuality, first by natural impulse, and then by self-induced and self-devised efforts (checked by its Karma), thus ascending through all the degrees of intelligence, from the lowest to the highest *Manas*, from mineral and plant, up to the holiest archangel (*Dhyani-Buddha*). The pivotal doctrine of the Esoteric philosophy admits no privileges or special gifts in man, save those won by his own Ego through personal effort and merit throughout a long series of metempsychoses and reincarnations. This is why the Hindus say that the Universe is Brahma and Brahmâ, for Brahma is in every atom of the universe, the six principles in Nature being all the outcome – the variously differentiated aspects – of the SEVENTH and ONE, the only reality in the Universe whether Cosmical or micro-cosmical, and also why the permutations (psychic, spiritual and physical), on the plane of manifestation and form, of the sixth (Brahmâ, the vehicle of Brahma) are viewed by metaphysical antiphrasis as illusive and Mayavic. For although the root of every atom individually and of every form collectively, is that seventh principle or the one Reality, still, in its manifested phenomenal and temporary appearance, it is no better than an evanescent illusion of our senses. (See, for clearer definition, Addendum "Gods, Monads and Atoms," and also "Theophania," "Bodhisatvas and Reincarnation," etc., etc.)"

SD, i 17-18

1

BEING AND NON-BEING

STANZA I (Continued)

7. THE CAUSES OF EXISTENCE HAD BEEN DONE AWAY WITH (a); THE VISIBLE THAT WAS, AND THE INVISIBLE THAT IS, RESTED IN ETERNAL NON-BEING, THE ONE BEING (b).

(a) "The Causes of Existence" mean not only the physical causes known to science, but the metaphysical causes, the chief of which is the desire to exist, an outcome of *Nidana* and *Maya*. This desire for a sentient life shows itself in everything, from an atom to a sun, and is a reflection of the Divine Thought propelled into objective existence, into a law that the Universe should exist. According to esoteric teaching, the real cause of that supposed desire, and of all existence, remains for ever hidden, and its first emanations are the most complete abstractions mind can conceive. These abstractions must of necessity be postulated as the cause of the material Universe which presents itself to the senses and intellect, and they underlie the secondary and subordinate powers of Nature, which, anthropomorphized, have been worshipped as God and gods by the common herd of every age. It is impossible to conceive anything without a cause; the attempt to do so makes the mind a blank.

This is virtually the condition to which the mind must come at last when we try to trace back the chain of causes and effects, but both science and religion jump to this condition of blankness much more quickly than is necessary, for they ignore the metaphysical abstractions which are the only conceivable cause of physical concretions. These abstractions become more and more concrete as they approach our plane of existence, until finally they phenomenalise in the form of the material Universe, by a process of conversion of metaphysics into physics, analogous to that by which steam can be condensed into water, and the water frozen into ice.

2

(*b*) The idea of Eternal Non-Being, which is the One Being, will appear a paradox to anyone who does not remember that we limit our ideas of being to our present consciousness of existence, making it a specific, instead of a generic term. An unborn infant, could it think in our acceptation of that term, would necessarily limit its conception of being, in a similar manner, to the intrauterine life which alone it knows, and were it to endeavour to express to its consciousness the idea of life after birth (death to it), it would, in the absence of data to go upon, and of faculties to comprehend such data, probably express that life as "Non-Being which is Real Being." In our case the One Being is the noumenon of all the noumena which we know must underlie phenomena, and give them whatever shadow of reality they possess, but which we have not the senses or the intellect to cognize at present. The impalpable atoms of gold scattered through the substance of a ton of auriferous quartz may be imperceptible to the naked eye of the miner, yet he knows that they are not only present there but that they alone give his quartz any appreciable value, and this relation of the gold to the quartz may faintly shadow forth that of the noumenon to the phenomenon. But the miner knows what the gold will look like when extracted from the quartz, whereas the common mortal can form no conception of the reality of things separated from the *Maya* which veils them, and in which they are hidden. Alone the Initiate, rich with the lore acquired by numberless generations of his predecessors, directs the "Eye of Dangma" toward the essence of things in which no *Maya* can have any influence. It is here that the teachings of esoteric philosophy in relation to the *Nidanas* and the Four Truths become of the greatest importance, but they are secret."

SD, i 44–45

ALAYA, THE UNIVERSAL SOUL

STANZA I (Continued)

9. BUT WHERE WAS THE DANGMA WHEN THE ALAYA OF THE UNIVERSE (*Soul as the basis of all, Anima Mundi*) WAS IN PARAMARTHA (*a*) (*Absolute Being and Consciousness which are Absolute Non-Being and Unconsciousness*) AND THE GREAT WHEEL WAS ANUPADAKA (*b*)?

(*a*) Here we have before us the subject of centuries of scholastic disputations. The two terms 'Alaya' and 'Paramârtha' have been the causes of dividing schools and splitting the truth into more different aspects than any other mystic terms. *Alaya* is literally the "Soul of the World" or *Anima Mundi*, the "Over-Soul" of Emerson, and according to esoteric teaching it changes periodically its nature. *Alaya*, though eternal and changeless in its inner essence on the planes which are unreachable by either men or Cosmic Gods (*Dhyani Buddhas*), alters during the active life period with respect to the lower planes, ours included. During that time not only the *Dhyani-Buddhas* are one with *Alaya* in Soul and Essence, but even the man strong in the Yoga (mystic meditation) "is able to merge his soul with it" (Aryasanga, the *Bumapa* school). This is not Nirvana, but a condition next to it. Hence the disagreement. Thus, while the *Yogâchâryas* (of the *Mahâyânâ* school) say that *Alaya* is the personification of the Voidness, and yet *Alaya* (*Nyingpo* and *Tsang* in Tibetan) is the basis of every visible and invisible thing, and that, though it is eternal and immutable in its essence, it reflects itself in every object of the Universe "like the moon in clear tranquil water"; other schools dispute the statement. The same for *Paramârtha*: the *Yogâchâryas* interpret the term as that which is also dependent upon other things (*paratantra*), and the *Madhyamikas* say that *Paramârtha* is limited to *Paranishpanna* or absolute perfection; i.e., in the exposition of these "two truths" (out of four), the former believe and maintain that (on this plane, at any rate) there exists only *Samvritisatya* or relative truth, and the latter teach the existence of *Paramârthasatya*, the "absolute truth."* "No Arhat, oh mendicants, can reach absolute knowledge before he becomes one with *Paranirvana*. *Parikalpita* and *Paratantra* are his two great enemies" (Aphorisms of the Bodhisattvas). *Parikalpita* (in Tibetan *Kun-ttag*) is error, made by those unable to realize the emptiness and illusionary nature of all, who believe something to exist which does not – e.g., the Non-Ego. And *Paratantra* is that, whatever it is, which exists only through a dependent or causal connexion, and which has to disappear as soon as the cause from which it proceeds is removed – e.g., the light of a wick. Destroy or extinguish it, and light disappears.

Esoteric philosophy teaches that everything lives and is conscious, but not that all life and consciousness are similar to those of human or even animal beings. Life we look upon as "the one form of existence," manifesting in what is called matter, or, as in man, what, incorrectly separating them, we name Spirit, Soul and Matter. Matter is the vehicle for the manifestation of soul on this plane of existence, and soul is the vehicle on a higher plane for the manifestation of spirit, and these three are a trinity synthesized by Life, which pervades them all. The idea of universal life is one of those ancient conceptions which are returning to the human mind in this century, as a consequence of its liberation from anthropomorphic theology. Science, it is true, contents itself with tracing or postulating the signs of universal life, and has not yet been bold enough even to whisper *"Anima Mundi!"* The idea of "crystalline life," now familiar to science, would have been scouted half a century ago. Botanists are now searching for the nerves of plants, not that they suppose that plants can feel or think as animals do, but because they believe that some structure, bearing the same relation functionally to plant life that nerves bear to animal life, is necessary to explain vegetable growth and nutrition. It hardly seems possible that science can disguise from itself much longer, by the mere use of terms such as

---

* *"Paramârtha"* is self-consciousness in Sanskrit, *Svasamvedana*, or the "self-analysing reflection" – from two words, *parama* (above everything) and *artha* (comprehension), *Satya* meaning absolute true being, or *Esse*. In Tibetan *Paramârthasatya* is *Dondampaidenpa*. The opposite of this absolute reality, or actuality, is *Samvritisatya* – the relative truth only – "*Samvriti*" meaning "false conception" and being the origin of illusion, *Maya*; in Tibetan *Kundzabchi-denpa*, "illusion-creating appearance."

"force" and "energy," the fact that things that have life are living things, whether they be atoms or planets.

But what is the belief of the inner esoteric Schools? the reader may ask. What are the doctrines taught on this subject by the Esoteric "Buddhists"? With them *"Alaya"* has a double and even a triple meaning. In the *Yogâchârya* system of the contemplative *Mahâyânâ* school, *Alaya* is both the Universal Soul (*Anima Mundi*) and the Self of a progressed adept. "He who is strong in the Yoga can introduce at will his *Alaya* by means of meditation into the true Nature of Existence." The *"Alaya* has an absolute eternal existence," says Aryâsanga – the rival of Nagârjuna.* In one sense it is *Pradhâna*, which is explained in *Vishnu Purâna* as: "that which is the unevolved cause, is emphatically called by the most eminent sages *Pradhâna*, original base, which is subtile *Prakriti*, viz., that which is eternal, and which at once is (or comprehends) what is and what is not, or is mere process." *'Prakriti'*, however, is an incorrect word, and *Alaya* would explain it better, for *Prakriti* is not the "uncognizable Brahma." † It is a mistake of those who know nothing of the Universality of the Occult doctrines from the very cradle of the human races, and especially so of those scholars who reject the very idea of a "primordial revelation," to teach that the *Anima Mundi*, the One Life or "Universal Soul," was made known only by Anaxagoras, or during his age. This philosopher brought the teaching forward simply to oppose the too materialistic conceptions on Cosmogony of Democritus, based on his exoteric theory of *blindly* driven atoms. Anaxagoras of Clazomene was not its inventor but only its propagator, as also was Plato. That which he called Mundane

---

* Aryasanga was a pre-Christian Adept and founder of a Buddhist esoteric school, though Csoma di Körös places him, for some reasons of his own, in the seventh centure A.D. There was another Aryâsanga, who lived during the first centuries of our era and the Hungarian scholar most probably confuses See Schwegler's *"Handbook of the History of Philosophy"* in Sterling's translation, p. 28.

† "The indiscreet cause which is uniform, and both cause and effect, and which those who are acquainted with first principles call *Pradhâna* and *Prakriti*, is the incognizable Brahma who was before all" (*Vâyu Purâna*); i.e., Brahma does not put forth evolution itself or create, but only exhibits various aspects of itself, one of which is *Prakriti*, an aspect of *Pradhâna*.

Intelligence, the *nous* (νους), the principle that according to his views is absolutely separated and free from matter and acts on design,‡ was called Motion, the ONE LIFE, or *Jivatma*, ages before the year 500 B.C. in India. Only the Aryan philosophers never endowed the principle, which with them is infinite, with the finite "attribute" of "thinking."

This leads the reader naturally to the "Supreme Spirit" of Hegel and the German Transcendentalists as a contrast that it may be useful to point out. The schools of Schelling and Fichte have diverged widely from the primitive archaic conception of an ABSOLUTE principle, and have mirrored only an aspect of the basic idea of the Vedanta. Even the "Absoluter Geist" shadowed forth by von Hartman in his pessimistic philosophy of the Unconscious, while it is, perhaps, the closest approximation made by European speculation to the Hindu Adwaitee Doctrines, similarly falls far short of the reality.

According to Hegel, the "Unconscious" would never have undertaken the vast and laborious task of evolving the Universe, except in the hope of attaining clear Self-consciousness. In this connection it is to be borne in mind that in designating Spirit, which the European Pantheists use as equivalent to *Parabrahm*, as unconscious, they do not attach to that expression of "Spirit" – one employed in the absence of a better to symbolise a profound mystery – the connotation it usually bears.

The "Absolute Consciousness," they tell us, "behind" phenomena, which is only termed unconsciousness in the absence of any element of personality, transcends human conception. Man, unable to form one concept except in terms of empirical phenomena, is powerless from the very constitution of his being to raise the veil that shrouds the majesty of the Absolute. Only the liberated Spirit is able to faintly realise the nature of the source whence it sprung and whither it must eventually return. . . . As the highest *Dhyan Chohan*, however, can but bow in ignorance before the awful mystery of Absolute Being, and since, even in that culmination of conscious existence – "the merging of the individual in the universal consciousness" – to use a phrase of Fichte's – the Finite cannot conceive the Infinite, nor can it apply

---

‡ Finite Self-consciousness, I mean. For how can the absolute attain it otherwise than as simply an aspect, the highest of which known to us is human consciousness?

to it its own standard of mental experiences, how can it be said that the "Unconscious" and the Absolute can have even an instinctive impulse or hope of attaining clear self-consciousness?* A Vedantin would never admit this Hegelian idea, and the Occultist would say that it applies perfectly to the awakened MAHAT, the Universal Mind already projected into the phenomenal world as the first aspect of the changeless ABSOLUTE, but never to the latter. "Spirit and Matter, or *Purusha* and *Prakriti* are but the two primeval aspects of the One and Secondless," we are taught.

The matter-moving *Nous*, the animating Soul, immanent in every atom, manifested in man, latent in the stone, has different degrees of power, and this pantheistic idea of a general Spirit-Soul pervading all Nature is the oldest of all the philosophical notions. Nor was the *Archaeus* a discovery of Paracelsus nor of his pupil Van Helmont, for it is again the same *Archaeus* or "Father-Ether," – the manifested basis and source of the innumerable phenomena of life – localised. The whole series of the numberless speculations of this kind are but variations on this theme, the keynote of which was struck in this primeval Revelation. (See Part II, "Primordial Substance.")"

SD, i 47–52

---

* See Schwegler's *"Handbook of the History of Philosophy"* in Sterling's translation, p. 28.

THE DRAGON AND THE LOGOI

"The "Dragon of Wisdom" is the One, the "*Eka*" (Sanskrit) or "*Saka*. It is curious that Jehovah's name in Hebrew should also be One, *Echod*. "His name is *Echod*", say the Rabbins. The philologists ought to decide which of the two is derived from the other – linguistically and symbolically: surely, not the Sanskrit? The "One" and the Dragon are expressions used by the ancients in connection with their respective *Logoi*. Jehovah – esoterically (as *Elohim*) – is also the Serpent or Dragon that tempted Eve, and the "Dragon" is an old glyph for "Astral Light" (Primordial Principle), "which is the Wisdom of Chaos." Archaic philosophy, recognizing neither Good nor Evil as a fundamental or independent power, but starting from the Absolute ALL (Universal Perfection eternally), traced both through the course of natural evolution to pure Light condensing gradually into form, hence becoming Matter or Evil. It was left with the early and ignorant Christian fathers to degrade the philosophical and highly scientific idea of this emblem (the Dragon) into the absurd superstition called the "Devil." They took it from the later Zoroastrians, who saw devils or the Evil in the Hindu *Devas*, and the word Evil thus became by a double transmutation D'Evil in every tongue (*Diabolos, Diable, Diavolo, Teufel*). But the Pagans have always shown a philosophical discrimination in their symbols. The primitive symbol of the serpent symbolised divine Wisdom and Perfection, and had always stood for psychical Regeneration and Immortality. Hence – Hermes, calling the serpent the most spiritual of all beings; Moses, initiated in the wisdom of Hermes, following suit in *Genesis*; the Gnostic's Serpent with the seven vowels over its head, being the emblem of the seven hierarchies of the Septenary or Planetary Creators. Hence, also, the Hindu serpent Sesha or Ananta, "the Infinite," a name of Vishnu, whose first *Vahan* or vehicle on the primordial waters is this serpent.† Yet they all made a difference between the good and the

---

† Like the *logoi* and the Hierarchies of Powers, however, the "Serpents" have to be distinguished one from the other. *Sesha* or *Ananta*, "the couch of Vishnu," is an

9

bad Serpent (the Astral Light of the Kabalists) – between the former, the embodiment of divine Wisdom in the region of the Spiritual, and the latter, Evil, on the plane of matter.* Jesus accepted the serpent as a synonym of Wisdom, and this formed part of his teaching: "Be ye wise as serpents," he says. "In the beginning, before Mother became Father-Mother, the fiery Dragon moved in the infinitudes alone" (*Book of Sarparajni*). The *Aitareya Brahmana* calls the Earth *Sarparâjni*, "the Serpent Queen," and "the Mother of all that moves." Before our globe became egg-shaped (and the Universe also) "a long trail of Cosmic dust (or fire mist) moved and writhed like a serpent in Space." The "Spirit of God moving on Chaos" was symbolized by every nation in the shape of a fiery serpent breathing fire and light upon the primordial waters, until it had incubated cosmic matter and made it assume the annular shape of a serpent with its tail in its mouth – which symbolises not only Eternity and Infinitude, but also the globular shape of all the bodies formed within the Universe from that fiery mist. The Universe, as well as the Earth and Man, cast off periodically, serpent-like, their old skins, to assume new ones after a time of rest. The serpent is, surely, a not less graceful or a more unpoetical image than the caterpillar and chrysalis from which springs the butterfly, the Greek emblem of *Psyche*, the human soul. The "Dragon" was also the symbol of the *Logos* with the Egyptians, as with the Gnostics. In the "*Book of Hermes*," Pymander, the oldest and the most spiritual of the *Logoi* of the Western Continent, appears to Hermes in the shape of a Fiery Dragon of "Light, Fire, and Flame." Pymander, the "Thought Divine" personified, says: The Light is me, I am the *Nous* (the mind or *Manu*), I am thy God, and I am far older than the human principle which escapes from the shadow ("*Darkness*," or the concealed Deity). I am the germ of thought, the resplendent

---

allegorical abstraction, symbolizing infinite Time in Space, which contains the germ and throws off periodically the efflorescence of this germ, the *manifested* Universe; whereas, the gnostic *Ophis* contained the same triple symbolism in its seven vowels as the One, Three and Seven-syllabled *Oeaohoo* of the Archaic doctrine; i.e., the One Unmanifested *Logos*, the Second manifested, the triangle concreting into the Quaternary or *Tetragrammaton*, and the rays of the latter on the material plane.

* The Astral Light, or the AEther, of the ancient pagans (for the name of Astral Light is quite modern) is Spirit . . . . Matter. Beginning with the pure spiritual plane, it becomes grosser as it descends until it becomes the *Maya* or the tempting and deceitful serpent on our plane.

Word, the *Son* of God. All that thus sees and hears in thee is the *Verbum* of the Master, it is the Thought (*Mahat*) which is God, the Father.[†]

The celestial Ocean, the AEther . . . . is the *Breath* of the Father, the life-giving principle, the *Mother,* the Holy Spirit, ...for these are not separated, and their union is LIFE."

Here we find the unmistakeable echo of the Archaic Secret Doctrine, as now expounded. Only the latter does not place at the head and Evolution of Life "the Father," who comes third and is the "Son of the Mother," but the "Eternal and Ceaseless Breath of the ALL." The *Mahat* (Understanding, Universal Mind, Thought, etc.), before it manifests itself as Brahmâ or Siva, appears as Vishnu, says *Sânkhya Sâra* (p. 16); hence *Mahat* has several aspects, just as the *logos* has. *Mahat* is called the Lord, in the *Primary* Creation, and is, in this sense, Universal Cognition or *Thought Divine,* but, "That *Mahat* which was first produced is (afterwards) called *Ego-ism,* when it is born as "I," that is said to be the *second* Creation" (*Anugîtâ,* ch. xxvi.). And the translator (an able and learned Brahmin, not a European Orientalist) explains in a footnote (6), "i.e., when *Mahat* develops into the feeling of Self-Consciousness – I – then it assumes the name of Egoism," which, translated into our esoteric phraseology, means when *Mahat* is transformed into the human *Manas* (or even that of the finite gods), and becomes *Aham*-ship. Why it is called the *Mahat* of the *Second* creation (or the *ninth,* that of the *Kumâra* in *Vishnu Purâna*) will be explained in Book II. The "Sea of Fire" is then the Super-Astral (i.e., noumenal) Light, the first radiation from the Root, the *Mulaprakriti,* the undifferentiated Cosmic Substance, which becomes *Astral* Matter. It is also called the "Fiery Serpent," as above described. If the student bears in mind that there is but One Universal Element, which is infinite, unborn, and undying, and that all the rest – as in the world of phenomena – are but so many various differentiated aspects and transformations (correlations, they are now called) of that One, from Cosmical down to microcosmical effects, from super-human down to human and sub-human beings,

---

† By "God, the Father," the seventh principle in Man and Kosmos are here unmistakeably meant, this principle being inseparable in its *Esse* and Nature from the seventh Cosmic principle. In one sense it is the *Logos* of the Greeks and the *Avalôkitêswara* of the esoteric Buddhists.

the totality, in short, of objective existence – then the first and chief difficulty will disappear and Occult Cosmology may be mastered.* All the Kabalists and Occultists, Eastern and Western, recognise (*a*) the identity of "Father-Mother" with primordial Æther or Akâsa, (Astral Light)[†], and (*b*) its homogeneity before the evolution of the "Son," cosmically *Fohat*, for it is Cosmic Electricity. "*Fohat* hardens and scatters the seven brothers" (Book III Dzyan), which means that the primordial Electric Entity – for the Eastern Occultists insist that Electricity is an Entity – electrifies into life, and separates primordial stuff or pregenetic matter into atoms, themselves the source of all life and consciousness. "There exists an universal *agent unique* of all forms and of life, that is called *Od*,[‡] *Ob*, and *Aour*, active and passive, positive and negative, like day and night: it is the first light in Creation" (Eliphas Lévi's *Kabala*): the first Light of the primordial *Elohim* – the Adam, "male and female" – or (scientifically) ELECTRICITY AND LIFE."

SD, i 73–76

---

* In the Egyptian as in the Indian theogony there was a *concealed* deity, the ONE, and the creative, androgynous god. Thus Shoo is the god of creation and Osiris is, in his original primary form, the "god whose name is unknown." (See Mariette's *Abydos* II, p. 63, and Vol. III, pp. 413, 414, No. 1122.)

† See next note.

‡ *Od* is the pure life-giving Light, or magnetic fluid; *Ob* the messenger of death used by the sorcerers, the nefarious evil fluid; *Aour* is the synthesis of the two, Astral Light proper. Can the Philologists tell why *Od* – a term used by Reichenbach to denominate the vital fluid – is also a Tibetan word meaning light, brightness, radiancy? It equally means "Sky" in an occult sense. Whence the root of the word? But *Akasa* is not quite *Ether*, but far higher than that, as will be shown.

NO MAN – NO GOD

STANZA V

1. THE PRIMORDIAL SEVEN, THE FIRST SEVEN BREATHS OF THE DRAGON OF WISDOM, PRODUCE IN THEIR TURN FROM THEIR HOLY CIRCUMGYRATING BREATHS THE FIERY WHIRLWIND (*a*).

(*a*) This is, perhaps, the most difficult of all the Stanzas to explain. Its language is comprehensible only to him who is thoroughly versed in Eastern allegory and its purposely obscure phraseology. The question will surely be asked, "Do the Occultists believe in all these 'Builders,' 'Lipika,' and 'Sons of Light' as Entities, or are they merely imageries?" To this the answer is given as plainly: "After due allowance for the imagery of personified Powers, we must admit the existence of these Entities, if we would not reject the existence of spiritual humanity within physical mankind. For the hosts of these Sons of Light and 'Mind-born Sons' of the first manifested Ray of the UNKNOWN ALL, are the very root of spiritual man." Unless we want to believe the unphilosophical dogma of a specially created soul for every human birth – a fresh supply of these pouring in daily, since "Adam" – we have to admit the occult teachings. This will be explained in its place. Let us see, now, what may be the occult meaning of this Stanza.

The Doctrine teaches that, in order to become a divine, fully conscious god – aye, even the highest – the Spiritual primeval INTELLIGENCES must pass through the human stage. And when we say human, this does not apply merely to our terrestrial humanity, but to the mortals that inhabit any world, i.e., to those Intelligences that have reached the appropriate equilibrium between matter and spirit, as we have now, since the middle point of the Fourth Root Race of the Fourth Round was passed. Each Entity must have won for itself the right of becoming divine, through self-experience. Hegel, the great German thinker, must have known or sensed intuitively this truth when saying, as he did, that the Unconscious evolved the Universe only "in the hope of

13

attaining clear self-consciousness," of becoming, in other words, MAN, for this is also the secret meaning of the usual Purânic phrase about Brahmâ being constantly "moved by the desire to create." This explains also the hidden Kabalistic meaning of the saying: "The *Breath* becomes a stone; the stone, a plant; the plant, an animal; the animal, a man; the man, a spirit; and the spirit, a god." The Mind-born Sons, the *Rishis*, the Builders, etc., were all men – of whatever forms and shapes – in other worlds and the preceding *Manvantaras*.

This subject, being so very mystical, is therefore the most difficult to explain in all its details and bearings, since the whole mystery of evolutionary creation is contained in it. A sentence or two in it vividly recalls to mind similar ones in the *Kabala* and the phraseology of the King Psalmist (civ.), as both, when speaking of God, show him making the wind his messenger and his "ministers a flaming fire." But in the Esoteric doctrine it is used figuratively. The "fiery Wind" is the incandescent Cosmic dust which only follows magnetically, as the iron filings follow the magnet, the directing thought of the "Creative Forces." Yet, this cosmic dust is something more, for every atom in the Universe has the potentiality of self-consciousness in it, and is, like the Monads of Leibnitz, a Universe in itself, and *for* itself. *It is an atom and an angel.*

In this connection it should be noted that one of the luminaries of the modern Evolutionist School, Mr. A. R. Wallace, when discussing the inadequacy of "natural selection" as the sole factor in the development of physical man, practically concedes the whole point here discussed. He holds that the evolution of man was directed and furthered by superior Intelligences, whose agency is a necessary factor in the scheme of Nature. But once the operation of these Intelligences is admitted in one place, it is only a logical deduction to extend it still further. No hard and fast line can be drawn."

SD, i 106–107

THE CLASSIFICATION
OF THE MONADS

The Japanese and the Chinese Buddhist ascetics and Initiates are, if possible, even more reticent in giving out their "Knowledge" than are the Hindus.

But the reader must not be allowed to lose sight of the Monads, and must be enlightened as to their nature, as far as permitted, without trespassing upon the highest mysteries, of which the writer does not in any way pretend to know the last or final word.

The Monadic Host may be roughly divided into three great classes:

1. The most developed Monads (the Lunar Gods or "Spirits," called, in India, the *Pitris*), whose function it is to pass in the first Round through the whole triple cycle of the mineral, vegetable, and animal kingdoms in their most ethereal, filmy, and rudimentary forms, in order to clothe themselves in, and assimilate, the nature of the newly formed chain. They are those who first reach the human form (if there can be any form in the realm of the almost subjective) on Globe A in the first Round. It is they, therefore, who lead and represent the human element during the second and third Rounds, and finally evolve their shadows at the beginning of the Fourth Round for the second class, or those who come behind them.

2. Those Monads that are the first to reach the human stage during the three and a half Rounds, and to become men.[*]

---

[*] We are forced to use here the misleading word "Men," and this is a clear proof of how little any European language is adapted to express these subtle distinctions.

It stands to reason that these "Men" did not resemble the men of to-day, either in form or nature. Why then, it may be asked, call them "Men" at all? Because there is no other term in any Western language which approximately conveys the idea intended. The word "Men" at least indicates that these beings were "*MANUS*," thinking entities, however they differed in form and intellection from ourselves.

15

3. The laggards, the Monads which are retarded, and which will not reach, by reason of Karmic impediments, the human stage at all during this cycle or Round, save one exception which will be spoken of elsewhere as already promised.

Now the evolution of the *external* form or body round the *astral* is produced by the terrestrial forces, just as in the case of the lower kingdoms, but the evolution of the internal or real MAN is purely spiritual. It is now no more a passage of the impersonal Monad through many and various forms of matter – endowed at best with instinct and consciousness on quite a different plane – as in the case of external evolution, but a journey of the "pilgrim soul" through various *states* of *not only matter* but Self-consciousness and self-perception, or of *perception* from apperception. (See "Gods, Monads and Atoms.")

The MONAD emerges from its state of spiritual and intellectual unconsciousness, and, skipping the first two planes – too near the ABSOLUTE to permit of any correlation with anything on a lower plane – it gets direct into the plane of Mentality. But there is no plane in the whole universe with a wider margin, or a wider field of action in its almost endless gradations of perceptive and apperceptive qualities, than this plane, which has in its turn an appropriate smaller plane for every "form," from the "mineral" monad up to the time when that monad blossoms forth by evolution into the DIVINE MONAD. But all the time it is still one and the same Monad, differing only in its

---

But in reality they were, in respect of spirituality and intellection, rather "gods" than "Men."

The same difficulty of language is met with in describing the "stages" through which the Monad passes. Metaphysically speaking, it is of course an absurdity to talk of the "development" of a Monad, or to say that *it* becomes "Man." But any attempt to preserve metaphysical accuracy of language in the use of such a tongue as the English would necessitate at least three extra volumes of this work, and would entail an amount of verbal repetition which would be wearisome in the extreme. It stands to reason that a MONAD cannot either progress or develop, or even be affected by the changes of states it passes through. *It is not of this world or plane*, and may be compared only to an indestructible star of divine light and fire, thrown down on to our Earth as a plank of salvation for the personalities in which it indwells. It is for the latter to cling to it; and thus partaking of its divine nature, obtain immortality. Left to itself the Monad will cling to no one; but, like the "plank," be drifted away to another incarnation by the unresting current of evolution.

incarnations, throughout its ever succeeding cycles of partial or total obscuration of spirit, or the partial or total obscuration of matter – two polar antitheses – as it ascends into the realms of mental spirituality, or descends into the depths of materiality.

To return to *"Esoteric Buddhism"*: It is there stated with regard to the enormous period intervening between the mineral epoch on Globe A, and the man epoch, [*] that: "The full development of the mineral epoch on Globe A, prepares the way for the vegetable development, and, as soon as this begins, the mineral life impulse overflows into Globe B. Then, when the vegetable development on Globe A is complete and the animal development begins, the vegetable life impulse overflows to Globe B, and the mineral impulse passes on to Globe C. Then finally comes the human life impulse on Globe A." (*Esoteric Buddhism*, page 49.)

And so it goes on for three Rounds, when it slackens, and finally stops at the threshold of our Globe, at the Fourth Round, because the human period (of the true physical men to be), the seventh, is now reached. This is evident, for as said, " . . . there are processes of evolution which precede the mineral kingdom, and thus a wave of evolution, indeed several waves of evolution, precede the mineral wave in its progress round the spheres" (*ibid.*).

And now we have to quote from another article, "The Mineral Monad" in *"Five Years of Theosophy,"* p. 273 *et seq.*

"There are seven kingdoms. The first group comprises three degrees of elementals, or nascent centres of forces – from the first stage of differentiation of (from) *Mulaprakriti* (or rather *Pradhâna*, primordial homogeneous matter) to its third degree – i.e., from full unconsciousness to semi-perception; the second or higher group embraces the kingdoms from vegetable to man; the mineral kingdom thus forming the central or turning point in the degrees of the "Monadic Essence," considered as an evolving energy. Three stages (sub-physical) on the elemental

---

[*] The term "Man epoch" is here used because of the necessity of giving a name to that fourth kingdom which follows the animal. But in truth the "Man" on Globe A during the First Round is no Man, but only his prototype or dimensionless image from the astral regions.

side; the mineral kingdom; three stages on the objective physical * side – these are the (first or preliminary) seven links of the evolutionary chain."

"Preliminary" because they are preparatory, and though belonging in fact to the natural, they yet would be more correctly described as sub-natural evolution. This process makes a halt in its stages at the Third, at the threshold of the Fourth stage, when it becomes, on the plane of the natural evolution, the first really manward stage, thus forming with the three elemental kingdoms, the ten, the *Sephirothal* number. It is at this point that begins:

"A descent of spirit into matter equivalent to an ascent in physical evolution; a re-ascent from the deepest depths of materiality (the mineral) towards its *status quo ante*, with a corresponding dissipation of concrete organism – up to Nirvana, the vanishing point of differentiated matter." ("*Five Years of Theosophy*," p. 276.)

Therefore it becomes evident why that which is pertinently called in *Esoteric Buddhism* "Wave of Evolution," and mineral-, vegetable-, animal- and man-"impulse," stops at the door of our Globe, at its Fourth cycle or Round. It is at this point that the Cosmic Monad (*Buddhi*) will be wedded to and become the vehicle of the Atmic Ray, i.e., it (*Buddhi*) will awaken to an apperception of it (*Atman*), and thus enter on the first step of a new septenary ladder of evolution, which will lead it eventually to the tenth (counting from the lowest upwards) of the *Sephiroth*al tree, the Crown.

Everything in the Universe follows analogy. "As above, so below"; Man is the microcosm of the Universe. That which takes place on the spiritual plane repeats itself on the Cosmic plane. Concretion follows the lines of abstraction: corresponding to the highest must be the lowest; the material to the spiritual. Thus, corresponding to the *Sephiroth*al Crown (or upper triad) there are the three elemental Kingdoms, which precede the Mineral (see diagram on p. 277 in *Five Years of Theosophy*), and which, using the language of the Kabalists,

---

* "Physical" here means differentiated for cosmical purposes and work; that "physical side," nevertheless, if objective to the apperception of beings from other planes, is yet quite subjective to us on our plane.

answer in the Cosmic differentiation to the worlds of Form and Matter from the Super-Spiritual to the Archetypal.

Now what is a "Monad?" And what relation does it bear to an Atom? The following reply is based upon the explanations given in answer to these questions in the above-cited article: "The Mineral Monad," written by the author.

"None whatever," is answered to the second question, "to the atom or molecule as existing in the scientific conception at present. It can neither be compared with the microscopic organism, once classed among polygastric infusoria, and now regarded as vegetable, and classed among Algae; nor is it quite the *Monas* of the Peripatetics. Physically or constitutionally the mineral monad differs, of course, from the human monad, which is neither physical nor can its constitution be rendered by chemical symbols and elements." In short, as the spiritual Monad is One, Universal, Boundless and Impartite, whose rays, nevertheless, form what we, in our ignorance, call the "Individual Monads" of men, so the Mineral Monad – being at the opposite point of the circle – is also One – and from it proceed the countless physical atoms, which Science is beginning to regard as individualized.

Otherwise how could one account for and explain mathematically the evolutionary and spiral progress of the Four Kingdoms? The "Monad" is the combination of the last two "principles" in man, the 6th and the 7th, and, properly speaking, the term "human monad" applies only to the dual soul (*Atma-Buddhi*), not to its highest spiritual vivifying Principle, *Atma*, alone. But since the Spiritual Soul, if divorced from the latter (*Atma*) could have no existence, no being, it has thus been called . . . . Now the Monadic, or rather Cosmic, Essence (if such a term be permitted) in the mineral, vegetable, and animal, though the same throughout the series of cycles from the lowest elemental up to the *Deva* Kingdom, yet differs in the scale of progression. It would be very misleading to imagine a Monad as a separate Entity trailing its slow way in a distinct path through the lower Kingdoms, and after an incalculable series of transformations flowering into a human being; in short, that the Monad of a Humboldt dates back to the Monad of an atom of horneblende. Instead of saying a "Mineral Monad," the more correct phraseology in physical Science, which differentiates every atom, would of course have been to call it "the Monad manifesting in that form of *Prakriti* called the Mineral Kingdom." The atom, as represented in the ordinary scientific hypothesis, is not a particle of something, animated by a psychic something, destined after aeons to blossom as a man. But it is a concrete manifestation of the Universal Energy which itself has not yet become individualized, a sequential manifestation of the one Universal *Monas*. The ocean (of matter) does not divide into its potential and constituent drops until the sweep of the life impulse reaches the evolutionary stage of man-birth. The tendency towards segregation into individual Monads is gradual, and in the higher animals comes almost to the point. The Peripatetics applied the word *Monas* to the whole Kosmos, in the pantheistic sense, and the Occultists, while accepting this thought for convenience sake, distinguish the progressive stages of the evolution of the concrete from the abstract by terms of which the "Mineral, Vegetable, Animal, (etc.), Monad" are examples. The term merely means that the tidal wave of spiritual evolution is passing through that arc of its circuit. The "Monadic Essence" begins to imperceptibly differentiate towards individual consciousness in the Vegetable Kingdom. As the Monads are uncompounded things, as correctly defined by Leibnitz, it is the spiritual essence which vivifies them in their degrees of differentiation, which properly constitutes the Monad – not the atomic aggregation, which is only the vehicle and the substance through which thrill the lower and the higher degrees of intelligence.

Leibnitz conceived of the Monads as elementary and indestructible units endowed with the power *of giving and receiving* with respect to other units, and thus of determining all spiritual and physical phenomena. It is he who invented the term apperception, which together with nerve- (not perception, but rather) sensation, expresses the state of the Monadic consciousness through all the Kingdoms up to Man.

Thus it may be wrong on strictly metaphysical lines to call *Atma-Buddhi* a MONAD, since in the materialistic view it is dual and therefore compound. But as Matter is Spirit, and *vice versa*; and since the Universe and the Deity which informs it are unthinkable apart from each other, so in the case of *Atma-Buddhi*. The latter being the vehicle of the former, *Buddhi* stands in the same relation to *Atma*, as

Adam Kadmon, the Kabalistic *Logos*, does to *En-Soph*, or *Mulaprakriti* to *Parabrahm*.

A few words more of the Moon.

What, it may be asked, are the "Lunar Monads," just spoken of? The description of the seven classes of *Pitris* will come later, but now some general explanations may be given. It must be plain to everyone that they are Monads, who, having ended their lifecycle on the lunar chain, which is inferior to the terrestrial chain, have incarnated on this one. But there are some further details which may be added, though they border too closely on forbidden ground to be treated of fully. The last word of the mystery is divulged only to the adepts, but it may be stated that our satellite is only the gross body of its invisible principles. Seeing then that there are 7 Earths, so there are 7 Moons, the last one alone being visible; the same for the Sun, whose visible body is called a *Maya*, a reflection, just as man's body is. "The real Sun and the real Moon are as invisible as the real man," says an occult maxim.

And it may be remarked *en passant* that those ancients were not so foolish after all who first started the idea of "the seven moons." For though this conception is now taken solely as an astronomical measure of time, in a very materialised form, yet underlying the husk there can still be recognised the traces of a profoundly philosophical idea.

In reality the Moon is only the satellite of the Earth in one respect, viz., that physically the Moon revolves round the Earth. But in every other respect it is the Earth which is the satellite of the Moon, and not *vice versa*. Startling as the statement may seem it is not without confirmation from scientific knowledge. It is evidenced by the tides, by the cyclic changes in many forms of disease which coincide with the lunar phases; it can be traced in the growth of plants, and is very marked in the phenomena of human gestation and conception. The importance of the Moon and its influence on the Earth were recognized in every ancient religion, notably the Jewish, and have been remarked by many observers of psychical and physical phenomena. But, so far as Science knows, the Earth's action on the Moon is confined to the physical attraction, which causes her to circle in her orbit. And should an objector insist that this fact alone is sufficient evidence that the

Moon is truly the Earth's satellite on other planes of action, one may reply by asking whether a mother, who walks round and round her child's cradle keeping watch over the infant, is the subordinate of her child or dependent upon it, though in one sense she is its satellite, yet she is certainly older and more fully developed than the child she watches.

It is, then, the Moon that plays the largest and most important part, as well in the formation of the Earth itself, as in the peopling thereof with human beings. The "Lunar Monads" or *Pitris*, the ancestors of man, become in reality man himself. They are the "Monads" who enter on the cycle of evolution on Globe A, and who, passing round the chain of planets, evolve the human form as has just been shown. At the beginning of the human stage of the Fourth Round on this Globe, they "ooze out" their astral doubles from the "ape-like" forms which they had evolved in Round III. And it is this subtle, finer form, which serves as the model round which Nature builds physical man. These "Monads" or "divine sparks" are thus the "Lunar" ancestors, the *Pitris* themselves. For these "Lunar Spirits" have to become "Men" in order that their "Monads" may reach a higher plane of activity and self-consciousness, i.e., the plane of the *Manasa-Putras*, those who endow the "senseless" shells, created and informed by the *Pitris*, with "mind" in the latter part of the Third Root Race.

In the same way the "Monads" or Egos of the men of the seventh Round of our Earth, after our own Globes A, B, C, D, *et seq.*, parting with their life energy, will have informed and thereby called to life other *laya* centres destined to live and act on a still higher plane of being – in the same way will the Terrene "Ancestors" create those who will become their superiors.

It now becomes plain that there exists in Nature a triple evolutionary scheme, for the formation of the three *periodical Upadhis*, or rather three separate schemes of evolution, which in our system are inextricably interwoven and interblended at every point. These are the Monadic (or spiritual), the intellectual, and the physical evolutions. These three are the finite aspects or the reflections on the field of Cosmic Illusion of ATMA, the seventh, the ONE REALITY.

1. The Monadic is, as the name implies, concerned with the growth

and development into still higher phases of activity of the Monad in conjunction with:

2. The Intellectual, represented by the *Manasa-Dhyanis* (the Solar *Devas*, or the *Agnishwatta Pitris*) the "givers of intelligence and consciousness" * to man and:

3. The Physical, represented by the *Chhayas* of the lunar *Pitris*, round which Nature has concreted the present physical body. This body serves as the vehicle for the "growth" (to use a misleading word) and the transformations through *Manas* and – owing to the accumulation of experiences – of the finite into the INFINITE, of the transient into the Eternal and Absolute.

Each of these three systems has its own laws, and is ruled and guided by different sets of the highest *Dhyanis* or "*Logoi*." Each is represented in the constitution of man, the Microcosm of the great Macrocosm, and it is the union of these three streams in him which makes him the complex being he now is.

"Nature," the physical evolutionary Power, could never evolve intelligence unaided – she can only create "senseless forms," as will be seen in our "ANTHROPOGENESIS." The "Lunar Monads" cannot progress, for they have not yet had sufficient touch with the forms created by "Nature" to allow of their accumulating experiences through its means. It is the *Manasa-Dhyanis* who fill up the gap, and they represent the evolutionary power of Intelligence and Mind, the link between "Spirit" and "Matter" – in this Round.

Also it must be borne in mind that the Monads which enter upon the evolutionary cycle upon Globe A, in the first Round, are in very different stages of development. Hence the matter becomes somewhat complicated. . . . Let us recapitulate.

The most developed Monads (the lunar) reach the human germ stage in the first Round, become terrestrial, though very ethereal human beings towards the end of the Third Round, remaining on it (the globe) through the "obscuration" period as the seed for future mankind in the Fourth Round, and thus become the pioneers of Humanity at the

---

* *Vide* CONCLUSION in Part II of this Book.

beginning of this, the Fourth Round. Others reach the Human stage only during later Rounds, i.e., in the second, third, or first half of the Fourth Round. And finally the most retarded of all, i.e., those still occupying animal forms after the middle turning point of the Fourth Round – will not become men at all during this Manwantara. They will reach to the verge of humanity only at the close of the seventh Round to be, in their turn, ushered into a new chain after *pralaya* – by older pioneers, the progenitors of humanity, or the Seed-Humanity (*Sishta*), viz., the men who will be at the head of all at the end of these Rounds.

The student hardly needs any further explanation on the part played by the fourth Globe and the fourth Round in the scheme of evolution."

SD, i 173–182

MAN, THE OLDEST SON
OF THE EARTH

"From the preceding diagrams, which are applicable, *mutatis mutandis*, to Rounds, Globes or Races, it will be seen that the fourth member of a series occupies a unique position. Unlike the others, the Fourth has no "sister" Globe on the same plane as itself, and it thus forms the fulcrum of the "balance" represented by the whole chain. It is the sphere of final evolutionary adjustments, the world of Karmic scales, the Hall of Justice, where the balance is struck which determines the future course of the Monad during the remainder of its incarnations in the cycle. And therefore it is, that, after this central turning point has been passed in the Great Cycle – i.e., after the middle point of the Fourth Race in the Fourth Round on our Globe – no more Monads can enter the human kingdom. The door is closed for this Cycle and the balance struck. For were it otherwise – had there been a new soul created for each of the countless milliards of human beings that have passed away, and had there been no reincarnation – it would become difficult indeed to provide room for the disembodied "Spirits," nor could the origin and cause of suffering ever be accounted for. It is the ignorance of the occult tenets and the enforcement of false conceptions under the guise of religious education, which have created materialism and atheism as a protest against the asserted divine order of things.

The only exceptions to the rule just stated are the "dumb races," whose Monads are already within the human stage, in virtue of the fact that these "animals" are later than, and even half descended from man, their last descendants being the anthropoid and other apes. These "human presentments" are in truth only the distorted copies of the early humanity. But this will receive full attention in the next Book.

As the Commentary, broadly rendered, says:

1. "*Every form on earth, and every speck (atom) in Space strives in its efforts towards self-formation to follow the model placed for it in the*

' HEAVENLY MAN.' . . . *Its (the atom's) involution and evolution, its external and internal growth and development, have all one and the same object – man; man, as the highest physical and ultimate form on this earth; the MONAD, in its absolute totality and awakened condition – as the culmination of the divine incarnations on Earth.*"

2. "*The Dhyanis (Pitris) are those who have evolved their BHUTA (doubles) from themselves, which RUPA (form) has become the vehicle of monads (seventh and sixth principles) that had completed their cycle of transmigration in the three preceding Kalpas (Rounds). Then, they (the astral doubles) became the men of the first Human Race of the Round. But they were not complete, and were senseless.*"

This will be explained in the Books that follow. Meanwhile man – or rather his Monad – has existed on the earth from the very beginning of this Round. But, up to our own Fifth Race, the external shapes which covered those divine astral doubles changed and consolidated with every sub-race, the form and physical structure of the fauna changing at the same time, as they had to be adapted to the ever-changing conditions of life on this globe during the geological periods of its formative cycle. And thus shall they go on changing with every Root Race and every chief sub-race down to the last one of the Seventh in this Round.

3. "*The inner, now concealed, man, was then (in the beginnings) the external man. The progeny of the Dhyanis (Pitris), he was 'the son like unto his father.' Like the lotus, whose external shape assumes gradually the form of the model within itself, so did the form of man in the beginning evolve from within without. After the cycle in which man began to procreate his species after the fashion of the present animal kingdom, it became the reverse. The human fœtus follows now in its transformations all the forms that the physical frame of man had assumed throughout the three Kalpas (Rounds) during the tentative efforts at Plastic formation around the monad by senseless, because imperfect, matter, in her blind wanderings. In the present age, the physical embryo is a plant, a reptile, an animal, before it finally becomes man, evolving within himself his own ethereal counterpart, in his turn. In the beginning it was that counterpart (astral man) which, being senseless, got entangled in the meshes of matter.*"

But this "man" belongs to the fourth Round. As shown, the MONAD had passed through, journeyed and been imprisoned in, every transitional form throughout every kingdom of nature during the three preceding Rounds. But the monad which becomes human *is not the Man*. In this Round – with the exception of the highest mammals after man, the anthropoids destined to die out in this our race, when their monads will be liberated and pass into the astral human forms (or the highest elementals) of the Sixth * and the Seventh Races, and then into lowest human forms in the fifth Round – no units of either of the kingdoms are animated any longer by monads destined to become human in their next stage, but only by the lower Elementals of their respective realms.†

The last human Monad incarnated before the beginning of the 5th Root Race.‡ The cycle of *metempsychosis* for the human monad is closed,

* Nature never repeats herself, therefore the anthropoids of our day have not existed at any time since the middle of the Miocene period; when, like all cross breeds, they began to show a tendency, more and more marked as time went on, to return to the type of their first parent, the black and yellow gigantic Lemuro-Atlantean. To search for the "Missing Link" is useless. To the scientists of the closing sixth Root Race, millions and millions of years hence, our modern races, or rather their fossils, will appear as those of small insignificant apes – an extinct species of the genus *homo*.

† These "Elementals" will become human Monads, in their turn, only at the next great planetary *Manvantara*.

‡ Such anthropoids form an exception because they were not intended by Nature, but are the direct product and creation of "senseless" man. The Hindus give a divine origin to the apes and monkeys because the men of the Third Race were gods from another plane who had become "senseless" mortals. This subject had already been touched upon in "*Isis Unveiled*" twelve years ago as plainly as was then possible. On pp. 278-279, the reader is referred "to the Brahmins, if he would know the reason of the regard they have for the monkeys. For then he (the reader) would perhaps learn – were the Brahman to judge him worthy of an explanation – that the Hindu sees in the ape but what *Manu* desired he should: the transformation of species most directly connected with that of the human family, a bastard branch engrafted on their own stock before the final perfection of the latter. He might learn, further, that in the eyes of the educated 'heathen' the spiritual or inner man is one thing, and his terrestrial physical casket another. That physical nature, the great combination of physical correlations of forces, ever creeping onward towards perfection, has to avail herself of the material at hand; she models and remodels as she proceeds, and finishing her crowning work in man, presents him alone as a fit tabernacle for the overshadowing of the divine Spirit."

for we are in the Fourth Round and the Fifth Root Race. The reader will have to bear in mind – at any rate one who has made himself acquainted with *"Esoteric Buddhism"* – that the Stanzas which follow in this Book and Book II speak of the evolution in our Fourth Round only. The latter is the cycle of the turning point, after which, matter, having reached its lowest depths, begins to strive onward and to get spiritualized with every new Race and with every fresh cycle. Therefore the student must take care not to see contradiction where there is none, as in *"Esoteric Buddhism"* Rounds are spoken of in general, while here only the Fourth, or our present Round, is meant. Then it was the work of formation; now it is that of reformation and evolutionary perfection.

Finally, to close this chapter anent various, but unavoidable misconceptions, we must refer to a statement in *"Esoteric Buddhism"* which has produced a very fatal impression upon the minds of many Theosophists. One unfortunate sentence from the work just referred to is constantly brought forward to prove the materialism of the doctrine. On p. 48, 5th Edition, the Author, referring to the progress of organisms on the Globes, says that "the mineral kingdom will no more develop the vegetable . . . than the Earth was able to develop man from the ape, till it received an impulse."

Moreover, a German scientific work is mentioned in a footnote on the same page. It says that a Hanoverian scientist had recently published a Book entitled *"Ueber die Auflosung der Arten durch Naturliche Zucht-wahl,"* in which he shows, with great ingenuity, that Darwin was wholly mistaken in tracing man back to the ape. On the contrary, he maintains that it is the ape which is evolved from man. He shows that, in the beginning, mankind were morally and physically the types and prototypes of our present Race, and of our human dignity, by their beauty of form, regularity of feature, cranial development, nobility of sentiments, heroic impulses, and grandeur of ideal conception. This is a purely Brahmanic, Buddhistic and Kabalistic philosophy. The Book is copiously illustrated with diagrams, tables, etc. It asserts that the gradual debasement and degradation of man, morally and physically, can be readily traced throughout the ethnological transformation down to our time. And, as one portion has already degenerated into apes, so the civilized man of the present day will at last, under the action of the inevitable law of necessity, be also succeeded by like descendants. If we may judge of the future by the actual Present, it certainly does seem possible that so unspiritual and materialistic a body should end as Simia rather than as Seraphs. But though the apes descend from man, it is certainly not the fact that the human Monad, which has once reached the level of humanity, ever incarnates again in the form of an animal.

Whether this sentence renders literally the thought of the author, or is simply (as we believe it is) a *lapsus calami*, may remain an open question.

It is really with surprise that we have ascertained the fact that *"Esoteric Buddhism"* was so little understood by some Theosophists, as to have led them into the belief that it thoroughly supported Darwinian evolution, and especially the theory of the descent of man from a pithecoid ancestor. As one member writes: "I suppose you realise that three-fourths of Theosophists and even outsiders imagine that, as far as the evolution of man is concerned, Darwinism and Theosophy kiss one another." Nothing of the kind was ever realised, nor is there any great warrant for it, so far as we know, in *"Esoteric Buddhism."* It has been repeatedly stated that evolution as taught by Manu and Kapila was the groundwork of the modern teachings, but neither Occultism nor Theosophy has ever supported the wild theories of the present Darwinists – least of all the descent of man from an ape. Of this, more hereafter. But one has only to turn to p. 47 of *"Esoteric Buddhism,"* 5th edition, to find there the statement that "Man belongs to a kingdom distinctly separate from that of the animals." With such a plain and unequivocal statement before him, it is very strange that any careful student should have been so misled unless he is prepared to charge the author with a gross contradiction.

Every Round repeats on a higher scale the evolutionary work of the preceding Round. With the exception of some higher anthropoids, as just mentioned, the Monadic inflow, or inner evolution, is at an end till the next *Manvantara*. It can never be too often repeated, that the full-blown human Monads have to be first disposed of, before the new crop of candidates appears on this Globe at the beginning of the next cycle. Thus there is a lull, and this is why, during the Fourth Round, man appears on Earth earlier than any animal creation, as will be described.

But it is still urged that the author of *"Esoteric Buddhism"* has "preached Darwinism" all along. Certain passages would undoubtedly seem to lend countenance to this inference. Besides which the Occultists themselves are ready to concede *partial* correctness to the Darwinian hypothesis, in later details, bye-laws of Evolution, and after the midway point of the Fourth Race. Of that which has taken place, physical science can really know nothing, for such matters lie entirely outside of its sphere of investigation. But what the Occultists have never admitted, nor will they ever admit, is that man was *an ape in this or in any other Round*, or that he ever could be one, however much he may have been "ape-like." This is vouched for by the very authority from whom the author of "*Esoteric Buddhism*" got his information.

Thus to those who confront the Occultists with these lines from the above-named volume: "It is enough to show that we may as reasonably – and that we must, if we would talk about these matters at all – conceive a life impulse giving birth to mineral form, as of the same sort of impulse concerned to *raise a race of apes into a race of rudimentary men*." To those who bring this passage forward as showing "decided Darwinism," the Occultists answer by pointing to the explanation of the Master (Mr. Sinnett's "teacher") which would contradict these lines, were they written in the spirit attributed to them. A copy of this letter was sent to the writer, together with others, two years ago (1886), with additional marginal remarks, to quote from, in the "*Secret Doctrine*." It begins by considering the difficulty experienced by the Western student, in reconciling some facts, previously given, with the evolution of man from the animal, i.e., from the mineral, vegetable and animal kingdoms, and advises the student to hold to the doctrine of analogy and correspondences. Then it touches upon the mystery of the *Devas*, and even Gods, having to pass through states which it was agreed to refer to as "Inmetallization, Inherbation, Inzoonization and finally Incarnation," and explains this by hinting at the necessity of failures even in the ethereal races of *Dhyan Chohans*. Concerning this it says:

"Still, as these 'failures' are too far progressed and spiritualized to be thrown back forcibly from Dhyan Chohanship into the vortex of a new primordial evolution through the lower kingdoms. . . ." After which only a hint is given about the mystery contained in the allegory of the fallen *Asuras*, which will be expanded and explained in Book II. When Karma has reached them at the stage of human evolution, "they will have to drink it to the last drop in the bitter cup of retribution. Then they become an active force and commingle with the Elementals, the progressed entities of the pure animal kingdom, to develop little by little the full type of humanity."

These *Dhyan Chohans*, as we see, do not pass through the three kingdoms as do the lower *Pitris*, nor do they incarnate in man until the Third Root Race. Thus, as the teaching stands:

"*Man in the First Round and First Race on Globe D, our Earth, was an ethereal being (a Lunar Dhyani, as man), non-intelligent but superspiritual, and correspondingly, on the law of analogy, in the First Race of the Fourth Round. In each of the subsequent races and sub-races . . . he grows more and more into an encased or incarnate being, but still preponderatingly ethereal. . . . He is sexless, and, like the animal and vegetable he develops monstrous bodies correspondential with his coarser surroundings.*

"*II. Round. He (Man) is still gigantic and ethereal but growing firmer and more condensed in body, a more physical man. Yet still less intelligent than spiritual (1), for mind is a slower and more difficult evolution than is the physical frame . . .*

"*III. Round. He has now a perfectly concrete or compacted body, at first the form of a giant ape, and now more intelligent, or rather cunning, than spiritual. For, on the downward arc, he has now reached a point where his primordial spirituality is eclipsed and overshadowed by nascent mentality (2). In the last half of the Third Round his gigantic stature decreases, and his body improves in texture, and he becomes a more rational being, though still more an ape than a Deva. . . . (All this is almost exactly repeated in the third Root Race of the Fourth Round.)*

"*IV. Round. Intellect has an enormous development in this Round. The (hitherto) dumb races acquire our (present) human speech on this globe, on which, from the Fourth Race, language is perfected and knowledge increases. At this half-way point of the Fourth Round (as of the Fourth Root, or Atlantean, race) humanity passes the axial point of the minor Manvantara cycle . . . . the world teeming with the results of intellectual activity and spiritual decrease....*"

This is from the authentic letter; what follows are the later remarks and additional explanations traced by the same hand in the form of footnotes.

(1.) "*. . . The original letter contained general teaching – a 'bird's eye view' – and particularized nothing. . . . To speak of 'physical man' while* *limiting the statement to the early Rounds would be drifting back to the miraculous and instantaneous 'coats of skin.' . . . The first 'Nature,' the first 'body,' the first 'mind' on the first plane of perception, on the first Globe in the first Round, is what was meant. For Karma and evolution have –*

' . . . centred in our make such strange extremes!
*From different Natures * marvellously mixed . . .'*

(2.) "Restore: he has now reached the point (by analogy, and as the Third Root Race in the Fourth Round) where his ("the angel"- man's) primordial spirituality is eclipsed and overshadowed by nascent human mentality, and you have the true version on your thumbnail. . ."

These are the words of the Teacher – text, words and sentences in brackets, and explanatory footnotes. It stands to reason that there must be an enormous difference in such terms as "objectivity" and "subjectivity," "materiality" and "spirituality," when the same terms are applied to different planes of being and perception. All this must be taken in its relative sense. And therefore there is little to be wondered at, if, left to his own speculations, an author, however eager to learn, yet quite inexperienced in these abstruse teachings, has fallen into an error. Neither was the difference between the "Rounds" and the "Races" sufficiently defined in the letters received, nor was there anything of the kind required before, as the ordinary Eastern disciple would have found out the difference in a moment. Moreover, to quote from a letter of the Master's (188-), "the teachings were imparted under protest. . . . They were, so to say, smuggled goods . . . and when I remained face to face with only one correspondent, the other, Mr. . . . ., had so far tossed all the cards into confusion, that little remained to be said without trespassing upon law." Theosophists, "whom it may concern," will understand what is meant.

The outcome of all this is that nothing had ever been said in the "letters" to warrant the assurance that the Occult doctrine has ever taught, or any Adept believed in, the preposterous modern theory of the descent of man from a common ancestor with the ape – an

---

* The *Natures* of the seven hierarchies or classes of *Pitris* and *Dhyan Chohans* which compose our nature and Bodies are here meant.

anthropoid of the actual animal kind, unless metaphorically. To this day the world is more full of "ape-like men" than the woods are of "men-like apes." The ape is sacred in India because its origin is well known to the Initiates, though concealed under a thick veil of allegory. Hanuman is the son of Pavana (Vayu, "the god of the wind") by Anjana, a monster called Kesarî, though his genealogy varies. The reader who bears this in mind will find in Book II *passim*, the whole explanation of this ingenious allegory. The "Men" of the Third Race (who separated) were "Gods" by their spirituality and purity, though senseless, and as yet destitute of mind, as men.

These "Men" of the Third Race – the ancestors of the Atlanteans – were just such ape-like, intellectually senseless giants as were those beings, who, during the Third Round, represented Humanity. Morally irresponsible, it was these third Race "men" who, through promiscuous connection with animal species lower than themselves, created that missing link which became ages later (in the tertiary period only) the remote ancestor of the real ape as we find it now in the pithecoid family.[†]

Thus the earlier teachings, however unsatisfactory, vague and fragmentary, did not teach the evolution of "man" from the "ape." Nor does the author of *"Esoteric Buddhism"* assert it anywhere in his work in so many words, but, owing to his inclination towards modern science, he uses language which might perhaps justify such an inference. The man who preceded the Fourth, the Atlantean race, however much he may have looked physically like a "gigantic ape" – "the counterfeit of man who hath not the life of a man" – was still a thinking and already a speaking man. The "Lemuro-Atlantean" was a highly civilized race, and if one accepts tradition, which is better history than the speculative fiction which now passes under that name, he was higher than we are

---

† And if this is found clashing with that other statement which shows the animal later than man, then the reader is asked to bear in mind that the placental mammal only is meant. In those days there were animals of which zoology does not even dream in our own; *and the modes of reproduction were not identical* with the notions which modern physiology has upon the subject. It is not altogether convenient to touch upon such questions in public, but there is *no* contradiction or impossibility in this whatever.

with all our sciences and the degraded civilization of the day: at any rate, the Lemuro-Atlantean of the closing Third Race was so."

SD, i 182–191

THE TREE FROM WHICH
THE ADEPTS GROW

(b) There are four grades of initiation mentioned in exoteric works, which are known respectively in Sanskrit as "*Sçrôtâpanna*," "*Sagardagan*," "*Anagamin*," and "*Arhan*" – the four paths to Nirvana, in this, our fourth Round, bearing the same appellations. The Arhan, though he can see the Past, the Present, and the Future, is not yet the highest Initiate, for the Adept himself, the *initiated* candidate, becomes *chela* (pupil) to a higher Initiate. Three further higher grades have to be conquered by the Arhan who would reach the apex of the ladder of *Arhat*ship. There are those who have reached it even in this fifth race of ours, but the faculties necessary for the attainment of these higher grades will be fully developed in the average ascetic only at the end of this Root Race, and in the Sixth and Seventh. Thus there will always be Initiates and the Profane till the end of this minor *Manvantara*, the present *lifecycle*. The *Arhats* of the "fire-mist" of the 7th rung are but one remove from the Root-Base of their Hierarchy – the highest on Earth, and our Terrestrial chain. This "Root-Base" has a name which can only be translated by several compound words into English" – "the ever-living-human-Banyan." This "Wondrous Being" descended from a "high region," they say, in the early part of the Third Age, before the separation of the sexes of the Third Race.

This Third Race is sometimes called collectively "the Sons of *Passive* Yoga," i.e., it was produced unconsciously by the second Race, which, as it was intellectually inactive, is supposed to have been constantly plunged in a kind of blank or abstract contemplation, as required by the conditions of the Yoga state. In the first or earlier portion of the existence of this third race, while it was yet in its state of purity, the "Sons of Wisdom," who, as will be seen, incarnated in this Third Race, produced by *Kriyasakti* a progeny called the "Sons of Ad" or "of the Fire-Mist," the "Sons of Will and Yoga," etc. They were a conscious production, as a portion of the race was already animated with the divine spark of spiritual, superior intelligence. It was not a Race, this

35

progeny. It was at first a wondrous Being, called the "Initiator," and after him a group of semi-divine and semi-human beings. "*Set apart*" in Archaic *genesis* for certain purposes, they are those in whom are said to have incarnated the highest *Dhyanis*, "*Munis* and *Rishis* from previous *Manvantaras*" – *to form the nursery for future human adepts*, on this earth and during the present cycle. These "Sons of Will and Yoga" born, so to speak, in an immaculate way, remained, it is explained, entirely apart from the rest of mankind.

The "BEING" just referred to, which has to remain nameless, is the *Tree* from which, in subsequent ages, all the great *historically* known Sages and Hierophants, such as the Rishi Kapila, Hermes, Enoch, Orpheus, etc., etc., have branched off. As objective *man*, he is the mysterious (to the profane – the ever invisible) yet ever present Personage about whom legends are rife in the East, especially among the Occultists and the students of the Sacred Science. It is he who changes form, yet remains ever the same. And it is he again who holds spiritual sway over the *initiated* Adepts throughout the whole world. He is, as said, the "Nameless One" who has so many names, and yet whose names and whose very nature are unknown. He is *the* "Initiator," called the "GREAT SACRIFICE." For, sitting at the threshold of LIGHT, he looks into it from within the circle of Darkness, which he will not cross, nor will he quit his post till the last day of this lifecycle. Why does the solitary Watcher remain at his self-chosen post? Why does he sit by the fountain of primeval Wisdom, of which he drinks no longer, as he has naught to learn which he does not know – aye, neither on this Earth, nor in its heaven? Because the lonely, sore-footed pilgrims on their way back to their *home* are never sure to the last moment of not losing their way in this limitless desert of illusion and matter called Earth Life. Because he would fain show the way to that region of freedom and light, from which he is a voluntary exile himself, to every prisoner who has succeeded in liberating himself from the bonds of flesh and illusion. Because, in short, he has sacrificed himself for the sake of mankind, though but a few Elect may profit by the GREAT SACRIFICE.

It is under the direct, silent guidance of this MAHA – (great) – GURU that all the other less divine Teachers and instructors of mankind became, from the first awakening of human consciousness, the guides of early Humanity. It is through these "Sons of God" that infant humanity got its first notions of all the arts and sciences, as well as of spiritual knowledge, and it is they who have laid the first foundation-stone of those ancient civilizations that puzzle so sorely our modern generation of students and scholars.*

---

* Let those who doubt this statement explain the mystery of the extraordinary knowledge possessed by the ancients – alleged to have developed from lower and animal-like savages, the *cave-men* of the Palaeolithic age – on any other equally reasonable grounds. Let them turn to such works as those of Vitruvius Pollio of the Augustan age, on architecture, for instance, in which all the rules of proportion are those *taught anciently at initiations*, if he would acquaint himself with the truly divine art, and understand the *deep esoteric significance hidden in every rule and law of proportion*. No man descended from a Palaeolithic cave-dweller could ever evolve such a science unaided, even in millenniums of thought and intellectual evolution. It is the pupils of those incarnated *Rishis* and *Devas* of the third Root Race, who handed their knowledge from one generation to another, to Egypt and Greece with its now *lost canon of proportion*; as it is the Disciples of the Initiates of the 4th, the Atlanteans, who handed it over to their *Cyclopes*, the "Sons of Cycles" or of the "Infinite," from whom the name passed to the still later generations of Gnostic priests. "It is owing to the divine perfection of those architectural proportions that the Ancients could build those wonders of all the subsequent ages, their Fanes, Pyramids, Cave-Temples, Cromlechs, Cairns, Altars, proving they had the powers of machinery and a knowledge of mechanics to which modern skill is like a child's play, and which that skill refers to itself as the 'works of hundred-handed giants.'" (See "*Book of God*," Kenealy.) Modern architects may not altogether have neglected those rules, but they have superadded enough empirical innovations to destroy those just proportions. It is Vitruvius who gave to posterity the rules of construction of the Grecian temples erected to the immortal gods; and the ten books of Marcus Vitruvius Pollio on Architecture, of one, in short, *who was an initiate*, can only be studied esoterically. The Druidical circles, the Dolmen, the Temples of India, Egypt and Greece, the Towers and the 127 towns in Europe which were found "Cyclopean in origin" by the French Institute, are all the work of initiated Priest-Architects, the descendants of those primarily taught by the "Sons of God," justly called "The Builders." This is what appreciative posterity says of those descendants. "They used neither mortar nor cement, nor steel nor iron to cut the stones with; and yet they were so artfully wrought that in many places the joints are not seen, though many of the stones, as in Peru, are 18 ft. thick, and in the walls of the fortress of Cuzco there are stones of a still greater size." (*Acosta*, vi., 14.) "Again, the walls of Syene, built 5,400 years ago, when that spot was exactly under the tropic, which it has now ceased to be, were so constructed that at noon, at the precise moment of the solar solstice, the entire disc of the Sun was seen reflected on their surface – a work which the united skill of all the astronomers of Europe would not now be able to effect." (Kenealy, "*Book of God*")

Although these matters were barely hinted at in "*Isis Unveiled*," it will be well to remind the reader of what was said in Vol. I, pp. 587 to 593, concerning a certain Sacred Island in Central Asia, and to refer him for further details to the chapter in Book II on "The Sons of God and the Sacred Island." A few more explanations, however, though thrown out in a fragmentary form, may help the student to obtain a glimpse into the present mystery.

To state at least one detail concerning these mysterious "Sons of God" in plain words. It is from them, these *Brahmaputras*, that the high *Dwijas*, the initiated Brahmins of old justly claimed descent, while the modern Brahmin would have the lowest castes believe literally that they issued direct from the mouth of Brahmâ. This is the esoteric teaching, which adds moreover that, although these descendants (spiritually of course) from the "sons of Will and Yoga," became in time divided into opposite sexes, as their "*Kriyasakti*" progenitors did themselves, later on, yet even their degenerate descendants have down to the present day retained a veneration and respect for the creative function, and still regard it in the light of a religious ceremony, whereas the more civilized nations consider it as a mere animal function. Compare the western views and practice in these matters with the *Institutions of Manu* in regard to the laws of *Grihasta* and married life. The true Brahmin is thus indeed "he whose seven forefathers have drunk the juice of the moon-plant (Soma)," and who is a "*Trisuparna*," for he has understood the secret of the *Vedas*.

And, to this day, such Brahmins know that, during its early beginnings, psychic and physical intellect being dormant and consciousness still undeveloped, the spiritual conceptions of that race were quite unconnected with its physical surroundings. That *divine* man dwelt in his animal – though externally human – form, and, if there was instinct in him, no self-consciousness came to enlighten the darkness of the latent fifth principle. When, moved by the law of Evolution, the Lords of Wisdom infused into him the spark of consciousness, the first feeling it awoke to life and activity was a sense of solidarity, of oneness with his spiritual creators. As the child's first feeling is for its mother and nurse, so the first aspirations of the awakening consciousness in primitive man were for those whose element he felt within himself, and who yet were outside, and independent of him. DEVOTION arose out of that feeling, and became the first and foremost motor in his nature, for it is the only one which is natural in our heart, which is innate in us, and which we find alike in human babe and the young of the animal. This feeling of irrepressible, instinctive aspiration in primitive man is beautifully, and one may say intuitively, described by Carlyle. "The great antique heart," he exclaims, "how like a child's in its simplicity, like a man's in its earnest solemnity and depth! heaven lies over him wheresoever he goes or stands on the earth, making all the earth a mystic temple to him, the earth's business all a kind of worship. Glimpses of bright creatures flash in the common sunlight; angels yet hover, doing God's messages among men . . . . . Wonder, miracle, encompass the man; he lives in an element of miracle * . . . . A great law of duty, high as these two infinitudes (heaven and hell), dwarfing all else, annihilating all else – it was a reality, and it is one: the garment only of it is dead; the essence of it lives through all times and all eternity!"

It lives undeniably, and has settled in all its ineradicable strength and power in the Asiatic Aryan heart from the Third Race direct through its first "mind-born" sons, the fruits of *Kriyasakti*. As time rolled on the holy caste of Initiates produced but rarely, and from age to age, such perfect creatures: beings apart, inwardly, though the same as those who produced them, outwardly.

While in the infancy of the third primitive race:

> "A creature of a more exalted kind
> Was wanting yet, and therefore was designed;
> Conscious of thought, of more capacious breast
> For empire formed and fit to rule the rest. . . . ."

It was called into being, a ready and perfect vehicle for the incarnating denizens of higher spheres, who took forthwith their abodes in these forms born of *Spiritual* WILL and the natural divine power in man.

---

* That which was *natural* in the sight of primitive man has become only now *miracle* to us; and that which was to him a miracle could never be expressed in our language.

It was a child of pure Spirit, mentally unalloyed with any tincture of earthly element. Its physical frame alone was of time and of life, as it drew its intelligence direct from above. It was the living tree of divine wisdom, and may therefore be likened to the Mundane Tree of the Norse Legend, which cannot wither and die until the last battle of life shall be fought, while its roots are gnawed all the time by the dragon Nidhogg; for even so, the first and holy Son of *Kriyasakti* had his body gnawed by the tooth of time, but the roots of his inner being remained for ever undecaying and strong, because they grew and expanded in heaven not on earth. He was the first of the FIRST, and he was the seed of all the others. There were other "Sons of *Kriyasakti*" produced by a second Spiritual effort, but the first one has remained to this day the Seed of divine Knowledge, the One and the Supreme among the terrestrial "Sons of Wisdom." Of this subject we can say no more, except to add that in every age – aye, even in our own – there have been great intellects who have understood the problem correctly.

How comes our physical body to the state of perfection it is found in now? Through millions of years of evolution, of course, yet never through, or from, animals, as taught by materialism. For, as Carlyle says: ". . . The essence of our being, the mystery in us that calls itself 'I,' – what words have we for such things? – it is a breath of Heaven, the highest Being reveals himself in man. This body, these faculties, this life of ours, is it not all as a vesture for the UNNAMED?"

The *breath* of heaven, or rather the breath of life, called in the *Bible Nephesh*, is in every animal, in every animate speck as in every mineral atom. But none of these has, like man, the consciousness of the nature of that highest Being,* as none has that divine harmony in its form which man possesses. It is, as Novalis said, and no one since has said it better, as repeated by Carlyle:

> "There is but one temple in the universe, and that is the body of man.
> Nothing is holier than that high form . . . . We touch heaven when we

---

* There is no nation in the world in which the feeling of devotion or of religious mysticism is more developed and prominent than in the Hindu people. See what Max Müller says of this idiosyncracy and national feature in his works. This is direct inheritance from the primitive *conscious* men of the Third Race."

lay our hand on a human body!" "This sounds like a mere flourish of rhetoric," adds Carlyle, "but it is not so. If well meditated it will turn out to be a scientific fact; the expression . . . of the actual truth of the thing. We are the miracle of miracles, the great inscrutable Mystery."

SD, i 206–212

THE HIERARCHIES OF SPIRITS

"1. BEHOLD THE BEGINNING OF SENTIENT FORMLESS LIFE (*a*).

FIRST, THE DIVINE (*vehicle*) (*b*), THE ONE FROM THE MOTHER-SPIRIT (*Atman*); THEN THE SPIRITUAL (*Atma-Buddhi, Spirit-soul*) * (*c*); (*again*) THE THREE FROM THE ONE (*d*), THE FOUR FROM THE ONE (*e*), AND THE FIVE (*f*), FROM WHICH THE THREE, THE FIVE AND THE SEVEN (*g*) – THESE ARE THE THREE-FOLD AND THE FOUR-FOLD DOWNWARD; THE "MIND-BORN SONS OF THE FIRST LORD (*Avalôkitêswara*) THE SHINING SEVEN (*the "Builders"*). † IT IS THEY WHO ARE THOU, ME, HIM, O LANOO; THEY WHO WATCH OVER THEE AND THY MOTHER, BHUMI (*the Earth*).

(*a*) The hierarchy of Creative Powers is divided into seven (or 4 and 3) esoteric, within the twelve great Orders, recorded in the twelve signs of the Zodiac, the seven of the manifesting scale being connected, moreover, with the Seven Planets. All this is subdivided into numberless groups of divine Spiritual, semi-Spiritual, and ethereal Beings.

The Chief Hierarchies among these are hinted at in the great Quaternary, or the "four bodies and the three faculties" of Brahma exoterically, and the *Panchasyam*, the five Brahmas, or the five *Dhyani-Buddhas* in the Buddhist system.

The highest group is composed of the divine Flames, so-called, also spoken of as the "Fiery Lions" and the "Lions of Life," whose esotericism is securely hidden in the Zodiacal sign of Leo. It is the *nucleole* of the superior divine World (see Commentary in first pages of *Addendum*). They are the formless Fiery Breaths, identical in one aspect

---

* This relates to the Cosmic principles.

† The seven creative *Rishis* now connected with the constellation of the Great Bear.

with the upper *Sephiroth*al TRIAD, which is placed by the Kabalists in the "Archetypal World."

The same hierarchy, with the same numbers, is found in the Japanese system, in the "Beginnings" as taught by both the Shinto and the Buddhist sects. In this system, Anthropogenesis precedes Cosmogenesis, as the Divine merges into the human, and creates – midway in its descent into matter – the visible Universe. The legendary personages – remarks reverentially Omoie – "having to be understood as the stereotyped embodiment of the higher (secret) doctrine, and its sublime truths." To state it at full length, however, would occupy too much of our space, but a few words on this old system cannot be out of place. The following is a short synopsis of this Anthropo-Cosmogenesis, and it shows how closely the most separated notions echoed one and the same Archaic teaching.

When all was as yet Chaos (*Kon-ton*) three spiritual Beings appeared on the stage of future creation: (1) *Ame no ani naka nushi no Kami*, "Divine Monarch of the Central Heaven"; (2) *Taka mi onosubi no Kami*, "Exalted, imperial Divine offspring of Heaven and the Earth"; and (3) *Kamu mi musubi no Kami*, "Offspring of the Gods," simply.

These were without form or substance (our *arupa* triad), as neither the celestial nor the terrestrial substance had yet differentiated, "nor had the essence of things been formed."

In the *Zohar* – which, as now arranged and re-edited by Moses de Leon, with the help of Syrian and Chaldean Christian Gnostics in the XIIth century, and corrected and revised still later by many Christian hands, is only a little less exoteric than the *Bible* itself – this divine "Vehicle" no longer appears as it does in the "Chaldean Book of Numbers." True enough, *Ain-Soph*, the ABSOLUTE ENDLESS NOTHING, uses also the form of the ONE, the manifested "Heavenly man" (the FIRST CAUSE) as its chariot (*Mercabah*, in Hebrew; *Vahan*, in Sanskrit) or vehicle to descend into, and manifest through, in the phenomenal world. But the Kabalists neither make it plain how the ABSOLUTE can use anything, or exercise any attribute whatever, since, as the Absolute, it is devoid of attributes; nor do they explain that in reality it is the First Cause (Plato's *Logos*) the original and eternal

IDEA, that manifests through Adam Kadmon, the *Second Logos,* so to speak. In the "Book of Numbers" it is explained that EN (or *Ain, Aior*) is the only self-existent, whereas its "Depth" (*Bythos* or *Buthon* of the Gnostics, called *Propator*) is only periodical. The latter is Brahma as differentiated from Brahma or *Parabrahm.* It is the Depth, the Source of Light, or Propator, which is the *unmanifested Logos* or the abstract *Idea,* and not *Ain-Soph, whose ray* uses Adam Kadmon or the *manifested Logos* (the objective Universe) "male and female" – as a chariot through which to manifest. But in the *Zohar* we read the following incongruity: "*Senior occultatus est et absconditus; Microprosopus manifestus est, et non manifestus.*" (Rosenroth, *Liber Mysterii,* IV., 1.) This is a fallacy, since *Microprosopus* or the *microcosm,* can only exist during its manifestations, and is destroyed during the *Maha-Pralayas.* Rosenroth's *Kabala* is no guide, but very often a puzzle.

(*b*) As in the Japanese system, in the Egyptian, and every old cosmogony – at this divine FLAME, The "One," are lit the three descending groups. Having their potential being in the higher group, they now become distinct and separate Entities. These are called the "Virgins of Life," the "Great Illusion," etc., etc., and collectively the "Six-pointed Star." The latter is the symbol, in almost every religion, of the *Logos* as the first emanation. It is that of Vishnu in India (the *Chakra,* or wheel), and the glyph of the *Tetragrammaton,* the "He of the four letters" or – metaphorically – "the limbs of *Microprosopos*" in the *Kabala,* which are ten and six respectively. The later Kabalists however, especially the Christian mystics, have played sad havoc with this magnificent symbol. * For the "*ten* limbs" of the Heavenly Man are the ten *Sephiroth;* but the first Heavenly Man is the unmanifested Spirit of the Universe, and ought never to be degraded into *Microprosopus* – the lesser Face or Countenance, the prototype of man on the terrestrial plane. † Of

---

* Indeed, the *Microprosopus* - who is, philosophically speaking, quite distinct from the unmanifested eternal *Logos* "one with the Father," - has been finally brought, by centuries of incessant efforts, of sophistry and paradoxes, to be considered as one with Jehovah, or the ONE living God (!), whereas Jehovah is no better than Binah, a female Sephiroth. This fact cannot be too frequently impressed upon the reader.

† The *Microprosopus* is, as just said, the *Logos* manifested, and of such there are many.

this, however, later on. The six-pointed Star refers to the six Forces or Powers of Nature, the six planes, principles, etc., etc., all synthesized by the seventh, or the central point in the Star. All these, the upper and lower hierarchies included, emanate from the "Heavenly or Celestial Virgin," ‡ the great mother in all religions, the Androgyne, the *Sephira-Adam Kadmon*. In its *Unity*, primordial light is the seventh, or highest, principle, *Daiviprakriti*, the light of the unmanifested *Logos*. But in its differentiation it becomes *Fohat*, or the "Seven Sons." The former is symbolised by the Central point in the double-Triangle; the latter by the hexagon itself, or the "six limbs" of the *Microprosopus* the Seventh being Malkuth, the "Bride" of the Christian Kabalists, or our Earth. Hence the expressions:

"The first after the 'One' is divine Fire; the second, Fire and Aether; the third is composed of Fire, Aether and Water; the fourth of Fire, Aether, Water, and Air." § *The One is not concerned with Man-bearing globes, but with the inner invisible Spheres. "The 'First Born' are the LIFE, the heart and pulse of the Universe; the Second are its MIND or Consciousness,"* ¶ as said in the Commentary.

(c) The second Order of Celestial Beings, those of Fire and Aether (corresponding to Spirit and Soul, or the *Atma-Buddhi*) whose names are legion, are still formless, but more definitely "substantial." They are the first differentiation in the Secondary Evolution or "Creation" – a misleading word. As the name shows, they are the prototypes of

---

‡ Sephira is the Crown, KETHER, in the abstract principle only, as a mathematical *x* (the unknown quantity). On the plane of differentiated nature she is the female counterpart of Adam Kadmon - the first Androgyne. The *Kabala* teaches that the words *"Fiat Lux"* (*Genesis* ch. i.) referred to the formation and evolution of the Sephiroth, and not to light as opposed to darkness. Rabbi Simeon says: "Oh companions, companions, man as an emanation was both man and woman, Adam Kadmon verily, and this is the sense of the words 'Let there be Light, and it was Light.' And this is the two-fold man." (*Auszuge aus dem Zohar*, pp. 13-15.)

§ See next footnote. These elements of Fire, Air, etc., are not our compound elements.

¶ This "Consciousness" has no relation to our consciousness. The consciousness of the "One manifested," if not absolute, is still unconditioned. *Mahat* (the Universal Mind) is the first production of the Brahma-Creator, but also of the *Pradhâna* (undifferentiated matter).

the incarnating *Jivas* or Monads, and are composed of the Fiery Spirit of Life. It is through these that passes, like a pure solar beam, the ray which is furnished by them with its future vehicle, the Divine Soul, *Buddhi*. These are directly concerned with the Hosts of the higher world of *our* system. From these twofold *Units* emanate the *threefold*.

In the cosmogony of Japan, when, out of the chaotic mass, an egg like nucleus appears, having within itself the germ and potency of all the universal as well as of all terrestrial life, it is the "three-fold" just named, which differentiates. "The male aethereal" (*Yo*) principle ascends and the female grosser or more material principle (*In*) is precipitated into the Universe of substance, when a separation occurs between the celestial and the terrestrial. From this the female, the mother, the first rudimentary objective being is born. It is ethereal, without form or sex, and yet it is from this and the mother that the Seven Divine Spirits are born, from whom will emanate *the seven creations*, just as in the *Codex Nazaraeus* from *Karabtanos* and the Mother *Spiritus* the seven *evilly disposed* (material) spirits are born. It would be too long to give here the Japanese names, but once translated they stand in this order:

(1.) The "Invisible Celibate," which is the creative logos of the noncreating "father," or the creative potentiality of the latter made manifest.

(2.) "The Spirit (or the God) of the rayless depths" (of Chaos); which becomes differentiated matter, or the world-stuff; also the mineral realm.

(3.) "The Spirit of the Vegetable Kingdom," of the "Abundant Vegetation."

(4.) This one is of dual nature, being at the same time "The Spirit of the Earth" and "the Spirit of the Sands," the former containing the potentiality of the male element, the latter that of the female element, the two forming a combined nature.

These two were ONE; yet unconscious of being two.

In this duality were contained (*a*) the male, dark and muscular Being, *Isu no gai no Kami*; and (*b*) *Eku gai no Kami*, the female, fair and weaker or more delicate Being. Then, the:

(5th and 6th.) Spirits who were androgynous or dual-sexed, and, finally:

(7.) The *Seventh* Spirit, the last emanated from the "mother," appears as the first divine human form distinctly male and female. It was the seventh creation, as in the *Purânas*, wherein man is the seventh creation of Brahma.

These, *Tsanagi-Tsanami*, descended into the Universe by the celestial Bridge (the milky way), and "Tsanagi, perceiving far below a chaotic mass of cloud and water, thrust his jewelled spear into the depths, and dry land appeared." Then the two separated to explore *Onokoro*, the newly-created island world; etc., etc. (*Omoie*).

Such are the Japanese exoteric fables, the rind that conceals the kernel of the same one truth of the Secret Doctrine.

(*d*) The *Third* order corresponds to the *Atma-Buddhi-Manas*: Spirit, Soul and Intellect, and is called the "Triads."

(*e*) The *Fourth* are substantial Entities. This is the highest group among the *Rupas* (Atomic Forms *). It is the nursery of the human,

---

* It is worthy of notice that, while rejecting as a superstition of Occultism, and religion too, the theory of substantial and invisible Beings called Angels, Elementals, etc. - without, of course, having ever looked into the philosophy of these incorporeal Entities, or thought over them - modern chemistry, owing to observation and discovery, should have unconsciously been forced to adopt and recognize the same ratio of progression and order in the evolution of chemical atoms as Occultism does, both for its *Dhyanis* and Atoms - analogy being its first law. As seen above, the very first group of the *Rupa* Angels is quaternary, an element being added to each in descending order. So are the atoms, adopting the phraseology of chemistry, monatomic, diatomic, and tetratomic, progressing downwards. Let it be remembered that Fire, Water, and Air, or the "Elements of primary Creation" so-called, are not the compound Elements they are on Earth, but noumenal homogeneous Elements - the Spirits thereof. Then follow the septenary groups or hosts. Placed on parallel lines in a diagram with Atoms, the Natures of those Beings would be seen to correspond in their downward scale of progression to composite elements in a mathematically identical manner, as to analogy. This refers, of course, only to diagrams made by the Occultists; for were the scale of Angelic Beings to be placed on a parallel line with the scale of the chemical atoms of Science - from the hypothetical Helium down to Uranium - they would of course be found to differ. For these have, as correspondents on the Astral plane, only the four lowest orders - the higher three principles in the atom, or rather molecule or chemical element,

conscious, spiritual Souls. They are called the "Imperishable *Jivas,*" and constitute, through the order below their own, the first group of the first septenary* host – the great mystery of human conscious and intellectual Being. For the latter are the field wherein lies concealed *in its privation* the germ *that will fall into generation.* That germ will become the spiritual potency in the physical cell that guides the development of the embryo, and which is the cause of the hereditary transmission of faculties and all the inherent qualities in man. The Darwinian theory, however, of the transmission of acquired faculties, is neither taught nor accepted in Occultism. Evolution, in it, proceeds on quite other lines; the physical, according to esoteric teaching, evolving gradually from the spiritual, mental, and psychic. This inner soul of the physical cell – this "spiritual plasm" that dominates the germinal plasm – is the key that must open one day the gates of the terra incognita of the Biologist, now called the dark mystery of Embryology. (See text and note *infra.*)

(*f*) The Fifth group is a very mysterious one, as it is connected with the Microcosmic Pentagon, the five-pointed star representing man. In India and Egypt these *Dhyanis* were connected with the Crocodile, and their abode is in Capricornus. These are convertible terms in Indian astrology, as this (tenth) sign of the Zodiac is called *Makara,* loosely translated "crocodile." The word itself is occultly interpreted in various ways, as will be shown further on. In Egypt the defunct man – whose symbol is the pentagram or the five-pointed star, the points of which represent the limbs of a man – was shown emblematically transformed into a crocodile: *Sebakh* or *Sevekh* "or seventh," as Mr. Gerald Massey

---

being perceptible only to the initiated *Dangma's* eye. But then, if Chemistry desired to find itself on the right path, it would have to correct its tabular arrangement by that of the Occultists - which it may refuse to do. In Esoteric Philosophy, every physical particle corresponds to and depends on its higher *noumenon* - the Being to whose essence it belongs; and above as below, the Spiritual evolves from the Divine, the psycho-mental from the Spiritual - tainted from its lower plane by the astral - the whole animate and (seemingly) inanimate Nature evolving on parallel lines, and drawing its attributes from above as well as from below.

* The number seven does not imply only seven Entities, but seven groups or Hosts, as explained before. The highest group, the *Asuras* born in Brahma's first body - which turned into "Night" - are septenary, i.e., divided like the *Pitris* into seven classes, three of which are *arupa* (bodiless) and four with bodies. (See *Vishnu Purâna,* Book I.) They are in fact more truly our *Pitris* (ancestors) than the *Pitris* who projected the first physical men. (See Book II.)

says, showing it as having been the type of intelligence, is a dragon in reality, not a crocodile. He is the "Dragon of Wisdom" or *Manas*, the "Human Soul," Mind, the Intelligent principle, called in our esoteric philosophy the "Fifth" principle.

Says the defunct "Osirified" in ch. lxxxviii, *"Book of the Dead,"* or the *Ritual*, under the glyph of a mummiform god with a crocodile's head:

> (1) "I am the god (crocodile) presiding at the fear . . . at the arrival of his Soul among men. I am the god-crocodile brought for destruction" (an allusion to the destruction of divine spiritual purity when man acquires the knowledge of good and evil; also to the "fallen" gods, or angels of every theogony).

> (2) "I am the fish of the great Horus (as *Mankara* is the "crocodile," the vehicle of Varuna). I am merged in *Sekten*."

This last sentence gives the corroboration of, and repeats the doctrine of, *Esoteric Buddhism*, for it alludes directly to the fifth principle (*Manas*), or the most spiritual part of its essence rather, which merges into, is absorbed by, and made one with *Atma-Buddhi* after the death of man. For Se-khen is the residence or *loka* of the god Khem (Horus-Osiris, or Father and Son), hence the *"Devachan"* of *Atma-Buddhi*. In the Ritual of the Dead the defunct is shown entering into *Sekhem* with Horus-Thot and "emerging from it as pure spirit" (lxiv, 29). Thus the defunct says (v. 130): "I see the forms of (myself, as various) men transforming eternally . . . I know this (chapter). He who knows it . . . takes all kinds of living forms." . . .

And in verse 35, addressing in magic formula that which is called, in Egyptian esotericism, the "ancestral heart," or the reincarnating principle, the permanent EGO, the defunct says:

> "Oh my heart, my ancestral heart necessary for my transformations, ... do not separate thyself from me before the guardian of the Scales. Thou art my personality within my breast, divine companion *watching over my fleshes* (bodies). . ."

It is in *Sekhem* that lies concealed "the Mysterious Face," or the real man concealed under the false personality, the triple crocodile of Egypt, the symbol of the higher Trinity or human Triad, *Atma, Buddhi* and

*Manas.** In all the ancient papyri the crocodile is called *Sebek* (Seventh), while the water is the fifth principle esoterically; and, as already stated, Mr. Gerald Massey shows that the crocodile was "the Seventh Soul, the supreme one of seven – the Seer unseen." Even exoterically *Sekhem* is the residence of the god Khem, and Khem is Horus avenging the death of his father Osiris, hence punishing the Sins of man when he becomes a disembodied Soul. Thus the defunct "Osirified" became the god Khem, who "gleans the field of *Aanroo*," i.e., he gleans either his reward or punishment, as that field is the celestial locality (*Devachan*) where the defunct is given *wheat*, the food of divine justice. The fifth group of the celestial Beings is supposed to contain in itself the dual attributes of both the spiritual and physical aspects of the Universe; the two poles, so to say, of *Mahat* the Universal Intelligence, and the dual nature of man, the spiritual and the physical. Hence its number Five, multiplied and made into ten, connecting it with *Makara*, the 10th sign of Zodiac.

(*g*) The sixth and seventh groups partake of the lower qualities of the Quaternary. They are conscious, ethereal Entities, as invisible as Ether, which are shot out like the boughs of a tree from the first central group of the four, and shoot out in their turn numberless side groups, the lower of which are the Nature-Spirits, or Elementals of countless kinds and varieties; from the formless and unsubstantial – the ideal THOUGHTS of their creators – down to the Atomic, though, to human perception, invisible organisms. The latter are considered as the "Spirits of Atoms" for they are the first remove (backwards) from the physical Atom – sentient, if not intelligent creatures. They are all subject to Karma, and have to work it out through every cycle. For, as the doctrine teaches, there are no such privileged beings in the universe, whether in our or in other systems, in the outer or the inner worlds,[†] as the angels of the Western Religion and the Judean. A *Dhyan*

---

* One of the explanations of the real though hidden meaning of this Egyptian religious glyph is easy. The crocodile is the first to await and meet the devouring fires of the morning sun, and very soon came to personify the solar heat. When the sun arose, it was like the arrival on earth and among men "of the divine soul which informs the Gods." Hence the strange symbolism. The mummy donned the head of a crocodile to show that it was a soul arriving from the earth.

† A world when called "a higher world" is not higher by reason of its location, but because it is superior in quality or essence. Yet such a world is generally understood

Chohan has to become one; he cannot be born or appear suddenly on the plane of life as a full-blown angel. The Celestial Hierarchy of the present *Manvantara* will find itself transferred in the next cycle of life into higher, superior worlds, and will make room for a new hierarchy, composed of the elect ones of our mankind. Being is an endless cycle within the one absolute eternity, wherein move numberless inner cycles finite and conditioned. Gods, created as such, would evince no personal merit in being gods. Such a class of beings, perfect only by virtue of the special immaculate nature inherent in them, in the face of suffering and struggling humanity, and even of the lower creation, would be the symbol of an eternal injustice quite Satanic in character, an ever present crime. It is an anomaly and an impossibility in Nature. Therefore the "Four" and the "Three" have to incarnate as all other beings have. This sixth group, moreover, remains almost inseparable from man, who draws from it all but his highest and lowest principles, or his spirit and body, the five middle human principles being the very essence of those *Dhyanis*.‡ Alone, the Divine Ray (the *Atman*) proceeds directly from the One. When asked how that can be? How is it possible to conceive that those "gods," or angels, can be at the same time their own emanations and their personal selves? Is it in the same sense in the material world, where the son is (in one way) his father, being his blood, the bone of his bone and the flesh of his flesh? To this the teachers answer "Verily it is so." But one has to go deep into the mystery of BEING before one can fully comprehend this truth.

SD, i 213–222

---

by the profane as "Heaven," and located above our heads.

‡ Paracelsus calls them the *Flagae*; the Christians, the "Guardian Angels;" the Occultist, the "Ancestors, the *Pitris*;" they are the sixfold *Dhyan Chohans*, having the six spiritual Elements in the composition of their bodies - in fact, men, minus the physical body.

SPIRIT FALLING INTO MATTER

"2. THE ONE RAY MULTIPLIES THE SMALLER RAYS.
LIFE PRECEDES FORM, AND LIFE SURVIVES THE LAST
ATOM (*of Form, Sthula sarira, external body*). THROUGH
THE COUNTLESS RAYS THE LIFE RAY, THE ONE, LIKE
A THREAD THROUGH MANY BEADS (*pearls*) (*a*).

(*a*) This sloka expresses the conception – a purely Vedantic one, as already explained elsewhere – of a life-thread, *Sutratma*, running through successive generations. How, then, can this be explained? By resorting to a simile, to a familiar illustration, though necessarily imperfect, as all our available analogies must be. Before resorting to it, however, I would ask whether it seems *unnatural*, least of all "supernatural," to any one of us, when we consider that process known as the growth and development of a foetus into a healthy baby weighing several pounds evolves from what? From the segmentation of an infinitesimally small *ovum* and a *spermatozoon*; and afterwards we see that baby develop into a six-foot man! This refers to the atomic and physical expansion from the microscopically small into something very large, from the – to the naked eye – unseen, into the visible and objective. Science has provided for all this; and, I dare say, her theories, embryological, biological, and physiological, are correct enough so far as exact observation of the material goes. Nevertheless, the two chief difficulties of the science of embryology – namely, what are the forces at work in the formation of the foetus, and the *cause* of "hereditary transmission" of likeness, physical, moral or mental – have never been properly answered; nor will they ever be solved till the day when scientists condescend to accept the Occult theories.* But if this

* The materialists and the evolutionists of the Darwinian school would be ill-advised to accept the newly worked-out theories of Professor Weissmann, the author of *Beitrage zur Descendenzlehre*, with regard to one of the two mysteries of Embryology, as above specified, which he seems to have solved — as he thinks. For, when it is solved, Science will have stepped over into the domain of the truly occult, and stepped for ever out of the realm of transformation, as taught by Darwin. The two are irreconcileable, from the standpoint of materialism. Regarded from that of

physical phenomenon astonishes no one, except in so far as it puzzles the Embryologists, why should our intellectual and inner growth, the evolution of the human-spiritual to the Divine-Spiritual, be regarded as, or seem, more impossible than the other? Now to the simile.

Complete the physical plasm, mentioned in the last footnote, the "Germinal Cell" of man with all its material potentialities, with the "spiritual plasm," so to say, or the fluid that contains the five lower principles of the six-principled Dhyan – and you have the secret, if you are spiritual enough to understand it.

"When the seed of the animal man is cast into the soil of the animal woman, that seed cannot germinate unless it has been fructified by the five virtues (the fluid of, or the emanation from the principles) of the six-fold Heavenly man. Wherefore the Microcosm is represented as a Pentagon, within the Hexagon Star, the "Macrocosm." (" Ἄνθρωπος," a work on Occult Embryology, Book I). Then: "The functions of *Jiva* on this Earth are of a five-fold character. In the mineral atom it is

---

the Occultists, it solves all these mysteries. Those who are not acquainted with the new discovery of Professor Weissman—at one time a fervent Darwinist—ought to hasten to repair the deficiency. The German Embryologist-philosopher shows—thus stepping over the heads of the Greek Hippocrates and Aristotle, right back into the teachings of the old Aryans—one infinitesimal cell, out of millions of others at work in the formation of an organism, determining alone and unaided, by means of constant segmentation and multiplication, the correct image of the future man (or animal) in its physical, mental, and psychic characteristics. It is that cell which impresses on the face and form of the new individual the features of the parents or of some distant ancestor; it is that cell again which transmits to him the intellectual and mental idiosyncracies of his sires, and so on. This Plasm is the immortal portion of our bodies—simply through the process of successive assimilations. Darwin's theory, viewing the embryological cell as an essence or the extract from all other cells, is set aside; it is incapable of accounting for hereditary transmission. There are but two ways of explaining the mystery of heredity; either the substance of the germinal cell is endowed with the faculty of crossing the whole cycle of transformations that lead to the construction of a separate organism and then to the reproduction of identical germinal cells; or, *those germinal cells do not have their genesis at all in the body of the individual, but proceed directly from the ancestral germinal cell passed from father to son through long generations.* It is the latter hypothesis that Weissmann accepted and has worked upon; and it is to this cell that he traces the immortal portion of man. So far, so good; and when this almost correct theory is accepted, how will Biologists explain the first appearance of this everlasting cell? Unless man "grew" like the "immortal Topsy," and was not born at all, but fell from the clouds, how was that embryological cell born in him?

connected with the lowest principles of the Spirits of the Earth (the six-fold *Dhyanis*); in the vegetable particle, with their second – the *Prana* (life); in the animal, with all these plus the third and the fourth; in man, the germ must receive the fruition of all the five. Otherwise he will be born no higher than an animal"; namely, a congenital idiot. Thus in man alone the *Jiva* is complete. As to his seventh principle, it is but one of the Beams of the Universal Sun. Each rational creature receives only the temporary loan of that which has to return to its source; while his physical body is shaped by the lowest terrestrial lives, through physical, chemical, and physiological evolution. "The Blessed Ones have nought to do with the purgations of matter." (*Kabala, Chaldean Book of Numbers*).

It comes to this: Mankind in its first prototypal, shadowy form, is the offspring of the *Elohim* of Life (or *Pitris*); in its qualitative and physical aspect it is the direct progeny of the "Ancestors," the lowest *Dhyanis*, or Spirits of the Earth; for its moral, psychic, and spiritual nature, it is indebted to a group of divine Beings, the name and characteristics of which will be given in Book II. Collectively, men are the handiwork of hosts of various spirits; distributively, the tabernacles of those hosts; and occasionally and singly, the vehicles of some of them. In our present all-material Fifth Race, the earthly Spirit of the Fourth is still strong in us; but we are approaching the time when the pendulum of evolution will direct its swing decidedly upwards, bringing Humanity back on a parallel line with the primitive third Root Race in Spirituality. During its childhood, mankind was composed wholly of that Angelic Host, who were the indwelling Spirits that animated the monstrous and gigantic tabernacles of clay of the Fourth Race built by (as they are now also) and composed of countless myriads of lives.* This sentence will be explained later on in the present Commentary. The "tabernacles" have improved in texture and symmetry of form, growing and developing with the globe that bore them; but the physical improvement took place at the expense of the spiritual inner man and nature. The three middle

---

* Science, dimly perceiving the truth, may find Bacteria and other infinitesimals in the human body, and see in them but occasional and abnormal visitors to which diseases are attributed. Occultism—which discerns a life in every atom and molecule, whether in a mineral or human body, in air, fire or water—affirms that our whole body is built of such lives, the smallest bacteria under the microscope being to them in comparative size like an elephant to the tiniest infusoria.

principles in earth and man became with every race more material; the Soul stepping back to make room for the physical intellect; the essence of elements becoming the material and composite elements now known.

Man is not, nor could he ever be, the complete product of the "Lord God"; but he *is* the child of the *Elohim*, so arbitrarily changed into the singular masculine gender. The first *Dhyanis*, commissioned to "create" man in their image, could only throw off their shadows, like a delicate model for the Nature Spirits of matter to work upon (See Book II). Man is, beyond any doubt, formed physically out of the dust of the Earth, but his creators and fashioners were many. Nor can it be said that the "Lord God breathed into his nostrils the breath of life," unless that God is identified with the "ONE LIFE," Omnipresent though invisible, and unless the same operation is attributed to "God" on behalf of every *living Soul* – or *Nephesh*, which is the *vital* Soul, not the divine Spirit or *Ruach*, which ensures to man alone a divine degree of immortality, that no animal, as such, could ever attain in this cycle of incarnation. It is the inadequate distinctions made by the Jews, and now by our Western metaphysicians, who, not knowing of, and being unable to understand, hence to accept, more than a triune man – Spirit, Soul, Body – thus confuse the "breath of life" with immortal Spirit.[†] This

---

† * The learned and very philosophical author of "New Aspects of Life" would impress upon his reader that the *Nephesh chaiah* (living soul), according to the Hebrews, "proceeded from, or was produced by, the infusion of the Spirit or Breath of Life into the quickening body of man, and was to supersede and take the place of that spirit in the thus constituted self, so that the spirit passed into, was lost sight of, and disappeared in the living Soul." The human body, he thinks, ought to be viewed as a matrix in which, and from which, the Soul (which he seems to place higher than the spirit) is developed—considered *functionally* and from the standpoint of activity, the Soul stands undeniably higher in this finite and conditioned world of Maya—the Soul, he says, "is ultimately produced from the animated body of man." Thus the author identifies "Spirit" (*Atma*) simply with "the breath of life." The Eastern Occultists will demur to this statement, for it is based on the erroneous conception that *Prana* and *Atma* or *Jivatma* are one and the same thing. The author supports the argument by showing that with the ancient Hebrews, Greeks and even Latins, *Ruach*, *Pneuma* and *Spiritus*—with the Jews undeniably, and with the Greeks and Romans very probably—meant Wind; the Greek word *Anemos* (wind) and the Latin *Anima* "Soul" having a suspicious relation.

This is very far fetched. A legitimate battle-field for deciding this question is hardly to be found, since Mr. Pratt seems to be a practical, matter-of-fact metaphysician,

applies also directly to the Protestant theologians, who, in translating verse 8 of Ch. III in the Fourth Gospel, have entirely perverted the meaning. Indeed the verse is made to say "The *wind* bloweth where it listeth," instead of "the *Spirit* goeth where it willeth," as in the original and also in the translation of the Greek Eastern Church.

Thus the philosophy of psychic, spiritual, and mental relations with man's physical functions is in almost inextricable confusion. Neither the old Aryan, nor the Egyptian psychology are now properly understood. Nor can they be assimilated without accepting the esoteric septenary, or, at any rate, the Vedantic quinquepartite division of the human inner principles. Failing which, it will be for ever impossible to understand the metaphysical and purely psychic and even physiological relations between the *Dhyan-Chohans*, or Angels, on the one plane, and humanity on the other. No Eastern (Aryan) esoteric works are so far published, but we possess the Egyptian papyri which speak clearly of the seven principles or the "Seven Souls of Man."* The *Book of the Dead* gives a complete list of the "transformations" that every defunct undergoes, while divesting himself, one by one, of all those principles – materialised for the sake of clearness into ethereal entities or bodies. We must, moreover, remind those who try to prove that the ancient Egyptians knew nothing of and did not teach Reincarnation, that the "Soul" (the *Ego* or *Self*) of the defunct is said to be living in Eternity: it is immortal, "co-eval with, and disappearing with the Solar boat," i.e., for the cycle of necessity. This "Soul" *emerges from the Tiaou* (the realm *of the cause of life*) and joins the living on Earth *by day*, to return to *Tiaou* every night. This expresses the periodical existences of the Ego. (*Book of the Dead*, cvxliii)

The *shadow*, the astral form, is annihilated, "devoured by the Uranus" (cxlix., 51), the *Manes* will be annihilated; the two twins (the 4th and 5th principles) will be scattered; but the Soul-bird, "the divine Swallow

---

a kind of Kabalist-Positivist, and the Eastern metaphysicians, especially the Vedantins, are all Idealists. The Occultists are also of the extreme esoteric Vedantin school, and they call the One Life (*Parabrahm*), the Great Breath and the Whirlwind; but they disconnect the seventh principle entirely from matter or any relation to, or connection with it.

* * Vide in Part II., Book II., "*The Seven Souls of Man*," the divisions made respectively by Messrs. Gerald Massey and Franz Lambert.

– and the Uranus of Flame" (*Manas* and *Atma-Buddhi*) will live in the eternity, for they are their mother's husbands.[†]

Like alone produces like. The Earth gives Man his body, the gods (*Dhyanis*) his five inner principles, the psychic Shadow, of which those gods are often the animating principle. SPIRIT (*Atman*) is one – and indiscrete. It is not in the *Tiaou*.

For what is the *Tiaou*? The frequent allusion to it in the "*Book of the Dead*" contains a mystery. *Tiaou* is the path of the Night Sun, the inferior hemisphere, or the infernal region of the Egyptians, placed by them on the *concealed side of the moon*. The human being, in their esotericism, came out from the moon (a triple mystery – astronomical, physiological, and psychical at once); he crossed the whole cycle of existence and then returned to his birth place before issuing from it again. Thus the defunct is shown arriving in the West, receiving his judgment before Osiris, resurrecting as the god Horus, and circling round the sidereal heavens, which is an allegorical assimilation to Ra, the Sun; then having crossed the *Noot* (the celestial abyss), returning once more to *Tiaou*: an assimilation to Osiris, who, as the God of life and reproduction, inhabits the moon. Plutarch (*Isis and Osiris*, ch. xliii) shows the Egyptians celebrating a festival called "The Ingress of Osiris into the moon." In chapter xli. life is promised after death; and the renovation of life is placed under the patronage of Osiris-Lunus, because the moon was the symbol of life-renewals or reincarnations, owing to its growth, waning, dying, and reappearance every month. In the *Dankmoe*, (iv. 5) it is said: "Oh, Osiris-Lunus! That renews to thee thy renewal." And Safekh says to Seti I. (*Mariette's Abydos*, plate 51),

---

[†] Another suggestive analogy between the Aryan or Brahmanical and the Egyptian esotericism. The former call the Pitris "the lunar ancestors" of men; and the Egyptians made of the Moon-God, Taht-Esmun, the first human ancestor. This "moon-god" "expressed the Seven nature-powers that were prior to himself, and were summed up in him as his seven souls, of which he was the manifestor as the eighth one (hence the eighth sphere). The seven rays of the Chaldean Heptakis or Iao, on the Gnostic stones indicate the same septenary of souls." . . . "The first form of the mystical SEVEN was seen to be figured in heaven, by the seven large stars of the Great Bear, the constellation assigned by the Egyptians to the Mother of Time, and of the seven elemental powers." (See *The Seven Souls*, etc.) As well known to every Hindu, this same constellation represents in India the Seven *Rishis*, and as such is called *Riksha*, and *Chitra-Sikhandinas*.

"Thou renewest thyself as the god Lunus when a babe." It is still better explained in a Louvre papyrus (P. Pierret, "*Etudes Egyptologiques*"): "Couplings and conceptions abound when he (Osiris-Lunus) is seen in heaven on that day." Says Osiris: "Oh, sole radiant beam of the moon! I issue from the circulating multitudes (of stars) . . . . . . Open me the *Tiaou*, for Osiris N. I will issue by day to do what I have to do amongst the living" ("*Book of the Dead*," ch. ii), i.e., to produce conceptions.

Osiris was "God manifest in generation," because the ancients knew, far better than the moderns, the real occult influences of the lunar body upon the mysteries of conception.* Later on, when the moon became connected with female goddesses † – with Diana, Isis, Artemis, Juno, etc., that connection was due to a thorough knowledge of physiology and female nature, physical as much as psychic. But, primarily, the Sun and Moon were the only visible and, so to say, *tangible* (by their effects) psychic and physiological deities – the Father and the Son, while Space and air in general, or that expanse of Heaven called *Noot* by the Egyptians, was the concealed Spirit or Breath of the two. These "Father and Son" were interchangeable in their functions and worked harmoniously together in their effects upon terrestrial nature and humanity; hence they were regarded as ONE, though TWO in personified Entities. They were both males, and both had their distinct and also collaborative work in the causative

---

* In the oldest systems we find the Moon always male. Thus Soma is, with the Hindus, a kind of sidereal Don Juan, a "King," and the father, albeit illegitimate, of Buddha—Wisdom, which relates to Occult Knowledge, a wisdom gathered through a thorough acquaintance with lunar mysteries including those of sexual generation. (See "*Holy of Holies.*")

† If instead of being taught in Sunday Schools useless lessons from the *Bible*, the armies of the ragged and the poor were taught Astrology—so far, at any rate, as the occult properties of the Moon and its hidden influences on generation are concerned, then there would be little need to fear increase of the population nor to resort to the questionable literature of the Malthusians for its arrest. For it is the Moon and her conjunctions that regulate conceptions, and every astrologer in India knows it. During the previous and the present races, at least at the beginning of this one, those who indulged in marital relations during certain lunar phases that made those relations sterile were regarded as sorcerers and sinners. But even now those sins of old, based on the Occult knowledge and the abuse of it, would appear preferable to the crimes of to-day, which are perpetrated because of the complete ignorance of, and disbelief in all such occult influences.

generation of Humanity. So much from the astronomical and cosmic standpoints viewed and expressed in symbolical language – which became in our last races theological and dogmatic. But behind this veil of Cosmic and Astrological symbols, there were the Occult mysteries of Anthropography and the primeval genesis of man. And in this, no knowledge of symbols – or even the key to the *post-diluvian* symbolical language of the Jews – will, or can help, save only with reference to that which was laid down in national scriptures for exoteric uses; the sum of which, however cleverly veiled, was only the smallest portion of the real primitive history of each people, often relating, moreover – as in the Hebrew Scriptures – merely to the terrestrial human, not divine life of that nation. That psychic and spiritual element belonged to MYSTERY and INITIATION. There were things never recorded in scrolls, but, as in Central Asia, on rocks and in subterranean crypts.

Nevertheless, there was a time when the whole world was "of one lip and of one knowledge," and Man knew more of his origin than he does now, and thus knew that the Sun and Moon, however large a part they do play in the constitution, growth and development of the human body, were not the direct causative agents of his appearance on Earth; these agents being, in truth, the living and intelligent Powers which the Occultists call *Dhyan Chohans*."

SD, i 222–230

WHAT INCARNATES IN ANIMAL MAN

Now every "Round" (on the descending scale) is but a repetition in a more concrete form of the Round which preceded it, as every globe – down to our fourth sphere (the actual earth) – is a grosser and more material copy of the more shadowy sphere which precedes it in their successive order, on the three higher planes. (See diagram in Stanza VI. Comm. 6). On its way upwards on the ascending arc, Evolution spiritualises and etherealises, so to speak, the general nature of all, bringing it on to a level with the plane on which the twin globe on the opposite side is placed; the result being, that when the seventh globe is reached (in whatever Round) the nature of everything that is evolving returns to the condition it was in at its starting point – plus, every time, a new and superior degree in the states of consciousness. Thus it becomes clear that the "origin of man," so-called, on this our present Round, or lifecycle on this planet, must occupy the same place in the same order – save details based on local conditions and time – as in the preceding Round. Again, it must be explained and remembered that, as the work of each Round is said to be apportioned to a different group of so-called "Creators" or "Architects," so is that of every globe; i.e., it is under the supervision and guidance of special "Builders" and "Watchers" – the various *Dhyan-Chohans*.

The group of the hierarchy which is commissioned to "create" * men is a special group, then; yet it evolved shadowy man in this cycle just as a higher and still more spiritual group evolved him in the Third Round. But as it is the Sixth – on the downward scale of Spirituality – the last and seventh being the terrestrial Spirits (elementals) which gradually form, build, and condense his physical body – this Sixth group evolves no more than the future man's shadowy form, a filmy, hardly

---

* Creation is an incorrect word to use, as no religion, not even the sect of the Visishta Adwaitees in India – one which anthropomorphises even *Parabrahmam* – believes in creation out of *nihil* as Christians and Jews do, but in evolution out of preexisting materials.

visible transparent copy of themselves. It becomes the task of the fifth Hierarchy – the mysterious beings that preside over the constellation Capricornus, *Makara*, or "Crocodile" in India as in Egypt – to inform the empty and ethereal animal form and make of it the Rational Man. This is one of those subjects upon which very little may be said to the general public. It is a MYSTERY, truly, but only to him who is prepared to reject the existence of intellectual and conscious spiritual Beings in the Universe, limiting full Consciousness to man alone, and that only as a "function of the Brain." Many are those among the Spiritual Entities, who have incarnated bodily in man, since the beginning of his appearance, and who, for all that, still exist as independently as they did before, in the infinitudes of Space. . . .

To put it more clearly: the invisible Entity may be bodily present on earth without abandoning, however, its status and functions in the supersensuous regions. If this needs explanation, we can do no better than remind the reader of like cases in Spiritualism, though such cases are very rare, at least as regards the nature of the Entity incarnating,[†] or taking temporary possession of a medium. Just as certain persons – men and women, reverting to parallel cases among living persons – whether by virtue of a peculiar organization, or through the power of acquired mystic knowledge, can be seen in their "double" in one place, while the body is many miles away; so the same thing can occur in the case of superior Beings.

Man, philosophically considered, is, in his outward form, simply an animal, hardly more perfect than his pithecoid-like ancestor of the third round. He is a living body, not a living being, since the realisation of existence, the "Ego-Sum," necessitates self-consciousness, and an animal can only have direct consciousness, or instinct. This was so well understood by the Ancients that the Kabalist even made of soul and body two lives, independent of each other.[‡] The soul, whose body

---

† The so-called "Spirits" that may occasionally possess themselves of the bodies of mediums are not the Monads or Higher Principles of disembodied personalities. Such a "Spirit" can only be either an Elementary, or – a *Nirmanakaya*.

‡ On p. 340-351 (*Genesis of the Soul*) in the "*New Aspects of Life*," the Author states the Kabalistic teaching: "They held that, functionally, Spirit and Matter of corresponding opacity and density tended to coalesce; and that the resultant created Spirits, in the

vehicle is the Astral, ethero-substantial envelope, could die and man be still living on earth – i.e., the soul could free itself from and quit the tabernacle for various reasons – such as insanity, spiritual and physical depravity, etc.* Therefore, that which living men (Initiates) can do, the *Dhyanis*, who have no physical body to hamper them, can do still better. This was the belief of the ante-diluvians, and it is fast becoming that of modern intellectual society, in Spiritualism, besides the Greek and Roman Churches, which teach the ubiquity of their angels. The Zoroastrians regarded their *Amshaspends* as dual entities (*Ferouers*), applying this duality – in esoteric philosophy, at any rate – to all the spiritual and invisible denizens of the numberless worlds in space which are visible to our eye. In a note of Damascius (sixth century) on the Chaldean oracles, we have a triple evidence of the universality of this doctrine, for he says: "In these oracles the seven *Cosmocratores* of the world, ('The World Pillars,') mentioned likewise by St. Paul, are double – one set being commissioned to rule the superior worlds the spiritual and the sidereal, and the other to guide and watch over the

---

disembodied state, were constituted on a scale in which the differing opacities and transparencies of Elemental or uncreated Spirit were reproduced. And that these Spirits in the disembodied state attracted, appropriated, digested and assimilated Elemental Spirit and Elemental Matter whose condition was conformed to their own." "They therefore taught that there was a wide difference in the condition of created Spirits; and that in the intimate association between the Spirit-world and the world of Matter, the more opaque Spirits in the disembodied state were drawn towards the more dense parts of the material world, and therefore tended towards the centre of the Earth, where they found the conditions most suited to their state; while the more transparent Spirits passed into the surrounding aura of the planet, the most rarified finding their home in its satellite."

This relates exclusively to our Elementary Spirits, and has naught to do with either the Planetary, Sidereal, Cosmic or Inter-Etheric Intelligent Forces or "Angels" as they are termed by the Roman Church. The Jewish Kabalists, especially the practical Occultists who dealt with ceremonial magic, busied themselves solely with the spirits of the Planets and the "Elementals" so-called. Therefore this covers only a portion of the Esoteric Teaching.

* The possibility of the "Soul" (i.e., the eternal Spiritual Ego) dwelling in the unseen worlds, while its body goes on living on Earth, is a pre-eminently occult doctrine, especially in Chinese and Buddhist philosophy. See "*Isis Unveiled*," vol. i., p. 602, for an illustration. Many are the *Soulless* men among us, for the occurrence is found to take place in wicked materialists as well as in persons "who advance in holiness and never turn back." (See *ibid* and also "*Isis*," vol. ii, p. 369.)

worlds of matter." Such is also the opinion of Jamblichus, who makes an evident distinction between the archangels and the "*Archontes.*" (See "*De Mysteriis,*" sec. ii, ch. 3.) The above may be applied, of course, to the distinction made between the degrees or orders of spiritual beings, and it is in this sense that the Roman Catholic Church tries to interpret and teach the difference; for while the archangels are in her teaching divine and holy, their doubles are denounced by her as devils.[†] But the word '*ferouer*' is not to be understood in this sense, for it means simply the reverse or the opposite side of some attribute or quality. Thus when the Occultist says that the "Demon is the lining of God" (evil, the reverse of the medal), he does not mean two separate actualities, but the two aspects or facets of the same Unity. Now the best man living would appear, side by side with an Archangel – as described in Theology – a fiend. Hence a certain reason to depreciate a lower "double," immersed far deeper in matter than its original. But there is still as little cause to regard them as devils, and this is precisely what the Roman Catholics maintain against all reason and logic."

SD, i 232–236

[†] This identity between the Spirit and its material "double" (in man it is the reverse) explains still better the confusion, alluded to already in this work, made in the names and individualities, as well as the numbers, of the *Rishis* and the *Prajâpatis*; especially between those of the *Satyayuga* and the Mahabhâratan period. It also throws additional light on what the Secret Doctrine teaches with regard to the Root and the Seed *Manus* (see Book ii, "On the primitive *Manus* of humanity".). Not only those progenitors of our mankind, but every human being, we are taught, has its prototype in the Spiritual Spheres; which prototype is the highest essence of his seventh principle. Thus the seven *Manus* become 14, the Root *Manu* being the Prime Cause, and the "Seed *Manu*" its effect; and when the latter reach from *Satyayuga* (the first stage) to the heroic period, these *Manus* or *Rishis* become 21 in number.

MANY BODIES BUT ONE SOUL

The chief difficulty which prevents men of science from believing in divine as well as in nature Spirits is their materialism. The main impediment before the Spiritualist which hinders him from believing in the same, while preserving a blind belief in the "Spirits" of the Departed, is the general ignorance of all, except some Occultists and Kabalists, about the true essence and nature of matter. It is on the acceptance or rejection of the theory of the *Unity of all in Nature, in its ultimate Essence*, that mainly rests the belief or unbelief in the existence around us of other conscious beings besides the Spirits of the Dead.

It is on the right comprehension of the primeval Evolution of Spirit-Matter and its real essence that the student has to depend for the further elucidation in his mind of the Occult Cosmogony, and for the only sure clue which can guide his subsequent studies.

In sober truth, as just shown, every "Spirit" so-called is either a *disembodied or a future man*. As from the highest Archangel (*Dhyan Chohan*) down to the last conscious "Builder" (the inferior class of Spiritual Entities), all such are *men*, having lived aeons ago, in other *Manvantaras*, on this or other Spheres; so the inferior, semi-intelligent and non-intelligent Elementals – are all *future* men. That fact alone – that a Spirit is endowed with intelligence – is a proof to the Occultist that that Being must have been a *man*, and acquired his knowledge and intelligence throughout the human cycle. There is but one indivisible and absolute Omniscience and Intelligence in the Universe, and this thrills throughout every atom and infinitesimal point of the whole finite Kosmos which hath no bounds, and which people call SPACE, considered independently of anything contained in it. But the first differentiation of its *reflection* in the manifested World is purely Spiritual, and the Beings generated in it are not endowed with a consciousness that has any relation to the one we conceive of. They can have no human consciousness or Intelligence before they have

64

acquired such, personally and individually. This may be a mystery, yet it is a fact, in Esoteric philosophy, and a very apparent one too.

The whole order of nature evinces a progressive march towards *a higher life*. There is design in the action of the seemingly blindest forces. The whole process of evolution with its endless adaptations is a proof of this. The immutable laws that weed out the weak and feeble species, to make room for the strong, and which ensure the "survival of the fittest," though so cruel in their immediate action – all are working toward the grand end. The very *fact* that adaptations *do* occur, that the fittest *do* survive in the struggle for existence, shows that what is called "unconscious Nature" * is in reality an aggregate of forces manipulated by semi-intelligent beings (Elementals) guided by High Planetary Spirits, (*Dhyan Chohans*), whose collective aggregate forms the manifested *verbum* of the unmanifested LOGOS, and constitutes at one and the same time the MIND of the Universe and its immutable LAW.

Three distinct representations of the Universe in its three distinct aspects are impressed upon our thought by the esoteric philosophy: the PRE-EXISTING (evolved from) the EVER-EXISTING; and the PHENOMENAL – the world of illusion, the reflection, and shadow thereof. During the great mystery and drama of life known as the *Manvantara*, real Kosmos is like the object placed behind the white screen upon which are thrown the Chinese shadows, called forth by the magic lantern. The actual figures and things remain invisible, while the wires of evolution are pulled by the unseen hands; and men and things are thus but the reflections, *on* the white field, of the realities *behind* the snares of *Mahamaya*, or the great Illusion. This was taught in every philosophy, in every religion, *ante-* as well as *post*-diluvian, in India and Chaldea, by the Chinese as by the Grecian Sages. In the former countries these three Universes were allegorized, in exoteric teachings, by the three trinities emanating from the Central eternal

---

* * Nature taken in its abstract sense, *cannot* be "unconscious," as it is the emanation from, and thus an aspect (on the manifested plane) of the ABSOLUTE consciousness. Where is that daring man who would presume to deny to vegetation and even to minerals *a consciousness of their own*. All he can say is, that this consciousness is beyond his comprehension.

germ and forming with it a Supreme Unity: the *initial*, the *manifested*, and the *Creative* Triad, or the three in One. The last is but the symbol, in its concrete expression, of the first *ideal* two. Hence Esoteric philosophy passes over the necessarianism of this purely metaphysical conception, and calls the first one, only, the Ever Existing. This is the view of every one of the six great schools of Indian philosophy – the *six principles of that unit body of* WISDOM *of which the "gnosis,"* the *hidden* knowledge, is the seventh.

The writer hopes that, superficially handled as may be the comments on the Seven Stanzas, enough has been given in this cosmogonic portion of the work to show Archaic teachings to be more *scientific* (in the modern sense of the word) on their very face, than any other ancient Scriptures left to be regarded and judged on their exoteric aspect. Since, however, as confessed before, this work *withholds far more than it gives out*, the student is invited to use his own intuitions. Our chief care is to elucidate that which has already been given out, and, to our regret, very incorrectly at times; to supplement the knowledge hinted at – whenever and wherever possible – by additional matter, and to bulwark our doctrines against the too strong attacks of modern Sectarianism, and more especially against those of our latter-day Materialism, very often miscalled Science, whereas, in reality, the words "Scientists" and "Sciolists" ought alone to bear the responsibility for the many illogical theories offered to the world. In its great ignorance, the public, while blindly accepting everything that emanates from "authorities," and feeling it to be its duty to regard every *dictum* coming from a man of Science as a proven fact – the public, we say, is taught to scoff at anything brought forward from "heathen" sources. Therefore, as materialistic Scientists can be fought solely with their own weapons – those of controversy and argument – an *Addendum* is added to every Book contrasting our respective views and showing how even great authorities may often err. We believe that this can be done effectually by showing the weak points of our opponents, and by proving their too frequent sophisms – made to pass for scientific *dicta* – to be incorrect. We hold to Hermes and his "Wisdom" – in its universal character; they – to Aristotle as against intuition and the experience of the ages, fancying that Truth is the exclusive property of the Western world. Hence the disagreement. As Hermes says, "Knowledge differs much from sense; for sense is of things that surmount it, but Knowledge (*gyi*) is the end of sense", i.e. of the illusion of our physical brain and its intellect; thus emphasizing the contrast between the laboriously acquired knowledge of the senses and mind (*manas*), and the intuitive omniscience of the Spiritual divine Soul – *Buddhi*."

SD, i 276–279

MATTER – THE SHADOW OF SPIRIT

Whatever may be the destiny of these actual writings in a remote future, we hope to have proven so far the following facts:

(1) The Secret Doctrine teaches no *Atheism*, except in the Hindu sense of the word *nastika*, or the rejection of *idols*, including every anthropomorphic god. In this sense every Occultist is a *Nastika*.

(2) It admits a *Logos* or a collective "Creator" of the Universe; a *Demiurgos* – in the sense implied when one speaks of an "Architect" as the "Creator" of an edifice, whereas that Architect has never touched one stone of it, but, while furnishing the plan, left all the manual labour to the masons; in our case the plan was furnished by the Ideation of the Universe, and the constructive labour was left to the Hosts of intelligent Powers and Forces. But that *Demiurgos* is no personal deity – i.e., an imperfect *extra-cosmic god* – but only the aggregate of the *Dhyan-Chohans* and the other forces.

As to the latter:

(3) They are dual in their character; being composed of *(a)* the irrational *brute energy*, inherent in matter, and *(b)* the intelligent soul or cosmic consciousness which directs and guides that energy, and which is the *Dhyan-Chohanic thought reflecting the Ideation of the Universal mind*. This results in a perpetual series of physical manifestations and *moral effects* on Earth, during manvantaric periods, the whole being subservient to Karma. As that process is not always perfect; and since, however many proofs it may exhibit of a guiding intelligence behind the veil, it still shows gaps and flaws, and even results very often in evident failures – therefore, neither the collective Host (*Demiurgos*), nor any of the working powers individually, are proper subjects for divine honours or worship. All are entitled to the grateful reverence of Humanity, however, and man ought to be ever striving to help the *divine evolution of Ideas*, by becoming to the best of his ability *a co-worker with nature* in the cyclic task. The ever unknowable and incognizable

Karana alone, the *Causeless* Cause of all causes, should have its shrine and altar on the holy and ever untrodden ground of our heart – invisible, intangible, unmentioned, save through "the still small voice" of our spiritual consciousness. Those who worship before it, ought to do so in the silence and the sanctified solitude of their Souls,* making their spirit the sole mediator between them and the *Universal Spirit*, their good actions the only priests, and their sinful intentions the only visible and objective sacrificial victims to the *Presence*. (See Part II, "On the Hidden Deity".)

(4) Matter is *Eternal*. It is the *Upadhi* (the physical basis) for the One infinite Universal Mind to build thereon its ideations. Therefore, the Esotericists maintain that there is no inorganic or *dead* matter in nature, the distinction between the two made by Science being as unfounded as it is arbitrary and devoid of reason. Whatever Science may think, however – and *exact* Science is a fickle dame, as we all know by experience – Occultism knows and teaches differently, from time immemorial – from Manu and Hermes down to Paracelsus and his successors.

Thus Hermes, the thrice great Trismegistus, says: "Oh, my son, matter *becomes*; formerly it *was*; for matter is the vehicle of becoming."†

---

* "When thou prayest, thou shalt not be as the hypocrites are ... but enter into *thine inner chamber and having shut thy door, pray to thy Father which is in secret*." Matt. vi.). Our Father is *within us* "in Secret," our 7th principle, in the "inner chamber" of our Soul perception. "The Kingdom of Heaven" and of God "*is within us*" says Jesus, *not outside*. Why are Christians so absolutely blind to the self-evident meaning of the words of wisdom they delight in mechanically repeating?

† To this the late Mrs. (Dr.) Kingsford, the able translator and compiler of the Hermetic Fragments (see "*The Virgin of the World*") remarks in a foot-note; "Dr. Menard observes that in Greek the same word signifies *to be born* and *to become*. The idea here is that the material of the world is in its essence eternal, but that before creation or 'becoming' it is in a passive and motionless condition. Thus it 'was' before being put into operation; now it 'becomes,' that is, it is mobile and progressive." And she adds the purely Vedantic doctrine of the Hermetic philosophy that "Creation is thus the period of activity (*Manvantara*) of God, who, according to Hermetic thought (or *which*, according to the Vedantin) has two modes—Activity or Existence, God evolved (*Deus explicitus*); and Passivity of Being (*Pralaya*) God involved (*Deus implicitus*). Both modes are perfect and complete, as are the waking and sleeping states of man. Fichte, the German philosopher, distinguished Being (*Seyn*) as One, which we know only through existence (*Daseyn*) as the Manifold.

Becoming is the mode of activity of the uncreate deity. Having been endowed with the germs of becoming, matter (objective) is brought into birth, for the creative force fashions it *according to the ideal forms*. Matter not yet engendered had no form; it becomes when it is put into operation." (*The Definitions of Asclepios*, p. 134, "Virgin of the World")

"Everything is the product of one universal creative effort. . . . There is nothing *dead*, in Nature. *Everything is organic and living*, and therefore the whole world appears to be a living organism." (Paracelsus, *"Philosophia ad Athenienes,"* F. Hartmann's translations, p. 44.)

(5.) The Universe was evolved out of its ideal plan, upheld through Eternity in the unconsciousness of that which the Vedantins call *Parabrahm*. This is practically identical with the conclusions of the highest Western Philosophy – "the innate, eternal, and self-existing Ideas" of Plato, now reflected by Von Hartmann. The "unknowable" of Herbert Spencer bears only a faint resemblance to that transcendental *Reality* believed in by Occultists, often appearing merely a personification of a *"force* behind phenomena" – an infinite and eternal *Energy* from which all things proceed, while the author of the "Philosophy of the Unconscious" has come (in this respect only) as near to a solution of the great *Mystery* as mortal man can. Few were those, whether in ancient or mediaeval philosophy, who have dared to approach the subject or even hint at it. Paracelsus mentions it inferentially. His ideas are admirably synthesized by Dr. F. Hartmann, F.T.S., in his *"Life of Paracelsus."*

All the *Christian* Kabalists understood well the Eastern root idea: The active Power, the "Perpetual motion of the great Breath" only awakens Kosmos at the dawn of every new Period, setting it into motion by means of the two contrary Forces, and thus causing it to become objective on the plane of Illusion. In other words, that dual motion transfers Kosmos from the plane of the Eternal Ideal into that of finite manifestation, or from the *Noumenal* to the *Phenomenal* plane. Everything that *is, was*, and *will be*, eternally IS, even the countless forms, which are finite and perishable only in their objective, not in their *ideal* Form. They existed as Ideas, in the Eternity, and, when they pass away, will exist as reflections. Neither the form of man, nor that of any animal, plant or stone has ever been *created*, and it is only on this plane of ours that it commenced "becoming," i.e., objectivising into its present materiality, or expanding *from within outwards*, from the most sublimated and supersensuous essence into its grossest appearance. Therefore *our* human forms have existed in the Eternity as astral orethereal prototypes; according to which models, the Spiritual Beings (or Gods) whose duty it was to bring them into objective being and terrestrial Life, evolved the protoplasmic forms of the future *Egos* from *their own essence*. After which, when this human *Upadhi*, or basic mould was ready, the natural terrestrial Forces began to work on those supersensuous moulds *which contained, besides their own, the elements of all the past vegetable and future animal forms of this globe in them*. Therefore, man's *outward* shell passed through every vegetable and animal body before it assumed the human shape. As this will be fully described in Book II, with the Commentaries thereupon, there is no need to say more of it here."

SD, i 279–283

THE SEVEN PRAKRITIS

If one turns to the "*Laws* (or Ordinances) *of Manu,*" one finds the prototype of all these ideas. Mostly lost (to the Western world) in their original form, disfigured by later interpolations and additions, they have, nevertheless, preserved quite enough of their ancient Spirit to show its character. "Removing the darkness, the Self-existent Lord" (*Vishnu, Narayana,* etc.) becoming manifest, and "wishing to produce beings from his Essence, created, in the beginning, water alone. In that he cast seed. . . . . That became a golden Egg." (V. 6, 7, 8, 9.) Whence this Self-existent Lord? It is called THIS, and is spoken of as "Darkness, imperceptible, without definite qualities, undiscoverable as if wholly in sleep." (V. 5.) Having dwelt in that Egg for a whole divine year, he "who is called in the world Brahmâ," splits that Egg in two, and from the upper portion he forms the heaven, from the lower the earth, and from the middle the sky and "the perpetual place of waters." (12, 13.)

But there is, directly following these verses, something more important for us, as it corroborates entirely our esoteric teachings. From verse 14 to 36, evolution is given in the order described in the Esoteric philosophy. This cannot be easily gainsaid. Even Medhâtithi, the son of Viraswâmin, and the author of the Commentary, the "*Manubhâsya,*" whose date, according to the western Orientalists, is 1,000 A.D., helps us with his remarks to the elucidation of the truth. He showed himself either unwilling to give out more, because he knew that truth which has to be kept from the profane, or else he was really puzzled. Still, what he does give out makes the septenary principle in men and nature plain enough.

Let us begin with Chapter 1. of the "Ordinances" or "Laws" after the Self-existent Lord, the *unmanifesting Logos* of the Unknown "Darkness," becomes manifested in the golden Egg. It is from this "Egg," from: (11.) That which is the undiscrete (undifferentiated) cause, eternal, which *Is and Is not*, from It issued that male who is called in the world Brahmâ.
. . . .

Here we find, as in all genuine philosophical systems, even the "Egg" or the Circle (or Zero), boundless Infinity, referred to as IT ,* and Brahmâ, the first *unit* only, referred to as the *male* god, i.e., the fructifying Principle. It is or 10 (ten) the Decade. On the plane of the Septenary *or our World* only, it is called Brahmâ. On that of the *Unified Decade* in the realm of Reality, this male Brahmâ is an illusion.

(14.) "From Self (*âtmanah*) he created mind, (*i*) *which is and is not*; (*ii*) and from mind, Ego-ism (*Self-Consciousness*) the ruler; (*iii*) the Lord."

(i) The mind is *Manas*. Medhâtithi, the commentator, justly observes here that it is the reverse of this and shows already interpolation and rearranging; for it is *Manas* that springs from *Ahamkara* or (Universal) Self-Consciousness, as *Manas* in the microcosm springs from *Mahat*, or *Maha-Buddha* (*Buddhi*, in man). For *Manas* is dual, and as shown and translated by Colebrooke, "is *serving both for sense and action*, is an organ by affinity, being cognate with the rest." "The rest" means, here, that *Manas*, our *fifth* principle (the fifth, because the body was named the *first*, which is the reverse of the true philosophical order)† is in affinity both with *Atma-Buddhi* and with the lower four principles. Hence, our teaching: namely, that *Manas* follows *Atma-Buddhi* to *Devachan*, and that the lower (dregs, the residue of) *Manas* remains with *Kama rupa*, in *Limbus*, or *Kama loka*, the abode of the "Shells."

(ii) Such is the meaning of *Manas*, which "*is, and is not.*"

(iii) Medhâtithi translates it as "the one conscious of the I," or Ego, not "ruler," as the Orientalists do. Thus they translate verse 16: "He also, having made the subtle parts of those six (the Great Self and the five organs of sense) of unmeasured brightness, to enter into the elements of Self (*Atmamâtrâsu*) created all beings."

When, according to Medhâtithi, it ought to read *mâtrâ-Chit* instead of "*Atmamâtrâsu*," and thus be made to say:

"He having pervaded the subtle parts of those six, of unmeasured brightness, by elements of self, created all beings."

---

* The ideal apex of the Pythagorean triangle: *Vide* Sections in Vol. II, "Cross and Circle," and the "Earliest Symbolics of the Cross."

† *Vide* A. Coke Burnell's translation, edited by Ed. W. Hopkins, Ph.D.

This latter reading must be the correct one, since he, the *Self*, is what we call *Atma*, and thus constitutes the seventh principle, the synthesis of the "*six*." Such is also the opinion of the editor of *Mânava Dharma Shastra*, who seems to have intuitively entered far deeper into the spirit of the philosophy than has the translator of the "*Ordinances of Manu*", the late Dr. Burnell. For he hesitates little between the text of Kulluka and the *Commentaries of Medhâtithi*. Rejecting the *tanmâtra*, or subtile elements, and the *âtmamâtrâsu* of Kulluka, he says, applying the principles to the Cosmic Self: "The six appear rather to be the *manas* plus the five principles of Ether, air, fire, water, earth"; "having united five portions of these six with the spiritual element (the seventh) he (thus) created all existing things;" *âtmamâtra* is therefore the spiritual atom as opposed to the elementary, not reflective "elements of himself." Thus he corrects the translation of verse –

> "17. As the subtile elements of bodily forms of This One depend on these six, so the wise call his form *çarira*" (*sharira*) –

and he says that "Elements" mean here portions or parts (or principles), which reading is borne out by verse 19, which says:

> 19. This non-eternal (Universe) arises then from the Eternal, by means of the subtile elements of forms of *those seven* very glorious principles" (*purusha*).

Commenting upon which, according to Medhâtithi, the Editor remarks that "the five elements plus mind (*Manas*) and Self-Consciousness (*Ahamkara*) * are meant;" "subtile elements," as before (meaning) "five portions of form" (or principles). For verse 20 shows it, when saying of these (five elements, or "five portions of form" (*rupa*, plus *Manas* and Self-Consciousness) that they constitute the "seven *purusha*," or *principles*, called in the *Purânas* the "Seven *Prâkritis*."

Moreover, these "five elements" or "five portions" are spoken of in verse 27 as "those which are called the atomic destructible portions" – therefore "distinct from the atoms of the *nyâya*."

---

* *Ahamkara*, as universal Self-Consciousness, has a triple aspect, as also *Manas*. For this conception of "I," or one's Ego, is either *sattwa*, "pure quietude," or appears as *rajas*, "active," or remains *tamas*, "stagnant," in darkness. It belongs to Heaven and Earth, and assumes the properties of either.

This creative Brahmâ, issuing from the mundane or golden egg, unites in himself both the male and the female principles. He is, in short, the same as all the creative *Protologoi*. Of Brahmâ, however, it could not be said, as of Dionysos: "πρωτόγονον διφυῆ τρίγονον Βακχεῖον Ανακτα Ἄγριον ἀρρητόνον κρύφιον δικέρωτα δίμορφον" – a lunar Jehovah – Bacchus truly, with David dancing nude before his *symbol* in the ark – because no licentious *Dionysia* were ever established in his name and honour. All such public worship was exoteric, and the great universal symbols were distorted universally, as those of Krishna are now by the Vallabachâryas of Bombay, the followers of the *infant* god. But are these popular gods the *true Deity*? Are *they* the Apex and synthesis of the seven-fold creation, man included? Never! Each and all are one of the rungs of that septenary ladder of Divine Consciousness, pagan as Christian. For *Ain-Soph* also is said to manifest through the *Seven Letters of Jehovah's name* who, having usurped the place of the Unknown Limitless, was given by his devotees his Seven Angels of the Presence – his *Seven Principles*. Yet they are mentioned in almost every school. In the pure *Sânkhya* philosophy *mahat, Ahamkara* and the five *tanmâtras* are called the *seven Prâkritis* (or Natures), and they are counted from *Maha-Buddhi* or *Mahat* down to Earth. (See *Sânkhya Karika* III and Commentaries.)

Nevertheless, however disfigured for Rabbinical purposes is the original *Elohistic* version by Ezra, however repulsive at times even the *esoteric* meaning in the Hebrew scrolls, which is far more so than its outward *veil* or *cloaking* may be † – once the *Jehovistic* portions are eliminated, the Mosaic books are found full of purely occult and priceless knowledge, especially in the first six chapters.

Read by the aid of the *Kabala* one finds a matchless temple of occult truths, a well of deeply concealed beauty hidden under a structure, the *visible* architecture of which, its apparent symmetry notwithstanding, is unable to stand the criticism of cold reason, or to reveal its age, for it belongs to all the ages. There is more wisdom concealed under the exoteric *fables* of *Purânas* and *Bible* than in all the exoteric *facts* and science in the literature of the world, and more OCCULT true Science, than there is of exact knowledge in all the academies. Or, in plainer

---

† See "*The Holy of Holies*".

and stronger language, there is as much esoteric wisdom in some portions of the *exoteric Purânas* and *Pentateuch*, as there is of nonsense and of designed childish fancy in it, when read only in the dead-letter murderous interpretations of great dogmatic religions, and especially of sects.

SD, i 333–336

THE ONE IS KNOWN BY THE MANY

. . . (T. Subba Row) explains what he means by this acting of something which is *nothing*, though it is the ALL, by a fine simile. He compares the *Logos* to the sun through which light and heat radiate, but whose energy, light and heat, exist in some unknown condition in Space and are diffused in Space only as *visible* light and heat, the sun being only the agent thereof. This is the first triadic hypostasis. The quaternary is made up by the *energizing light* shed by the *Logos*.

The Hebrew Kabalists give it in a shape which esoterically is identical with the Vedantic. AIN-SOPH, they taught, could not be comprehended, could not be located, nor named, though the causeless cause of all. Hence its name – AIN-SOPH – is a term of negation, "the inscrutable, the incognizable, and the unnameable." They made of it, therefore, a boundless circle, a sphere, of which human intellect, with the utmost stretch, could only perceive the vault. In the words of one who has unriddled much in the Kabalistical system, in one of its meanings thoroughly, in its numerical and geometrical esotericism: "Close your eyes, and from your own consciousness of perception try and think outward to the extremest limits in every direction. You will find that equal lines or rays of perception extend out evenly in all directions, so that the utmost effort of perception will terminate in the *vault of a sphere*. The limitation of this sphere will, of necessity, be a great *Circle*, and the direct rays of thought in any and every direction must be *right line radii* of the circle. This, then, *must* be, humanly speaking, the extremest all-embracing conception of the *Ain-Soph manifest*, which formulates itself as a *geometrical figure*, viz., of a circle, with its elements of curved circumference and right line diameter divided into radii. Hence, a geometrical shape is the first recognisable means of connection between the *Ain-Soph* and the intelligence of man."*

This great circle (which Eastern Esotericism reduces to the point within the Boundless Circle) is the *Avalôkitêswara*, the *Logos* or *Verbum*

---

* From the *Masonic Review* for June, 1886.

of which Mr. Subba Row speaks. But this circle or manifested God is as unknown to us, except through its *manifested* universe, as the ONE, though easier, or rather more possible to our highest conceptions. This *Logos* which sleeps in the bosom of *Parabrahmam* during *Pralaya*, as our "*Ego* is latent (in us) at the time *of sushupti*, sleep"; which cannot cognize *Parabrahmam* otherwise than as *Mulaprakriti* – the latter being a cosmic veil which is "the mighty expanse of cosmic matter" – is thus only an organ in cosmic creation, through which radiate the energy and wisdom of *Parabrahmam*, unknown to the *Logos*, as it is to ourselves. Moreover, as the *Logos* is as unknown to us as *Parabrahmam* is unknown in reality to the *Logos*, both Eastern Esotericism and the *Kabala* – in order to bring the *Logos* within the range of our conceptions – have resolved the abstract synthesis into concrete images, viz., into the reflections or multiplied aspects of that *Logos* or *Avalôkitêswara*, Brahmâ, Ormazd, Osiris, Adam Kadmon, call it by any of these names – which aspects or Manvantaric emanations are the *Dhyan Chohans*, the *Elohim*, the *Devas*, the *Amshaspends*, &c., &c. Metaphysicians explain the root and germ of the latter, according to Mr. Subba Row, as the first manifestation of *Parabrahmam*, "the highest trinity that we are capable of understanding," which is *Mulaprakriti* (the veil), the *Logos*, and the conscious energy "of the latter," or its power and light[*]; or "matter, force and the Ego, or the one root of self, of which every other kind of self is but a manifestation or a reflection." It is then only in this "light" (of consciousness) of mental and physical perception, that practical Occultism can throw this into visibility by geometrical figures; which, when closely studied, will yield not only a scientific explanation of the real, objective, existence [†] of the "Seven sons of the divine Sophia," which is this light of the *Logos*, but show by means of other yet undiscovered keys that, with regard to Humanity, these "Seven Sons" and their numberless emanations, centres of energy personified, are an absolute necessity. Make away with them, and the mystery of Being and Mankind will never be unriddled, not even closely approached.

It is through this light that everything is created. This ROOT of mental SELF is also the root of physical Self, for this light is the permutation, in our manifested world, of *Mulaprakriti*, called Aditi in

---

* Called, in the *Bhagavad-Gita, Daiviprakriti.*

† Objective—in the world of *Maya*, of course; still as real as we are.

the *Vedas*. In its third aspect it becomes Vâch‡, the daughter and the mother of the *Logos*, as Isis is the daughter and the mother of Osiris, who is Horus; and Mout, the daughter, wife, and mother of Ammon, in the Egyptian Moon-glyph. In the *Kabala*, *Sephira* is the same as Shekinah, and is, in another synthesis, the wife, daughter, and mother of the "Heavenly man," Adam Kadmon, and is even identical with him, just as Vâch is identical with Brahmâ, and is called the female *Logos*. In the *Rig Veda*, Vâch is "mystic speech," by whom Occult Knowledge and Wisdom are communicated to man, and thus Vâch is said to have "entered the *Rishis*." She is "generated by the gods;" she is the divine Vâch – the "Queen of gods"; and she is associated – like *Sephira* with the *Sephiroth* – with the *Prajâpati* in their work of creation. Moreover, she is called "the mother of the *Vedas*," "since it is through her power (as mystic speech) that Brahmâ revealed them, and also owing to her power that he produced the universe" – i.e., through speech, and words (synthesized by the "WORD") and numbers.§

SD, i 428–430

---

‡ "In the course of cosmic manifestation, this *Daiviprakriti*, instead of being the mother of the *Logos*, should, strictly speaking, be called his daughter." ("*Notes on the Bhagavad-Gita*," p. 305, *Theosophist*.)

§ The wise men, like Stanley Jevons amongst the moderns, who invented the scheme which makes the incomprehensible assume a tangible form, could only do so by resorting to numbers and geometrical figures.

MANY VERSIONS OF THE ONE TRUTH

In India these creations were described as follows:

(I.) *Mahat-tattwa* creation – so-called because it was the primordial self-evolution of that which had to become *Mahat* – the "divine MIND, conscious and intelligent"; esoterically, "the spirit of the Universal soul." ... "Worthiest of ascetics, through its potency (the potency of that cause); every produced cause comes by its proper nature." (*Vishnu Purâna.*) "Seeing that the potencies of all beings are understood only through the knowledge of That (Brahma), which is beyond reasoning, creation, and the like, such potencies are referable to Brahma." THAT, then, precedes the manifestation. "The first was *Mahat*," says *Linga Purâna*; for the ONE (the That) is neither first nor last, but ALL. Exoterically, however, this manifestation is the work of the "Supreme One" (a natural effect, rather, of an Eternal Cause); or, as the Commentator says, it might have been understood to mean that Brahmâ was then created (?), being identified with *Mahat*, active intelligence or the operating will of the Supreme. Esoteric philosophy renders it "the operating LAW."

It is on the right comprehension of this tenet in the *Brâhmanas* and *Purânas* that hangs, we believe, the apple of discord between the three Vedantin Sects: the *Advaita*, *Dwaita*, and the *Visishtadvaitas*. The first arguing rightly that *Parabrahman*, having no relation, as the absolute all, to the manifested world – the Infinite having no connection with the finite – can neither will nor create; that, therefore, Brahmâ, *Mahat*, *Iswara*, or whatever name the creative power may be known by, creative gods and all, are simply an illusive aspect of *Parabrahmam* in the conception of the conceivers; while the other sects identify the impersonal Cause with the Creator, or *Iswara*.

Mahat (or Maha-*Buddhi*) is, with the *Vaishnavas*, however, divine mind in active operation, or, as Anaxagoras has it, "an ordering and disposing mind, which was the cause of all things" – Νοῦς ὅ διακοσμῶντε και παντων ἄιτιος.

Wilson saw at a glance the suggestive connection between *Mahat* and the Phœnician *Mot,* or *Mut,* who was female with the Egyptians – the Goddess Mout, the "Mother" – "which, like *Mahat,*" he says, "was the first product of the mixture (?) of Spirit and matter, and the first rudiment of Creation": "*Ex connexione autem ejus spiritus prodidit Mot . . . . . .* From whose seed were created all living things" – repeats Brucker (I., 240) – giving it a still more materialistic and anthropomorphic colouring.

Nevertheless, the esoteric sense of the doctrine is seen through every exoteric sentence on the very face of the old Sanscrit texts that treat of primordial Creation. "The Supreme Soul, the all permeant (*Sarvaga*) Substance of the World, having entered (been drawn) into matter (*prakriti*) and Spirit (*purusha*), agitated the mutable and the immutable principles the season of Creation (*manvantara*) having arrived."* . . .

---

* The *nous* of the Greeks, which is (spiritual or divine) mind, or *mens,* "*Mahat,*" operates upon matter in the same way; it "enters into" and agitates it:

"*Spiritus intus alit, totamque infusa per artus,*

Mens agitat molem, et magno se corpore miscet."

In the Phœnician Cosmogony, "Spirit mixing with its own principles gives rise to – creation" also; (Brucker, I., 240); the Orphic triad shows an identical doctrine: for there *Phanes* (or *Eros*), *Chaos,* containing crude undifferentiated Cosmic matter, and *Chronos* (time), are the three co-operating principles, emanating from the Unknowable and concealed point, which produce the work of "Creation." And they are the Hindu *Purusha* (*Phanes*), *Pradhâna* (*chaos*), and *Kala* (*Chronos*) or time. The good Professor Wilson does not like the idea, as no Christian clergyman, however liberal, would. He remarks that "as presently explained,. the mixture (of the Supreme Spirit or Soul) is not mechanical; it is an influence or effect exerted upon intermediate agents which produce effects." The sentence in *Vishnu Purâna*: "As fragrance affects the mind from its proximity merely, and not from any immediate operation upon mind itself, so the Supreme influenced the elements of creation," the reverend and erudite Sanscritist correctly explains . . . : "As perfumes do not delight the mind by actual contact, but by the impression they make upon the sense of smelling, which communicates it to the mind," adding: "The entrance of the Supreme into spirit, as well as matter, is less intelligible than the view elsewhere taken of it, as the infusion of spirit, identified with the supreme, into *Prakriti* or matter alone." He prefers the verse in *Padma Purâna*: "He who is called the male (spirit) of *Prakriti* . . . that same divine Vishnu entered into *Prakriti.*" This "view" is certainly more akin to the plastic character of certain verses in the *Bible* concerning the Patriarchs, such as Lot (*Gen.* xix., 34-38) and even Adam (iv., v. 1), and others of a still more anthropomorphic nature. But it is just that which led Humanity to Phallicism, Christian religion being honeycombed with it, from the first chapter of *Genesis* down to the *Revelation.*

Esoteric doctrine teaches that the *Dhyan Chohans* are the collective aggregate of divine Intelligence or primordial mind, and that the first *Manus* – the seven "mind-born" Spiritual Intelligences – are identical with the former. Hence the "Kwan-shi-yin" – "the golden Dragon in whom are the seven," of Stanza III – is the primordial *Logos*, or Brahmâ, the first manifested creative Power; and the Dhyani-Energies are the *Manus*, or *Manu-Swayambhuva* collectively. The direct connection, moreover, between the "*Manus*" and "*Mahat*" is easy to see. *Manu* is from the root man, "to think"; and thinking proceeds from the mind. It is, in Cosmogony, the pre-nebular period.

(II.) "The second Creation," "*Bhûta*," was of the rudimental principles (*Tanmatras*), thence termed the elemental creation (*Bhûta-sarga*)* It is the period of the first breath of the differentiation of the pre-Cosmic Elements or matter. *Bhûtadi* means literally "the origin of the Elements," and precedes *Bhûta-sarga* – the "creation" or differentiation of those Elements in primordial "*Akâsa*" (Chaos or Vacuity).† In the "*Vishnu Purâna*" it is said to proceed along, and belong to, the triple aspect of *Ahankâra*, translated Egotism, but meaning rather that untranslateable term the "I-AM-NESS," that which first issues from "*Mahat*," or divine mind; the first shadowy outline of Self-hood, for "pure" *Ahankâra* becomes "passionate" and finally "rudimental" (initial); it is "the origin of conscious as of all unconscious being," though the Esoteric school rejects the idea of anything being "unconscious" – save on this (our) plane of illusion and ignorance. At this stage of the Second Creation, the second hierarchy of the *Manus* appear, the *Dhyan Chohans* or *Devas*, who are the origin of Form (*rupa*): the *Chitrasikhandina* (bright-crested) or the *Riksha* – those *Rishis* who have become the informing souls of the seven stars (of the Great Bear)‡ In astronomical and Cosmogonical language this Creation relates to the first stage of Cosmic-life, the Fire-

---

* All these sentences are quoted from "*Vishnu Purâna*," Book I., ch. v.

† Vishnu is both Bhûtesa, "Lord of the Elements, and all things," and *Viswarûpa*, "Universal Substance or Soul."

‡ See concerning their post-types, the Treatise written by Trithemius (Agrippa's master, 16th cent.). "Concerning the seven secondaries, or Spiritual Intelligences, who, after God, actuate the Universe;" giving out, besides secret cycles and several prophecies, certain facts and beliefs about the *Genii*, or the *Elohim*, which preside over and guide the septenary stages of the World's Course.

Mist Period after its Chaotic stage,§ when atoms issue from *Laya*.

(III.) The third (the *Indriya*) was the modified form of *Ahankâra*, the conception of "I," (from "*Aham*," "I") termed the organic Creation, or creation of the senses (*Aindriyaka*). "These three were the *Prâkrita* creation, the (discrete) developments of indiscrete nature preceded by the indiscrete principle." "Preceded by," ought to be replaced here with "beginning by," *Buddhi*; for the latter is neither a discrete nor an indiscrete quantity, but partakes of the nature of both, in man as in Kosmos: a unit – a human MONAD on the plane of illusion – when once freed from the three forms of *Ahankâra* and liberated from its terrestrial *manas*, *Buddhi* becomes truly a continued quantity, both in duration and extension, because eternal and immortal. Earlier it is stated, that the third Creation "abounding with the quality of goodness, is termed *Urdhvasrotas*"; and a page or two further the *Urdhvasrotas* creation is referred to as "the sixth creation . . . that of the divinities" (p. 75). This shows plainly that earlier as well as later *manvantaras* have been purposely confused, to prevent the profane from perceiving the truth. This is called "incongruity" and "contradictions" by the Orientalists.¶

---

§ From the first, the Orientalists have found themselves beset by great difficulties with regard to any possible order in the Purânic Creations. Brahma is very often confused with Brahmâ, by Wilson, for which he is criticised by his successors. The "Original Sanscrit Texts" are preferred by Mr. Fitzedward Hall for the translation of *Vishnu Purâna* and texts, to those used by Wilson. "Had Professor Wilson enjoyed the advantages which are now at the command of the student of Indian philosophy, unquestionably he would have expressed himself differently," as said by the editor of his works. This reminds one of the answer given by one of Thomas Taylor's admirers to those scholars who criticised his translations of Plato. "Thomas Taylor may have had less knowledge of the Greek than his critics have, but he understood Plato far better than they do," he said. Our present Orientalists disfigure the mystic sense of the Sanskrit texts far more than Wilson ever did, though the latter is undeniably guilty of very gross errors.

¶ "The three Creations beginning with Intelligence are elemental, but the six creations which proceed from the series of which Intellect is the first are the work of Brahmâ" (*Vâyu Purâna*). Here "creations" mean everywhere stages of Evolution. *Mahat*, "Intellect" or mind (which corresponds with *Manas*, the former being on the Cosmic, and the latter on the human plane) stands here, too, lower than *Buddhi* or Supra-divine Intelligence. Therefore, when we read in *Linga Purâna* that "the first Creation was that of *Mahat*, Intellect being the first in manifestation," we must refer that (specified) creation to the first evolution of our system or even our Earth, none of the preceding ones being discussed in the *Purânas*, but only occasionally hinted at.

This "creation" of the immortals, the "*Deva-Sarga*," is the last of the first series, and has a universal reference; namely, to Evolutions in general, not specifically to our *Manvantara*; but the latter begins with the same over and over again, showing that it refers to several distinct *Kalpas*. For it is said "at the close of the past (*Padma*) *Kalpa* the divine Brahmâ awoke from his night of sleep and beheld the universe void." Then Brahmâ is shown going once more over the "seven creations" in the secondary stage of evolution, repeating the first three on the objective plane.

(IV.) The *Mukhya*, the Primary as it begins the series of four. Neither the word "inanimate" bodies nor yet immovable things, as translated by Wilson, gives a correct idea of the Sanskrit terms used. Esoteric philosophy is not the only one to reject the idea of any atom being inorganic, for it is found also in orthodox Hinduism. Moreover, Wilson himself says (in his collected Works, vol. iii, p. 381): "All the Hindu systems consider vegetable bodies as endowed with life . . . " *Charâchara*, or the synonymous *sthâvara* and *jangama*, is, therefore, inaccurately rendered by "animate and inanimate," "sentient beings," and "unconscious," or "conscious and unconscious beings," etc., etc. "Locomotive and fixed" would be better, since trees are considered to possess souls." *Mukhya* is the "creation" or organic evolution of the vegetable kingdom. In this secondary Period, the three degrees of Elemental or Rudimental Kingdoms are evolved in this world, corresponding inversely in order to the three Prakritic creations during the Primary period of Brahmâ's activity. As in that period, in the words of "*Vishnu Purâna*": "The first creation was that of *Mahat* (Intellect), the second, of *Tanmâtras* (rudimental principles), and the third, that of the senses (*Aindriyaka*)"; in this one, the order of the Elemental Forces stands thus: (1) The nascent centres of Force (intellectual and physical); (2) the rudimental principles – nerve force, so to say; and (3) nascent apperception, which is the *Mahat* of the lower kingdoms, especially developed in the third order of Elementals; these are succeeded by the objective kingdom of minerals, in which latter that apperception is entirely latent, to re-develop only in the plants). The *Mukhya* "Creation," then, is the middle point between the three lower and the three higher kingdoms, which represent the seven esoteric kingdoms of Kosmos, as of Earth.

(V.) The *Tiryaksrotas* (or *Tairyagyonya*) creation,* that of the "(sacred) animals," corresponding only on Earth, to the dumb animal creation. That which is meant by "animals," in primary Creation, is the germ of awakening consciousness or of apperception, that which is faintly traceable in some sensitive plants on Earth and more distinctly in the protistic *monera*.† On our globe, during the first round, animal "creation" precedes that of man, while the former (or mammal) evolves from the latter in our fourth round – on the physical plane: in Round I, the animal atoms are drawn into a cohesion of human physical form; while in Round IV, the reverse occurs according to magnetic conditions developed during life. And this is metempsychosis (See "Mineral Monad" in *"Five Years of Theosophy,"* p. 276). This fifth stage of evolution, called exoterically "Creation," may be viewed in both the Primary and Secondary periods, one as the Spiritual and Cosmic, the other as the material and terrestrial. It is Archibiosis, or life-origination – "origination," so far, of course, as the manifestation of life on all the seven planes is concerned. It is at this period of Evolution that the absolutely eternal universal motion, or vibration, that which is called in Esoteric language "the GREAT BREATH," differentiates in the primordial, first manifested ATOM. More and more, as chemical and physical sciences progress, does this occult axiom find its corroboration in the world of knowledge: the scientific hypothesis, that even the simplest elements of matter are identical in nature and differ from each other only owing to the variety of the distributions of atoms in the molecule or speck of substance, or by the modes of its atomic vibration, gains every day more ground.

Thus, as the differentiation of the primordial germ of life has to precede the evolution of the *Dhyan Chohan* of the third group or hierarchy of Being in Primary Creation, before those "gods" can become

---

* Professor Wilson translates it, as though animals were higher on the scale of "creation" than divinities, or angels, although the truth about the *devas* is very plainly stated further on. This "creation," says the text, is both primary (*Prâkrita*) and secondary (*Vaikrita*). It is the latter, as regards the origin of the gods from Brahmâ (the personal anthropomorphic creator of our material universe); it is the former (primary) as affecting Rudra, who is the immediate production of the first principle. Rudra is not alone a title of Siva, but embraces agents of creation, angels and men, as will be shown further on.

† Neither plant nor animal, but an existence between the two.

rupa (embodied in their first ethereal form), so animal creation has to precede, for that same reason, divine MAN on earth. And this is why we find in the *Purânas*: "The fifth, the *Tairyagyonya* creation, was that of animals, and –

(VI). The *Urdhvasrotas* creation, or that of divinities (*Vishnu Purâna*, Book I, Chp. i.). But these (divinities) are simply the prototypes of the First Race, the fathers of their "mind-born" progeny with the soft bones.* It is these who became the Evolvers of the "Sweat-born" – an expression explained in Book II. Finally, the sixth "Creation" is followed, and "Creation in general, closed by –

(VII.) The evolution of the *"Arvaksrotas* beings, which was the seventh, and was that of man" (*Vishnu Purâna*, Book I.)."

SD, i 450–456

---

* "Created beings" – explains *Vishnu Purâna* – "although they are destroyed (in their individual forms) at the periods of dissolution, yet being affected by the good or evil acts of former existences, are never exempted from their consequences. And when Brahmâ produces the world anew, they are the progeny of his will. . ." "Collecting his mind into itself (Yoga willing), Brahmâ creates the four orders of beings, termed gods, demons, progenitors, and MEN" . . . "progenitors" meaning the prototypes and Evolvers of the first Root Race of men. The progenitors are the *Pitris*, and are of seven classes. They are said in exoteric mythology to be born of Brahmâ's side, like Eve from the rib of Adam.

WHO ARE THE KUMARAS?

The "eighth creation" mentioned is no Creation at all; it is a blind again, for it refers to a purely mental process: the cognition of the "ninth" creation, which, in its turn, is an effect, manifesting in the secondary of that which was a "Creation" in the Primary (*Prâkrita*) Creation.[†] The Eighth, then, called *Anûgraha* (the *Pratyayasarga* or the intellectual creation of the *Sankhyas*, explained in *Karika*, v. 46, p. 146), is "that creation of which we have a perception" – in its esoteric aspect – and "to which we give intellectual assent (*Anûgraha*) in contradistinction to organic creation." It is the correct perception of our relations to the whole range of "gods" and especially of those we bear to the *Kumâras* – the so-called "Ninth Creation" – which is in reality an aspect of or reflection of the sixth in our *manvantara* (the *Vaivasvata*). "There is a ninth, the *Kumâra* Creation, which is both primary and secondary," says *Vishnu Purâna*, the oldest of such texts.[‡] "The *Kumâras*," explains an esoteric text, "are the *Dhyanis*, derived immediately from the supreme Principle, who reappear in the *Vaivasvata Manu* period, for the progress of mankind." [§] The commentator of the *Vishnu Purâna* corroborates it, by remarking that "these sages live as long as Brahmâ; and they are only created by him in the first *Kalpa*, although their generation is very commonly and inconsistently introduced in the *Varaha*, or *Padma Kalpa*"

---

† "These notions," remarks Dr. Wilson, "the birth of Rudra and the saints, seem to have been borrowed from the *Saivas*, and to have been awkwardly engrafted upon the *Vaishnava* system." The esoteric meaning ought to have been consulted before venturing such a hypothesis.

‡ Parâsara, the Vedic *Rishi*, who received the *Vishnu Purâna* from Pulastya and taught it to Maitreya, is placed by the Orientalists at various epochs. As correctly observed, in the *Hindu Class. Dict*: – "Speculations as to his era differ widely from 575 B.C. to 1391 B.C., and cannot be trusted." Quite so; but no less, however, than any other date as assigned by the Sanskritists, so famous in this department of arbitrary fancy.

§ They may indeed mark a "special" or extra creation, since it is they who, by incarnating themselves within the senseless human shells of the two first Root Races, and a great portion of the Third Root Race – create, so to speak, a new race: that of thinking, self-conscious and divine men.

(the secondary). Thus, the *Kumâras* are, exoterically, "the creation of Rudra or Nilalohita, a form of Siva, by Brahmâ, and of certain other mind-born sons of Brahmâ. But, in the esoteric teaching, they are the progenitors of the true spiritual SELF in the physical man – the higher *Prajâpati*, while the *Pitris*, or lower *Prajâpati*, are no more than the fathers of the model, or type of his physical form, made "in their image." Four (and occasionally five) are mentioned freely in the exoteric texts, three *Kumâras* being secret. * (Compare what is said of "The Fallen Angels" in Book II).

The Exoteric four are: Sanât-Kumâra, Sananda, Sanaka, and Sanatana; and the esoteric three are: Sana, Kapila, and Sanat-Sujâta. Special attention is once more drawn to this class of *Dhyan Chohans*, for herein lies the mystery of generation and heredity hinted at in Book I. (See the four "Orders of Angelic Beings", Comment on Stanza VII). Book II explains their position in the divine Hierarchy. Meanwhile, let us see what the exoteric texts say about them.

They do not say much; nothing to him who fails to read between the lines. "We must have recourse, here, to other *Purânas* for the elucidation of this term," remarks Wilson, who does not suspect for one moment that he is in the presence of the "Angels of Darkness," the mythical "great enemy" of his Church. Therefore, he contrives to elucidate no more than that these (divinities) DECLINING TO CREATE PROGENY†

---

* "The four *Kumâras* (are) the mind-born Sons of Brahmâ. Some specify seven" (*H. Class. Dict.*). All these seven Vaidhatra, the patronymic of the *Kumâras*, "the Maker's Sons," are mentioned and described in Iswara Krishna's "*Sânkhya Kârika*" with the Commentary of Gaudapâdâcharya (Sankarâchârya's Paraguru) attached to it. It discusses the nature of the *Kumâras*, though it refrains from mentioning by name all the seven *Kumâras*, but calls them instead "the seven sons of Brahmâ," which they are, as they are created by Brahmâ in Rudra. The list of names it gives us is: Sanaka, Sanandana, Sanatana, Kapila, Ribhu, and Panchasikha. But these are again all aliases.

† So untrustworthy are some translations of the Orientalists that in the French Translation of Hari-Vamsa, it is said "The seven *Prajâpati*, Rudra, Skanda (his son) and Sanat-Kumâra proceeded to create beings." Whereas, as Wilson shows, the original is: "These seven . . . created progeny; and so did Rudra, but Skanda and Sanat Kumâra, restraining their power, abstained from creation." The "four orders of beings" are referred to sometimes as "*Ambhamsi*," which Wilson renders: "literally Waters," and believes it "a mystic term." It is one, no doubt; but he evidently failed to catch the real esoteric meaning. "Waters" and "water" stand as the symbol for

(and thus rebelling against Brahmâ), remained, as the name of the first implies, ever boys, *Kumâras*: that is, ever pure and innocent, whence their creation is also called the "*Kumâra.*" (Book I. chap. v., *Vishnu Purâna.*) The *Purânas*, however, may afford a little more light. "Being ever as he was born, he is here called a youth; and hence his name is well known as Sanat-Kumâra" (*Linga Purâna*, prior section LXX. 174.) In the *Saiva Purâna*, the *Kumâras* are always described as Yogins. The *Kurma Purâna*, after enumerating them, says: "These five, O Brahmans, were Yogins, who acquired entire exemption from passion." They are five, because two of the *Kumâras* fell.

Of all the seven great divisions of *Dhyan-Chohans*, or *Devas*, there is none with which humanity is more concerned than with the *Kumâras*. Imprudent are the Christian Theologians who have degraded them into fallen Angels, and now call them "Satan" and Demons; as among these heavenly denizens who refuse to create, the Archangel Michael – the greatest patron Saint of Western and Eastern Churches, under his double name of St. Michael and his supposed copy on earth, St. George conquering the DRAGON – has to be allowed one of the most prominent places. (See Book II, "The Sacred Dragons and their Slayers.")

The *Kumâras*, the "mind-born Sons" of Brahmâ-Rudra (or Siva) the

---

Akâsa, the "primordial Ocean of Space," on which Narâyana, the self-born Spirit, moves: reclining on that which is its progeny (See *Manu*). "Water is the body of Nara; thus we have heard the name of water explained. Since Brahmâ rests on the water, therefore he is termed Narâyana" (*Linga, Vayu,* and *Markandeya Purânas*) ". . . Pure, *Purusha* created the Waters pure . . ." at the same time Water is the third principle in material Kosmos, and the third in the realm of the Spiritual: Spirit of Fire, Flame, *Akâsa*, Ether, Water, Air, Earth, are the cosmic, sidereal, psychic, spiritual and mystic principles, pre-eminently occult, in every plane of being. "Gods, Demons, *Pitris* and men," are the four orders of beings to whom the term *Ambhamsi* is applied (in the *Vedas* it is a synonym of gods): because they are all the product of WATERS (mystically), of the Akâsic Ocean, and of the Third Principle in nature. *Pitris* and men on earth are the transformations (rebirths) of gods and demons (Spirits) on a higher plane. Water is, in another sense, the feminine principle. Venus Aphrodite is the personified Sea, and the mother of the god of love, the generator of all the gods as much as the Christian Virgin Mary is *Mare* (the sea), the mother of the Western God of Love, Mercy and Charity. If the student of Esoteric philosophy thinks deeply over the subject he is sure to find out all the suggestiveness of the term *Ambhamsi*, in its manifold relations to the Virgin in Heaven, to the Celestial Virgin of the Alchemists, and even to the "Waters of Grace" of the modern Baptist.

howling and terrific destroyer of human passions and physical senses, which are ever in the way of the development of the higher spiritual perceptions and the growth of the inner eternal man – mystically,* are the progeny of Siva, the Mahayogi, the great patron of all the Yogis and mystics of India. They themselves, being the "Virgin-Ascetics," refuse to create the material being MAN. Well may they be suspected of a direct connection with the Christian Archangel Michael, the "Virgin Combatant" of the Dragon Apophis, whose victim is every soul united too loosely to its immortal Spirit, the Angel who, as shown by the Gnostics, refused to create just as the *Kumâras* did. (See Book II, "The Mystic Dragons and their Slayers.") . . . Does not that patron-Angel of the Jews preside over Saturn (Siva or Rudra), and the Sabbath, the day of Saturn? Is he not shown of the same essence with his father (Saturn), and called the "Son of Time," KRONOS, or *Kâla* (time), a form of Brahmâ (Vishnu and Siva)?" And is not "Old Time" of the Greeks, with its scythe and sand-glass, identical with the "Ancient of Days" of the Kabalists, the latter "Ancient" being one with the Hindu "Ancient of Days," Brahmâ (in his triune form), whose name is also "*Sanat*," the Ancient? Every *Kumâra* bears the prefix of Sanat and Sana; and Sanaischara is Saturn, the planet (*Sani* and *Sarra*), the King Saturn whose Secretary in Egypt was Thot-Hermes the first. They are thus identified both with the planet and the god (Siva), who are, in their turn, shown the prototypes of Saturn, who is the same as Bel, Baal, Siva, and Jehovah Sabbaoth, The angel of whose face is MIKAEL ("who is as God"). He is the patron, and guardian Angel of the Jews, as Daniel tells us (v. 21); and, before the *Kumâras* were degraded, by those who were ignorant of their very name, into demons and fallen angels, the Greek Ophites, the occultly inclined predecessors and precursors of the Roman Catholic Church after its secession and separation from the primitive Greek Church, had identified Michael with their

---

* Siva-Rudra is the Destroyer, as Vishnu is the preserver; and both are the regenerators of spiritual as well as of physical nature. To live as a plant, the seed must die. To live as a conscious entity in the Eternity, the passions and senses of man must first DIE before his body does. "To live is to die and to die is to live," has been too little understood in the West. Siva, the destroyer, is the creator and the Saviour of Spiritual man, as he is the good gardener of nature. He weeds out the plants, human and cosmic, and kills the passions of the physical, to call to life the perceptions of the spiritual, man.

Ophiomorphos, the rebellious and opposing spirit. This means nothing more than the reverse aspect (symbolically) of Ophis – divine Wisdom or Christos. In the Talmud, Mikael (Michael) is "Prince of Water" and the chief of the seven Spirits, for the same reason that his prototype (among many others) Sanat-Sujâta – the chief of the *Kumâras* – is called *Ambhamsi*, "Waters" – according to the commentary on *Vishnu Purâna*. Why? Because the "Waters" is another name of the "Great Deep," the primordial Waters of space or Chaos, and also means "Mother," *Amba*, meaning Aditi and *Akâsa*, the Celestial Virgin-Mother of the visible universe. Furthermore, the "Waters of the flood" are also called "the GREAT DRAGON," or Ophis, Ophio-Morphos.

The *Rudras* will be noticed in their Septenary character of "Fire-Spirits" in the "Symbolism" attached to the Stanzas in Book II. There we shall also consider the Cross (3 + 4) under its primeval and later forms, and shall use for purposes of comparison the Pythagorean numbers side by side with Hebrew Metrology. The immense importance of the number seven will thus become evident, as the root number of nature. We shall examine it from the standpoints of the *Vedas* and the Chaldean Scriptures, as it existed in Egypt thousands of years B.C., and as treated in the Gnostic records; we shall show how its importance as a basic number has gained recognition in physical Science; and we shall endeavour to prove that the importance attached to the number seven throughout all antiquity was due to no fanciful imaginings of uneducated priests, but to a profound knowledge of natural law."

SD, i 456–460

GODS, MONADS, AND ATOMS – I

On page 429 of *Isis Unveiled*, Vol. I., we said that "the mystery of first creation, which was ever the despair of Science, is unfathomable unless they (the Scientists) accept the doctrine of Hermes. They will have to follow in the footsteps of the Hermetists." Our prophecy begins to assert itself.

But between Hermes and Huxley there is a middle course and point. Let the men of Science only throw a bridge half-way, and think seriously over the theories of Leibnitz. We have shown our theories with regard to atomic evolution – their last formation into compound chemical molecules being produced within our terrestrial workshops in the earth's atmosphere and not elsewhere – as strangely agreeing with the evolution of atoms shown on Mr. Crookes' plates. Several times already it was stated in this volume that *Marttanda* (the Sun) had evolved and aggregated, together with his smaller seven Brothers, from his Mother's (Aditi's) bosom, that bosom being prima MATER-ia – the lecturer's primordial protyle. Esoteric doctrines teach the existence of "an antecedent form of energy having periodic cycles of ebb and swell, rest and activity" (p. 21) – and behold a great scholar in Science now asking the world to accept this as one of the postulates. We have shown the "Mother," fiery and hot, becoming gradually cool and radiant, and that same Scientist claims as his second postulate, a scientific necessity, it would seem – "an internal action akin to cooling, operating slowly in the protyle." Occult Science teaches that "Mother" lies stretched in infinity (during *Pralaya*) as the great Deep, the "dry Waters of Space," according to the quaint expression in the Catechism, and becomes wet only after the separation and the moving over its face of *Narayana*, the "Spirit which is invisible Flame, which never burns, but sets on fire all that it touches, and gives it life and generation." * And now Science tells us that "the first-born element . . . most nearly allied to protyle" . . . would be "hydrogen . . . which for some time would be the only existing

---

* "The Lord is a consuming fire." . . . "In him was life, and the life was the light of men."

form of matter" in the Universe. What says Old Science? It answers: just so; but we would call hydrogen and oxygen (which instils the fire of life into the "Mother" by incubation) in the pregenetic and even pre-geological ages – the Spirit, the noumenon of that which becomes in its grossest form oxygen and hydrogen and nitrogen on Earth – nitrogen being of no divine origin, but merely an earth-born cement to unite other gases and fluids, and serve as a sponge to carry in itself the breath of LIFE – pure air.[†] Before these gases and fluids become what they are in our atmosphere, they are interstellar Ether; still earlier and on a deeper plane – something else, and so on *in infinitum*. The eminent and learned gentleman must pardon an Occultist for quoting him at such length; but such is the penalty of a Fellow of the Royal Society who approaches so near the precincts of the Sacred *Adytum* of Occult mysteries as virtually to overstep the forbidden boundaries.

But it is time to leave modern physical science and turn to the psychological and metaphysical side of the question. We would only remark that to the "two very reasonable postulates" required by the eminent lecturer, "to get a glimpse of some few of the secrets so darkly hidden" behind "the door of the Unknown" – a third should be added[‡] – lest no battering at it should avail; the postulate that Leibnitz, in his speculations, stood on a firm groundwork of fact and truth. The admirable and thoughtful synopsis of these speculations – as given by John Theodore Merz in his "Leibnitz" – shows how nearly he has brushed the hidden secrets of esoteric Theogony in his *Monadologie*. And yet that philosopher has hardly risen in his speculations above the first planes, the lower principles of the Cosmic Great Body. His theory soars to no loftier heights than those of the manifested life, self-consciousness and intelligence, leaving the regions of the earlier post-genetic mysteries untouched, as his ethereal fluid is post-planetary.

But this third postulate will hardly be accepted by the modern men of Science; and, like Descartes, they will prefer keeping to the

---

† Which if separated ALCHEMICALLY would yield the Spirit of Life, and its Elixir.

‡ § Foremost of all, the postulate that there is no such thing in Nature as inorganic substances or bodies. Stones, minerals, rocks, and even chemical "atoms" are simply organic units in profound lethargy. Their coma has an end and their inertia becomes activity.

properties of external things, which, like extension, are incapable of explaining the phenomenon of motion, rather than accept the latter as an independent Force. They will never become anti-Cartesian in this generation; nor will they admit that "this property of inertia is not a purely geometrical property, that it points to the existence of something in external bodies which is not extension merely." This is Leibnitz's idea as analyzed by Mertz, who adds that he called this something Force, and maintained that external things were endowed with Force, and that in order to be the bearers of this force they must have a substance, for they are not lifeless and inert masses, but the centres and bearers of form, a purely esoteric claim, since force was with Leibnitz an active principle, the division between mind and matter disappearing by this conclusion. But:

> "The mathematical and dynamical inquiries of Leibnitz would not have led to the same result in the mind of a purely scientific inquirer. But Leibnitz was not a scientific man in the modern sense of the word. Had he been so, he might have worked out the conception of energy, defined mathematically the ideas of force and mechanical work, and arrived at the conclusion that even for purely scientific purposes it is desirable to look upon force, not as a primary quantity, but as a quantity derived from some other value."

But, luckily for truth –

> "Leibnitz was a philosopher; and as such he had certain primary principles, which biassed him in favour of certain conclusions, and his discovery that external things were substances endowed with force was at once used for the purpose of applying these principles. One of these principles was the law of continuity, the conviction that all the world was connected, that there were no gaps and chasms which could not be bridged over. The contrast of extended thinking substances was unbearable to him. The definition of the extended substances had already become untenable: it was natural that a similar inquiry was made into the definition of mind, the thinking substance..."

The divisions made by Leibnitz, however incomplete and faulty from the standpoint of Occultism, show a spirit of metaphysical intuition to which no man of science, not Descartes not even Kant – has ever reached. With him there existed ever an infinite gradation of thought. Only a small portion of the contents of our thoughts, he said, rises into the clearness of apperception, "into the light of perfect consciousness." Many remain in a confused or obscure state, in the state of "perceptions;" but they are there . . . Descartes denied soul to the animal, Leibnitz endowed, as the Occultists do, "the whole creation with mental life, this being, according to him, capable of infinite gradations." And this, as Mertz justly observes, "at once widened the realm of mental life, destroying the contrast of animate and inanimate matter; it did yet more – it reacted on the conception of matter, of the extended substance. For it became evident that external or material things presented the property of extension to our senses only, not to our thinking faculties. The mathematician, in order to calculate geometrical figures, had been obliged to divide them into an infinite number of infinitely small parts, and the physicist saw no limit to the divisibility of matter into atoms. The bulk through which external things seemed to fill space was a property which they acquired only through the coarseness of our senses. . . . Leibnitz followed these arguments to some extent, but he could not rest content in assuming that matter was composed of a finite number of very small parts. His mathematical mind forced him to carry out the argument *in infinitum*. And what became of the atoms then? They lost their extension and they retained only their property of resistance; they were the centres of force. They were reduced to mathematical points . . . but if their extension in space was nothing, so much fuller was their inner life. Assuming that inner existence, such as that of the human mind, is a new dimension, not a geometrical but a metaphysical dimension . . . having reduced the geometrical extension of the atoms to nothing, Leibnitz endowed them with an infinite extension in the direction of their metaphysical dimension. After having lost sight of them in the world of space, the mind has, as it were, to dive into a metaphysical world to find and grasp the real essence of what appears in space merely as a mathematical point. . . . As a cone stands on its point, or a perpendicular straight line cuts a horizontal plane only in one mathematical point, but may extend infinitely in height and depth, so the essences of things real have only a punctual existence in this physical world of space; but have an infinite depth of inner life in the metaphysical world of thought . . . " (p. 144).

This is the spirit, the very root of occult doctrine and thought. The "Spirit-Matter" and "Matter-Spirit" extend infinitely in depth, and like "the essence of things" of Leibnitz, our essence of things real is at the seventh depth; while the unreal and gross matter of Science and the external world, is at the lowest end of our perceptive senses. The Occultist knows the worth or worthlessness of the latter."

SD, i 625–628

GODS, MONADS, AND ATOMS – II

The student must now be shown the fundamental distinction between the system of Leibnitz* and that of occult philosophy, on the question of the Monads, and this may be done with his Monadology before us. It may be correctly stated that were Leibnitz' and Spinoza's systems reconciled, the essence and Spirit of esoteric philosophy would be made to appear. From the shock of the two – as opposed to the Cartesian system – emerge the truths of the Archaic doctrine. Both opposed the metaphysics of Descartes. His idea of the contrast of two substances – Extension and Thought – radically differing from each other and mutually irreducible, was too arbitrary and too unphilosophical for them. Thus Leibnitz made of the two Cartesian substances two attributes of one universal unity, in which he saw God. Spinoza recognised but one universal indivisible substance and absolute ALL, like *Parabrahmam*. Leibnitz, on the contrary perceived the existence of a plurality of substances. There was but ONE for Spinoza; for Leibnitz, an infinitude of Beings, from, and in, the One. Hence, though both admitted but one real Entity, while Spinoza made it impersonal and indivisible, Leibnitz divided his personal Deity into a number of divine and semi-divine Beings. Spinoza was a subjective, Leibnitz an objective Pantheist, yet both were great philosophers in their intuitive perceptions.

Now, if these two teachings were blended together and each corrected by the other – and foremost of all the One Reality weeded of its personality – there would remain as sum total a true spirit of esoteric philosophy in them; the impersonal, attributeless, absolute divine essence which is no "Being," but the root of all being. Draw a deep line in your thought between that ever-incognizable essence, and the, as invisible, yet comprehensible Presence (*Mulaprakriti*), or *Schekinah*, from beyond and through which vibrates the Sound of the *Verbum*, and from which evolve the numberless hierarchies of intelligent Egos,

---

* The real spelling of the name – as spelt by himself – is Leibniz. He was of Slavonian descent though a German by birth.

of conscious as of semi-conscious, perceptive and apperceptive Beings, whose essence is spiritual Force, whose Substance is the Elements and whose Bodies (when needed) are the atoms – and our doctrine is there. For, says Leibnitz, "the primitive Element of every material body being Force, which has none of the characteristics of (objective) matter – it can be conceived but can never be the object of any imaginative representation." That which was for him the primordial and ultimate element in every body and object was thus not the material atoms, or molecules, necessarily more or less extended, as those of Epicurus and Gassendi, but, as Mertz shows, immaterial and metaphysical atoms, 'mathematical points', or real souls – as explained by Henri Lachelier (Professeur agrege de Philosophie), his French biographer. "That which exists outside of us in an absolute manner, are Souls whose essence is force," (*Monadologie*, Introduction).

Thus, reality in the manifested world is composed of a unity of units, so to say, immaterial (from our stand-point) and infinite. This Leibnitz calls "Monads," Eastern philosophy "*Jivas*" –and Occultism gives it, with the Kabalists and all the Christians, a variety of names.

They are with us, as with Leibnitz – "the expression of the universe,"[*] and every physical point is but the phenomenal expression of the noumenal, metaphysical point. His distinction between perception and apperception, is the philosophical though dim expression of the Esoteric teachings. His "reduced universes," of which "there are as many as there are Monads" – is the chaotic representation of our Septenary System with its divisions and sub-divisions.

As to the relation his Monads bear to our *Dhyan-Chohans*, Cosmic Spirits, *Devas* and Elementals, we may reproduce briefly the opinion of a learned and thoughtful theosophist, Mr. H. A. Bjerregaard, on the subject. In an excellent paper "On the Elementals, the Elementary Spirits, and the relationship between them and Human Beings," read by him before the "Aryan Theosophical Society of New York" (see *Path*, Nos. 10 and 11, of Jan. and Feb. 1887), Mr. Bjerregaard formulates distinctly his opinion. . . . . "To Spinoza, substance is dead and inactive,

---

[*] "Leibnitz's Dynamism," says Professor Lachelier, "would offer but little difficulty if, with him, the Monad had remained a simple atom of blind force. But . . . ." One perfectly understands the perplexity of modern materialism!

but to Leibnitz's penetrating mind everything is living activity and active energy. In holding this view, he comes infinitely nearer the Orient than any other thinker of his day, or after him. His discovery that an active energy forms the essence of Substance is a principle that places him in direct relationship to the Seers of the East."

And the lecturer proceeds to show that to Leibnitz atoms and elements are centres of force, or rather "spiritual beings whose very nature is to act," for the elementary particles are not acting mechanically, but from an internal principle. They are incorporeal spiritual units ("substantial," however, but not immaterial in our sense) inaccessible to all changes from without, and indestructible by any external force. Leibnitz's monads, adds the lecturer, "differ from atoms in the following particulars, which are very important for us to remember, otherwise we shall not be able to see the difference between elementals and mere matter." . . . . "Atoms are not distinguished from each other, they are qualitatively alike; but one monad differs from every other monad qualitatively; and every one is a peculiar world to itself. Not so with atoms; they are absolutely alike quantitatively and qualitatively, and possess no individuality of their own.[†] Again, the atoms (molecules, rather) of materialistic philosophy can be considered as extended and divisible, while the monads are mere mathematical points and indivisible. Finally, and this is a point where these monads of Leibnitz closely resemble the elementals of mystic philosophy – these monads are representative Beings. Every monad reflects every other. Every monad is a living mirror of the Universe within its own sphere. And mark this, for upon it depends the power possessed by these monads, and upon this depends the work they can do for us; in mirroring

---

† Leibnitz was an absolute Idealist in maintaining that "material atoms are contrary to reason" (*Systeme Nouveau*, Erdmann, p. 126. col. 2). For him matter was a simple representation of the monad, whether human or atomic. Monads, he thought (as we do), are everywhere. Thus the human soul is a monad, and every cell in the human body has its monad, as every cell in animal, vegetable, and even in the (so-called) inorganic bodies. His atoms are the molecules of modern Science, and his monads those simple atoms that materialistic Science takes on faith, though it will never succeed in interviewing them – except in imagination. But Leibnitz is rather contradictory in his views about Monads. He speaks of his Metaphysical Points and Formal Atoms, at one time as realities, occupying space; at another as pure Spiritual ideas; then again endows them with tivity and aggregates and positions in their co-relations.

the world, the monads are not mere passive reflective agents, but spontaneously self-active; they produce the images spontaneously, as the soul does a dream. In every monad, therefore, the adept may read everything, even the future. Every monad or Elemental is a looking-glass that can speak. . ."

It is at this point that Leibnitz's philosophy breaks down. There is no provision made, nor any distinction established, between the "Elemental" monad and that of a high Planetary Spirit, or even the human monad or Soul. He even goes so far as to sometimes doubt whether "God has ever made anything but Monads or substances without extension." (*Examen des Principes du P. Malebranche*) He draws a distinction between Monads and Atoms,* because, as he repeatedly states, "bodies with all their qualities are only phenomenal, like the rainbow. . . . *Corpora omnia cum omnibus qualitatibus suis non sunt aliud quam phenomena bene fundata, ut Iris*" (Letter to Father Desbosses, *Correspondence*, Letter xviii) – but soon after he finds a provision for this in a substantial correspondence, a certain metaphysical bond between the monads – vinculum substantiale. Esoteric philosophy, teaching an objective Idealism – though it regards the objective Universe and all in it as *Maya*, temporary illusion –draws a practical distinction between collective illusion, *Mahamaya*, from the purely metaphysical stand-point, and the objective relations in it between various conscious Egos so long as this illusion lasts. The adept, therefore, may read the future in an Elemental Monad, but he has to draw for this object a great number of them, as each monad represents only a portion of the Kingdom it belongs to. "It is not in the object, but in the modification of the cognition of the object that the Monads are limited. They all go confusedly to the infinite, to the all, but they are all limited and distinguished by the degrees of distinct perceptions." (§ 60, *Monadologie*)† And as Leibnitz explains, "All the portions of the Universe are distinctly represented

---

* The atoms of Leibnitz have, in truth, nothing but the name in common with the atoms of the Greek Materialists, or even the molecules of modern Science. He calls them formal atoms, and compares them to the substantial forms of Aristotle. (See *Systeme Nouveau*, § 3.) degrees of distinct perceptions."

† Leibnitz, like Aristotle, calls the created or emanated monads (the Elementals issued from Cosmic Spirits or Gods) – *Entelechies, Entelecheia* – and "incorporeal automata." (§ 18, *Monadologie*)

in the Monads, but some are reflected in one monad, some in another;" but a number of monads could represent simultaneously the thoughts of the two millions of inhabitants of Paris.

But what say the Occult Sciences to this, and what do they add?

They say that what is called collectively Monads by Leibnitz – roughly viewed, and leaving every subdivision out of calculation, for the present‡ – may be separated into three distinct Hosts, which, counted from the highest planes, are, firstly, "gods," or conscious, spiritual Egos; the intelligent architects, who work after the plan in the Divine Mind. Then come the Elementals, or Monads, who form collectively and unconsciously the grand Universal Mirrors of everything connected with their respective realms. Lastly, the atoms, or material molecules, which are informed in their turn by their apperceptive monads, just as every cell in a human body is so informed. (See the closing pages of Book I.) There are shoals of such informed atoms which, in their turn, inform the molecules; an infinitude of monads, or Elementals proper, and countless spiritual Forces – Monadless, for they are pure incorporealities,§ except under certain laws, when they assume a form – not necessarily human. Whence the substance that clothes them – the apparent organism they evolve around their centres? The Formless ("*Arupa*") Radiations, existing in the harmony of Universal Will, and being what we term the collective or the aggregate of Cosmic Will on the plane of the subjective Universe, unite together an infinitude of

---

‡ These three "rough divisions" correspond to spirit, mind (or soul), and body, in the human constitution.

§ Brother C. H. A. Bjerregaard, in his lecture (already mentioned), warns his audience not to regard the Sephiroth too much as individualities, but to avoid at the same time seeing in them abstractions. "We shall never arrive at the truth," he says, "much less the power of associating with those celestials, until we return to the simplicity and fearlessness of the primitive ages, when men mixed freely with the gods, and the gods descended among men and guided them in truth and holiness" (No. 10, *Path*) . . . . "There are several designations for 'angels' in the *Bible* which clearly show that beings like the Elementals of the *Kabala* and the monads of Leibnitz, must be understood by that term rather than that which is commonly understood. They are called 'morning stars,' 'flaming fires,' 'the mighty ones,' and St. Paul sees them in his cosmogonic vision as 'Principalities and Powers.' Such names as these preclude the idea of personality, and we find ourselves compelled to think of them as impersonal Existences . . . as an influence, a spiritual substance, or conscious Force." (*Path*, No. 11, p. 322.)

monads – each the mirror of its own Universe – and thus individualize for the time being an independent mind, omniscient and universal; and by the same process of magnetic aggregation they create for themselves objective, visible bodies, out of the interstellar atoms. For atoms and Monads, associated or dissociated, simple or complex, are, from the moment of the first differentiation, but the principles, corporeal, psychic and Spiritual, of the "Gods," – themselves the Radiations of primordial nature. Thus, to the eye of the Seer, the higher Planetary Powers appear under two aspects: the subjective – as influences, and the objective – as mystic FORMS, which, under Karmic law, become a Presence, Spirit and Matter being One, as repeatedly stated. Spirit is matter on the seventh plane; matter is Spirit – on the lowest point of its cyclic activity; and both – are MAYA.

Atoms are called "Vibrations" in Occultism; also "Sound" – collectively. This does not interfere with Mr. Tyndall's scientific discovery. He traced, on the lower rung of the ladder of monadic being, the whole course of the atmospheric vibrations – and this constitutes the objective part of the process in nature. He has traced and recorded the rapidity of their motion and transmission; the force of their impact; their setting up vibrations in the tympanum and their transmission of these to the stolithes, etc., etc., till the vibration of the auditory nerve commences – and a new phenomenon now takes place: the subjective side of the process or the sensation of Sound. Does he perceive or see it? No; for his speciality is to discover the behaviour of matter. But why should not a psychic see it, a spiritual seer, whose inner Eye is opened, and who can see through the veil of matter? The waves and undulations of Science are all produced by atoms propelling their molecules into activity from within. Atoms fill the immensity of Space, and by their continuous vibration are that MOTION which keeps the wheels of Life perpetually going. It is that inner work that produces the natural phenomena called the correlation of Forces. Only, at the origin of every such "force," there stands the conscious guiding noumenon thereof – Angel or God, Spirit or Demon – ruling powers, yet the same.

As described by Seers – those who can see the motion of the interstellar shoals, and follow them in their evolution clairvoyantly – they are dazzling, like specks of virgin snow in radiant sunlight. Their velocity is swifter than thought, quicker than any mortal physical eye could follow, and, as well as can be judged from the tremendous rapidity of their course, the motion is circular. . . . . Standing on an open plain, on a mountain summit especially, and gazing into the vast vault above and the spacial infinitudes around, the whole atmosphere seems ablaze with them, the air soaked through with these dazzling coruscations. At times, the intensity of their motion produces flashes like the Northern lights during the Aurora Borealis. The sight is so marvellous, that, as the Seer gazes into this inner world, and feels the scintillating points shoot past him, he is filled with awe at the thought of other, still greater mysteries, that lie beyond, and within, this radiant ocean. . . . .

However imperfect and incomplete this explanation on "Gods, Monads and Atoms," it is hoped that some students and theosophists, at least, will feel that there may be indeed a close relation between materialistic Science, and Occultism, which is the complement and missing soul of the former.

SD, i 628–634

ON THE ARCHAIC STANZAS

"Facies totius Universi, quamvis infinitis modis variet,
Manet tamen semper eadem." Spinoza

THE Stanzas, with the Commentaries thereon, in this Book, the second, are drawn from the same Archaic Records as the Stanzas on Cosmogony in Book I. As far as possible a verbatim translation is given; but some of the Stanzas were too obscure to be understood without explanation. Hence, as was done in Book I., while they are first given in full as they stand, when taken verse by verse with their Commentaries an attempt is made to make them clearer, by words added in brackets, in anticipation of the fuller explanation of the Commentary.

As regards the evolution of mankind, the Secret Doctrine postulates three new propositions, which stand in direct antagonism to modern science as well as to current religious dogmas: it teaches (*a*) the simultaneous evolution of seven human groups on seven different portions of our globe; (*b*) the birth of the *astral*, before the *physical* body: the former being a model for the latter; and (*c*) that man, in this Round, preceded every mammalian — the anthropoids included — in the animal kingdom.* The Secret Doctrine is not alone in speaking of primeval MEN born

---

* See *Genesis* ch. ii., v. 19. Adam is formed in verse 7, and in verse 19 it is said: "Out of the *ground* the Lord God formed *every beast of the field, and every fowl of the air; and brought them unto Adam* to see what he would call them." Thus man was created *before* the animals; for the animals mentioned in chapter i. are the signs of the Zodiac, while the man, "male and female," is not *man,* but the Host of the Sephiroth; FORCES, or Angels, "made in his (God's) image and after his likeness." The Adam, man, is not made in that likeness, nor is it so asserted in the *Bible.* Moreover, the Second Adam is esoterically a septenary which represents seven men, or rather groups of men. For the first Adam — the *Kadmon* — is the synthesis of the *ten Sephiroth.* Of these, the upper triad remains in the Archetypal World as the future "Trinity," while the seven lower *Sephiroth* create the manifested material world; and *this septenate is the second Adam. Genesis,* and the mysteries upon which it was fabricated, came from Egypt. The "God" of the 1st chapter of *Genesis* is the *Logos,* and the "Lord God" of the 2nd chapter the Creative *Elohim* — the *lower* powers.

simultaneously on the seven divisions of our Globe. In the *Divine "Pymander"* of Hermes we find the same Seven primeval men[†] evolving from Nature and "Heavenly Man," in the collective sense of the word, namely, from the Creative Spirits; and in the fragments (collected by George Smith) of Chaldean tablets on which is inscribed the Babylonian Legend of Creation, in the first column of the *Cutha* tablet, seven human beings with the faces of ravens (black, swarthy complexions), whom "the (Seven) great gods created," are mentioned. Or, as explained in lines 16 and 18 — "In the midst of the Earth they grew up and became great . . . . Seven kings, brothers of the same family." These are the Seven Kings of Edom to whom reference is made in the *Kabala*; the first race, which was *imperfect, i.e.,* was born before the "balance" (sexes) existed, and which was therefore destroyed. (*Zohar, Siphrah Dzeniouta, Idrah Suta,* 2928, *La Kabbale,* p. 205.) *"Seven Kings,* brethren, appeared and begat children, 6,000 in number were their peoples" (*Hibbert Lectures,* p. 372). The god Nergas (death) destroyed them. "How did he destroy them?" "By bringing into equilibrium (or balance) those who did not yet exist" (*Siphrah Dzeniouta*). They were "destroyed," as a race, by being merged in their own progeny (by exudation); that is to say, the sexless race reincarnated in the bisexual (potentially); the latter in the Androgynes; these again in the sexual, the later third Race; (for further explanation, *vide infra*). Were the tablets less mutilated, they would be found to contain word for word the same account as given in the archaic records and in Hermes, at least as regards the fundamental facts, if not as regards minute details; for Hermes is a good deal disfigured by mistranslations.

---

† Thus saith Pymander: "This is the mystery that to this day was hidden. Nature being mingled with the Heavenly man (Elohim, or Dhyanis), brought forth a wonder . . . . *Seven men,* all males and females (Hermaphrodite) . . . according to the nature of the seven Governors" (Book II. v. 29) — or the seven Hosts of the *Pitris* or *Elohim,* who projected or created him. This is very clear, but yet, see the interpretations of even our modern theologians, men supposed to be intellectual and learned! In the *"Theological and philosophical works of Hermes Trismegistus, Christian (?) Neoplatonist,"* a work compiled by John David Chambers, of Oriel College, Oxford, the translator wonders "for whom these *seven men* are intended?" He solves the difficulty by concluding that, as "the original pattern man (*Adam Kadmon of ch. i. Genesis*) was masculine-feminine, the seven may signify the succeeding patriarchs named in *Genesis*" (p. 9) . . . A truly theological way of cutting the Gordian knot.

It is quite certain that the seeming supernaturalism of these teachings, although allegorical, is so diametrically opposed to the dead-letter statements of the *Bible* * as well as to the latest hypotheses of science, that it will evoke passionate denial. The Occultists, however, know that the traditions of Esoteric Philosophy must be the right ones, simply because they are the most logical, and reconcile every difficulty. Besides, we have the Egyptian *"Books of Thoth,"* and *"Book of the Dead,"* and the Hindu *Purânas* with the seven Manus, as well as the Chaldeo-Assyrian accounts, whose tiles mention seven primitive men, or Adams, the real meaning of which name may be ascertained through the *Kabala.* Those who know anything of the Samothracian mysteries will also remember that the generic name of the Kabiri was the "Holy Fires," which created on seven localities of the island of *Electria* (or Samothrace) the "Kabir born of the Holy Lemnos" (the island sacred to *Vulcan*).

According to Pindar *(See "Philosophomena," Miller's edition, p. 98),* this Kabir, whose name was Adamas, was, in the traditions of Lemnos, the type of the primitive man born from the bosom of the Earth. He was the Archetype of the first males in the order of generation, and was one of the seven autochthonous ancestors or progenitors of mankind *(ibid, p.* 108). If, while coupling with this the fact that Samothrace was colonised by the Phœnicians, and before them by the mysterious Pelasgians who came from the East, one remembers also the identity of the *mystery* gods of the Phœnicians, Chaldeans, and Israelites, it will be easy to discover whence came also the confused account of the Noachian deluge. It has become undeniable of late that the Jews, who obtained their primitive ideas about creation from Moses, who had them from the Egyptians, compiled their Genesis and first Cosmogonic traditions — when these were rewritten by Ezra and others — from the Chaldeo-Akkadian account. It is, therefore, sufficient to examine the Babylonian and Assyrian cuneiform and other inscriptions to find also therein, scattered here and there, not only the original meaning

---

* As it is now asserted that the Chaldean tablets, which give the allegorical description of Creation, the Fall, and the Flood, even to the legend of the Tower of Babel, were written "before the time of Moses" (*See G. Smith's "Chaldean Account of Genesis,"* p. 86), how can the Pentateuch be called a *revelation?* It is simply another version of the same story.

of the name Adam, Admi, or Adami,[†] but also the creation of seven Adams or roots of men, born of Mother Earth, physically, and of the *divine fire* of the progenitors, spiritually or astrally. The Assyriologists, ignorant of the esoteric teachings, could hardly be expected to pay any greater attention to the mysterious and ever-recurring number seven on the Babylonian cylinders, than they paid to it on finding the same in *Genesis* and the *Bible*. Yet the number of the ancestral spirits and their seven groups of human progeny are there, notwithstanding the dilapidated condition of the fragments, as plainly as they are to be found in "*Pymander*" and in the "*Book of the Concealed Mystery*" of the Kabala. In the latter Adam Kadmon is the Sephirothal TREE, as also the "Tree of the Knowledge of Good and Evil." And that "*Tree*," says verse 32, "hath around it seven columns," or palaces, of the seven creative Angels operating in the spheres of the seven planets on our Globe. As Adam Kadmon is a *collective* name, so also is the name of the man Adam. Says George Smith in his "*Chaldean Account of Genesis:*"

"The word Adam used in these legends for the first human being is evidently *not a proper name, but is only used as a term for mankind*. Adam appears as a proper name in Genesis, but certainly in some passages is only used in the same sense as the Assyrian word" (*p.* 86).

Moreover, neither the Chaldean nor the Biblical deluge (the stories of Xisuthrus and Noah) is based on the universal or even on the Atlantean deluges, recorded in the Indian allegory of Vaivaswata Manu. They are the *exoteric allegories based on the esoteric mysteries* of Samothrace. If the older Chaldees knew the esoteric truth concealed in the Purânic legends, the other nations were aware only of the Samothracian mystery, and allegorised it. They adapted it to their astronomical and anthropological, or rather phallic, notions. Samothrace is known *historically* to have been famous in antiquity for a deluge, which submerged the country and reached the top of the highest mountains; an event which happened before the age of the Argonauts. It was overflowed very suddenly by the waters of the Euxine, regarded up to that time as a lake.[‡] But the Israelites had, moreover, another legend

---

† *Vide* § "Adam-Adami," in Part II. of this volume.

‡ See Pliny, 4, c. 12; Strabo, 10; Herodotus, 7, c. 108; Pausanias, 7, c. 4, etc.

upon which to base their allegory: the "deluge," that transformed the present Gobi Desert into a sea *for the last time,* some 10 or 12,000 years ago, and which drove many Noahs and their families on to the surrounding mountains. As the Babylonian accounts are now only restored from hundreds of thousands of broken fragments (the mound of *Kouyunjik* alone having yielded to Layard's excavations over twenty thousand fragments of inscriptions), the proofs here cited are comparatively scanty; yet such as they are, they corroborate almost every one of our teachings, certainly three, at least. These are:

(1.) That the race which was the first to fall into generation was a *dark Race (Zalmat Gaguadi),* which they call the *Adami* or dark Race, and that *Sarku,* or the light Race, remained pure for a long while subsequently.

(2.) That the Babylonians recognised *two principal Races* at the time of the Fall, the Race of the Gods (the Ethereal *doubles of the Pitris*), having preceded these two. This is Sir H. Rawlinson's opinion. These "Races" are our second and third Root-races.

(3) That these seven Gods, each of whom created a *man,* or group of men, were "the gods *imprisoned* or incarnated." These gods were: the god *Zi;* the god *Ziku* (noble life, Director of purity); the god *Mirku* (noble crown) "Saviour from death of the gods" (later on) imprisoned, and the creator of "the dark Race which his hand has made;" the god *Libzu* "wise among the gods"; the god *Nissi* . . . . and the god *Suhhab;* and *Hea* or *Sa,* their synthesis, the god of wisdom and of the Deep, identified with *Oannes-Dagon,* at the time of the fall, and called (collectively) the Demiurge, or Creator. (*See Chaldean Account Genesis,* p. 82.)

There are two "Creations" so called, in the Babylonian fragments, and *Genesis* having adhered to this, one finds its first two chapters distinguished as the Elohite and the Jehovite creations. Their proper order, however, is not preserved in these or in any other exoteric accounts. Now these "Creations," according to the occult teachings, refer respectively to the formation of the primordial seven *men* by the progenitors (the Pitris, or Elohim): and to that of the human groups after the fall.

SD, ii 1-5

MAN, THE THIRD LOGOS

STANZA I*

1. THE LHA (*a*) WHICH TURNS THE FOURTH (*Globe, or our Earth*) IS SERVANT TO THE LHA(S) OF THE SEVEN (*the planetary Spirits*) (*b*), THEY WHO REVOLVE, DRIVING THEIR CHARIOTS AROUND THEIR LORD, THE ONE EYE (*Loka-Chakshub*) OF OUR WORLD. HIS BREATH GIVES LIFE TO THE SEVEN (*gives light to the planets*). IT GAVE LIFE TO THE FIRST (*c*). "THEY ARE ALL DRAGONS OF WISDOM," adds the Commentary (*d*).

(*a*) *Lha* is the ancient word in trans-Himalayan regions for "Spirit," any celestial or *superhuman* Being, and it covers the whole series of heavenly hierarchies, from Archangel, or *Dhyani*, down to an angel of darkness, or terrestrial Spirit.

(*b*) This expression shows in plain language that the Spirit-Guardian of our globe, which is the fourth in the chain, is subordinate to the chief Spirit (or God) of the Seven Planetary Genii or Spirits. As already explained, the ancients had, in their *Kyriel* of gods, seven chief Mystery-gods, whose chief was, *exoterically*, the visible Sun, or the eighth, and, *esoterically*, the *second Logos*, the Demiurge. The seven (who have now become the "Seven Eyes of the Lord" in the Christian religion) were the regents of the seven *chief* planets; but these were not reckoned according to the enumeration devised later by people who

---

* All the words and sentences placed in brackets in the Stanzas and Commentaries are the writer's. In some places they may be incomplete and even inadequate from the Hindu standpoint; but in the meaning attached to them in Trans-Himalayan Esotericism they are correct. In every case the writer takes any blame upon herself. Having never claimed personal infallibility, that which is given on her own authority may leave much to be desired, in the very abstruse cases where too deep metaphysics is involved. The teaching is offered as it is understood; and as there are seven keys of interpretation to every symbol and allegory, that which may not fit a meaning, say from the psychological or astronomical aspect, will be found quite correct from the physical or metaphysical.

had forgotten, or who had an inadequate notion of, the real *Mysteries*, and included neither the sun, the moon, nor the earth. The sun was the chief, exoterically, of the twelve great gods, or zodiacal constellations; and, esoterically, the Messiah, the *Christos* (the subject *anointed* by the Great BREATH, or the ONE) surrounded by his twelve subordinate powers, also subordinate, in turn, to each of the seven "Mystery-gods" of the planets.

"The seven higher make the Seven Lhas create the world," states a Commentary; which means that our Earth, leaving aside the rest, was *created* or fashioned by terrestrial spirits, the "Regents" being simply the supervisors. This is the first germ, the seed of that which grew later into the Tree of Astrology and Astrolatry. The Higher ones were the *Kosmocratores*, the fabricators of our solar system. This is borne out by all the ancient Cosmogonies: that of Hermes, of the Chaldees, of the Aryans, of the Egyptians, and even of the Jews. Heaven's belt, the signs of the Zodiac (the *Sacred animals*), are as much the *Bne' Alhim* (Sons of the Gods or the *Elohim*) as the Spirits of the Earth; but they are prior to them. Soma and Sin, Isis and Diana, are all lunar gods or goddesses, called the fathers and mothers of our Earth, which is subordinate to them. But these, in their turn, are subordinate to their "Fathers" and "Mothers" — the latter interchangeable and varying with each nation — the gods and their planets, such as Jupiter, Saturn Bel, Brihaspati, etc.

(*c*) "His breath gave life to the seven," refers as much to the sun, who gives life to the Planets, as to the "High One," the *Spiritual Sun*, who gives life to the whole Kosmos. The astronomical and astrological keys opening the gate leading to the mysteries of Theogony can be found only in the later glossaries, which accompany the Stanzas.

In the apocalyptic Slokas of the Archaic Records, the language is as symbolical, if less mythical, than in the *Purânas*. Without the help of the later *commentaries*, compiled by generations of adepts, it would be impossible to understand the meaning correctly. In the ancient Cosmogonies, the visible and the invisible worlds are the double links of one and the same chain. As the invisible *Logos*, with its seven hierarchies (represented or personified each by its chief angel or rector), form one POWER, the inner and the invisible; so, in the world of Forms, the Sun and the seven chief Planets constitute the visible and active potency; the latter "Hierarchy" being, so to speak, the visible and objective *Logos* of the invisible and (except in the lowest grades) ever-subjective angels.

Thus — to anticipate a little by way of illustration — every Race in its evolution is said to be born under the direct influence of one of the Planets: Race the first receiving its breath of life from the Sun, as will be seen later on; while the third humanity — those who fell into generation, or from androgynes became separate entities, one male and the other female — are said to be under the direct influence of Venus, "*the little sun* in which the solar orb stores his light."

The summation of the Stanzas in Book I. showed the genesis * of Gods and men taking rise in, and from, one and the same Point, which is the One Universal, Immutable, Eternal, and absolute UNITY. In its primary manifested aspect we have seen it become: (1) in the sphere of objectivity and Physics, Primordial Substance and Force (centripetal and centrifugal, positive and negative, male and female, etc., etc.); (2) in the world of Metaphysics, the SPIRIT OF THE UNIVERSE, or Cosmic Ideation, called by some the LOGOS.

This LOGOS is the apex of the Pythagorean triangle. When the triangle is complete it becomes the Tetraktis, or the Triangle in the Square, and is the dual symbol of the four-lettered *Tetragrammaton* in the manifested Kosmos, and of its radical triple RAY in the unmanifested, or its *noumenon*.

Put more metaphysically, the classification given here of Cosmic Ultimates, is more one of convenience than of absolute philosophical accuracy. At the commencement of a great *Manvantara, Parabrahm* manifests as *Mulaprakriti* and then as the *Logos*. This *Logos* is equivalent to the "Unconscious Universal Mind," etc., of Western Pantheists. It constitutes the Basis of the SUBJECT-side of manifested Being, and is the source of all manifestations of individual consciousness. *Mulaprakriti* or Primordial Cosmic Substance, is the foundation of

---

* According to Dr. A. Wilder's learned definition, *Genesis*, γενεσις, is not generation, but "*a coming out of the eternal* into the Kosmos and Time": "a coming from *esse* into *exsistere*," or "from BE-NESS into 'being' " — as a Theosophist would say.

the OBJECT-side of things — the basis of all objective evolution and Cosmogenesis. Force, then, does not emerge with Primordial Substance from Parabrahmic Latency. It is *the transformation into energy of the supra-conscious thought of the Logos,* infused, so to speak, into the objectivation of the latter out of potential latency in the One Reality. Hence spring the wondrous laws of matter: hence the "primal impress" so vainly discussed by Bishop Temple. Force thus is *not synchronous with the first objectivation of Mulaprakriti.* But as, apart from it, the latter is absolutely and necessarily inert — *a mere abstraction* — it is unnecessary to weave too fine a cobweb of subtleties as to the order of succession of the Cosmic Ultimates. Force *succeeds* Mulaprakriti; but, *minus* Force, *Mulaprakriti* is for all practical intents and purposes non-existent. *

The "Heavenly Man" (*Tetragrammaton*) who is the *Protogonos, Tikkoun,* the firstborn from the passive deity and the first manifestation of that deity's shadow, is the universal form and idea, which engenders the manifested *Logos,* Adam Kadmon, or the four-lettered symbol, in the *Kabala,* of the *Universe itself,* also called the *second Logos.* The second springs from the first and develops the third triangle (see the Sephirothal Tree); from the last of which (the lower host of Angels) MEN are generated. It is with this third aspect that we shall deal at present.

The reader must bear in mind that there is a great difference between the LOGOS and the *Demiurgos,* for one is *Spirit* and the other is *Soul;* or as Dr. Wilder has it: "*Dianoia* and *Logos* are synonymous, *Nous* being superior and closely in affinity with Tò ἀγαθον, one being the superior apprehending, the other the comprehending — one noetic and the other phrenic."

Moreover, Man was regarded in several systems as the *third Logos.* The esoteric meaning of the word *Logos* (speech or word, *Verbum*) is the rendering in objective expression, as in a photograph, of the concealed thought. The *Logos* is the mirror reflecting DIVINE MIND, and the Universe is the mirror of the Logos, though the latter is the *esse*

---

* For a clearer explanation of the origins, as contained in the esotericism of the *Bhagavad Gita,* see the *Notes* thereon published in the *"Theosophist"* for February, March and June, 1887, Madras.

of that Universe. As the *Logos* reflects *all* in the Universe of Pleroma, so man reflects in himself all that he sees and finds in *his* Universe, the Earth. It is the three Heads of the Kabala: "*Unum intra alterum, et alterum super alterum*" (*Zohar, Idra Suta,* sec. VII). "Every Universe (world or planet) has its own *Logos,*" says the doctrine. The Sun was always called by the Egyptians "the eye of Osiris," and was himself the *Logos,* the first-begotten, or light made manifest to the world, "which is the Mind and divine intellect of the Concealed." It is only by the seven-fold Ray of this light that we can become cognizant of the *Logos* through the Demiurge, regarding the latter as the *creator* of our planet and everything pertaining to it, and the former as the guiding Force of that "Creator" — good and bad at the same time, the origin of good and the origin of evil. This "Creator" is neither good nor bad *per se,* but its differentiated aspects in nature make it assume one or the other character. With the invisible and the unknown Universes disseminated through space, none of the sun-gods had anything to do. The idea is expressed very clearly in the "Books of Hermes," and in every ancient folk lore. It is symbolised generally by the Dragon and the Serpent — the Dragon of Good and the Serpent of Evil, represented on Earth by the right and the left-hand Magic. In the epic poem of Finland, the Kalewala,[†] the origin of the Serpent of Evil is given: it is born from the "spittle of Suoyatar . . . . and endowed with a living Soul by the Principle of Evil," Hisi. A strife is described between the two, the "thing of Evil" (the Serpent or Sorcerer), and Ahti, the Dragon, "Magic Lemminkainen." The latter is one of the seven sons of Ilmatar, the virgin "daughter of the air," she "who fell from heaven into the sea," before Creation, *i.e.,* Spirit transformed into the matter of sensuous life. There is a world of meaning and Occult thought in these few lines, admirably rendered by Dr. J. M. Crawford, of Cincinnati. The hero Lemminkainen, the good magician,

> "Hews the wall with might of magic,
> Breaks the palisade in pieces,
> Hews to atoms *seven* pickets,
> Chops the *Serpent wall* to fragments.
>
> .   .   .   .   .   .
>
> When the monster little heeding,

---

† * J. W. Alden, New York.

. . . . . .

Pounces with his mouth of venom
At the head of Lemminkainen.
But the hero, quick recalling,
Speaks the *Master words of Knowledge,*
Words that came from distant ages,
Words his ancestors had taught him. . "

(d) In China the men of Fohi (or the "Heavenly Man") are called
the twelve Tien-Hoang, the twelve hierarchies of Dhyanis or Angels,
with human Faces, and Dragon bodies; the dragon standing for divine
Wisdom or Spirit *; and they create men by incarnating themselves in
seven figures of clay — earth and water — made in the shape of those
Tien-hoang,a third allegory; (compare the "Symbols of the Bonzes").
The twelve ÆSERS of the Scandinavian Eddas do the same. In the
Secret Catechism of the Druses of Syria — a legend which is repeated
word for word by the oldest tribes about and around the Euphrates
— men were created by the "Sons of God" descending on Earth, where,

---

* It has been repeatedly stated that the Serpent is the symbol of wisdom and of
Occult knowledge. "The Serpent has been connected with the god of wisdom from
the earliest times of which we have any historical notice," writes Staniland Wake.
"This animal was the especial symbol of Thot or Taut . . . and of all those *gods,* such
as Hermes (?) and Seth who can be connected with him. This is also the primitive
Chaldean triad Hea or Hoa." According to Sir Henry Rawlinson, the most important
titles of this deity refer to "his functions as the source of all knowledge and science."
Not only is he "the intelligent fish," but his name may be read as signifying both
"life" and a serpent (an initiated adept), and he may be considered as "figured
by the great serpent which occupies so conspicuous a place among the symbols
of the gods on the black stones recording Babylonian benefactions." Esculapius,
Serapis, Pluto, Knoum and Kneph, are all deities with the attributes of the serpent.
Says Dupuis, "They are all *healers,* givers of health, spiritual and physical, and of
enlightenment." The crown formed of an asp, the *Thermuthis,* belongs to Isis, goddess
of Life and Healing. The *Upanishads* have a treatise on the *Science of Serpents* —
in other words, the Science of Occult knowledge; and the *Nagas* of the exoteric
Buddhist are not "the fabulous *creatures* of the nature of serpents . . . beings superior
to men and the protectors of the law of Buddha," as Schlagintweit believes, but real
living men, some superior to men by virtue of their Occult knowledge, and the
protectors of Buddha's law, inasmuch as *they interpret his metaphysical tenets correctly,*
others inferior morally as being *black* magicians. Therefore it is truly declared that
Gautama Buddha "is said to have taught them a more philosophical religious
system than to men, who were not sufficiently advanced to understand it at the
time of his appearance." (Schlagintweit's *"Tibetan Buddhism."*)

after culling seven *Mandragoras,* they animated these roots, which became forthwith men.*

All these allegories point to one and the same origin — to the dual and the triple nature of man; dual, as male and female; triple — as being of spiritual and psychic essence *within,* and of a material fabric without.

SD, ii 22-25

CREATION OF DIVINE BEINGS IN THE EXOTERIC ACCOUNTS

In the *Vishnu Purâna* – which is certainly the earliest of all the scriptures of that name – we find, as in all the others, Brahmâ assuming as the male God, for purposes of creation, "four bodies invested by three qualities."* It is said: "In this manner, *Maitreya, Jyotsna* (dawn), *Ratri* (night), *Ahan* (day), and *Sandhya* (evening twilight) are the four bodies of Brahmâ" . . (p. 81, Vol. I., Wilson's translation). As Parasâra explains it, when Brahmâ wants to create the world anew and construct progeny through his will, in the fourfold condition (or the four orders of beings) termed gods (*Dhyan Chohans*), Demons† (i.e., more material *Devas*), Progenitors (*Pitris*) and men, "he collects Yoga-like (*Yúyujè*) his mind."

Strange to say, he begins by creating DEMONS, who thus take precedence over the angels or gods. This is no incongruity, nor is it due to inconsistency, but has, like all the rest, a profound esoteric meaning, quite clear to one free from Christian theological prejudice. He who bears in mind that the principle MAHAT, or Intellect, the "Universal Mind" (literally "the great"), which esoteric philosophy explains as the "manifested Omniscience" – the "first product" of *Pradhâna* (primordial matter) as *Vishnu Purâna* says, but the first Cosmic aspect of *Parabrahm* or the esoteric SAT, the Universal Soul,‡ as Occultism teaches – is at the root of SELF-Consciousness, will understand the reason why. The so-called "Demons" – who are (esoterically) the Self-asserting and

---

* This has in esotericism a direct bearing upon the seven principles of the manifested Brahmâ, or universe, in the same order as in man. Exoterically, it is only four principles.

† Demons is a very loose word to use, as it applies to a great number of inferior – i.e., more material – Spirits, or minor Gods, who are so termed because they "war" with the higher ones; but they are no devils.

‡ The same order of principles in man: – *Atma* (Spirit), *Buddhi* (Soul), its vehicle, as Matter is the *Vahan* of Spirit, and *Manas* (mind), the third, or the fifth microcosmically. On the plane of personality, *Manas* is the first.

116

(intellectually) active Principle – are the positive poles of creation, so to say; hence, the first produced. This is in brief the process as narrated allegorically in the *Purânas*.

> "Having concentrated his mind into itself and the quality of darkness pervading Brahmâ's assumed body, the *Asuras*, issuing from his thigh, were first produced; after which, abandoning this body, it was transformed into NIGHT." (See Part II, Section "The Fallen Angels.")

Two important points are involved herein: *(a)* Primarily in the *Rig Veda*, the "*Asuras*" are shown as spiritual divine beings; their etymology is derived from asu (breath), the "Breath of God," and they mean the same as the Supreme Spirit or the Zoroastrian Ahura. It is later on, for purposes of theology and dogma, that they are shown issuing from Brahmâ's thigh, and that their name began to be derived from a, privative, and sura, god (solar deities), or not-a-god, and that they became the enemies of the gods. Every ancient theogony without exception – from the Aryan and the Egyptian down to that of Hesiod – places, in the order of Cosmogonical evolution, Night before the Day; even *Genesis*, where "darkness is upon the face of the deep" before "the first day." The reason for this is that every Cosmogony – except in the Secret Doctrine – begins by the "Secondary Creation" so-called: to wit, the manifested Universe, the genesis of which has to open by a marked differentiation between the eternal Light of Primary Creation, whose mystery must remain for ever "Darkness" to the prying finite conception and intellect of the profane, and the Secondary Evolution of manifested visible nature. The *Veda* contains the whole philosophy of that division without having ever been correctly explained by our Orientalists, because it has never been understood by them.

Continuing to create, Brahmâ assumes another form, that of the Day, and creates from his breath the gods, who are endowed with the quality of goodness (passivity)§. In his next body the quality of great passivity prevailed, which is also (negative) goodness, and from the side of that personage issued the *Pitris*, the progenitors of men, because, as the text explains, "Brahmâ thought of himself (during the

---

§ Thus, says the Commentary, the saying "by day the gods are most powerful, and by night the demons," is purely allegorical.

process) as the father of the world."* This is *Kriyasakti* – the mysterious Yoga power explained elsewhere. This body of Brahmâ when cast off became the *Sandhya* (evening twilight), the interval between day and night.

Finally Brahmâ assumed his last form pervaded by the quality of foulness, "and from this MEN, in whom foulness and passion predominate, were produced." This body when cast off became the dawn, or morning twilight – the twilight of Humanity. Here Brahmâ stands esoterically for the *Pitris*. He is collectively the *Pitar,* "father."

The true esoteric meaning of this allegory must now be explained. Brahmâ here symbolizes personally the collective creators of the World and Men – the universe with all its numberless productions of things movable and (seemingly) immovable.† He is collectively the *Prajâpatis,* the Lords of Being; and the four bodies typify the four classes of creative powers or *Dhyan Chohans,* described in the Commentary directly following Stanza VII in Book I. The whole philosophy of the so-called "Creation" of the good and evil in this world and of the whole cycle of Manvantaric results therefrom, hangs on the correct comprehension of these Four bodies of Brahmâ.

The reader will now be prepared to understand the real, the esoteric significance of what follows. Moreover there is an important point to be cleared up. Christian theology having arbitrarily settled and agreed that Satan with his Fallen Angels belonged to the earliest creation, Satan being the first-created, the wisest and most beautiful of God's Archangels, the word was given, the keynote struck. Henceforth all the pagan scriptures were made to yield the same meaning, and all were shown to be demoniacal, and it was and is claimed that truth and fact belong to, and commence only with, Christianity. Even the

---

* This thinking of oneself as this, that, or the other, is the chief factor in the production of every kind of psychic or even physical phenomena. The words "whosoever shall say to this mountain be thou removed and cast into the sea, and shall not doubt . . . . that thing will come to pass," are no vain words. Only the word "faith" ought to be translated by WILL. Faith without Will is like a wind-mill without wind – barren of results.

† The same idea is found in the first four chapters of *Genesis,* with their "Lord" and "God," which are the *Elohim* and the Androgynous *Eloha.*

Orientalists and Mythologists, some of them no Christians at all but "infidels," or men of science, entered unconsciously to themselves, and by the mere force of association of ideas and habit, into the theological groove. Purely Brahmanical considerations, based on greed of power and ambition, allowed the masses to remain in ignorance of great truths; and the same causes led the Initiates among the early Christians to remain silent, while those who had never known the truth disfigured the order of things, judging of the hierarchy of "Angels" by their exoteric form. Thus as the *Asuras* had become the rebellious inferior gods fighting the higher ones in popular creeds, so the highest archangel, in truth the Agathodaemon, the eldest benevolent *Logos*, became with theology the "Adversary" or Satan. But is this warranted by the correct interpretation of any old Scripture? The answer is, most certainly not. As the Mazdean Scriptures of the *Zend Avesta*, the *Vendidad* and others correct and expose the later cunning shuffling of the gods in the Hindu Pantheon, and restore through AHURA the *Asuras* to their legitimate place in theogony, so the recent discoveries of the Chaldean tablets vindicate the good name of the first divine Emanations. This is easily proved. Christian Angelology is directly and solely derived from that of the Pharisees, who brought their tenets from Babylonia. The Sadducees, the real guardians of the Laws of Moses, knew not of, and rejected, any angels, opposing even the immortality of the human Soul (not impersonal Spirit). In the *Bible* the only "Angels" spoken of are the "Sons of God" mentioned in *Genesis* vi. (who are now regarded as the *Nephilim*, the Fallen Angels), and several angels in human form, the "Messengers" of the Jewish God, whose own rank needs a closer analysis than heretofore given. (*Vide Supra*, Stanza I., sub-sections 2, 3, *et seq.*, where it is shown that the early Akkadians called *Ea*, Wisdom, that which was disfigured by the later Chaldees and Semites into *Tismat, Tisalat* and the *Thallath* of Berosus, the female Sea Dragon, now Satan.) Truly – "How art thou fallen (by the hand of man), O bright star and son of the morning"!

Now what do the Babylonian accounts of "Creation," as found on the Assyrian fragments of tiles, tell us, those very accounts upon which the Pharisees built their angelology? But compare Mr. G. Smith's "Assyrian Discoveries," p. 398, and his "*Chaldean Account of Genesis*," p. 107. The "Tablet with the story of the Seven Wicked Gods or Spirits," has the following account (we print the important passages in italics):

1. In the *first days* the evil Gods,

2. the *angels, who were in rebellion,* who *in the lower part of heaven*

3. *had been created,*

4. they caused their evil work

5. devising with wicked heads . . . . etc.

Thus we are shown, as plainly as can be, on a fragment which remained unbroken, so that there can be no dubious reading, that the "rebellious angels" had been created in the lower part of heaven, i.e., that they belonged and do belong to a material plane of evolution, although as it is not the plane of which we are made cognizant through our senses, it remains generally invisible to us, and is thus regarded as subjective. Were the Gnostics so wrong, after this, in affirming that this our visible world, and especially the Earth, had been created by lower angels, the inferior *Elohim,* of which, as they taught, the God of Israel was one. These Gnostics were nearer in time to the records of the Archaic Secret Doctrine, and therefore ought to be allowed to have known better than non-initiated Christians, who took upon themselves, hundreds of years later, to remodel and correct what was said. But let us see what the same Tablet says further on:

7. There were seven of them (the wicked gods) . . . . (then follows the description of these, the fourth being a "serpent," the phallic symbol of the *fourth* Race in human Evolution).

15. The seven of them, messengers of the God *Anu*, their king.

Now *Anu* belongs to the Chaldean trinity, and is identical with *Sin*, the "Moon," in one aspect. And the Moon in the Hebrew *Kabala* is the *Argha* of the seed of all material life, and is still more closely connected, kabalistically, with Jehovah, who is double-sexed as *Anu* is. They are both represented in Esotericism and viewed from a dual aspect: male or spiritual, female or material, or Spirit and Matter, the two antagonistic principles. Hence the "Messengers of *Anu*," (who is *Sin*, the "Moon,") are shown, in verses 28 to 41, as being finally overpowered by the same *Sin* with the help of *Bel* (the Sun) and *Ishtar* (Venus). This is regarded as a contradiction by the Assyriologists, but is simply metaphysics in the esoteric teaching.

There is more than one interpretation, for there are seven keys to the mystery of the Fall. Moreover there are two "Falls" in Theology: the rebellion of the Archangels and their "Fall," and the "Fall" of Adam and Eve. Thus the lower as well as the higher Hierarchies are charged with a supposed crime. The word "supposed" is the true and correct term, for in both cases it is founded on misconception. Both are considered in Occultism as Karmic effects, and both belong to the law of Evolution: intellectual and spiritual on the one hand, physical and psychic on the other. The "Fall" is a universal allegory. It sets forth at one end of the ladder of Evolution the "rebellion," i.e., the action of differentiating intellection or consciousness on its various planes, seeking union with matter; and at the other, the lower end, the rebellion of matter against Spirit, or of action against spiritual inertia. And here lies the germ of an error which has had such disastrous effects on the intelligence of civilized societies for over 1,800 years. In the original allegory it is matter – hence the more material angels – which was regarded as the conqueror of Spirit, or the Archangels who "fell" on this plane. "They of the flaming sword (or animal passions) had put to flight the Spirits of Darkness." Yet it is the latter who fought for the supremacy of the conscious and divine spirituality on Earth and failed, succumbing to the power of matter. But in theological dogma we see the reverse. It is Michael, "who is like unto God," the representative of Jehovah, who is the leader of the celestial hosts – as Lucifer, in Milton's fancy, is of the infernal hosts – who has the best of Satan. It is true that the nature of Michael depends upon that of his Creator and Master. Who the latter is, one may find out by carefully studying the allegory of the "War in Heaven" with the astronomical key. As shown by Bentley, the "War of the Titans against the gods" in Hesiod, and also the war of the *Asuras* (or the *Târakâmaya*) against the *devas* in Purânic legend, are identical in all save the names. The aspects of the stars show (Bentley taking the year 945 B.C. as the nearest date for such conjunction) that "all the planets, except Saturn, were on the same side of the heavens as the Sun and Moon," and hence were his opponents. And yet it is Saturn, or the Jewish "Moon god," who is shown as prevailing, both by Hesiod and Moses, neither of whom was understood. Thus it was that the real meaning became distorted.

SD, ii 58 – 63

MAN, A GOD IN ANIMAL FORM

13. THEY (the Moon gods) WENT, EACH ON HIS ALLOTTED LAND: SEVEN OF THEM, EACH ON HIS LOT. THE LORDS OF THE FLAME REMAINED BEHIND. THEY WOULD NOT GO, THEY WOULD NOT CREATE (a).

(a) The Secret teachings show the divine Progenitors creating men on seven portions of the globe "each on his lot" – i.e., each a different race of men externally and internally, and on different zones. This polygenistic claim is considered elsewhere (Vide Stanza VII). But who are "They" who create, and the "Lords of the Flame," "who do not"? Occultism divides the "Creators" into twelve classes; of which four have reached liberation to the end of the "Great Age," the fifth is ready to reach it, but still remains active on the intellectual planes, while seven are still under direct Karmic law. These last act on the man-bearing globes of our chain.

Exoteric Hindu books mention seven classes of Pitris, and among them two distinct kinds of Progenitors or Ancestors: the Barhishad and the Agnishwatta; or those possessed of the "sacred fire" and those devoid of it. Hindu ritualism seems to connect them with sacrificial fires, and with Grihasta Brahmins in earlier incarnations: those who have, and those who have not attended as they should to their household sacred fires in their previous births. The distinction, as said, is derived from the Vedas. The first and highest class (esoterically) the Agnishwatta, are represented in the exoteric allegory as Grihasta (Brahman householders) who, in their past births in other Manvantaras having failed to maintain their domestic fires and to offer burnt sacrifices, have lost every right to have oblations with fire presented to them. Whereas the Barhishad, being Brahmins who have kept up their household sacred fires, are thus honoured to this day. Thence the Agnishwatta are represented as devoid of, and the Barhishad as possessed of, fires.

But esoteric philosophy explains the original qualifications as being due to the difference between the natures of the two classes: the

Agnishwatta Pitris are devoid of fire (i.e., of creative passion), because too divine and pure (*Vide supra*, Sloka 11th); whereas the *Barhishad*, being the lunar spirits more closely connected with Earth, became the creative *Elohim* of form, or the Adam of dust.

The allegory says that Sanandana and other *Vedhas*, the Sons of Brahmâ, his first progeny, "were without desire or passion, inspired with the holy wisdom, estranged from the Universe and undesirous of progeny" (*Vishnu Purâna*, Book I. vii). This also is what is meant in Sloka 11 by the words: "They would not create," and is explained as follows: "The primordial Emanations from the creative Power are too near the absolute Cause. They are transitional and latent forces, which will develop only in the next and subsequent removes." This makes it plain. Hence Brahmâ is said to have felt wrathful when he saw that those "embodied spirits, produced from his limbs (gatra), would not multiply themselves." After which, in the allegory, he creates other seven mind-born Sons (see "*Moksha-Darma*" and "*Mahabhârata*"), namely, *Marichi, Atri, Angiras, Pulastya, Pulaha, Kratu* and *Vasishta*, the latter being often replaced by *Daksha*, the most prolific of the creators. In most of the texts these Seven Sons of *Vasishta-Daksha* are called the seven *Rishis* of the Third *Manvantara*; the latter referring both to the Third Round and also to the third Root Race and its branch Races in the Fourth Round. These are all the creators of the various beings on this Earth, the *Prajâpati*, and at the same time they appear as divers reincarnations in the early *Manvantaras* or races.

It thus becomes clear why the *Agnishwatta*, devoid of the grosser creative fire, hence unable to create physical man, having no double, or astral body, to project, since they were without any form, are shown in exoteric allegories as Yogis, *Kumâras* (chaste youths), who became "rebels," *Asuras*, fighting and opposing gods,* etc., etc. Yet it is they

---

* Because, as the allegory shows, the Gods who had no personal merit of their own, dreading the sanctity of those self-striving incarnated Beings who had become ascetics and Yogis, and thus threatened to upset the power of the former by their self-acquired powers – renounced them. All this has a deep philosophical meaning and refers to the evolution and acquirement of divine powers through self-exertion. Some *Rishi*-Yogis are shown in the *Purânas* to be far more powerful than the gods. Secondary gods or temporary powers in Nature (the Forces) are doomed to disappear; it is only the spiritual potentiality in man which can lead him to become one with the INFINITE and the ABSOLUTE.

alone who could complete man, i.e., make of him a self-conscious, almost a divine being – god on Earth. The *Barhishad*, though possessed of creative fire, were devoid of the higher MAHAT-mic element. Being on a level with the lower principles – those which precede gross objective matter – they could only give birth to the outer man, or rather to the model of the physical, the astral man. Thus, though we see them intrusted with the task by Brahmâ (the collective *Mahat* or Universal Divine Mind), the "Mystery of Creation" is repeated on Earth, only in an inverted sense, as in a mirror. It is those who are unable to create the spiritual immortal man, who project the senseless model (the Astral) of the physical Being; and, as will be seen, it was those who would not multiply, who sacrificed themselves to the good and salvation of Spiritual Humanity. For, to complete the septenary man, to add to his three lower principles and cement them with the spiritual Monad – which could never dwell in such a form otherwise than in an absolutely latent state – two connecting principles are needed: *Manas* and *Kama*. This requires a living Spiritual Fire of the middle principle from the fifth and third states of *Pleroma*. But this fire is the possession of the Triangles, not of the (perfect) Cubes, which symbolize the Angelic Beings:* the former having from the first creation got hold of it and being said to have appropriated it for themselves, as in the allegory of Prometheus. These are the active, and therefore – in Heaven – no longer "pure" Beings. They have become the independent and free Intelligences, shown in every Theogony as fighting for that independence and freedom, and hence – in the ordinary sense – "rebellious to the divine passive law." These are then those "Flames" (the *Agnishwatta*) who, as shown in Sloka 13, "remain behind" instead of going along with the others to create men on Earth. But the true esoteric meaning is that most of them were destined to incarnate as the Egos of the forthcoming crop of Mankind. The human Ego is neither *Atman* nor *Buddhi*, but the higher *Manas*: the intellectual fruition and the efflorescence of the intellectual self-conscious Egotism – in the higher spiritual sense. The ancient works refer to it as *Karana Sarira* on the plane of *Sutratma*, which is the golden thread on which, like beads, the various personalities of this higher Ego are strung.

---

* See Book I, Stanzas III to V. The triangle becomes a Pentagon (five-fold) on Earth.

If the reader were told, as in the semi-esoteric allegories, that these Beings were returning Nirvanees, from preceding *Maha-Manvantaras* – ages of incalculable duration which have rolled away in the Eternity, a still more incalculable time ago – he would hardly understand the text correctly; while some Vedantins might say: "This is not so; the Nirvanee can never return"; which is true during the *Manvantara* he belongs to, and erroneous where Eternity is concerned. For it is said in the Sacred Slokas:

> "The thread of radiance which is imperishable and dissolves only in Nirvana, re-emerges from it in its integrity on the day when the Great Law calls all things back into action. . . ."

Hence, as the higher "*Pitris* or *Dhyanis*" had no hand in his physical creation, we find primeval man, issued from the bodies of his spiritually fireless progenitors, described as aëriform, devoid of compactness, and MINDLESS. He had no middle principle to serve him as a medium between the highest and the lowest, the spiritual man and the physical brain, for he lacked *Manas*. The Monads which incarnated in those empty SHELLS, remained as unconscious as when separated from their previous incomplete forms and vehicles. There is no potentiality for creation, or self-Consciousness, in a pure Spirit on this our plane, unless its too homogeneous, perfect, because divine, nature is, so to say, mixed with, and strengthened by, an essence already differentiated. It is only the lower line of the Triangle – representing the first triad that emanates from the Universal MONAD – that can furnish this needed consciousness on the plane of differentiated Nature. But how could these pure Emanations, which, on this principle, must have originally been themselves unconscious (in our sense), be of any use in supplying the required principle, as they could hardly have possessed it themselves? The answer is difficult to comprehend, unless one is well acquainted with the philosophical metaphysics of a beginningless and endless series of Cosmic Rebirths; and becomes well impressed and familiarised with that immutable law of Nature which is ETERNAL MOTION, cyclic and spiral, therefore progressive even in its seeming retrogression. The one divine Principle, the nameless THAT of the *Vedas*, is the universal Total, which, neither in its spiritual aspects and emanations, nor in its physical atoms, can ever be at "absolute rest" except during the "Nights" of Brahmâ. Hence, also, the "first born" are those who are first set in motion at the beginning of a *Manvantara*, and thus the first to fall into the lower spheres of materiality. They who are called in Theology "the Thrones," and are the "Seat of God," must be the first incarnated men on Earth; and it becomes comprehensible, if we think of the endless series of past *Manvantaras*, to find that the last had to come first, and the first last. We find, in short, that the higher Angels had broken, countless aeons before, through the "Seven Circles," and thus robbed them of the Sacred fire; which means in plain words, that they had assimilated during their past incarnations, in lower as well as in higher worlds, all the wisdom therefrom – the reflection of MAHAT in its various degrees of intensity. No Entity, whether angelic or human, can reach the state of Nirvana, or of absolute purity, except through aeons of suffering and the knowledge of EVIL as well as of good, as otherwise the latter remains incomprehensible.

Between man and the animal – whose Monads (or *Jivas*) are fundamentally identical – there is the impassable abyss of Mentality and Self-consciousness. What is human mind in its higher aspect, whence comes it, if it is not a portion of the essence – and, in some rare cases of incarnation, the very essence – of a higher Being: one from a higher and divine plane? Can man – a god in the animal form – be the product of Material Nature by evolution alone, even as is the animal, which differs from man in external shape, but by no means in the materials of its physical fabric, and is informed by the same, though undeveloped, Monad – seeing that the intellectual potentialities of the two differ as the Sun does from the Glow worm? And what is it that creates such difference, unless man is an animal plus a living god within his physical shell? Let us pause and ask ourselves seriously the question, regardless of the vagaries and sophisms of both the materialistic and the psychological modern sciences.

To some extent, it is admitted that even the esoteric teaching is allegorical. To make the latter comprehensible to the average intelligence, requires the use of symbols cast in an intelligible form. Hence the allegorical and semi-mythical narratives in the exoteric, and the (only) semi-metaphysical and objective representations in the esoteric teachings. For the purely and transcendentally spiritual conceptions are adapted only to the perceptions of those who "see without eyes, hear without ears, and sense without organs," according to the graphic expression of the Commentary. The too puritan idealist is at liberty to spiritualise the tenet, whereas the modern psychologist would simply try to spirit away our "fallen," yet still divine, human Soul in its connection with *Buddhi*.

The mystery attached to the highly spiritual ancestors of the divine man within the earthly man is very great. His dual creation is hinted at in the *Purânas*, though its esoteric meaning can be approached only by collating together the many varying accounts, and reading them in their symbolical and allegorical character. So it is in the *Bible*, both in *Genesis* and even in the Epistles of Paul. For that creator, who is called in the second chapter of *Genesis* the "Lord God," is in the original the *Elohim*, or Gods (the Lords), in the plural; and while one of them makes the earthly Adam of dust, the other breathes into him the breath of life, and the third makes of him a living soul (ii 7), all of which readings are implied in the plural number of the *Elohim*.* "The first man is of the Earth, the second (the last, or rather highest) is from heaven," says Paul in *I. Corinthians* xv. 47.

In the Aryan allegory the rebellious Sons of Brahmâ are all represented as holy ascetics and Yogis. Reborn in every *Kalpa*, they generally try to impede the work of human procreation. When *Daksha*, the chief of the *Prajâpati* (creators), brings forth 10,000 sons for the purpose of peopling the world, Narada – a son of Brahmâ, the great *Rishi*, and virtually a "Kumara," if not so in name – interferes with, and twice frustrates *Daksha's* aim, by persuading those Sons to remain holy ascetics and eschew marriage. For this, *Daksha* curses Narada to be reborn as a man, as Brahmâ had cursed him before for refusing to marry, and obtain progeny, saying: "Perish in thy present (*Deva* or angelic) form and take up thy abode in the womb," i.e., become a man

---

* Seth, as Bunsen and others have shown, is not only the primitive god of the Semites – early Jews included – but also their "semi-divine ancestor." For, says Bunsen ("*God in History*," vol. i, pp. 233, 234), "the Seth of *Genesis*, the father of Enoch (the man) must be considered as originally running parallel with that derived from the *Elohim*, Adam's father." "According to Bunsen, the Deity (the god Seth) was the primitive god of Northern Egypt and Palestine" (Staniland Wake, "*The Great Pyramid*"). And Seth became considered in the later Theology of the Egyptians as "AN EVIL DAEMON," says the same Bunsen, for he is one with Typhon and one with the Hindu demons as a logical sequel.

(*Vâyu Purâna; Harivamsa*, 170). Notwithstanding several conflicting versions of the same story, it is easy to see that Narada belongs to that class of Brahma's, "first born," who have all proven rebellious to the law of animal procreation, for which they had to incarnate as men. Of all the Vedic *Rishis*, Narada, as already shown, is the most incomprehensible, because the most closely connected with the occult doctrines – especially with the secret cycles and *Kalpas* (*Vide supra*).

Certain contradictory statements about this Sage have much distracted the Orientalists. Thus he is shown as refusing positively to create (have progeny), and even as calling his father Brahmâ "a false teacher" for advising him to get married ("*Narada-Pancha-Râtra*"); nevertheless, he is referred to as one of the *Prajâpati*, "progenitors"! In *Naradiya Purâna*, he describes the laws and the duties of the celibate adepts; and as these occult duties do not happen to be found in the fragment of about 3,000 Stanzas in the possession of European museums, the Brahmins are proclaimed liars; the Orientalists forgetting that the *Naradiya* is credited with containing 25,000 Stanzas, and that it is not very likely that such MSS. should be found in the hands of the Hindu profane, those who are ready to sell any precious olla for a red pottage. Suffice it to say, that Narada is the *Deva-Rishi* of Occultism par excellence; and that the Occultist who does not ponder, analyse, and study Narada from his seven esoteric facets, will never be able to fathom certain anthropological, chronological, and even Cosmic Mysteries. He is one of the Fires above-mentioned, and plays a part in the evolution of this *Kalpa* from its incipient, down to its final stage. He is an actor who appears in each of the successive acts (Root Races) of the present Manvantaric drama, in the world allegories which strike the keynote of esotericism, and are now becoming more familiar to the reader."

SD, ii 77–83

SEVEN CLASSES OF PITRIS

The Progenitors of Man, called in India "Fathers," *Pitara* or *Pitris*, are the creators of our bodies and lower principles. They are ourselves, as the first personalities, and we are they. Primeval man would be "the bone of their bone and the flesh of their flesh," if they had body and flesh. As stated, they were "lunar Beings."

The Endowers of man with his conscious, immortal EGO, are the "Solar Angels" – whether so regarded metaphorically or literally. The mysteries of the Conscious EGO or human Soul are great. The esoteric name of these "Solar Angels" is, literally, the "Lords" (*Nath*) of "persevering ceaseless devotion" (*pranidhâna*). Therefore they of the fifth principle (*Manas*) seem to be connected with, or to have originated the system of the Yogis who make of *pranidhâna* their fifth observance (see Yoga Shastra, II, 32.) It has already been explained why the trans-Himalayan Occultists regard them as evidently identical with those who in India are termed *Kumâras, Agnishwattas*, and the *Barhishads*.

How precise and true is Plato's expression, how profound and philosophical his remark on the (human) soul or EGO, when he defined it as "a compound of the same and the other." And yet how little this hint has been understood, since the world took it to mean that the soul was the breath of God, of Jehovah. It is "the same and the other," as the great Initiate-Philosopher said; for the EGO (the "Higher Self" when merged with and in the Divine Monad) is Man, and yet the same as the "OTHER," the Angel in him incarnated, as the same with the universal MAHAT. The great classics and philosophers felt this truth, when saying that "there must be something within us which produces our thoughts. Something very subtle; it is a breath; it is fire; it is ether; it is quintessence; it is a slender likeness; it is an intellection; it is a number; it is harmony. . . . . " (Voltaire).

All these are the *Manasam* and *Rajasas*: the *Kumâras, Asuras,* and other rulers and *Pitris*, who incarnated in the Third Race, and in this and various other ways endowed mankind with Mind.

There are seven classes of *Pitris*, as shown below, three incorporeal and four corporeal; and two kinds, the *Agnishwatta* and the *Barhishad*. And we may add that, as there are two kinds of *Pitris*, so there is a double and a triple set of *Barhishad* and *Agnishwatta*. The former, having given birth to their astral doubles, are reborn as Sons of Atri, and are the "*Pitris* of the Demons," or corporeal beings, on the authority of *Manu* (III, 196); while the *Agnishwatta* are reborn as Sons of Marichi (a son of Brahmâ), and are the *Pitris* of the Gods (*Manu* again, *Matsya* and *Padma Purânas* and Kulluka in the *Laws of the Manavas*, III, 195) *. Moreover, the *Vâyu Purâna* declares all the seven orders to have originally been the first gods, the *Vairajas*, whom Brahmâ "with the eye of Yoga, beheld in the eternal spheres, and who are the gods of gods"; and the *Matsya* adds that the Gods worshipped them; while the *Harivansa* (S. 1, 935) distinguishes the *Virâjas* as one class of the *Pitris* only – a statement corroborated in the Secret Teachings, which, however, identify the *Virâjas* with the elder *Agnishwattas[†]* and the *Rajasas*, or *Abhuta Rajasas*, who are incorporeal without even an astral phantom. Vishnu is said, in most of the MSS., to have incarnated in and through them. "In the *Raivata Manvantara*, again, Hari, best of gods, was born of Sambhuti, as the divine *Manasas* – originating with the deities called *Rajasas*." Sambhuti was a daughter of *Daksha*, and wife of Marichi, the father of the *Agnishwatta*, who, along with the *Rajasas*, are ever associated with *Manasas*. As remarked by a far more able Sanskritist than Wilson, Mr. Fitzedward Hall, "*Manasa* is no inappropriate name for a deity associated with the *Rajasas*. We appear to have in it *Manasam* – the same as *Manas* – with the change of termination required to express male personification" (*Vishnu Purâna* Bk. III, ch. I., p. 17 footnote). All the sons of Virâja are *Manasa*, says Nilakantha. And Virâja is Brahmâ, and, therefore, the incorporeal *Pitris* are called *Vairâjas* from being the sons of Virâja, says *Vâyu Purâna*.

---

* We are quite aware that the *Yayu* and *Matsya Purânas* identify (agreeably to Western interpretation) the *Agnishwatta* with the seasons, and the *Barhishad* Pitris with the months; adding a fourth class — the *Kavyas* — cyclic years. But do not Christian, Roman Catholics identify their Angels with planets, and are not the seven *Rishis* become the *Saptarshi* — a constellation? They are deities presiding over all the cyclic divisions.

† † The *Vayu Purâna* shows the region called *Virâja-loka* inhabited by the *Agnishwattas*.

We could multiply our proofs *ad infinitum*, but it is useless. The wise will understand our meaning, the unwise are not required to. There are thirty-three crores, or 330 millions, of gods in India. But, as remarked by the learned lecturer on the *Bhagavad Gitâ*, "they may be all *devas*, but are by no means all 'gods', in the high spiritual sense one attributes to the term." "This is an unfortunate blunder," he remarks, "generally committed by Europeans. *Deva* is a kind of spiritual being, and because the same word is used in ordinary parlance to mean god, it by no means follows that we have to worship thirty-three crores of gods." And he adds suggestively: "These beings, as may be naturally inferred have a certain affinity with one of the three component *Upadhis* (basic principles) into which we have divided man." – (*Vide Theosophist*, Feb., 1887, *et seq.*)."

SD, ii 88–90

WHAT PROMETHEUS SYMBOLIZED

STANZA IV – (Continued)

15. SEVEN TIMES SEVEN SHADOWS (*Chhayas*) OF
FUTURE MEN (or *AManasas*) (*a*) WERE (*thus*) BORN,
EACH OF HIS OWN COLOUR (*complexion*) AND KIND
(*b*). EACH (*also*) INFERIOR TO HIS FATHER (*creator*).
THE FATHERS, THE BONELESS, COULD GIVE NO LIFE
TO BEINGS WITH BONES. THEIR PROGENY WERE
BHUTA (*phantoms*) WITH NEITHER FORM NOR MIND,
THEREFORE THEY WERE CALLED THE CHHAYA
(*image or shadow*) RACE (*c*).

(*a*) *Manu*, as already remarked, comes from the root "man" to think,
hence "a thinker." It is from this Sanskrit word very likely that sprung
the Latin "*mens*," mind, the Egyptian "*Menes*," the "Master-Mind," the
Pythagorean *Monas*, or conscious "thinking unit," mind also, and even
our "*Manas*" or mind, the fifth principle in man. Hence these shadows
are called *amanasa*, "mindless."

With the Brahmins the *Pitris* are very sacred, because they are the
Progenitors,* or ancestors of men – the first *Manushya* on this Earth
– and offerings are made to them by the Brahmin when a son is born
unto him. They are more honoured and their ritual is more important
than the worship of the gods (See the "*Laws of Manu*," Bk. III, p. 203).

May we not now search for a philosophical meaning in this dual
group of progenitors?

The *Pitris* being divided into seven classes, we have here the mystic
number again. Nearly all the *Purânas* agree that three of these are

---

* This was hinted at in *Isis Unveiled*, Vol. I., p. xxxviii, though the full explanation
could not then be given: "The *Pitris* are not the ancestors of the present living men,
but those of the first human kind or Adamic race; the spirits of human races, which,
on the great scale of descending evolution, preceded our races of men, and were
physically as well as spiritually, far superior to our modem pigmies. In *Manava
Dharma Shastra* they are called the Lunar ancestors."

arupa, formless, while four are corporeal; the former being intellectual and spiritual, the latter material and devoid of intellect. Esoterically, it is the *Asuras* who form the first three classes of *Pitris* – "born in the body of night" – whereas the other four were produced from the body of twilight. Their fathers, the gods, were doomed to be born fools on Earth, according to *Vâyu Purâna*. The legends are purposely mixed up and made very hazy: the *Pitris* being in one the sons of the gods, and, in another, those of Brahmâ; while a third makes them instructors of their own fathers. It is the Hosts of the four material classes who create men simultaneously on the seven zones.

Now, with regard to the seven classes of *Pitris*, each of which is again divided into seven, a word to students and a query to the profane. That class of the "Fire *Dhyanis*," which we identify on undeniable grounds with the *Agnishwattas*, is called in our school the "Heart" of the Dhyan-Chohanic Body, and it is said to have incarnated in the third race of men and made them perfect. The esoteric Mystagogy speaks of the mysterious relation existing between the hebdomadic essence or substance of this angelic Heart and that of man, whose every physical organ, and psychic, and spiritual function, is a reflection, so to say, a copy on the terrestrial plane of the model or prototype above. Why, it is asked, should there be such a strange repetition of the number seven in the anatomical structure of man? Why should the heart have four lower "cavities and three higher divisions," answering so strangely to the septenary division of the human principles, separated into two groups, the higher and the lower; and why should the same division be found in the various classes of *Pitris*, and especially our Fire *Dhyanis*? For, as already stated, these Beings fall into four corporeal (or grosser) and three incorporeal (or subtler) "principles," or call them by any other name you please. Why do the seven nervous plexuses of the body radiate seven rays? Why are there these seven plexuses, and why seven distinct layers in the human skin?

"Having projected their shadows and made men of one element (ether), the progenitors re-ascend to *Maha-loka*, whence they descend periodically, when the world is renewed, to give birth to new men.

"The subtle bodies remain without understanding (*Manas*) until the advent of the *Suras* (Gods) now called *Asuras* (not Gods)," says the Commentary.

"Not-gods," for the Brahmins, perhaps, but the highest Breaths, for the Occultist; since those progenitors (*Pitar*), the formless and the intellectual, refuse to build man, but endow him with mind; the four corporeal classes creating only his body.

This is very plainly shown in various texts of the Rig Veda – the highest authority for a Hindu of any sect whatever. Therein *Asura* means "spiritual divine," and the word is used as a synonym for Supreme Spirit, while in the sense of a "God," the term *"Asura"* is applied to Varuna and Indra and pre-eminently to Agni – the three having been in days of old the three highest gods, before Brahmanical Theo-Mythology distorted the true meaning of almost everything in the Archaic Scriptures. But, as the key is now lost, the *Asuras* are hardly mentioned.

In the Zendavesta the same is found. In the Mazdean, or Magian, religion, *"Asura"* is the lord *Asura Visvavedas*, the "all-knowing" or "omniscient Lord"; and *Asura-Mazdha*, become later *Ahura-Mazdha*, is, as Benfey shows, "the Lord who bestows Intelligence" – *Asura-Medha* and Ahura-Mazdao. Elsewhere in this work it is shown, on equally good authority, that the Indo-Iranian *Asura* was always regarded as seven-fold. This fact, combined with the name *Mazdha*, as above, which makes of the seven-fold *Asura* the "Lord," or "Lords" collectively "who bestow Intelligence," connects the *Amshaspends* with the *Asuras* and with our incarnating *Dhyan Chohans*, as well as with the *Elohim*, and the seven informing gods of Egypt, Chaldea, and every other country.

Why these "gods" refused to create men is not, as stated in exoteric accounts, because their pride was too great to share the celestial power of their essence with the children of Earth, but for reasons already suggested. However, allegory has indulged in endless fancies and theology taken advantage thereof in every country to make out its case against these first born, or the *logoi*, and to impress it as a truth on the minds of the ignorant and credulous. (Compare also what is said about *Makara* and the *Kumâras* in connection with the Zodiac.)

The Christian system is not the only one which has degraded them into demons. Zoroastrianism and even Brahmanism have profited thereby to obtain hold over the people's mind. Even in Chaldean exotericism, Beings who refuse to create, i.e., who are said to oppose thereby the *Demiurgos*, are also denounced as the Spirits of Darkness. The *Suras*, who win their intellectual independence, fight the *Suras* who are devoid thereof, who are shown as passing their lives in profitless ceremonial worship based on blind faith – a hint now ignored by the orthodox Brahmins – and forthwith the former become *A-Suras*. The first and mind-born Sons of the Deity refuse to create progeny, and are cursed by Brahmâ to be born as men. They are hurled down to Earth, which, later on, is transformed, in theological dogma, into the infernal regions. Ahriman destroys the Bull created by Ormazd – which is the emblem of terrestrial illusive life, the "germ of sorrow" – and, forgetting that the perishing finite seed must die, in order that the plant of immortality, the plant of spiritual, eternal life, should sprout and live, Ahriman is proclaimed the enemy, the opposing power, the devil. Typhon cuts Osiris into fourteen pieces, in order to prevent his peopling the world and thus creating misery; and Typhon becomes, in the exoteric, theological teaching, the Power of Darkness. But all this is the exoteric shell. It is the worshippers of the latter who attribute to disobedience and rebellion the effort and self-sacrifice of those who would help men to their original status of divinity through self-conscious efforts; and it is these worshippers of Form who have made demons of the Angels of Light.

Esoteric philosophy, however, teaches that one third * of the *Dhyanis* – i.e., the three classes of the *Arupa Pitris*, endowed with intelligence, "which is a formless breath, composed of intellectual not elementary substances" (see *Harivamsa*, 932) – was simply doomed by the law of Karma and evolution to be reborn (or incarnated) on Earth.† Some of

---

* Whence the subsequent assertions of St. John's vision, referred to in his *Apocalypse*, about "the great red Dragon having seven heads and ten horns, and seven crowns upon his heads," whose "tail drew the third part of the stars of heaven and did cast them to the earth" (ch. xii).

† The verse "did cast them to the Earth," plainly shows its origin in the grandest and oldest allegory of the Aryan mystics, who, after the destruction of the Atlantean giants and sorcerers, concealed the truth – astronomical, physical, and divine, as it is a page out of pre-cosmic theogony – under various allegories. Its esoteric, true interpretation is a veritable Theodice of the "Fallen Angels," so called; the willing

these were *Nirmanakayas* from other *Manvantaras*. Hence we see them, in all the *Purânas*, reappearing on this globe, in the third *Manvantara*, as Kings, *Rishis* and heroes (read Third Root Race). This tenet, being too philosophical and metaphysical to be grasped by the multitudes, was, as already stated, disfigured by the priesthood for the purpose of preserving a hold over them through superstitious fear.

The supposed "rebels," then, were simply those who, compelled by Karmic law to drink the cup of gall to its last bitter drop, had to incarnate anew, and thus make responsible thinking entities of the astral statues projected by their inferior brethren. Some are said to have refused, because they had not in them the requisite materials – i.e., an astral body – since they were *arupa*. The refusal of others had reference to their having been Adepts and Yogis of long past preceding *Manvantaras*; another mystery. But, later on, as *Nirmanakayas*, they sacrificed themselves for the good and salvation of the Monads which were waiting for their turn, and which otherwise would have had to linger for countless ages in irresponsible, animal-like, though in appearance human, forms. It may be a parable and an allegory within an allegory. Its solution is left to the intuition of the student, if he only reads that which follows with his spiritual eye.

As to their fashioners or "Ancestors" – those Angels who, in the exoteric legends, obeyed the law – they must be identical with the *Barhishad Pitris*, or the *Pitar-Devata*, i.e., those possessed of the physical creative fire. They could only create, or rather clothe, the human Monads with their own astral Selves, but they could not make man in their image and likeness. "Man must not be like one of us," say the creative gods, entrusted with the fabrication of the lower animal but

---

and the unwilling, the creators and those who refused to create, being now mixed up most perplexingly by Christian Catholics, who forget that their highest Archangel, St. Michael, who is shown to conquer (to master and to assimilate) the DRAGON OF WISDOM and of divine Self-sacrifice (now miscalled and calumniated as Satan), WAS THE FIRST TO REFUSE TO CREATE! This led to endless confusion. So little does Christian theology understand the paradoxical language of the East and its symbolism, that it even explains, in its dead letter sense, the Chinese Buddhist and Hindu exoteric rite of raising a noise during certain eclipses to scare away the "great red Dragon," which laid a plot to carry away the light! But here "Light" means esoteric Wisdom, and we have sufficiently explained the secret meaning of the terms Dragon, Serpent, etc., etc., all of which refer to Adepts and Initiates.

higher; (see Gen. and Plato's *Timaeus*). Their creating the semblance of men out of their own divine Essence means, esoterically, that it is they who became the first Race, and thus shared its destiny and further evolution. They would not, simply because they could not, give to man that sacred spark which burns and expands into the flower of human reason and self-consciousness, for they had it not to give. This was left to that class of *Devas* who became symbolised in Greece under the name of Prometheus, to those who had nought to do with the physical body, yet everything with the purely spiritual man. (See Part II of this volume, "The Fallen Angels"; also "The Gods of Light proceed from the Gods of Darkness.")

Each class of Creators endows man with what it has to give: the one builds his external form; the other gives him its essence, which later on becomes the Human Higher Self owing to the personal exertion of the individual; but they could not make men as they were themselves – perfect, because sinless; sinless, because having only the first, pale shadowy outlines of attributes, and these all perfect – from the human standpoint – white, pure and cold as the virgin snow. Where there is no struggle, there is no merit. Humanity, "of the Earth earthy," was not destined to be created by the angels of the first divine Breath: therefore they are said to have refused to do so, and man had to be formed by more material creators,* who, in their turn, could give only what they had in their own natures, and no more. Subservient to eternal law, the pure gods could only project out of themselves shadowy men, a little

---

* In spite of all efforts to the contrary, Christian theology – having burdened itself with the Hebrew esoteric account of the creation of man, which is understood literally – cannot find any reasonable excuse for its "God, the Creator," who produces a man devoid of mind and sense; nor can it justify the punishment following an act, for which Adam and Eve might plead non compos. For if the couple is admitted to be ignorant of good and evil before the eating of the forbidden fruit, how could it be expected to know that disobedience was evil? If primeval man was meant to remain a half-witted, or rather witless, being, then his creation was aimless and even cruel, if produced by an omnipotent and perfect God. But Adam and Eve are shown, even in *Genesis*, to be created by a class of lower divine Beings, the *Elohim*, who are so jealous of their personal prerogatives as reasonable and intelligent creatures, that they will not allow man to become "as one of us." This is plain, even from the dead-letter meaning of the *Bible*. The Gnostics, then, were right in regarding the Jewish God as belonging to a class of lower, material and not very holy denizens of the invisible World.

less ethereal and spiritual, less divine and perfect than themselves – shadows still. The first humanity, therefore, was a pale copy of its progenitors; too material, even in its ethereality, to be a hierarchy of gods; too spiritual and pure to be MEN, endowed as it is with every negative (*Nirguna*) perfection. Perfection, to be fully such, must be born out of imperfection, the incorruptible must grow out of the corruptible, having the latter as its vehicle and basis and contrast. Absolute light is absolute darkness, and vice versa. In fact, there is neither light nor darkness in the realms of truth. Good and Evil are twins, the progeny of Space and Time, under the sway of *Maya*. Separate them, by cutting off one from the other, and they will both die. Neither exists per se, since each has to be generated and created out of the other, in order to come into being; both must be known and appreciated before becoming objects of perception, hence, in mortal mind, they must be divided.

Nevertheless, as the illusionary distinction exists, it requires a lower order of creative angels to "create" inhabited globes – especially ours – or to deal with matter on this earthly plane. The philosophical Gnostics were the first to think so, in the historical period, and to invent various systems upon this theory. Therefore in their schemes of creation, one always finds their Creators occupying a place at the very foot of the ladder of spiritual Being. With them, those who created our earth and its mortals were placed on the very limit of mayavic matter, and their followers were taught to think – to the great disgust of the Church Fathers – that for the creation of those wretched races, in a spiritual and moral sense, which grace our globe, no high divinity could be made responsible, but only angels of a low hierarchy,* to which class they relegated the Jewish God, Jehovah.

Mankinds different from the present are mentioned in all the ancient Cosmogonies. Plato speaks, in the *Phaedrus*, of a winged race of men. Aristophanes (in Plato's *Banquet*), speaks of a race androgynous and with round bodies. In *Pymander*, all the animal kingdom even is double-

---

* In *Isis Unveiled* several of these Gnostic systems are given. One is taken from the *Codex Nazaraeus*, the Scriptures of the Nazarenes, who, although they existed long before the days of Christ, and even before the laws of Moses, were Gnostics, and many of them Initiates. They held their "Mysteries of Life" in Nazara (ancient and modern Nazareth), and their doctrines are a faithful echo of the teachings of the Secret Doctrine – some of which we are now endeavouring to explain.

sexed. Thus in § 18, it is said: "The circuit having been accomplished, the knot was loosened. . . . and all the animals, which were equally androgynous, were untied (separated) together with man. . . . ." for. . . . "the causes had to produce effects on earth."[†] Again, in the ancient Quiche Manuscript, the *Popol Vuh* – published by the late Abbé Brasseur de Bourbourg – the first men are described as a race "whose sight was unlimited, and who knew all things at once": thus showing the divine knowledge of Gods, not mortals. The Secret Doctrine, correcting the unavoidable exaggerations of popular fancy, gives the facts as they are recorded in the Archaic symbols.

(*b*) These "shadows" were born "each of his own colour and kind," each also "inferior to his creator," because the latter was a complete being of his kind. The Commentaries refer the first sentence to the colour or complexion of each human race thus evolved. In *Pymander*, the Seven primitive men, created by Nature from the "heavenly Man," all partake of the qualities of the "Seven Governors," or Rulers, who loved Man – their own reflection and synthesis.

In the Norse Legends, one recognizes in *Asgard*, the habitat of the gods, as also in the *Ases* themselves, the same mystical *loci* and personifications woven into the popular "myths," as in our Secret Doctrine; and we find them in the *Vedas*, the *Purânas*, the Mazdean Scriptures and the *Kabala*. The *Ases* of Scandinavia, the rulers of the world which preceded ours, whose name means literally the "pillars of the world," its "supports," are thus identical with the Greek *Cosmocratores*, the "Seven Workmen or Rectors" of Pymander, the seven *Rishis* and *Pitris* of India, the seven Chaldean gods and seven evil spirits, the seven Kabalistic *Sephiroth* synthesised by the upper triad, and even the seven Planetary Spirits of the Christian mystics. The *Ases* create the earth, the seas, the sky and the clouds, the whole visible world, from the remains of the slain giant Ymir; but they do not create MAN, but only his form from the *Ask* or ash tree. It is Odin who endows him with life and soul, after Lodur had given him blood and bones, and finally it is Honir who furnishes him with his intellect (*manas*) and with his conscious senses. The Norse

---

† See the translation from the Greek by Francois, Monsieur de Foix, Evesque d'Ayre: the work dedicated to Marguerite de France, Reine de Navarre. Edition of 1579, Bordeaux.

Ask, the Hesiodic Ash tree, whence issued the men of the generation of bronze, the Third Root Race, and the Tzite tree of the Popol-Vuh, out of which the Mexican third race of men was created, are all one.*
This may be plainly seen by any reader. But the Occult reason why the Norse *Yggdrasil*, the Hindu *Aswatha*, the *Gogard*, the Hellenic tree of life, and the Tibetan *Zampun*, are one with the Kabalistic *Sephirothal* Tree, and even with the Holy Tree made by *Ahura Mazda*, and the Tree of Eden – who among the western scholars can tell? † Nevertheless, the fruits of all those "Trees," whether *Pippala* or *Haoma* or yet the more prosaic apple, are the "plants of life," in fact and verity. The prototypes of our races were all enclosed in the microcosmic tree, which grew and developed within and under the great mundane macrocosmic tree;‡ and the mystery is half revealed in the *Dirghotamas*, where it is said: "*Pippala*, the sweet fruit of that tree upon which come spirits who love the science, and where the gods produce all marvels." As in the *Gogard*, among the luxuriant branches of all those mundane trees, the "Serpent" dwells. But while the Macroscosmic tree is the Serpent of Eternity and of absolute Wisdom itself, those who dwell in the Microcosmic tree are the Serpents of the manifested Wisdom. One is the One and All; the others are its reflected parts. The "tree" is man himself, of course, and the Serpents dwelling in each, the conscious *Manas*, the connecting link between Spirit and Matter, heaven and earth.

Everywhere, it is the same. The creating powers produce Man, but fail in their final object. All these *logoi* strive to endow man with conscious immortal spirit, reflected in the Mind (*manas*) alone; they fail, and they are all represented as being punished for the failure, if not for the attempt. What is the nature of the punishment? A sentence of imprisonment in the lower or nether region, which is our earth; the lowest in its chain; an "eternity" – meaning the duration of the life cycle – in the darkness of matter, or within animal Man. It has pleased the half ignorant and half designing Church Fathers to disfigure the graphic symbol. They took advantage of the metaphor and allegory found in every old religion to turn them to the benefit of the new one.

---

* See Max Muller's review of the *Popol-Vuh*.

† Mr. James Darmesteter, the translator of the *Vendidad*, speaking of it, says: "The tree, whatever it is . . ." (p. 209).

‡ Plato's "*Timaeus*".

Thus man was transformed into the darkness of a material hell; his divine consciousness, obtained from his indwelling Principle (the *Manasa*), or the incarnated *Deva*, became the glaring flames of the infernal region; and our globe that Hell itself. *Pippala, Haoma,* the fruit of the Tree of Knowledge, were denounced as the forbidden fruit, and the "Serpent of Wisdom," the Voice of reason and consciousness, remained identified for ages with the Fallen Angel, which is the old Dragon, the Devil! (*Vide* Part II, "The Evil Spirit, who, or what?")"

SD, ii 90–98

THE DIVINE REBELS

16. HOW ARE THE *(real)* MANUSHYAS BORN? THE MANUS WITH MINDS, HOW ARE THEY MADE? *(a)* THE FATHERS *(Barhishad (?))* CALL TO THEIR HELP THEIR OWN FIRE *(the Kavyavahana, electric fire)*, WHICH IS THE FIRE WHICH BURNS IN EARTH. THE SPIRIT OF THE EARTH CALLED TO HIS HELP THE SOLAR FIRE *(Suchi, the spirit in the Sun)*. THESE THREE *(the Pitris and the two fires)* PRODUCED IN THEIR JOINT EFFORTS A GOOD RUPA. IT *(the form)* COULD STAND, WALK, RUN, RECLINE AND FLY. YET IT WAS STILL BUT A CHHAYA, A SHADOW WITH NO SENSE *(b)* . . . . . .

(a) Here an explanation again becomes necessary in the light, and with the help of the exoteric added to the esoteric scriptures. The *"Manushyas"* (men) and the *Manus* are here equivalent to the Chaldean "Adam" – this term not meaning at all the first man, as with the Jews, or one solitary individual, but mankind collectively, as with the Chaldeans and Assyrians. It is the four orders or classes of *Dhyan Chohans* out of the seven, says the Commentary, "who were the progenitors of the concealed man," i.e., the subtle inner man. The *"Lha"* of the Moon, the lunar spirits, were, as already stated, only the ancestors of his form, i.e., of the model according to which Nature began her external work upon him. Thus primitive man was, when he appeared, only a senseless *Bhuta* * or a "Phantom." This "creation" was a failure, the reason of which will be explained in the Commentary on Sloka 20.

(b) This attempt was again a failure. It allegorizes the vanity of physical nature's unaided attempts to construct even a perfect animal –

---

* It is not clear why *"Bhûtas"* should be rendered by the Orientalists as meaning "evil Spirits" in the *Purânas*. In the *Vishnu Purâna*, Book I, ch. 5, the Sloka simply says: "*Bhûtas* – fiends, frightful from being monkey-coloured and carnivorous"; and the word in India now means ghosts, ethereal or astral phantoms, while in esoteric teaching it means elementary substances, something made of attenuated, noncompound essence, and, specifically, the astral double of any man or animal. In this case these primitive men are the doubles of the first ethereal *Dhyanis* or *Pitris*.

142

let alone man. For the "Fathers," the lower Angels, are all Nature Spirits and the higher Elementals also possess an intelligence of their own; but this is not enough to construct a THINKING man. "Living Fire" was needed, that fire which gives the human mind its self-perception and self-consciousness, or *Manas*; and the progeny of Pârvaka and Suchi are the animal electric and solar fires, which create animals, and could thus furnish but a physical living constitution to that first astral model of man. The first creators, then, were the Pygmalions of primeval man: they failed to animate the statue – intellectually.

This Stanza we shall see is very suggestive. It explains the mystery of, and fills the gap between, the informing principle in man – the HIGHER SELF or human Monad – and the animal Monad, both one and the same, although the former is endowed with divine intelligence, the latter with instinctual faculty alone. How is the difference to be explained, and the presence of that HIGHER SELF in man accounted for?

"The Sons of MAHAT are the quickeners of the human Plant. They are the Waters falling upon the arid soil of latent life, and the Spark that vivifies the human animal. They are the Lords of Spiritual Life eternal." . . . . "In the beginning (in the Second Race) some (of the Lords) only breathed of their essence into *Manushya* (men), and some took in man their abode."

This shows that not all men became incarnations of the "divine Rebels," but only a few among them. The remainder had their fifth principle simply quickened by the spark thrown into it, which accounts for the great difference between the intellectual capacities of men and races. Had not the "sons of *Mahat*," speaking allegorically, skipped the intermediate worlds, in their impulse toward intellectual freedom, the animal man would never have been able to reach upward from this earth, and attain through self-exertion his ultimate goal. The cyclic pilgrimage would have to be performed through all the planes of existence half unconsciously, if not entirely so, as in the case of the animals. It is owing to this rebellion of intellectual life against the morbid inactivity of pure spirit, that we are what we are – self-conscious, thinking men, with the capabilities and attributes of Gods in us, for good as much as for evil. Hence the REBELS are our saviours.

Let the philosopher ponder well over this, and more than one mystery will become clear to him. It is only by the attractive force of the contrasts that the two opposites – Spirit and Matter – can be cemented on Earth, and, smelted in the fire of self-conscious experience and suffering, find themselves wedded in Eternity. This will reveal the meaning of many hitherto incomprehensible allegories, foolishly called "fables." (*Vide infra*, "The Secret of Satan.")

It explains, to begin with, the statement made in *Pymander*, that the "heavenly MAN," the "Son of the Father," who partook of the nature and essence of the Seven Governors, or creators and Rulers of the material world, "peeped through the Harmony and, breaking through the Seven Circles of Fire, made manifest the downward-born nature." * It explains every verse in that Hermetic narrative, as also the Greek allegory of Prometheus. Most important of all, it explains the many allegorical accounts about the "Wars in Heaven," including that of Revelation with respect to the Christian dogma of the fallen angels. It explains the "rebellion" of the oldest and highest Angels, and the meaning of their being cast down from Heaven into the depths of Hell, i.e., MATTER. It even solves the recent perplexity of the Assyriologists, who express their wonder through the late George Smith.

"My first idea of this part" (of the rebellion), he says, "was that the wars with the powers of Evil preceded the Creation; I now think it followed the account of the fall" (*Chaldean Account of Genesis*, p. 92). In this work Mr. George Smith gives an engraving, from an early Babylonian cylinder, of the Sacred Tree, the Serpent, man and woman. The tree has seven branches: three on the man's side, four on that of the female. These branches are typical of the seven Root Races, in the third of which, at its very close, occurred the separation of the sexes and the so-called FALL into generation. The three earliest Races were sexless, then hermaphrodite; the other four, male and female, as distinct from each other. "The Dragon," says Mr. G. Smith, "which in the Chaldean account of the creation leads man to sin, is the creation of *Tiamat*, the living principle of the Sea, or Chaos . . . which was opposed to the deities at the creation of the world." This is an error. The Dragon is the male principle, or Phallus, personified, or rather animalized; and

---

* See "*Pymander*," Bk. II, verses 17 to 29.

Tiamat, "the embodiment of the Spirit of Chaos," of the deep, or Abyss, is the female principle, the Womb. The "Spirit of Chaos and Disorder" refers to the mental perturbation which it led to. It is the sensual, attractive, magnetic principle which fascinates and seduces, the ever living active element which throws the whole world into disorder, chaos, and sin. The Serpent seduces the woman, but it is the latter who seduces man, and both are included in the Karmic curse, though only as a natural result of a cause produced. Says George Smith: "It is clear that the Dragon is included in the curse for the Fall, and that the Gods" (the *Elohim*, jealous at seeing the man of clay becoming a Creator in his turn, like all the animals,) "invoke on the head of the human Race all the evils which afflict humanity. Wisdom and knowledge shall injure him, he shall have family quarrels, he will anger the gods, he shall submit to tyranny. . . . he shall be disappointed in his desires, he shall pour out useless prayers, he shall commit future sin. . No doubt subsequent lines continue this topic, but again our narrative is broken, and it re-opens only where the gods are preparing for war with the powers of evil, which are led by *Tiamat* (the woman). . . . " (*Babylonian Legend of Creation*, p. 92.)

This account is omitted in *Genesis*, for monotheistic purposes. But it is a mistaken policy – born no doubt of fear, and regard for dogmatic religion and its superstitions – to have sought to restore the Chaldean fragments by *Genesis*, whereas it is the latter, far younger than any of the fragments, which ought to be explained by the former.

> 17. THE BREATH (*human Monad*) NEEDED A FORM; THE FATHERS GAVE IT. THE BREATH NEEDED A GROSS BODY; THE EARTH MOULDED IT. THE BREATH NEEDED THE SPIRIT OF LIFE; THE SOLAR LHAS BREATHED IT INTO ITS FORM. THE BREATH NEEDED A MIRROR OF ITS BODY (*astral shadow*); "WE GAVE IT OUR OWN," SAID THE DHYANIS. THE BREATH NEEDED A VEHICLE OF DESIRES (*Kama rupa*); "IT HAS IT," SAID THE DRAINER OF WATERS (*Suchi, the fire of passion and animal instinct*). THE BREATH NEEDS A MIND TO EMBRACE THE UNIVERSE; "WE CANNOT GIVE THAT," SAID THE FATHERS. "I NEVER HAD IT," SAID THE SPIRIT OF THE EARTH. "THE FORM WOULD

BE CONSUMED WERE I TO GIVE IT MINE," SAID THE
GREAT (*solar*) FIRE . . . . (*nascent*) MAN REMAINED AN
EMPTY, SENSELESS BHÛTA . . . . THUS HAVE THE
BONELESS GIVEN LIFE TO THOSE WHO BECAME
(*later*) MEN WITH BONES IN THE THIRD (*race*) (*a*).

As a full explanation is found in Stanza V. (*Vide* paragraph (*a*)), a few remarks will now suffice. The "Father" of primitive physical man, or of his body, is the vital electric principle residing in the Sun. The Moon is its Mother, because of that mysterious power in the Moon which has as decided an influence upon human gestation and generation, which it regulates, as it has on the growth of plants and animals. The "Wind" or Ether, standing in this case for the agent of transmission by which those influences are carried down from the two luminaries and diffused upon Earth, is referred to as the "nurse", while "Spiritual Fire" alone makes of man a divine and perfect entity.

Now what is that "Spiritual Fire"? In alchemy it is HYDROGEN, in general, while in esoteric actuality it is the emanation or the Ray which proceeds from its noumenon, the "Dhyan of the first Element." Hydrogen is gas only on our terrestrial plane. But even in chemistry hydrogen "would be the only existing form of matter, in our sense of the term," * and is very nearly allied to protyle, which is our *layam*. It is the father and generator, so to say, or rather the *Upadhi* (basis), of both AIR and WATER, and is "fire, air and water," in fact: one under three aspects, hence the chemical and alchemical trinity. In the world of manifestation or matter it is the objective symbol and the material emanation from the subjective and purely spiritual entitative Being in the region of noumena. Well might Godfrey Higgins have compared Hydrogen to, and even identified it with, the TO ON, the "One" of the Greeks. For, as he remarks, Hydrogen is not Water, though it generates it; Hydrogen is not fire, though it manifests or creates it; nor is it Air, though air may be regarded as a product of the union of Water and Fire – since Hydrogen is found in the aqueous element of the atmosphere. It is three in one.

If one studies comparative Theogony, it is easy to find that the secret

---

* See "*Genesis of the Elements*," by Prof. W. Crookes, p. 21.

of these "Fires" was taught in the Mysteries of every ancient people, pre-eminently in Samothrace. There is not the smallest doubt that the *Kabiri*, the most arcane of all the ancient deities, gods and men, great deities and Titans, are identical with the *Kumâras* and *Rudras* headed by Kartikeya – a *Kumâra* also. This is quite evident even exoterically, and these Hindu deities were, like the *Kabiri*, the personified sacred Fires of the most occult powers of Nature. The several branches of the Aryan Race, the Asiatic and the European, the Hindu and the Greek, did their best to conceal their true nature, if not their importance. As in the case of the *Kumâras*, the number of the *Kabiri* is uncertain. Some say that there were three or four only, others say seven. Aschieros, Achiosersa, Achiochersus, and Camillus may very well stand for the alter egos of the four *Kumâras* – Sanat-Kumâra, Sananda, Sanaka, and Sanâtana. The former deities, whose reputed father was Vulcan, were often confounded with the *Dioscuri*, *Corybantes*, *Anaces*, etc., just as the *Kumâra*, whose reputed father is Brahmâ, (or rather, the "Flame of his Wrath," which prompted him to perform the ninth or *Kumâra* creation, resulting in Rudra or Nilalohita (Siva) and the *Kumâras*), were confounded with the *Asuras*, the *Rudras*, and the *Pitris*, for the simple reason that they are all one – i.e., correlative Forces and Fires. There is no space to describe these "fires" and their real meaning here, though we may attempt to do so if the third and fourth volumes of this work are ever published. Meanwhile a few more explanations may be added.

The foregoing are all mysteries which must be left to the personal intuition of the student for solution, rather than described. If he would learn something of the secret of the FIRES, let him turn to certain works of the Alchemists, who very correctly connect fire with every element, as do the Occultists. The reader must remember that the ancients considered religion, and the natural sciences along with philosophy, to be closely and inseparably linked together. AEsculapius was the Son of Apollo – the Sun or FIRE of Life, at once Helios, Pythios, and the god of oracular Wisdom. In exoteric religions, as much as in esoteric philosophy, the Elements – especially fire, water, and air – are made the progenitors of our five physical senses, and hence are directly connected (in an occult way) with them. These physical senses pertain even to a lower creation than the one called in the *Purânas Pratisarga*, or secondary Creation. "Liquid fire proceeds from indiscrete fire," says an Occult axiom.

"The Circle is the THOUGHT; the diameter (or the line) is the WORD; and their union is LIFE." In the *Kabala*, Bath-Kol is the daughter of the Divine Voice, or primordial light, Shekinah. In the *Purânas* and Hindu exotericism, Vâch (the Voice) is the female *Logos* of Brahmâ – a permutation of Aditi, primordial light. And if Bath-Kol, in Jewish mysticism, is an articulate preter-natural voice from heaven, revealing to the "chosen people" the sacred traditions and laws, it is only because Vâch was called, before Judaism, the "Mother of the *Vedas*," who entered into the *Rishis* and inspired them by her revelations, just as Bath-Kol is said to have inspired the prophets of Israel and the Jewish High Priests. And both exist to this day, in their respective sacred symbologies, because the ancients associated sound or Speech with the Ether of Space, of which Sound is the characteristic. Hence Fire, Water and Air are the primordial Cosmic Trinity. "I am thy Thought, thy God, more ancient than the moist principle, the light that radiates within Darkness (Chaos), and the shining Word of God (Sound) is the Son of the Deity." ("*Pymander*," § 6.) *

Thus we have to study well the "Primary creation," before we can understand the Secondary. The first Race had three rudimentary elements in it, and no fire as yet, because, with the Ancients, the evolution of man, and the growth and development of his spiritual and physical senses, were subordinate to the evolution of the elements on the Cosmic plane of this Earth. All proceeds from *Prabhavâpyaya*, the evolution of the creative and sentient principles in the gods, and even of the so-called creative deity himself. This is found in the names and appellations given to Vishnu in exoteric scriptures. As the *Protologos* (the Orphic), he is called *Pûrvaja*, "pregenetic," and then the

---

* The opponents of Hinduism may call the above Pantheism, Polytheism, or anything they may please. If Science is not entirely blinded by prejudice, it will see in this account a profound knowledge of natural Sciences and Physics, as well as of Metaphysics and Psychology. But to find this out, one has to study the personifications, and then convert them into chemical atoms. It will then be found to satisfy both physical and even purely materialistic Science, as well as those who see in evolution the work of the "Great Unknown Cause" in its phenomenal and illusive aspects.

other names connect him in their descending order more and more with matter.

The following order on parallel lines may be found in the evolution of the Elements and the Senses, or in Cosmic terrestrial "MAN" or "Spirit," and mortal physical man:

1. Ether ... Hearing ... Sound.
2. Air ... Touch ... Sound and Touch.
3. Fire, or Light, Sight ... Sound, Touch and Colour.
4. Water ... Taste ... Sound, Touch, Colour and Taste ...
5. Earth ... Smell ... Sound, Touch, Colour, Taste and Smell.

As seen, each Element adds to its own characteristics, those of its predecessor, as each Root Race adds the characterizing sense of the preceding Race. The same is true in the septenary creation of man, who evolves gradually in seven stages, and on the same principles, as will be shown further on.

Thus, while Gods or *Dhyan Chohans* (*Devas*) proceed from the First Cause – which is not *Parabrahm*, for the latter is the ALL CAUSE, and cannot be referred to as the "First Cause" – which First Cause is called in the Brahmanical Books *Jagad-Yoni*, "the womb of the world," mankind emanates from these active agents in Kosmos. But men, during the first and the second races, were not physical beings, but merely rudiments of the future men: *Bhûtas*, which proceeded from *Bhûtadi*, "origin," or the "original place whence sprung the Elements." Hence they proceeded with all the rest from *Prabhavâpyaya*, "the place whence is the origination, and into which is the resolution of all things," as explained by the Commentator. Whence also our physical senses. Whence even the highest "created" deity itself, in our philosophy. As one with the Universe, whether we call him Brahmâ, Iswara, or Purusha, he is a manifested deity – hence created, or limited and conditioned. This is easily proven, even from the exoteric teachings.

After being called the incognizable, eternal Brahma (neuter or abstract), the *Punda-Rikaksha*, "supreme and imperishable glory," once that instead of *Sadaika-Rupa*, "changeless" or "immutable" Nature, he is addressed as *Ekanaka-Rupa*, "both single and manifold," he, the cause, becomes merged with his own effects; and his names, if placed in esoteric order, show the following descending scale:

1. *Mahapurusha* or *Paramatman* . . . Supreme Spirit.

2. *Atman* or *Pûrvaja* (*Protologos*) . . . The living Spirit of Nature.

3. *Indriyâtman*, or *Hrishikesa* . . . Spiritual or intellectual soul (One with the senses).

5. *Bhutâtman* . . . The living, or Life Soul.

6. *Kshetragna* . . . Embodied soul, or the Universe of Spirit and Matter.

7. *Bhrântidarsanatah* . . . False perception – Material Universe.

The last name means something perceived or conceived of, owing to false and erroneous apprehension, as a material form, but, in fact, only *Maya*, illusion, as all is in our physical universe.

It is in strict analogy with ITS attributes in both the spiritual and material worlds, that the evolution of the Dhyan Chohanic Essences takes place, the characteristics of the latter being reflected, in their turn, in Man, collectively, and in each of his principles, every one of which contains in itself, in the same progressive order, a portion of their various "fires" and elements."

SD, ii 102–108

THE DEVAS CAST NO SHADOWS

18. THE FIRST (*Race*) WERE THE SONS OF YOGA. THEIR SONS, THE CHILDREN OF THE YELLOW FATHER AND THE WHITE MOTHER.

In the later Commentary, the sentence is translated: desire to live. It is a strange law of Nature that, on this plane, the higher (Spiritual) Nature should be, so to say, in bondage to the lower. Unless the Ego takes refuge in the *Atman*, the ALL-SPIRIT, and merges entirely into the essence thereof, the personal Ego may goad it to the bitter end. This cannot be thoroughly understood unless the student makes himself familiar with the mystery of evolution, which proceeds on triple lines – spiritual, psychic and physical.

That which propels towards, and forces evolution, i.e., compels the growth and development of Man towards perfection, is (*a*) the MONAD, or that which acts in it unconsciously through a force inherent in itself; and (*b*) the lower astral body or the personal SELF. The former, whether imprisoned in a vegetable or an animal body, is endowed with, is indeed itself, that force. Owing to its identity with the ALL-FORCE, which, as said, is inherent in the Monad, it is all potent on the *Arupa*, or formless plane. On our plane, its essence being too pure, it remains all-potential, but individually becomes inactive: e.g., the rays of the Sun, which contribute to the growth of vegetation, do not select this or that plant to shine upon. Uproot the plant and transfer it to a piece of soil where the sunbeam cannot reach it, and the latter will not follow it. So with the *Atman*: unless the higher Self or EGO gravitates towards its Sun – the Monad – the lower Ego, or personal Self, will have the upper hand in every case. For it is this Ego, with its fierce Selfishness and animal desire to live a Senseless life (*Tanha*), which is "the maker of the tabernacle," as Buddha calls it in *Dhammapada* (153 and 154). Hence the expression, "the Spirits of the Earth clothed the shadows and expanded them." To these "Spirits" belong temporarily the human astral selves, and it is they who give, or build, the physical tabernacle of man, for the

Monad and its conscious principle, *Manas*, to dwell in. But the "Solar" *Lhas*, Spirits, warm them, the shadows. This is physically and literally true; metaphysically, or on the psychic and spiritual plane, it is equally true that the *Atman* alone warms the inner man; i.e., it enlightens it with the ray of divine life and alone is able to impart to the inner man, or the reincarnating Ego, its immortality. Thus, as we shall find, for the first three and a half Root Races, up to the middle or turning point, it is the astral shadows of the "progenitors," the lunar *Pitris*, which are the formative powers in the Races, and which build and gradually force the evolution of the physical form towards perfection – this, at the cost of a proportionate loss of spirituality. Then, from the turning point, it is the Higher Ego, or incarnating principle, the *Nous* or Mind, which reigns over the animal Ego, and rules it whenever it is not carried down by the latter. In short, Spirituality is on its ascending arc, and the animal or physical impedes it from steadily progressing on the path of its evolution only when the selfishness of the personality has so strongly infected the real inner man with its lethal virus, that the upward attraction has lost all its power on the thinking reasonable man. In sober truth, vice and wickedness are an abnormal, unnatural manifestation, at this period of our human evolution at least they ought to be so. The fact that mankind was never more selfish and vicious than it is now, civilized nations having succeeded in making of the first an ethical characteristic, of the second an art, is an additional proof of the exceptional nature of the phenomenon.

The entire scheme is in the "*Chaldean Book of Numbers*," and even in the *Zohar*, if one only understood the meaning of the apocalyptic hints. First comes *En Soph*, the "Concealed of the Concealed," then the Point, *Sephira* and the later *Sephiroth*; then the Atzilatic World, a World of Emanations that gives birth to three other worlds – called the Throne, the abode of pure Spirits; the second, the World of Formation, or *Jetzira*, the habitat of the Angels who sent forth the Third, or World of Action, the Asiatic World, which is the Earth or our World; and yet it is said of it that this world, also called *Kliphoth*, containing the (six other) Spheres, בלבלים, and matter, is the residence of the "Prince of Darkness." This is as clearly stated as can be, for *Metatron*, the Angel of the second or Briatic World, means Messenger *agg*, Angel, called the great Teacher, and under him are the Angels of the third World,

Jetzira, whose ten and seven classes are the *Sephiroth**, of whom it is said that "they inhabit and vivify this world as Essential Entities and Intelligences, whose correlatives and contraries inhabit the third or Asiatic World." These "Contraries" are called "the Shells," בלּיפה, or demons[†],who inhabit the seven habitations called Sheba Hachaloth, which are simply the seven zones of our globe. Their prince is called in the *Kabala* Samael, the Angel of Death, who is also the seducing serpent Satan, but that Satan is also Lucifer, the bright angel of Light, the Light and Life-bringer, the "Soul" alienated from the Holy Ones, the other angels, and for a period, anticipating the time when they would have descended on Earth to incarnate in their turn.

"The Souls (Monads) are pre-existent in the world of Emanations," (*Book of Wisdom* viii, 20), and the *Zohar* teaches that in the "Soul" "is the real man, i.e., the Ego and the conscious I AM: '*Manas*.' "

"They descend from the pure air to be chained to bodies," says Josephus repeating the belief of the Essenes (*De Bello Judâo*, 11, 12). "The air is full of Souls," states Philo, "they descend to be tied to mortal bodies, being desirous to live in them" (*De Gignat*, 222 c.; *De Somniis*, p. 455)[‡], because through and in the human form they will become progressive beings, whereas the nature of the angel is purely intransitive; therefore, man has in him the potency of transcending the faculties of the Angels. Hence the Initiates in India say that it is the Brahmin, the twice-born, who rules the gods or *devas*, and Paul repeated it in *I Corinthians* vi., 3: "Know ye not that we (the Initiates) shall judge angels"?

Finally, it is shown in every ancient scripture and Cosmogony that man evolved primarily as a luminous incorporeal form, over which, like the molten brass round the clay model of the sculptor, the physical

---

* See Vol. 1. Part III., "Gods, Monads and Atoms." It is symbolised in the Pythagorean Triangle, the 10 dots within, and the seven points of the Triangle and the Cube.

† Whence the Kabalistic name of Shells given to the astral form, the body called *Kama Rupa*, left behind by the higher angels in the shape of the higher *Manas*, when the latter leaves for *Devachan*, forsaking its residue.

‡ Which shows that the Essenes believed in re-birth and many reincarnations on Earth, as Jesus himself did, a fact we can prove from the *New Testament* itself.

frame of his body was built by, through, and from, the lower forms and types of animal terrestrial life. "The Soul and the Form when descending on Earth put on an earthly garment," says the *Zohar*. His protoplastic body was not formed of that matter of which our mortal frames are fashioned. "When Adam dwelt in the garden of Eden, he was clothed in the celestial garment, which is the garment of heavenly light. . . . light of that light which was used in the garden of Eden," (*Zohar* II 229 B). "Man (the heavenly Adam) was created by the ten *Sephiroth* of the Jetziric world, and by the common power they (the seven angels of a still lower world) engendered the earthly Adam . . . . First Samael fell, and then deceiving (?) man, caused his fall also."

(*b*) The sentence: "They were the shadows of the shadows of the Lords," i.e., the progenitors created man out of their own astral bodies, explains an universal belief. The *Devas* are credited in the East with having no shadows of their own. "The *devas* cast no shadows," and this is the sure sign of a good holy Spirit.

Why had they "no fire or water of their own"?* Because –

(*c*) That which Hydrogen is to the elements and gases on the objective plane, its noumenon is in the world of mental or subjective phenomena, since its trinitarian latent nature is mirrored in its three

---

* * It is corroborated, however, as we have shown, by the esotericism of *Genesis*. Not only are the animals created therein after the "Adam of Dust," but vegetation is shown in the Earth before "the heavens and the Earth were created." "Every plant of the field before it (the day that the heavens and the Earth were made, v. 4) was in the Earth" (v. 5). Now, unless the Occult interpretation is accepted, which shows that in this 4th Round the Globe was covered with vegetation, and the first (astral) humanity was produced before almost anything could grow and develop thereon, what can the dead letter mean? Simply that the grass was in the earth of the Globe before that Globe was created? And yet the meaning of verse 6, which says that "there went up a mist from the Earth" and watered the whole face of the Earth before it rained, and caused the trees, etc., to grow, is plain enough. It shows also in what geological period it occurred, and further what is meant by "Heaven and Earth." It meant the firmament and dry incrustated land, separated and ridden of its vapours and exhalations. Moreover, the student must bear in mind that, as *Adam Kadmon*, "the male and female being" of *Genesis*, ch. I., is no physical human being but the host of the *Elohim*, among which was Jehovah himself — so the animals mentioned in that chapter as "created" before man in the dead letter text, were no animals, but the Zodiacal signs and other sidereal bodies.

active emanations from the three higher principles in man, namely, "Spirit, Soul, and Mind," or *Atma, Buddhi,* and *Manas.* It is the spiritual and also the material human basis. Rudimentary man, having been nursed by the "air" or the "wind," becomes the perfect man later on, when, with the development of "Spiritual fire," the noumenon of the "Three in One" within his Self, he acquires from his inner Self, or Instructor, the Wisdom of Self-Consciousness, which he does not possess in the beginning. Thus here again divine Spirit is symbolised by the Sun or Fire; divine Soul by Water and the Moon, both standing for the Father and Mother of *Pneuma,* human Soul, or Mind, symbolised by the Wind or air, for *Pneuma,* means "breath.

Hence in the *Smaragdine Tablet,* disfigured by Christian hands –

"The Superior agrees with the Inferior, and the Inferior with the Superior, to effect that one truly wonderful Work" – which is MAN. For the secret work of Chiram, or King Hiram in the *Kabala,* "one in Essence, but three in Aspect," is the Universal Agent or *Lapis Philosophorum.* The culmination of the Secret Work is Spiritual Perfect Man, at one end of the line; the union of the three elements is the Occult Solvent in the "Soul of the World," the Cosmic Soul or Astral Light, at the other, and, on the material plane, it is Hydrogen in its relation to the other gases. The TO ON, truly, the ONE "whom no person has seen except the Son", this sentence applying both to the metaphysical and physical Kosmos, and to the spiritual and material Man. For how could the latter understand the TO ON the "One Father," if his *Manas,* the "Son," does not become (as) "One with the Father," and through this absorption receive enlightenment from the "divine instructor," Guru – *Atma-Buddhi?*

SD, ii 109–113

THE SONS OF YOGA

"The first race of men were, then, simply the images, the astral doubles, of their Fathers, who were the pioneers, or the most progressed Entities from a preceding though lower sphere, the shell of which is now our Moon. But even this shell is all-potential, for, having generated the Earth, it is the phantom of the Moon which, attracted by magnetic affinity, sought to form its first inhabitants, the pre-human monsters, (*Vide supra*, Stanza II). To assure himself of this, the student has again to turn to the Chaldean *Fragments*, and read what Berosus says. Berosus obtained his information, he tells us, from Ea, the male-female deity of Wisdom. While the gods were generated in its androgynous bosom (*Svâbhâvat*, Mother-space) its (the Wisdom's) reflections became on Earth the woman Omoroka, who is the Chaldean Thavatth, or the Greek Thalassa, the Deep or the Sea, which esoterically and even exoterically is the Moon. It was the Moon (Omoroka) who presided over the monstrous creation of nondescript beings which were slain by the Dyanis. (*Vide Hibbert Lectures*, p. 370 *et seq.*; also in Part II "Adam-Adami.")

Evolutionary law compelled the lunar "Fathers" to pass, in their monadic condition, through all the forms of life and being on this globe, but at the end of the Third Round, they were already human in their divine nature, and were thus called upon to become the creators of the forms destined to fashion the tabernacles of the less progressed Monads, whose turn it was to incarnate. These "Forms" are called "Sons of Yoga," because Yoga (union with Brahmâ exoterically) is the supreme condition of the passive infinite deity, since it contains all the divine energies and is the essence of Brahmâ, who is said (as Brahmâ) to create everything through Yoga power. Brahmâ, Vishnu and Siva are the most powerful energies of God, Brahma, the Neuter, says a Purânic text. Yoga here is the same as *Dhyâna*, which word is again synonymous with Yoga in the Tibetan text, where the "Sons of Yoga" are called "Sons of *Dhyâna*," or of that abstract meditation through which the *Dhyani-Buddhas* create their celestial sons, the *Dhyani-Bodhisattvas*. All the creatures in the world have each a superior above. "This superior, whose inner pleasure it is to emanate into them, cannot impart efflux until they have adored" – i.e., meditated as during Yoga. (*Sepher M'bo Ska-arim*, translated by Isaac Myer, *Qabbalah*, pp. 109–111.)

> 19. THE SECOND RACE (*was*) THE PRODUCT BY BUDDING AND EXPANSION; THE ASEXUAL (*form*) FROM THE SEXLESS (*shadow*). THUS WAS, O LANOO, THE SECOND RACE PRODUCED (*a*).

(*a*) What will be most contested by scientific authorities is this asexual Race, the Second, the fathers of the "Sweat born" so-called, and perhaps still more the Third Race, the "Egg-born" androgynes. These two modes of procreation are the most difficult to comprehend, especially for the Western mind. It is evident that no explanation can be attempted for those who are not students of Occult metaphysics. European language has no words to express things which Nature repeats no more at this stage of evolution, things which therefore can have no meaning for the materialist. But there are analogies. It is not denied that in the beginning of physical evolution there must have been processes in Nature, spontaneous generation, for instance, now extinct, which are repeated in other forms. Thus we are told that microscopic research shows no permanence of any particular mode of reproducing life. For "it shows that the same organism may run through various metamorphoses in the course of its lifecycle, during some of which it may be sexual, and in others asexual, i.e., it may reproduce itself alternately by the co-operation of two beings of opposite sex, and also by fissure or budding from one being only, which is of no sex."* "Budding" is the very word used in the Stanza. How could these *Chhayas* reproduce themselves otherwise, viz., procreate the Second Race, since they were ethereal, asexual, and even devoid, as yet, of the vehicle of desire, or *Kama rupa*, which evolved only in the Third Race? They evolved the Second Race unconsciously, as do some plants. Or, perhaps, as the Amâba, only on a more ethereal, impressive, and larger scale. If, indeed, the cell theory applies equally to Botany and Zoology, and extends to Morphology, as well as to the Physiology of organisms,

---

* See Laing's "*Modern Science and Modern Thought*," p. 90.

and if the microscopic cells are looked upon by physical science as independent living beings – just as Occultism regards the "fiery lives"* – there is no difficulty in the conception of the primitive process of procreation.

Consider the first stages of the development of a germ cell. Its nucleus grows, changes, and forms a double cone or spindle, thus – X – within the cell. This spindle approaches the surface of the cell, and one half of it is extruded in the form of what are called the "polar cells." These polar cells now die, and the embryo develops from the growth and segmentation of the remaining part of the nucleus which is nourished by the substance of the cell. Then why could not beings have lived thus, and been created in this way – at the very beginning of human and mammalian evolution?

This may, perhaps, serve as an analogy to give some idea of the process by which the Second Race was formed from the First.

The astral form clothing the Monad was surrounded, as it still is, by its egg-shaped sphere of aura, which here corresponds to the substance of the germ cell or ovum. The astral form itself is the nucleus, now, as then, instinct with the principle of life.

When the season of reproduction arrives, the sub-astral "extrudes" a miniature of itself from the egg of surrounding aura. This germ grows and feeds on the aura till it becomes fully developed, when it gradually separates from its parent, carrying with it its own sphere of aura, just as we see living cells reproducing their like by growth and subsequent division into two.

The analogy with the "polar cells" would seem to hold good, since their death would now correspond to the change introduced by the separation of the sexes, when gestation *in utero,* i.e., within the cell, became the rule.

"The early Second (Root) Race were the Fathers of the 'Sweat born'; the later Second (Root) Race were 'Sweat born' themselves."

This passage from the Commentary refers to the work of evolution from the beginning of a Race to its close. The "Sons of Yoga," or

---

* See Book I. Part I. Stanza VII Commentary 10.

the primitive astral race, had seven stages of evolution racially, or collectively, as every individual Being in it had, and has now. It is not Shakespeare only who divided the ages of man into a series of seven, but Nature herself. Thus the first sub-races of the Second Race were born at first by the process described on the law of analogy, while the last began gradually, *pari passu* with the evolution of the human body, to be formed otherwise. The process of reproduction had seven stages also in each Race, each covering aeons of time. What physiologist or biologist could tell whether the present mode of generation, with all its phases of gestation, is older than half a million, or at most one million of years, since their cycle of observation began hardly half a century ago.

Primeval human hermaphrodites are a fact in Nature well known to the ancients, and form one of Darwin's greatest perplexities. Yet there is certainly no impossibility, but, on the contrary, a great probability that hermaphroditism existed in the evolution of the early races, while on the grounds of analogy, and on that of the existence of one universal law in physical evolution, acting indifferently in the construction of plant, animal, and man, it must be so. The mistaken theories of monogenesis, and the descent of man from the mammals instead of the reverse, are fatal to the completeness of evolution as taught in modern schools on Darwinian lines, and they will have to be abandoned in view of the insuperable difficulties which they encounter. Occult tradition – if the terms Science and Knowledge are denied in this particular to antiquity – can alone reconcile the inconsistencies and fill the gap. "If thou wilt know the invisible, open thine eye wide on the visible," says a Talmudic axiom.

In the *"Descent of Man"*† occurs the following passage, which shows how near Darwin came to the acceptance of this ancient teaching.

> It has been known that in the vertebrate kingdom one sex bears rudiments of various accessory parts appertaining to the reproductive system, which properly belong to the opposite sex. . . . Some remote progenitor of the whole vertebrate kingdom appears to have been hermaphrodite or androgynous ‡ . . . But here we encounter a singular

---

† Second Edition, p. 161.

‡ And why not all the progenitive first Races, human as well as animal; and why

difficulty. In the mammalian class the males possess rudiments of a uterus with the adjacent passages in the *Vesiculae prostaticae*; they bear also rudiments of *mammae*, and some male marsupials have traces of a marsupial sac. Other analogous facts could be added. Are we then to suppose that some extremely ancient mammal continued androgynous after it had acquired the chief distinctions of its class, and therefore after it had diverged from the lower classes of the vertebrate kingdom? This seems very improbable[*], for we have to look to fishes, the lowest of all the classes, to find any still existent androgynous forms.

Mr. Darwin is evidently strongly disinclined to adopt the hypothesis which the facts so forcibly suggest, viz., that of a primeval androgynous stem from which the mammalia sprang. His explanation runs: "The fact that various accessory organs proper to each sex, are found in a rudimentary condition in the opposite sex may be explained by such organs having been gradually acquired by the one sex and then transmitted in a more or less imperfect condition to the other." He instances the case of "spurs, plumes, and brilliant colours, acquired for battle or for ornament by male birds" and only partially inherited by their female descendants. In the problem to be dealt with, however, the need of a more satisfactory explanation is evident, the facts being of so much more prominent and important a character than the mere superficial details with which they are compared by Darwin. Why not candidly admit the argument in favour of the hermaphroditism which characterises the old fauna? Occultism proposes a solution which embraces the facts in a most comprehensive and simple manner. These relics of a prior androgyne stock must be placed in the same category as the pineal gland, and other organs as mysterious, which afford us silent testimony as to the reality of functions which have long since become atrophied in the course of animal and human progress, but which once played a signal part in the general economy of primeval life."

SD, ii 115–119

---

one "remote progenitor"?

[*] Obviously so, on the lines of Evolutionism, which traces the mammalia to some amphibian ancestor.

THE VIRGIN THIRD RACE

"What say the old sages, the philosopher-teachers of antiquity? Aristophanes speaks thus on the subject in Plato's *"Banquet"*: "Our nature of old was not the same as it is now. It was androgynous, the form and name partaking of, and being common to both the male and female. . . . Their bodies were round, and the manner of their running circular[†]. They were terrible in force and strength and had prodigious ambition. Hence Zeus divided each of them into two, making them weaker; Apollo, under his direction, closed up the skin."

Meshia and Meshiane were but a single individual with the old Persians. "They also taught that man was the product of the tree of life, growing in androgynous pairs, till they were separated at a subsequent modification of the human form[‡]."

In the Toleduth (generation) of Adam, the verse "God created (*bara*, brought forth) man in his image, in the image of God created he him, male and female created he them," if read esoterically will yield the true sense, viz.: "The *Elohim* (Gods) brought forth from themselves (by modification) man in their image . . . . created they him (collective humanity, or Adam), male and female created he (collective deity) them[§]." This will show the esoteric point. The sexless Race was their first

---

† Compare Ezekiel's vision (chap. i) of the four divine beings who "had the likeness of a man" and yet had the appearance of a wheel, "when they went they went upon their four sides . . . . for the spirit of the living creature was in the wheel."

‡ See Prof. Wilder's Essay *"The Primeval Race Double-Sexed."*

§ Eugibinus, a Christian, and the Rabbis Samuel, Manasseh ben Israel, and Maimonides taught that "Adam had two faces and one person, and from the beginning he was both male and female — male on one side and female on the other (like Manu's Brahmâ), but afterwards the parts were separated." The one hundred and thirty-ninth *Psalm of David* recited by Rabbi Jeremiah ben Eliazar is evidence of this. "Thou hast fashioned me behind and before," not beset as in the *Bible*, which is absurd and meaningless, and this shows, as Prof. Wilder thinks, "that the primeval form of mankind was androgynous."

161

production, a modification of and from themselves, the pure spiritual existences, and this was Adam *solus*. Thence came the second Race: Adam-Eve or Jod-Heva, inactive androgynes; and finally the Third, or the "Separating Hermaphrodite," Cain and Abel, who produce the Fourth, Seth-Enos, etc. It is that Third, the last semi-spiritual race, which was also the last vehicle of the divine and innate Wisdom, ingenerate in the Enochs, the Seers of that Mankind. The Fourth, which had tasted from the fruit of the Tree of Good and Evil – Wisdom united already to earthy, and therefore impure, intelligence* had consequently to acquire that Wisdom by initiation and great struggle. And the union of Wisdom and Intelligence, the former ruling the latter, is called in the Hermetic books "the God possessing the double fecundity of the two sexes." Mystically Jesus was held to be man-woman. See also in the Orphic hymns, sung during the Mysteries, we find:

"Zeus is a male, Zeus is an immortal maid." The Egyptian Ammon was the goddess Neâth, in his other half. Jupiter has female breasts, Venus is bearded in some of her statues, and Ila, the goddess, is also Su-Dyumna, the god, as *Vaivasvata's* progeny.

"The name Adam," says Professor A. Wilder, "or man, itself implies this double form of existence. It is identical with Athamas, or Thomas (Tamil *Tam*), which is rendered by the Greek *Didumos*, a twin; if, therefore, the first woman was formed subsequently to the first man, she must, as a logical necessity, be 'taken out of man' . . . and the side which the *Elohim* had taken from man, 'made he a woman' (*Gen*. ii). The Hebrew word here used is *Tzala*, which bears the translation we have given. It is easy to trace the legend in Berosus, who says that Thalatth (the Omoroca, or Lady of Urka) was the beginning of creation. She was also Melita, the queen of the Moon. . . . The two twin births of *Genesis*, that of Cain and Abel, and of Esau and Jacob, shadow the same idea. The name 'Hebel' is the same as Eve, and its characteristic seems to be feminine," continues the author. "Unto thee shall be his desire,"

---

* See the union of *Chochmah*, Wisdom, with *Binah*, Intelligence, or Jehovah, the *Demiurge*, called Understanding in the *Proverbs of Solomon*, ch. vii. Unto men Wisdom (divine occult Wisdom) crieth: "Oh, ye simple, understand Wisdom; and ye fools, be of an understanding heart." It is spirit and matter, the nous and the psyche; of the latter of which St. James says that it is "earthly, sensual, and devilish."

said the Lord God to Cain, "and thou shalt rule over him." The same language had been uttered to Eve: "Thy desire shall be to thy husband, and he shall rule over thee." . . .

Thus the pristine bi-sexual unity of the human Third Root Race is an axiom in the Secret Doctrine. Its virgin individuals were raised to "Gods," because that Race represented their "divine Dynasty." The moderns are satisfied with worshipping the male heroes of the Fourth Race, who created gods after their own sexual image, whereas the gods of primeval mankind were "male and female."

As stated in Book I, the humanities developed coordinately, and on parallel lines with the four Elements, every new Race being physiologically adapted to meet the additional element. Our Fifth Race is rapidly approaching the Fifth Element – call it interstellar ether, if you will – which has more to do, however, with psychology than with physics. We men have learned to live in every climate, whether frigid or tropical, but the first two Races had nought to do with climate, nor were they subservient to any temperature or change therein. And thus, we are taught, men lived down to the close of the Third Root Race, when eternal spring reigned over the whole globe, such as is now enjoyed by the inhabitants of Jupiter, a "world," says M. Flammarion, "which is not subject like our own to the vicissitudes of seasons nor to abrupt alternations of temperature, but which is enriched with all the treasures of eternal spring." (*"Pluralite des Mondes,"* p. 69.) Those astronomers who maintain that Jupiter is in a molten condition, in our sense of the term, are invited to settle their dispute with this learned French Astronomer.[†] It must, however, be always borne in mind that

_____

† An hypothesis evolved in 1881 by Mr. Mattieu Williams seems to have impressed Astronomers but little. Says the author of *"The Fuel of the Sun,"* in *Knowledge,* Dec. 23, 1881: "Applying now the researches of Dr. Andrews to the conditions of Solar existence . . . I conclude that the Sun has *no nucleus,* either solid, liquid, or gaseous, but is composed of dissociated matter in the critical state, surrounded, first, by a flaming envelope, due to the recombination of the dissociated matter, and outside of this, by another envelope of vapours due to this combination."

This is a novel theory to be added to other hypotheses, *all scientific and orthodox.* The meaning of the *"critical* state" is explained by Mr. M. Williams in the same journal (Dec. 9, 1881), in an article on *"Solids, Liquids, and Gases."* Speaking of an experiment by Dr. Andrews on carbonic acid, the scientist says that "when 88º is reached, the boundary between liquid and gas vanished; *liquid and gas have blended into one mysterious intermediate fluid; an indefinite fluctuating something is there filling the whole of the tube — an etherealised liquid or a visible gas*. Hold a red-hot poker between your eye and the light; you will see an upflowing wave of movement of what appears like liquid air. The appearance of the *hybrid* fluid in the tube resembles this, but is sensibly denser, and evidently stands between the liquid and gaseous states of matter, as pitch or treacle stands between solid and liquid."

The *temperature at which this occurs has been named by Dr. Andrews the "critical temperature"*; here the gaseous and the liquid states are "*continuous*," and it is probable that *all other substances capable of existing* in both states have their own particular critical temperatures.

Speculating further upon this "critical" state, Mr. Mattieu Williams emits some quite occult theories about Jupiter and other planets. He says: "*Our notions of solids, liquids, and gases are derived from our experiences of the state of matter here upon this Earth. Could we be removed to another planet, they would be curiously changed.* On Mercury water would rank as one of the condensible gases; on Mars, as a fusible solid; but what on Jupiter?"

"Recent observations justify us in regarding this as a miniature sun, with an external envelope of cloudy matter, apparently of partially-condensed water, but red-hot, or probably still hotter within. His vaporous atmosphere is evidently of enormous depth, and the force of gravitation being on his visible outer surface two-and-a-half times greater than that on our Earth's surface, the atmospheric pressure, in descending below this visible surface, must soon reach that at which the vapour of water would be brought to its critical condition. Therefore we may infer that *the oceans of Jupiter are neither of frozen, liquid, nor gaseous water, but are oceans or atmospheres of critical water. If any fish or birds swim or fly therein, they must be very critically organized*."

As the whole mass of Jupiter is 300 times greater than that of the Earth, and its compressing energy towards the centre proportional to this, its materials, if similar to those of the Earth, and no hotter, would be considerably more dense, and the whole planet would have a higher specific gravity; but we know by the movement of its satellites that, instead of this, its specific gravity is less than a fourth of that of the Earth. This justifies the conclusion that it is intensely hot; for even hydrogen, if cold, would become denser than Jupiter under such pressure.

"As all elementary substances may exist as solids, liquids, or gases, or, critically, according to the conditions of temperature and pressure, I am justified in hypothetically concluding that *Jupiter is neither a solid, a liquid, nor a gaseous planet, but a critical planet, or an orb composed internally of associated elements in the critical state, and surrounded by a dense atmosphere of their vapours* and those of some of their compounds such as water. The same reasoning applies to Saturn and other large and rarified planets."

It is gratifying to see how *scientific imagination* approaches every year more closely to the borderland of our occult teachings.

the "eternal spring" referred to is only a condition cognised as such by the Jovians. It is not "spring" as we know it. In this reservation is to be found the reconciliation between the two theories here cited. Both embrace partial truths.

It is thus a universal tradition that mankind has evolved gradually into its present shape from an almost transparent condition of texture, and neither by miracle nor by sexual intercourse. Moreover, this is in full accord with the ancient philosophies, from those of Egypt and India with their Divine Dynasties down to that of Plato. And all these universal beliefs must be classed with the "presentiments" and "obstinate conceptions," some of them ineradicable, in popular faiths. Such beliefs, as remarked by Louis Figuier, are "frequently the outcome of the wisdom and observation of an infinite number of generations of men." For, "a tradition which has an uniform and universal existence, has all the weight of scientific testimony." [*] And there is more than one such tradition in the Purânic allegories, as has been shown. Moreover, the doctrine that the first Race of mankind was formed out of the *Chhayas* (astral images) of the *Pitris*, is fully corroborated in the *Zohar*. "In the *Tzalam* (shadow image) of *Elohim* (the *Pitris*), was made Adam (man). (Cremona, Ed. iii, 76a; Brody, Ed. iii, 159a; "*Qabbalah*," Isaac Myer, p. 420.)

It has been repeatedly urged as an objection that, however high the degree of metaphysical thought in ancient India, yet the old Egyptians had nothing but crass idolatry and zoolatry to boast of; Hermes, as alleged, being the work of mystic Greeks who lived in Egypt. To this, one answer can be given – a direct proof that the Egyptians believed in the Secret Doctrine is, that it was taught to them at Initiation. Let the objectors open the "*Eclogae Physicae et Ethicae*" of Stobaeus, the Greek compiler of ancient fragments, who lived in the fifth century, A.D. The following is a transcription by him of an old Hermetic fragment, showing the Egyptian theory of the Soul. Translated word for word, it says:

From one Soul, that of ALL, spring all the Souls, which spread

---

[*] "*The Day After Death,*" p. 23.

themselves as if purposely distributed through the world. These souls undergo many transformations; those which are already creeping creatures turn into aquatic animals; from these aquatic animals are derived land animals, and from the latter the birds. From the beingswho live aloft in the air (heaven) men are born. On reaching that status of men, the Souls receive the principle of (conscious) immortality, become Spirits, then pass into the choir of gods.

SD, ii 133–138

CREATORS AND SUB-CREATORS

STANZA VII

FROM THE SEMI-DIVINE DOWN TO THE
FIRST HUMAN RACES

§§ (24) The higher creators reject in their pride the forms evolved by the "Sons of Yoga." (25) They will not incarnate in the early "Egg-born"... (26) They select the later androgynes. (27) The first man endowed with mind.

24. THE SONS OF WISDOM, THE SONS OF NIGHT (*issued from the body of Brahmâ when it became Night*), READY FOR RE-BIRTH, CAME DOWN. THEY SAW THE (*intellectually*) VILE FORMS OF THE FIRST THIRD (*still senseless Race*) (*a*). "WE CAN CHOOSE," SAID THE LORDS, "WE HAVE WISDOM." SOME ENTERED THE CHHAYAS. SOME PROJECTED A SPARK. SOME DEFERRED TILL THE FOURTH (*Race*). FROM THEIR OWN ESSENCE THEY FILLED (*intensified*) THE KAMA (*the vehicle of desire*). THOSE WHO RECEIVED BUT A SPARK REMAINED DESTITUTE OF (*higher*) KNOWLEDGE. THE SPARK BURNT LOW (*b*). THE THIRD REMAINED MIND-LESS. THEIR JIVAS (*Monads*) WERE NOT READY. THESE WERE SET APART AMONG THE SEVEN (*primitive human species*). THEY (*became the*) NARROW-HEADED. THE THIRD WERE READY. IN THESE SHALL WE DWELL, SAID THE LORDS OF THE FLAME AND OF THE DARK WISDOM (*c*).

This Stanza contains, in itself, the whole key to the mysteries of evil, the so-called Fall of the angels, and the many problems that have puzzled the brains of the philosophers from the time that the memory of man began. It solves the secret of the subsequent inequalities of intellectual capacity, of birth or social position, and gives a logical explanation to the incomprehensible Karmic course throughout the aeons which followed. The best explanation which can be given, in view of the difficulties of the subject, shall now be attempted.

(*a*) Up to the Fourth Round, and even to the later part of the Third Race in this Round, Man – if the ever-changing forms that clothed the Monads during the first three Rounds and the first two and a half races of the present one can be given that misleading name – is, so far, only an animal intellectually. It is only in the actual midway Round that he develops in himself entirely the fourth principle as a fit vehicle for the fifth. But *Manas* will be relatively fully developed only in the following Round, when it will have an opportunity of becoming entirely divine until the end of the Rounds. As Christian Schoettgen says in *Horae Hebraic*, etc., the first terrestrial Adam "had only the breath of life," *Nephesh*, but not the living Soul.

(*b*) Here the inferior Races, of which there are still some analogues left – as the Australians (now fast dying out) and some African and Oceanic tribes – are meant. "They were not ready" signifies that the Karmic development of these Monads had not yet fitted them to occupy the forms of men destined for incarnation in higher intellectual Races. But this is explained later on.

(*c*) The *Zohar* speaks of "Black Fire," which is Absolute Light-Wisdom. To those who, prompted by old theological prejudice, may say: "But the *Asuras* are the rebel *Devas*, the opponents of the Gods – hence devils, and the spirits of Evil," it is answered: Esoteric philosophy admits neither good nor evil *per se*, as existing independently in nature. The cause for both is found, as regards the Kosmos, in the necessity of contraries or contrasts, and with respect to man, in his human nature, his ignorance and passions. There is no devil or the utterly depraved, as there are no Angels absolutely perfect, though there may be spirits of Light and of Darkness, thus LUCIFER – the spirit of Intellectual Enlightenment and Freedom of Thought – is metaphorically the guiding beacon, which helps man to find his way through the rocks and sandbanks of Life, for Lucifer is the LOGOS in his highest, and the "Adversary" in his lowest aspect – both of which are reflected in our Ego. Lactantius, speaking of the Nature of Christ, makes the LOGOS, the Word, the first-born brother of Satan, the "first of all creatures." (Inst. div. Book II, c. viii, "*Qabbalah,*" 116.)

The *Vishnu Purâna* describes these primeval creatures (the *Arvaksrota*) with crooked digestive canals: They were "endowed with inward manifestations, but mutually in ignorance about their kind and nature." The twenty-eight kinds of *Badha*, or imperfections, do not apply, as Wilson thought, to the animals now known and specified by him,* for these did not exist in those geological periods. This is quite plain in the said work, in which the first created (on this globe) are the "five-fold immovable creation," minerals and vegetables; then come those fabulous animals, *Tiryaksrota*, (the monsters of the abyss slain by the "Lords," see Stanzas II and III); then the *Urdhwasrotas*, the happy celestial beings, which feed on ambrosia; then lastly, the *Arvaksrotas*, human beings – Brahmâ's seventh creation so-called. But these "creations," including the latter, did not occur on this globe, wherever else they may have taken place. It is not Brahmâ who creates things and men on this Earth, but the chief and Lord of the *Prajâpati*, the Lords of Being and terrestrial Creation.† Obeying the command of Brahmâ, *Daksha* (the synthesis, or the aggregate, of the terrestrial creators and progenitors, *Pitris* included) made superior and inferior (*vara* and *avara*) things "referring to *putra*" progeny, and "bipeds and quadrupeds, and subsequently by his will (the Sons of Will and Yoga) made females," i.e., separated the androgynes. Here again, we have "bipeds" or men, created before the "quadrupeds" as in the esoteric teachings. (*Vide supra* and Stanza XII as explained.)

Since, in the exoteric accounts, the *Asuras* are the first beings created from the "body of night," while the *Pitris* issue from that of Twilight, the "gods" being placed by Parâsara (*Vishnu Purâna*) between the two, and shown to evolve from the "body of the day," it is easy to discover a determined purpose to veil the order of creation. Man is the *Arvaksrota* coming from the "Body of the Dawn"; and elsewhere, man is again referred to, when the creator of the world, Brahmâ, is shown "creating fierce beings, denominated *Bhûtas* and eaters of flesh," or as the text has

---

* See Book I., chap. v., p. 71.

† "*Vishnu Purâna*", Book I, chap xv of vol. 2.

it, "fiends frightful from being monkey-coloured and carnivorous."* Whereas the *Râkshasas* are generally translated by "Evil Spirits" and "the enemies of the gods," which identifies them with the *Asuras*. In the *Ramâyana*, when Hanuman is reconnoitering the enemy in Lanka, he finds there *Râkshasas*, some hideous, "while some were beautiful to look upon," and, in *Vishnu Purâna*, there is a direct reference to their becoming the Saviours of "Humanity," or of Brahmâ.

The allegory is very ingenious. Great intellect and too much knowledge are a two-edged weapon in life, and instruments for evil as well as for good. When combined with Selfishness, they will make of the whole of Humanity a footstool for the elevation of him who possesses them, and a means for the attainment of his objects; while, applied to altruistic humanitarian purposes, they may become the means of the salvation of many. At all events, the absence of self-consciousness and intellect will make of man an idiot, a brute in human form. Brahmâ is *Mahat* – the universal Mind – hence the too-selfish among the *Râkshasas* showing the desire to become possessed of it all – to "devour" *Mahat*. The allegory is transparent.

At any rate, esoteric philosophy identifies the pre-Brahmanical *Asuras, Rudras,*† *Râkshasas* and all the "Adversaries" of the Gods in the allegories, with the Egos, which, by incarnating in the still witless man of the Third Race, made him consciously immortal. They are, then, during the cycle of Incarnations, the true dual *Logos* – the conflicting and two-faced divine Principle in Man. The Commentary that follows, and the next Stanzas may, no doubt, throw more light on this very difficult tenet, but the writer does not feel competent to give it out fully. Of the succession of Races, however, they say:

"First come the SELF-EXISTENT on this Earth. They are the 'Spiritual Lives' projected by the absolute WILL and LAW, at the dawn of every rebirth of the worlds. These LIVES are the divine '*Sishta,*' (the seed-*Manus*, or the *Prajâpati* and the *Pitris*)."

---

* *Ibid.*, Book I., chap. v.

† Whom *Manu* calls "our paternal grandfathers" (III, 284). The *Rudras* are the seven manifestations of Rudra-Siva, "the destroying god," and also the grand Yogi and ascetic.

From these proceed –

1. The First Race, the "Self born," which are the (astral) shadows of their Progenitors. ‡ The body was devoid of all understanding (mind, intelligence, and will). The inner being (the higher self or Monad), though within the earthly frame, was unconnected with it. The link, the *Manas*, was not there as yet.

2. From the First (race) emanated the second, called the "Sweat born"§ and the "Boneless." This is the Second Root Race, endowed

---

‡ See § II, §§ 1, *Commentary*.

§ To speak of life as having arisen, and of the human race as having originated, in this absurdly unscientific way, in the face of the modern Pedigrees of Man, is to court instantaneous annihilation. The esoteric doctrine risks the danger, nevertheless, and even goes so far as to ask the impartial reader to compare the above hypothesis (if it is one) with Haeckel's theory – now fast becoming an axiom with science – which is quoted verbatim:

". . . How did life, the living world of organisms, arise? And, secondly, the special question: How did the human race originate? The first of these two inquiries, that as to the first appearance of living beings, can only be decided empirically (! !) by proof of the so-called Archebiosis, or equivocal generation, or the spontaneous production of organisms of the simplest conceivable kind. Such are the *Monera* (Protogenes, Protamoeba, etc), exceedingly simple microscopic masses of protoplasm without structure or organisation, which take in nutriment and reproduce themselves by division. Such a Moneron as that primordial organism discovered by the renowned English zoologist Huxley, and named *Bathybius Haeckelii*, appears as a continuous thick protoplasmic covering at the greatest depths of the ocean, between 3,000 and 30,000 feet. It is true that the first appearance of such *Monera* has not up to the present moment been actually observed; but there is nothing intrinsically improbable in such an evolution." (The *"Pedigree of Man,"* Aveling's translation, p 33.) The Bathybius protoplasm having recently turned out to be no organic substance at all, there remains little to be said. Nor, after reading this, does one need to consume further time in refuting the further assertion that . . . . "in that case man also has beyond a doubt (to the minds of Haeckel and his like) arisen from the lower mammalia, apes and the earlier simian creatures, the still earlier *Marsupialia, Amphibia, Pisces*, by progressive transformations," all produced by "a series of natural forces working blindly. . . . . aim, without design" (p. 36).

The above-quoted passage bears its criticism on its own face. Science is made to teach that which, up to the present time, "has never been actually observed." She is made to deny the phenomenon of an intelligent nature and a vital force independent of form and matter, and to find it more scientific to teach the miraculous performance of "natural forces working blindly without aim or design." If so, then we are led to think that the physico-mechanical forces of the brains of certain eminent Scientists

by the preservers (*Râkshasas*) * and the incarnating gods (*Asuras* and the *Kumâras*) with the first primitive and weak spark (the germ of intelligence) . . And from these in turn proceeds:

3. The Third Root Race, the "Two-fold" (Androgynes). The first Races hereof are shells, till the last is "inhabited" (i.e., informed) by the *Dhyanis*.

The Second Race, as stated above, being also sexless, evolved out of itself, at its beginning, the Third Androgyne Race by an analogous, but already more complicated process. As described in the Commentary, the very earliest of that race were:

"*The 'Sons of Passive Yoga'.* † *They issued from the second Manushyas*

---

are leading them on as blindly to sacrifice logic and common sense on the altar of mutual admiration. Why should the protoplasmic Moneron producing the first living creature through self-division be held as a very scientific hypothesis, and an ethereal pre-human race generating the primeval men in the same fashion be tabooed as unscientific superstition? Or has materialism obtained a sole monopoly in Science?

* The *Râkshasas*, regarded in Indian popular theology as demons, are called the "Preservers" beyond the Himalayas. This double and contradictory meaning has its origin in a philosophical allegory, which is variously rendered in the *Purânas*. It is stated that when Brahmâ created the demons, *Yakshas* (from *Yaksh*, to eat) and the *Râkshasas*, both of which kinds of demons, as soon as born, wished to devour their creator, those among them that called out "Not so! oh, let him be saved (preserved)" were named *Râkshasas* (*Vishnu Purâna* Book I. ch. v.). The *Bhagavata Purâna* (III, 20, 19-21) renders the allegory differently. Brahmâ transformed himself into night (or ignorance) invested with a body, upon which the *Yakshas* and *Râkshasas* seized, exclaiming "Do not spare it; devour it." Brahmâ then cried out, "Do not devour me, spare me." This has an inner meaning of course. The "body of Night" is the darkness of ignorance, and it is the darkness of silence and secrecy. Now the *Râkshasas* are shown in almost every case to be Yogis, pious *Saddhus* and Initiates, a rather unusual occupation for demons. The meaning then is that while we have power to dispel the darkness of ignorance, "devour it," we have to preserve the sacred truth from profanation. "Brahmâ is for the Brahmins alone," says that proud caste. The moral of the fable is evident.

† The gradual evolution of man in the Secret Doctrine shows that all the later (to the profane the earliest) Races have their physical origin in the early Fourth Race. But it is the sub-race, which preceded the one that separated sexually, that is to be regarded as the spiritual ancestors of our present generations, and especially of the Eastern Aryan Races. Weber's idea that the Indo-Germanic Race preceded the Aryan Vedic Race is, to the Occultist, grotesque to the last degree.

(human race), and became oviparous. The emanations that came out of their bodies during the seasons of procreation were ovulary; the small spheroidal nuclei developing into a large soft, egg-like vehicle, gradually hardened, when, after a period of gestation, it broke and the young human animal issued from it unaided, as the fowls do in our race."

This must seem to the reader ludicrously absurd. Nevertheless, it is strictly on the lines of evolutionary analogy, which science perceives in the development of the living animal species. First the moneron-like procreation by self-division (*Vide* Haeckel); then, after a few stages, the oviparous, as in the case of the reptiles, which are followed by the birds; then, finally, the mammals with their ovoviviparous modes of producing their young ones.

If the term ovoviviparous is applied to some fish and reptiles, which hatch their eggs within their bodies, why should it not be applied to female mammalians, including woman? The ovule, in which, after impregnation, the development of the fœtus takes place, is an egg.

At all events, this conception is more philosophical than that of Eve with a suddenly created placenta giving birth to Cain, because of the Apple, when even the marsupial, the earliest of mammals, is not placental yet.

Moreover, the progressive order of the methods of reproduction, as unveiled by science, is a brilliant confirmation of esoteric Ethnology. It is only necessary to tabulate the data in order to prove our assertion. (Cf. especially Schmidt's *"Doctrine of Descent and Darwinism,"* p. 39, *et. seq.*, and Laing's *"A Modern Zoroastrian,"* pp. 102–111.)

1. Fission:

(*a*) As seen in the division of the homogeneous speck of protoplasm, known as Moneron or Amoeba, into two.

(*b*) As seen in the division of the nucleated cell, in which the cell nucleus splits into two sub-nuclei, which either develop within the original cell wall or burst it, and multiply outside as independent entities. (Cf., the First Root Race.)

II. Budding:

A small portion of the parent structure swells out at the surface and finally parts company, growing to the size of the original organism, e.g., many vegetables, the sea anemone, etc. (Cf., the Second Root Race.)*

III. Spores:

A single cell thrown off by the parent organism, which develops into a multicellular organism reproducing the features of the latter, e.g., bacteria and mosses.

IV. Intermediate Hermaphroditism:

Male and female organs inhering in the same individual, e.g., the majority of plants, worms, and snails, etc., allied to budding. (Cf. Second and early Third Root Races.)

V. True sexual union:

(Cf. later Third Root Race.)

We now come to an important point with regard to the double evolution of the human race. The Sons of Wisdom, or the spiritual *Dhyanis*, had become "intellectual" through their contact with matter, because they had already reached, during previous cycles of incarnation, that degree of intellect which enabled them to become independent and self-conscious entities, on this plane of matter. They were reborn only by reason of Karmic effects. They entered those who were "ready," and became the *Arhats*, or sages, alluded to above. This needs explanation.

It does not mean that Monads entered forms in which other Monads already were. They were "Essences," "Intelligences," and conscious spirits, entities seeking to become still more conscious by uniting with more developed matter. Their essence was too pure to be distinct from the universal essence, but their "Egos," or *Manas* (since they are called *Manasaputra*, born of "*Mahat*," or Brahmâ) had to pass through

---

* Every process of healing and cicatrization in the higher animal groups – even in the case of reproduction of mutilated limbs with the Amphibians – is effected by fission and gemmation of the elementary morphological elements.

earthly human experiences to become all-wise, and be able to start on the returning ascending cycle. The Monads are not discrete principles, limited or conditioned, but rays from that one universal absolute Principle. The entrance into a dark room through the same aperture of one ray of sunlight following another will not constitute two rays, but one ray intensified. It is not in the course of natural law that man should become a perfect septenary being, before the seventh race in the seventh Round. Yet he has all these principles latent in him from his birth. Nor is it part of the evolutionary law that the Fifth principle (*Manas*), should receive its complete development before the Fifth Round. All such prematurely developed intellects (on the spiritual plane) in our Race are abnormal; they are those whom we call the "Fifth Rounders." Even in the coming seventh Race, at the close of this Fourth Round, while our four lower principles will be fully developed, that of *Manas* will be only proportionately so. This limitation, however, refers solely to the spiritual development. The intellectual, on the physical plane, was reached during the Fourth Root Race. Thus, those who were "half ready," who received "but a spark," constitute the average humanity which has to acquire its intellectuality during the present Manvantaric evolution, after which they will be ready in the next for the full reception of the "Sons of Wisdom." While those which "were not ready" at all, the latest Monads, which had hardly evolved from their last transitional and lower animal forms at the close of the Third Round, remained the "narrow-brained" of the Stanza. This explains the otherwise unaccountable degrees of intellectuality among the various races of men – the savage Bushman and the European – even now. Those tribes of savages, whose reasoning powers are very little above the level of the animals, are not the unjustly disinherited, or the unfavoured, as some may think – nothing of the kind. They are simply those latest arrivals among the human Monads, which were not ready: which have to evolve during the present Round, as on the three remaining globes (hence on four different planes of being) so as to arrive at the level of the average class when they reach the Fifth Round. One remark may prove useful, as food for thought to the student in this connection. The MONADS of the lowest specimens of humanity, the "narrow-brained"[*] savage South Sea Islander, the African, the Australian) had no Karma to work out when first born as men, as their more favoured brethren in intelligence had. The former are spinning out Karma only now; the latter are burdened with past, present, and future Karma. In this respect the poor savage is more fortunate than the greatest genius of civilised countries.

Let us pause before giving any more such strange teachings. Let us try and find out how far any ancient Scriptures, and even Science, permit the possibility of, or even distinctly corroborate, such wild notions as are found in our Anthropogenesis.

Recapitulating that which has been said we find: That the Secret Doctrine claims for man: (1) a polygenetic origin; (2) a variety of modes of procreation before humanity fell into the ordinary method of generation; (3) that the evolution of animals – of the mammalians at any rate – follows that of man instead of preceding it. And this is diametrically opposed to the now generally accepted theories of evolution and the descent of man from an animal ancestor.

Let us, by giving to Caesar what is Caesar's, examine, first of all, the chances for the polygenetic theory among the men of science.

Now the majority of the Darwinian evolutionists incline to a polygenetic explanation of the origin of Races. On this particular question, however, scientists are, as in many other cases, at sixes and sevens; they agree to disagree.

"Does man descend from one single couple or from several groups

---

[*] The term here means neither the dolicho-cephalic nor the brachyo-cephalic, nor yet skulls of a smaller volume, but simply brains devoid of intellect generally. The theory which would judge of the intellectual capacity of a man according to his cranial capacity, seems absurdly illogical to one who has studied the subject. The skulls of the stone period, as well as those of African Races (Bushmen included) show that the first are above rather than below the average of the brain capacity of the modern man, and the skulls of the last are on the whole (as in the case of Papuans and Polynesians generally) larger by one cubic inch than that of the average Frenchman. Again, the cranial capacity of the Parisian of to-day represents an average of 1437 cubic centimetres compared to 1523 of the Auvergnat.

– monogenism or polygenism? As far as one can venture to pronounce on what in the absence of witnesses (?) will never be known (?), the second hypothesis is far the most probable." † Abel Hovelacque, in his *"Science of Language,"* comes to a similar conclusion, arguing from the evidence available to a linguistic enquirer.

In an address delivered before the British Association, Professor W. H. Flower remarked on this question:

"The view which appears best to accord with what is now known of the characters and distribution of the races of man . . . . is a modification of the monogenistic hypothesis (!). Without entering into the difficult question of the method of man's first appearance upon the world, we must assume for it a vast antiquity, at all events as measured by any historical standard. If we had any approach to a complete palaeontological record, the history of Man could be re-constructed, but nothing of the kind is forthcoming."

Such an admission must be regarded as fatal to the dogmatism of the physical Evolutionists, and as opening a wide margin to occult speculations. The opponents of the Darwinian theory were, and still remain, polygenists. Such "intellectual giants" as John Crawford and James Hunt discussed the problem and favoured polygenesis, and in their day there was a far stronger feeling in favour of than against this theory. It is only in 1864 that Darwinians began to be wedded to the theory of unity, of which Messrs. Huxley and Lubbock became the first coryphaei.

As regards that other question, of the priority of man to the animals in the order of evolution, the answer is as promptly given. If man is really the Microcosm of the Macrocosm, then the teaching has nothing so very impossible in it, and is but logical. For, man becomes that Macrocosm for the three lower kingdoms under him. Arguing from a physical standpoint, all the lower kingdoms, save the mineral – which is light itself, crystallised and immetallised – from plants to the creatures which preceded the first mammalians, all have been consolidated in their physical structures by means of the

---

† A. Lefevre, *"Philosophy,"* p. 498.

"cast-off dust" of those minerals, and the refuse of the human matter, whether from living or dead bodies, on which they fed and which gave them their outer bodies. In his turn, man grew more physical, by re-absorbing into his system that which he had given out, and which became transformed in the living animal crucibles through which it had passed, owing to Nature's alchemical transmutations. There were animals in those days of which our modern naturalists have never dreamed, and the stronger became physical material man, the giants of those times, the more powerful were his emanations. Once that Androgyne "humanity" separated into sexes, transformed by Nature into child-bearing engines, it ceased to procreate its like through drops of vital energy oozing out of the body. But while man was still ignorant of his procreative powers on the human plane, (before his Fall, as a believer in Adam would say,) all this vital energy, scattered far and wide from him, was used by Nature for the production of the first mammal-animal forms. Evolution is an eternal cycle of becoming, we are taught, and nature never leaves an atom unused. Moreover, from the beginning of the Round, all in Nature tends to become Man. All the impulses of the dual, centripetal and centrifugal Force are directed towards one point – MAN. The progress in the succession of beings, says Agassiz, "consists in an increasing similarity of the living fauna, and, among the vertebrates, especially, in the increasing resemblance to man. Man is the end towards which all animal creation has tended from the first appearance of the first palaeozoic fishes." *

Just so, but "the palaeozoic fishes" being at the lower curve of the arc of the evolution of forms, this Round began with astral man, the reflection of the *Dhyan Chohans*, called the "Builders." Man is the alpha and the omega of objective creation. As said in *"Isis Unveiled,"* "all things had their origin in spirit – evolution having originally begun from above and proceeding downwards, instead of the reverse, as taught in the Darwinian theory."† Therefore, the tendency spoken of by the eminent naturalist above quoted, is one inherent in every atom. Only, were one to apply it to both sides of the evolution, the observations

---

* *"Principles of Zoology,"* p. 206.

† *Isis Unveiled*, Vol. I, p. 154.

made would greatly interfere with the modern theory, which has now almost become (Darwinian) law.

But in citing the passage from Agassiz' work with approval, it must not be understood that the occultists are making any concession to the theory, which derives man from the animal kingdom. The fact that in this Round he preceded the mammalia is obviously not impugned by the consideration that the latter (mammalia) follow in the wake of man.

SD, ii 161–170

THE HISTORY OF THE FOURTH RACE

§§ (38) The Birth of the Fourth, Atlantean Race. (39) The sub-races of the Fourth Humanity begin to divide and interblend; they form the first mixed races of various colours. (40) The superiority of the Atlantean over other races. (41) They fall into sin and beget children and monsters. (42) The first germs of Anthropomorphism and sexual religion. They lose their "third Eye."

38. THUS TWO BY TWO, ON THE SEVEN ZONES, THE THIRD (*Race*) GAVE BIRTH TO THE FOURTH (*Race men*). THE GODS BECAME NO-GODS (*Sura became a-Sura*) (*a*).

39. THE FIRST (Race) ON EVERY ZONE WAS MOON-COLOURED (*yellow-white*); THE SECOND, YELLOW, LIKE GOLD; THE THIRD, RED; THE FOURTH, BROWN, WHICH BECAME BLACK WITH SIN. * THE FIRST SEVEN (*human*) SHOOTS WERE ALL OF ONE COMPLEXION IN THE BEGINNING. THE NEXT (*seven, the sub-races*) BEGAN MIXING THEIR COLOURS (*b*).

(*a*) To understand this verse 38, it must be read together with the three verses of Stanza IX. Up to this point of evolution man belongs more to

---

* Strictly speaking, it is only from the time of the Atlantean, brown and yellow giant Races, that one ought to speak of MAN, since it was the Fourth race only which was the first completely human species, however much larger in size than we are now. In "*Man*" (by two *chelas*), all that is said of the Atlanteans is quite correct. It is chiefly that race which became "black with sin" that brought the divine names of the *Asuras*, the *Râkshasas* and the *Daityas* into disrepute, and passed them on to posterity as the names of fiends. For, as said, the *Suras* (gods) or *Devas* having incarnated in the wise men of Atlantis, the names of *Asuras* and *Râkshasas* were given to the Atlanteans; which names, owing to their incessant conflicts with the last remnants of the Third Race and the "Sons of Will and Yoga," have led to the later allegories about them in the *Purânas*. "*Asura* was the generic appellation of all the Atlanteans who were the enemies of the spiritual heroes of the Aryans (gods)." ("*Man*," p. 97.)

metaphysical than physical nature. It is only after the so-called FALL, that the races began to develop rapidly into a purely human shape. And, in order that he may correctly comprehend the full meaning of the Fall, so mystic and transcendental is it in its real significance, the student must be told at once the details which preceded this event, of which event modern theology has formed a pivot on which its most pernicious and absurd dogmas and beliefs are made to turn.

The archaic commentaries explain, as the reader must remember, that, of the Host of *Dhyanis*, whose turn it was to incarnate as the Egos of the immortal, but, on this plane, senseless monads – that some "obeyed" (the law of evolution) immediately when the men of the Third Race became physiologically and physically ready, i.e., when they had separated into sexes. These were those early conscious Beings who, now adding conscious knowledge and will to their inherent Divine purity, created by *Kriyasakti* the semi-Divine man, who became the seed on earth for future adepts. Those, on the other hand, who, jealous of their intellectual freedom (unfettered as it then was by the bonds of matter), said: "We can choose . . . we have wisdom" (See verse 24), and incarnated far later – these had their first Karmic punishment prepared for them. They got bodies (physiologically) inferior to their astral models, because their *Chhayas* had belonged to progenitors of an inferior degree in the seven classes. As to those "Sons of Wisdom" who had "deferred" their incarnation till the Fourth Race, which was already tainted (physiologically) with sin and impurity, they produced a terrible cause, the Karmic result of which weighs on them to this day. It was produced in themselves, and they became the carriers of that seed of iniquity for aeons to come, because the bodies they had to inform had become defiled through their own procrastination. (See verses 32, 36.)

This was the "Fall of the angels," because of their rebellion against Karmic Law. The "fall of man" was no fall, for he was irresponsible. But "Creation" having been invented on the dualistic system as the "prerogative of God alone," the legitimate attribute patented by theology in the name of an infinite deity of their own making, this power had to be regarded as "Satanic," and as an usurpation of divine rights. Thus, the foregoing, in the light of such narrow views, must naturally be considered as a terrible slander on man, "created in the image of God," a still more dreadful blasphemy in the face of the dead-letter dogma. "Your doctrine," the Occultists were already told, "makes of man, created out of dust in the likeness of his God, a vehicle of the Devil, from the first." "Why did you make of your god a devil – both, moreover, created in your own image?" is our reply. The esoteric interpretation of the *Bible*, however, sufficiently refutes this slanderous invention of theology; the Secret Doctrine must some day become the just Karma of the Churches – more anti-Christian than the representative assemblies of the most confirmed Materialists and Atheists.

The old doctrine about the true meaning of the "Fallen Angels," in its anthropological and evolutionary sense, is contained in the *Kabala*, and explains the *Bible*. It is found pre-eminent in *Genesis* when the latter is read in a spirit of research for truth, with no eye to dogma, and in no mood of preconception. This is easily proven. In *Genesis* (vi.) the "Sons of God" – *B'ne Aleim* – become enamoured of the daughters of men, marry, and reveal to their wives the mysteries unlawfully learnt by them in heaven, according to Enoch, and this is the "Fall of Angels."*

---

* In general, the so-called orthodox Christian conceptions about the "fallen" angels or Satan, are as remarkable as they are absurd. About a dozen could be cited, of the most various character as to details, and all from the pen of educated lay authors, "University graduates" of the present quarter of our century. Thus, the author of "*Earth's Earliest Ages*," J. H. Pember, M.A., devotes a thick volume to proving Theosophists, Spiritualists, Metaphysicians, Agnostics, Mystics, poets, and every contemporary author on oriental speculations, to be the devoted servants of the "Prince of the Air," and irretrievably damned. He describes Satan and his Antichrist in this wise:

"Satan is the 'Anointed Cherub' of old. . . . God created Satan, the fairest and wisest of all his creatures in this part of His Universe, and made him Prince of the World, and of the Power of the Air. . . . He was placed in an Eden, which was both far anterior to the Eden of *Genesis*. . . and of an altogether different and more substantial character, resembling the New Jerusalem. Thus, Satan being perfect in wisdom, and beauty, His vast empire is our earth, if not the whole solar system. . . Certainly no other angelic power of greater or even equal dignity has been revealed to us. The Archangel Michael himself is quoted by Jude as preserving towards the Prince of Darkness the respect due to a superior, however wicked he may be, until God has formally commanded his deposition." Then we are informed that "Satan was from the moment of his creation surrounded by the insignia of royalty" (! !): that he "awoke to consciousness to find the air filled with the rejoicing music of those whom God had appointed . . . ." Then the Devil "passes from the royalty to

But what is, in reality, the *"Book of Enoch"* itself, from which the author of *Revelation* and even the St. John of the Fourth Gospel have so profusely quoted? (e.g., verse 8, in chapter 10, about all who have come before Jesus, being "thieves and robbers.") Simply a Book of Initiation, giving out in allegory and cautious phraseology the programme of certain archaic mysteries performed in the inner temples. The author of the *"Sacred Mysteries among the Mayas and Quiches"* very justly suggests that the so-called "Visions" of Enoch relate to his (Enoch's) experience at initiation, and what he learned in the mysteries, while he very erroneously states his opinion that Enoch had learned them before being converted to Christianity (!); furthermore, he believes that this book was written "at the beginning of the Christian era, when . . . the customs and religion of the Egyptians fell into decadency"! This is hardly possible, since Jude quotes in his epistle from the *"Book of Enoch"* (verse 14), and, therefore, as Archbishop Laurence, the translator of the *Book of Enoch* from the Ethiopic version, remarks, it "could not have been the production of a writer who lived after . . . or was even coeval with" the writers of the *New Testament*: unless, indeed, *Jude* and the Gospels, and all that follows, was also a production of the already established Church – which, some critics say, is not impossible. But we are now concerned with the "fallen Angels" of Enoch, rather than with Enoch himself.

In Indian exotericism, these angels (*Asuras*) are also denounced as "the enemies of the gods," those who oppose sacrificial worship offered to the latter. In Christian theology they are broadly referred to as the "Fallen Spirits," the heroes of various conflicting and contradictory legends about them, gathered from Pagan sources. The *coluber tortuosus*, "the tortuous snake," a qualification said to have originated with the

---

his priestly dignity" (! ! !) "Satan was also a priest of the Most High," etc., etc. And now – "Antichrist will be Satan incarnate" (pp. 56-59). The Pioneers of the coming Apollyon have already appeared – they are the Theosophists, the Occultists, the authors of the "Perfect Way," of *"Isis Unveiled,"* of the *"Mystery of the Ages,"* and even of the *"Light of Asia"*! ! The author notes the "avowed origin" (of Theosophy) from the "descending angels," from the "Nephilim," or the angels of the VIth ch. of *Genesis*, and the Giants. He ought to note his own descent from them also, as the present Secret Doctrine endeavours to show – unless he refuses to belong to the present humanity.

Jews, had quite another meaning before the Roman Church distorted it: among others, a purely astronomical meaning.

The "Serpent" fallen from on high, "*deorsum fluens*," was credited with the possession of the Keys of the Empire of the Dead, τοῦ πανάατου ἀρχή to that day, when Jesus saw it "falling like lightning from heaven" (*Luke* x. 17, 18), the Roman Catholic interpretation of *cadebat ut fulgur* to the contrary, notwithstanding, and it means indeed that even "the devils are subject" to the *Logos* – who is WISDOM, but who, as the opponent of ignorance, is Satan or Lucifer at the same time. This remark refers to divine Wisdom falling like lightning on, and quickening the intellects of those who fight the devils of ignorance and superstition. Up to the time when Wisdom, in the shape of the incarnating Spirits of MAHAT, descended from on high to animate and call the Third Race to real conscious life, humanity – if it can be so called in its animal, senseless state – was of course doomed to – moral as well as to physical death. The Angels fallen into generation are referred to metaphorically as Serpents and Dragons of Wisdom. On the other hand, regarded in the light of the LOGOS, the Christian Saviour, like Krishna, whether as man or *logos*, may be said to have saved those who believed in the secret teachings from "eternal death," to have conquered the Kingdom of Darkness, or Hell, as every Initiate does. This in the human, terrestrial form of the Initiates, and also because the *logos* is Christos, that principle of our inner nature which develops in us into the Spiritual Ego – the Higher Self – being formed of the indissoluble union of *Buddhi* (the sixth) and the spiritual efflorescence of *Manas*, the fifth principle. * "The *Logos* is passive Wisdom in Heaven and Conscious, Self-Active Wisdom on Earth," we are taught. It is the Marriage of "Heavenly man" with the "Virgin of the World" – Nature, as described in *Pymander*, the result of which is their progeny – immortal man. It is this which is called in St. John's *Revelation* the marriage of the lamb with his bride. (xix. 7.) That "wife" is now identified with the

---

* It is not correct to refer to Christ – as some theosophists do – as the sixth principle in man – *Buddhi*. The latter per se is a passive and latent principle, the spiritual vehicle of *Atman*, inseparable from the manifested Universal Soul. It is only in union and in conjunction with Self-consciousness that *Buddhi* becomes the Higher Self and the divine, discriminating Soul. Christos is the seventh principle, if anything.

Church of Rome owing to the arbitrary interpretations of her votaries. But they seem to forget that her linen may be fine and white outwardly (like the "whitened sepulchre"), but that the rottenness she is inwardly filled with, is not "the righteousness of Saints" (v. 8. *ibid.*), but rather the blood of the Saints she has "slain upon the earth" (chap. xviii 24.) Thus the remark made by the great Initiate (in *Luke* x. 18) – one that referred allegorically to the ray of Enlightenment and reason, falling like lightning from on high into the hearts and minds of the converts to that old wisdom religion then presented in a new form by the wise Galilean Adept [†] – was distorted out of recognition (as was his own personality), and made to fit in with one of the most cruel as the most pernicious of all theological dogmas. (*Vide* at the end of Stanza XI. "SATANIC MYTHS.")

But if Western theology alone holds the patent for, and copyright of SATAN – in all the dogmatic horror of that fiction – other nationalities and religions have committed equal errors in their misinterpretation of this tenet, which is one of the most profoundly philosophical and ideal conceptions of ancient thought. For they have both disfigured and hinted at the correct meaning of it in their numerous allegories

---

† To make it plainer, any one who reads that passage in Luke, will see that the remark follows the report of the seventy, who rejoice that "even the devils (the spirit of controversy and reasoning, or the opposing power, since Satan means simply "adversary" or opponent) are subject unto us through thy name." (*Luke* x. 17.) Now, "thy name" means the name of Christos, or *Logos*, or the spirit of true divine wisdom, as distinct from the spirit of intellectual or mere materialistic reasoning – the HIGHER SELF in short. And when Jesus remarks to this that he has "beheld Satan as lightning fall from heaven," it is a mere statement of his clairvoyant powers, notifying them that he already knew it, and a reference to the incarnation of the divine ray (the gods or angels) which falls into generation. For not all men, by any means, benefit by that incarnation, and with some the power remains latent and dead during the whole life. Truly "No man knoweth who the Son is, but the Father; and who the Father is, but the Son" as added by Jesus then and there (*Ibid.* v. 22) – the Church "of Christ" less than any one else. The Initiates alone understood the secret meaning of the term "Father and the Son," and knew that it referred to Spirit and Soul on the Earth. For the teachings of Christ were occult teachings, which could only be explained at the initiation. They were never intended for the masses, for Jesus forbade the twelve to go to the Gentiles and the Samaritans (*Matt.* x. 8), and repeated to his disciples that the "mysteries of Heaven" were for them alone, not for the multitudes (*Mark* iv. 11).

touching the subject. Nor have the semi-esoteric dogmas of Purânic Hinduism failed to evolve very suggestive symbols and allegories concerning the rebellious and fallen gods. The *Purânas* teem with them, and we find a direct hint at the truth in the frequent allusions of Parâsara (*Vishnu Purâna*), to all those *Rudras, Rishis, Asuras, Kumâras* and *Munis,* having to be born in every age, to reincarnate in every *Manvantara.* This (esoterically) is equivalent to saying that the FLAMES born of the Universal Mind (*Mahat*), owing to the mysterious workings of Karmic Will and an impulse of Evolutionary Law, had, as in *Pymander* – without any gradual transition – landed on this Earth, having broken through the seven Circles of fire, or the seven intermediate Worlds, in short.

There is an eternal cyclic law of rebirths, and the series is headed at every new Manvantaric dawn by those who had enjoyed their rest from reincarnations in previous *Kalpas* for incalculable AEons – by the highest and the earliest Nirvanees. It was the turn of those "Gods" to incarnate in the present *Manvantara*; hence their presence on Earth, and the ensuing allegories; hence, also, the perversion of the original meaning. * The Gods who had fallen into generation, whose mission it was to complete divine man, are found represented later on as Demons, evil Spirits, and fiends, at feud and war with Gods, or the irresponsible agents of the one Eternal law. But no conception of such creatures as the devils and Satan of the Christian, Jewish, and Mahomedan religions

---

* So, for instance, in the *Purânas*, "Pulastya," a *Prajâpati*, or son of Brahmâ – the progenitor of the *Râkshasas*, and the grandfather of Ravana, the Great King of Lanka (see *Ramayana*) – had, in a former birth, a son named Dattoli, "who is now known as the sage Agastya" – says *Vishnu Purâna*. This name of Dattoli alone, has six more variants to it, or seven meanings. He is called respectively, Dattoi, Dattâli, Dattotti, Dattotri, Dattobhri, Dambhobhi and Dambholi – which seven variants have each a secret sense, and refer in the esoteric comments to various ethnological classifications, and also to physiological and anthropological mysteries of the primitive races. For, surely, the *Râkshasas* are not demons, but simply the primitive and ferocious giants, the Atlanteans, who were scattered on the face of the globe as the Fifth Race is now. Vasishta is a warrant to this, if his words addressed to Parâsara, who attempted a bit of JADOO (sorcery), which he calls "sacrifice," for the destruction of the *Râkshasas*, mean anything. For he says, "Let no more of these unoffending 'Spirits Darkness' be destroyed." (see for details Adiparvan, s. 176, *Mahabhârata*; also the *Linga Purâna* "Purvârdha," s. 64.)

was ever intended under those thousand and one Aryan allegories.[†]
(See "The Fallen Angels" and "The Mystic Dragons" in Part II.)

SD, ii 227–232

[†] We have a passage from a Master's letter which has a direct bearing upon these incarnating angels. Says the letter: "Now there are, and there must be, failures in the ethereal races of the many classes of Dhyan-Chohans, or *Devas* (progressed entities of a previous planetary period), as well as among men. But still, as the failures are too far progressed and spiritualized to be thrown back forcibly from Dhyan-Chohanship into the vortex of a new primordial evolution through the lower Kingdoms, this then happens. Where a new solar system has to be evolved these Dhyan-Chohans are borne in by influx 'ahead' of the Elementals (Entities . . . to be developed into humanity at a future time) and remain as a latent or inactive spiritual force, in the aura of a nascent world . . . until the stage of human evolution is reached. . . . Then they become an active force and commingle with the Elementals, to develop little by little the full type of humanity." That is to say, to develop in, and endow man with his Self-conscious mind, or *Manas*."

MAN, THE PALE SHADOW OF GOD

"Now, as everything proceeds cyclically, the evolution of man like everything else, the order in which he is generated is described fully in the Eastern teachings, whereas it is only hinted at in the *Kabala*. Says the *Book of Dzyan* with regard to primeval man when first projected by the "Boneless," the incorporeal Creator: "First, the Breath, then *Buddhi*, and the Shadow-Son (the Body) were 'CREATED.' But where was the pivot (the middle principle, *Manas*)? Man is doomed. When alone, the indiscrete (undifferentiated Element) and the *Vahan* (*Buddhi*) – the cause of the causeless – break asunder from manifested life" – "unless cemented and held together by the middle principle, the vehicle of the personal consciousness of JIVA", explains the Commentary. In other words, the two higher principles can have no individuality on Earth, cannot be man, unless there is (*a*) the Mind, the *Manas*-Ego, to cognize itself, and (*b*) the terrestrial false personality, or the body of egotistical desires and personal Will, to cement the whole, as if round a pivot (which it is, truly), to the physical form of man. It is the Fifth and the Fourth principles* – *Manas* and *Kama rupa* – that contain the dual personality: the real immortal Ego (if it assimilates itself to the two higher) and the false and transitory personality, the mayavi or astral body, so-called, or the animal-human Soul – the two having to be closely blended for purposes of a full terrestrial existence. Incarnate the Spiritual Monad of a Newton grafted on that of the greatest saint on earth – in a physical body the most perfect you can think of – i.e., in a two or even a three-principled body composed of its *Sthula Sarira*, *prana* (life principle), and *linga sarira* – and, if it lacks its middle and fifth principles, you will have created an idiot – at best a beautiful, soulless, empty and unconscious appearance. "*Cogito, ergo sum*" – can find no room in the brain of such a creature, not on this plane, at any rate.

There are students, however, who have long ago understood the

---

* The Fourth, and the Fifth from below beginning by the physical body; the Third and the Fourth, if we reckon from *Atma*.

philosophical meaning underlying the allegory – so tortured and disfigured by the Roman Church – of the Fallen Angels. "The Kingdom of Spirits and spiritual action which flows from and is the product of Spirit Volition, is outside and contrasted with and in contradiction to the Kingdom of (divine) Souls and divine action." † As said in the text:

> Like produces like and no more at the genesis of being, and evolution with its limited conditioned laws comes later. The Self-Existent ‡ are called CREATIONS, for they appear in the Spirit Ray, manifested through the potency inherent in its UNBORN Nature, which is beyond time and (limited or conditioned) Space. Terrene products, animate and inanimate, including mankind, are falsely called creation and creatures: they are the development (evolution) of the discrete elements. (Com. xiv.)

Again:

> The Heavenly *rupa* (*Dhyan Chohan*) creates (man) in his own form; it is a spiritual ideation consequent on the first differentiation and awakening of the universal (manifested) Substance; that form is the ideal shadow of Itself: and this is THE MAN OF THE FIRST RACE.

To express it in still clearer form, limiting the explanation to this earth only, it was the duty of the first "differentiated Egos" – the Church calls them Archangels – to imbue primordial matter with the evolutionary impulse and guide its formative powers in the fashioning of its productions. This it is which is referred to in the sentences both in the Eastern and Western tradition – "the Angels were commanded to create." After the Earth had been made ready by the lower and more material powers, and its three Kingdoms fairly started on their way to be "fruitful and multiply," the higher powers, the Archangels or *Dhyanis*, were compelled by the evolutionary Law to descend on Earth, in order to construct the crown of its evolution – MAN. Thus the "Self-created" and the "Self-existent" projected their pale shadows, but group the Third, the Fire-Angels, rebelled and refused to join their Fellow *Devas*.

---

† "*New Aspects of Life.*"

‡ Angelic, Spiritual Essences, immortal in their being because unconditioned in Eternity; periodical and conditioned in their Manvantaric manifestations.

Hindu exotericism represents them all as Yogins, whose piety inspired them to refuse creating, as they desired to remain eternally *Kumâras*, "Virgin Youths," in order to, if possible, anticipate their fellows in progress towards Nirvana – the final liberation. But, agreeably to esoteric interpretation, it was a self-sacrifice for the benefit of mankind. The "Rebels" would not create will-less irresponsible men, as the "obedient" angels did, nor could they endow human beings with only the temporary reflections of their own attributes, for even the latter, belonging to another and a so much higher plane of consciousness, would leave man still irresponsible, hence interfere with any possibility of a higher progress. No spiritual and psychic evolution is possible on earth – the lowest and most material plane – for one who on that plane, at all events, is inherently perfect and cannot accumulate either merit or demerit. Man remaining the pale shadow of the inert, immutable, and motionless perfection, the one negative and passive attribute of the real I am that I am, would have been doomed to pass through life on earth as in a heavy dreamless sleep, hence a failure on this plane. The Beings, or the Being, collectively called *Elohim*, who first (if ever) pronounced the cruel words, "Behold, the man is become as one of us, to know good and evil, and now, lest he put forth his hand and take also of the tree of life and eat and live for ever . . . " must have been indeed the Ilda-Baoth, the Demiurge of the Nazarenes, filled with rage and envy against his own creature, whose reflection created Ophiomorphos. In this case it is but natural – even from the dead letter standpoint – to view Satan, the Serpent of *Genesis*, as the real creator and benefactor, the Father of Spiritual mankind. For it is he who was the "Harbinger of Light," bright radiant Lucifer, who opened the eyes of the automaton created by Jehovah, as alleged, and he who was the first to whisper: "in the day ye eat thereof ye shall be as *Elohim*, knowing good and evil" – can only be regarded in the light of a Saviour. An "adversary" to Jehovah the "personating spirit," he still remains in esoteric truth the ever-loving "Messenger" (the angel), the *Seraphim* and *Cherubim* who both knew well, and loved still more, and who conferred on us spiritual, instead of physical immortality – the latter a kind of static immortality that would have transformed man into an undying "Wandering Jew."

As narrated in King's "*Gnostics*," Ilda-Baoth, whom several sects regarded as the God of Moses, was not a pure spirit, he was ambitious and proud, and rejecting the spiritual light of the middle space offered him by his mother Sophia-Achamoth, he set himself to create a world of his own. Aided by his sons, the six planetary genii, he fabricated man, but this one proved a failure. It was a monster, soulless, ignorant, and crawling on all fours on the ground like a material beast. Ilda-Baoth was forced to implore the help of his spiritual mother. She communicated to him a ray of her divine light, and so animated man and endowed him with a soul. And now began the animosity of Ilda-Baoth toward his own creature. Following the impulse of the divine light, man soared higher and higher in his aspirations; very soon he began presenting not the image of his creator Ilda-Baoth but rather that of the Supreme Being, the 'primitive man,' Ennoia. Then the *Demiurgos* was filled with rage and envy, and fixing his jealous eye on the abyss of matter, his looks envenomed with passion were suddenly reflected as in a mirror; the reflection became animate, and there arose out of the abyss Satan, serpent, Ophiomorphos – 'the embodiment of envy and cunning. He is the union of all that is most base in matter, with the hate, envy, and craft of a spiritual intelligence.' " This is the exoteric rendering of the Gnostics, and the allegory, though a sectarian version, is suggestive, and seems true to life. It is the natural deduction from the dead letter text of chapter iii of *Genesis*.

Hence the allegory of Prometheus, who steals the divine fire so as to allow men to proceed consciously on the path of spiritual evolution, thus transforming the most perfect of animals on earth into a potential god, and making him free to "take the kingdom of heaven by violence." Hence also, the curse pronounced by Zeus against Prometheus, and by Jehovah-Ilda-Baoth against his "rebellious son," Satan. The cold, pure snows of the Caucasian mountain and the never-dying, singeing fire and flames of an extinguishable hell. Two poles, yet the same idea; the dual aspect of a refined torture: a fire producer – the personified emblem of Φωσφόρος of the astral fire and light in the *anima mundi* – (that element of which the German materialist philosopher Moleschott said: "*ohne phosphor kein gedanke*," i.e., without phosphorus no thought), burning in the fierce flames of his terrestrial passions; the conflagration fired by his Thought, discerning as it now does good from evil, and yet a slave to the passions of its earthly Adam; feeling the vulture of doubt and full consciousness gnawing at its heart – a Prometheus indeed, because a conscious, hence a responsible entity. * The curse of life is great, yet how few are those men, outside some Hindu and Sufi mystics, who would exchange all the tortures of conscious life, all the evils of a responsible existence, for the unconscious perfection of a passive (objectively) incorporeal being, or even the universal static Inertia personified in Brahmâ during his "night's" rest. For, to quote from an able article by one † who, confusing the planes of existence and consciousness, fell a victim to it:

> "Satan, or Lucifer, represents the active, or, as M. Jules Baissac calls it, the 'Centrifugal Energy of the Universe' in a cosmic sense. He is Fire, Light, Life, Struggle, Effort, Thought, Consciousness, Progress, Civilization, Liberty, Independence. At the same time he is pain, which is the Re-action of the pleasure of action, and death – which is the revolution of life – Satan, burning in his own hell, produced by the fury of his own momentum – the expansive disintegration of the nebulae which is to concentrate into new worlds. And fitly is he again and again baffled by the eternal Inertia of the passive energy of the Kosmos – the inexorable 'I AM' – the flint from which the sparks are beaten out. Fitly is he . . . and his adherents . . . consigned to the 'sea of fire,' because it is the Sun (in one sense only in the Cosmic allegory), the fount of life in our system, where they are purified (disintegrated) and churned up to rearrange them for another life (the resurrection); that Sun which, as the origin of the active principle of our Earth, is at once the Home and the Source of the Mundane Satan. . ." To

---

* The history of Prometheus, Karma, and human consciousness, is found further on.

† By an Englishman whose erratic genius killed him. The son of a Protestant clergyman, he became a Mahomedan, then a rabid atheist, and after meeting with a master, a Guru, he became a mystic; then a theosophist who doubted, despaired; threw up white for black magic, went insane and joined the Roman Church. Then again turning round, anathematized her, re-became an atheist, and died cursing humanity, knowledge, and God, in whom he had ceased to believe. Furnished with all the esoteric data to write his "War in Heaven," he made a semi-political article out of it, mixing Malthus with Satan, and Darwin with the astral light. Peace be to his – Shell. He is a warning to the *chelas* who fail. His forgotten tomb may now be seen in the Mussulman burial ground of the Joonagad, Kathiawar, in India.

demonstrate furthermore the accuracy of Baissac's general theory (in *Le Diable et Satan*) cold is known to have a 'Centripetal' effect. "Under the influence of cold everything contracts. . . . Under it life hybernates, or dies out, thought congeals, and fire is extinguished. Satan is immortal in his own Fire-Sea – it is only in the '*Nifl-heim*' (the cold Hell of the Scandinavian *Eddas*) of the 'I AM' that he cannot exist. But for all that there is a kind of Immortal Existence in the *Nifl-heim*, and that existence must be painless and peaceful, because it is Unconscious and Inactive. In the Kingdom of Jehovah (if this God were all that the Jews and Christians claim for him) there is no Misery, no War, no marrying and giving in marriage, no change, no Individual Consciousness. ‡ All is absorbed in the spirit of the most Powerful. It is emphatically a kingdom of Peace and loyal Submission as that of the 'Arch-Rebel' is one of War and Revolution. . . It (the former) is in fact what Theosophy calls Nirvana. But then Theosophy teaches that separation from the Primal Source having once occurred, Reunion can only be achieved by Will – Effort – which is distinctly Satanic in the sense of this essay."

It is "Satanic" from the standpoint of orthodox Romanism, for it is owing to the prototype of that which became in time the Christian Devil – to the Radiant Archangels, *Dhyan-Chohans*, who refused to create, because they wanted Man to become his own creator and an immortal god – that men can reach Nirvana and the haven of heavenly divine Peace.

To close this rather lengthy comment, the Secret Doctrine teaches that the Fire-*Devas*, the *Rudras*, and the *Kumâras*, the "Virgin-Angels," (to whom Michael and Gabriel, the Archangels, both belong), the divine "Rebels" – called by the all-materializing and positive Jews, the Nahash or "Deprived" – preferred the curse of incarnation and the long cycles of terrestrial existence and rebirths, to seeing the misery (even if unconscious) of the beings (evolved as shadows out of their Brethren) through the semi-passive energy of their too spiritual Creators. If "man's uses of life should be such as neither to animalize

---

‡ The author talks of the active, fighting, damning Jehovah as though he were a synonym of *Parabrahm*! We have quoted from this article to show where it dissents from theosophic teachings; otherwise it would be quoted some day against us, as everything published in the *Theosophist* generally is.

nor to spiritualize, but to humanize Self," * before he can do so, he must be born human not angelic. Hence, tradition shows the celestial Yogis offering themselves as voluntary victims in order to redeem Humanity – created god-like and perfect at first – and to endow him with human affections and aspirations. To do this they had to give up their natural status and, descending on our globe, take up their abode on it for the whole cycle of the *Mahayuga*, thus exchanging their impersonal individualities for individual personalities – the bliss of sidereal existence for the curse of terrestrial life. This voluntary sacrifice of the Fiery Angels, whose nature was Knowledge and Love, was construed by the exoteric theologies into a statement that shows "the rebel angels hurled down from heaven into the darkness of Hell" – our Earth. Hindu philosophy hints at the truth by teaching that the *Asuras* hurled down by Siva, are only in an intermediate state in which they prepare for higher degrees of purification and redemption from their wretched condition; but Christian theology, claiming to be based on the rock of divine love, charity, and justice of him it appeals to as its Saviour – has invented, to enforce that claim paradoxically, the dreary dogma of hell, that Archimedean lever of Roman Catholic philosophy.

As to Rabbinical Wisdom – than which there is none more positive, materialistic, or grossly terrestrial, as it brings everything down to physiological mysteries – it calls these Beings, the "Evil One," and the Kabalists – Nahash, "Deprived," as just said, and the Souls, that have thrown themselves, after having been alienated in Heaven from the Holy One, into an abyss at the dawn of their very existence, and have anticipated the time when they are to descend on earth. (*Zohar*, iii 61, C.)

---

* Explaining the *Kabala*, Dr. H. Pratt says, "Spirit was to man (to the Jewish Rabbin, rather â) a bodiless, disembodied, or deprived, and degraded being, and hence was termed by the ideograph *Nahash*, 'Deprived;' represented as appearing to and seducing the human race – men through the Woman. . . . In the picture from this *Nahash*, this spirit was represented by a serpent, because from its destitution of bodily members, the Serpent was looked upon as a deprived and depraved and degraded creature" ("*New Aspects*," p. 235). Symbol for symbol there are those who would prefer that of the serpent – the symbol of wisdom and eternity, deprived of limbs as it is – to the *Jod* (ו) – the poetical ideograph of Jehovah in the *Kabala* – the god of the male symbol of generation.

And let me explain at once that our quarrel is not with the *Zohar* and the *Kabala* in their right interpretation – for the latter is ours – but only with the gross, pseudo-esoteric explanations of the later, and especially those of the Christian Kabalists.

"Our earth and man," says the Commentary, "being the products of the three Fires" – whose three names answer, in Sanskrit, to "the electric fire, the Solar fire, and the fire produced by friction," – these three fires, explained on the Cosmic and human planes, are Spirit, Soul, and Body, the three great Root groups, with their four additional divisions. These vary with the Schools, and become – according to their applications – the *Upadhis* and the vehicles, or the noumena of these. In the exoteric accounts, they are personified by the "three sons of surpassing brilliancy and splendour" of Agni Abhimanin, the eldest son of Brahmâ, the Cosmic LOGOS, by Swaha, one of *Daksha's*[†] daughters. In the metaphysical sense the "Fire of friction" means the Union between *Buddhi*, the sixth, and *Manas*, the fifth, principles, which thus are united or cemented together, the fifth merging partially into and becoming part of the monad; in the physical, it relates to the creative spark, or germ, which fructifies and generates the human being. The three Fires, it is said (whose names are *Pâvaka*, *Pavamâna* and *Suchi*) were condemned by a curse of Vasishta, the great sage, "to be born over and over again." (*Bhagavata-Purâna* iv. 24, 4.) This is clear enough.

Therefore, the FLAMES, whose functions are confused in the exoteric books, and who are called indifferently *Prajâpati, Pitris, Manus, Asuras, Rishis, Kumâras,* [‡] etc. etc., are said to incarnate personally in

---

† *Daksha*, the "intelligent, the competent." "This name generally carries with it the idea of creative power." He is a son of Brahmâ, and of Aditi, and agreeably to other versions, a self-born power, which, like Minerva, sprang from his father's body. He is the chief of the *Prajâpati* – the Lords or Creators of Being. In *Vishnu Purâna*, Parâsara says of him, "in every Kalpa (or *manvantara*) Daksha and the rest are born and are again destroyed." And the *Rig Veda* says that "*Daksha* sprang from Aditi and Aditi from *Daksha*," a reference to the eternal cyclic re-birth of the same divine Essence.

‡ No one of these orders is distinct from the *Pitris* or Progenitors, as says *Manu* (iii 284). "The wise call our fathers *Vasus*; our paternal grandfathers, *Rudras*; our paternal great grandfathers, *Adityas*; agreeably to a text of the *Vedas*," or "this is an

the Third Root Race and thus find themselves "reborn over and over again." In the Esoteric doctrine they are generally named the *Asuras*, or the *Asura Devata* or *Pitar-devata* (gods) for, as said, they were first Gods – and the highest – before they became "no-gods," and had from Spirits of Heaven fallen into Spirits of the Earth * – exoterically, note well, in orthodox dogma.

No Theologian, any more than an Orientalist, can ever understand the genealogies of the *Prajâpati*, the *Manus*, and the *Rishis*, nor the direct connection of these – or their correlation rather – with the Gods, unless he has the key to the old primitive Cosmogony and Theogony, which all the Nations originally had in common. All these gods and demi-gods are found reborn on earth, in various *Kalpas* and in as various characters, each, moreover, having his Karma distinctly traced, and every effect assigned to its cause.

Before other Stanzas could be explained, it was, as seen, absolutely necessary to show that the sons of "Dark Wisdom," though identical with the Archangels which Theology has chosen to call the "Fallen," are as divine and as pure and more so than all the Michaels and Gabriels so glorified in the churches. The "old Book" goes into various details of Astral life, which at this juncture would be quite incomprehensible to the reader. It may, therefore, be left for later explanations, and the First and Second Races can now only receive bare notice. Not so for the Third Race – the Root Race which separated into sexes, and which was the first to be endowed with reason. Men evolving *pari passu* with the globe, and the latter having "incrustated" more than a hundred million of years before – the first human sub-race had already begun to materialize or solidify, so to say. But, as the Stanza has it: "the inner man (the conscious Entity) was not." This "Conscious Entity" Occultism says, comes from, nay, in many cases is, the very entire essence and *esse* of the high Intelligences condemned, by the undeviating law of Karmic evolution, to reincarnate in this *manvantara*.

---

everlasting Vedic text" in another translation.

* As now discovered by the late G. Smith in the Babylonian cylinder literature, it was the same in Chaldean theogony. Ishtar, "eldest of Heaven and of Earth." Below him the *Igaga* or Angels of Heaven, and the *Anunnaki*, or angels of Earth. Below these again various classes of Spirits and "Genii" called *Sadu, Vadukku, Ekimu, Gallu* – of which some were good, some evil. (See "*Babylonian Mythology.*")

(*b*) This verse (thirty-ninth) relates exclusively to the racial divisions. Strictly speaking, esoteric philosophy teaches a modified polygenesis. For, while it assigns to humanity a oneness of origin, in so far that its forefathers or "Creators" were all divine beings – though of different classes or degrees of perfection in their hierarchy – men were nevertheless born on seven different centres of the continent of that period. Though all of one common origin, yet for reasons given their potentialities and mental capabilities, outward or physical forms, and future characteristics, were very different. † As to their complexions, there is a suggestive allegory told in *Linga Purâna*. The *Kumâra* – the Rudra gods, so called (see further), are described as incarnations of Siva, the destroyer (of outward forms), named also Vamadeva. The latter, as a *Kumâra*, the "Eternal Celibate," the chaste Virgin youth, springs from Brahmâ in each great *Manvantara*, and "again becomes four", a reference to the four great divisions of the human races, as regards complexion and type – and three chief variations of these. Thus in the 29th *Kalpa* – in this case a reference to the transformation and evolution of the human form which Siva ever destroys and remodels periodically, down to the manvantaric great turning point about the middle of the Fourth (Atlantean) Race – in the 29th *Kalpa*, Siva, as Swetalohita, the root *Kumâra*, becomes, from moon-coloured, white; in his next transformation – he is red (and in this the exoteric version differs from the Esoteric teaching); in the third – yellow; in the fourth – black.

Esotericism now classes these seven variations, with their four great divisions, into only three distinct primeval races – as it does not take into consideration the First Race, which had neither type nor colour, and hardly an objective, though colossal form. The evolution of these races, their formation and development, went *pari passu* and on parallel lines with the evolution, formation, and development of three geological strata, from which the human complexion was as much derived as it was determined by the climates of those zones. It names three great

---

† Some superior, others inferior, to suit the Karma of the various reincarnating Monads which could not be all of the same degree of purity in their last births in other worlds. This accounts for the difference of races, the inferiority of the savage, and other human varieties.

divisions, namely, the RED-YELLOW, the BLACK, and the BROWN-WHITE. * The Aryan races, for instance, now varying from dark brown, almost black, red-brown-yellow, down to the whitest creamy colour, are yet all of one and the same stock – the Fifth Root Race – and spring from one single progenitor, called in Hindu exotericism by the generic name of *Vaivasvata Manu*: the latter, remember, being that generic personage, the Sage, who is said to have lived over 18,000,000 years ago, and also 850,000 years ago – at the time of the sinking of the last remnants of the great continent of Atlantis [†] (See the Root and Seed Manus further on), and who is said to live even now in his mankind. (*Vide* at the end of this Stanza, "THE PRIMEVAL MANUS OF HUMANITY.") The light yellow is the colour of the first SOLID human race, which appeared after the middle of the Third Root Race (after its fall into generation – as just explained), bringing on the final changes. For, it is only at that period that the last transformation took place, which brought forth man as he is now, only on a magnified scale. This Race gave birth to the Fourth Race, "Siva" gradually transforming that portion of Humanity which became "black with sin" into red-yellow (the red Indians and the Mongolians being the descendants of these) and finally into Brown-white races – which now, together with the yellow Races, form the great bulk of Humanity. The allegory in *Linga Purâna* is curious, as showing the great ethnological knowledge of the ancients.

When reading of "the last transformation," let the reader consider at this juncture, if that took place 18,000,000 years ago, how many millions more it must have required to reach that final stage? And if man, in his

---

* "There are," says Topinard (English edition of "*Anthropology*," with preface by Professor Broca), "THREE fundamental elements of colour in the human organism – namely, the red, the yellow, and the black, which, mixed in variable quantities with the white of the tissues, give rise to those numerous shades seen in the human family." Here is science unintentionally supporting Occultism again.

[†] It must be remembered that the "last remnants" here spoken of, refer to those portions of the "great continent" which still remained, and not to any of the numerous islands which existed contemporaneously with the continent. Plato's "island" was, for instance, one of such remnants; the others having sunk at various periods previously. An occult "tradition" teaches that such submersions occur whenever there is an eclipse of the "spiritual sun."

gradual consolidation, developed *pari passu* with the earth, how many millions of years must have elapsed during the First, Second, and the first half of the Third Race? For the Earth was in a comparatively ethereal condition before it reached its last consolidated state; the archaic teachings, moreover, telling us that, during the middle period of the Lemuro-Atlantean Race, three and a half Races after the genesis of man, the Earth, man, and everything on the Globe was of a still grosser and more material nature, while such things as corals and some shells were still in a semi-gelatinous, astral state. The cycles that intervened since then, have already carried us onward, on the opposite ascending arc, some steps toward our dematerialization, as the spiritualists would say. The Earth, ourselves, and all things have softened since then – aye, even our brains. But it has been objected by some theosophists that an ethereal Earth even some 15, or 20,000,000 years ago, does not square with Geology, which teaches us that winds blew, rains fell, waves broke on the shore, sands shifted and accumulated, etc., etc., that, in short, all natural causes now in operation were then in force, "in the very earliest ages of geological time, aye, that of the oldest palaeozoic rocks." To this the following answers are given. Firstly, what is the date assigned by geology to those "oldest palaezoic rocks"? And secondly, why could not the winds blow, rain fall, and waves (of carbonic acid apparently, as science seems to imply) break on the shore, on an Earth semi-astral, i.e., viscid? The word "astral" does not necessarily mean as thin as smoke, in occult phraseology, but rather "starry," shining or pellucid, in various and numerous degrees, from a quite filmy to a viscid state, as just observed. But it is further objected: How could an astral Earth have affected the other planets in this system? Would not the whole process get out of gear now if the attraction of one planet was suddenly removed? The objection is evidently invalid, since our system is composed of older and younger planets, some dead (like the moon), others in process of formation, for all astronomy knows to the contrary. Nor has the latter ever affirmed, so far as we know, that all the bodies of our system have sprung into existence and developed simultaneously. The Cis-Himalayan secret teachings differ from those of India in this respect. Hindu Occultism teaches that the *Vaivasvata Manu* Humanity is eighteen million and odd years old. We say, yes, but only so far as physical, or approximately physical, man is concerned, who dates from the close of the Third Root Race. Beyond that period MAN, or his filmy image, may have existed for 300 million years, for all we know, since we are not taught figures which are and will remain secret with the Masters of Occult Science, as justly stated in "*Esoteric Buddhism*." Moreover, whereas the Hindu *Purânas* speak of one *Vaivasvata Manu*, we affirm that there were several, the name being a generic one. (*Vide supra*).

We must now say a few more words on the physical evolution of man.

SD, ii 241–251

THE INHERENT LAW OF PROGRESSIVE DEVELOPMENT

That man originates like other animals in a cell and develops "through stages undistinguishable from those of fish, reptile, and mammal until the cell attains the highly specialized development of the quadrumanous and at last the human type," is an Occult axiom thousands of years old. The Kabalistic axiom, "A stone becomes a plant; a plant a beast; a beast a man; a man a God," holds good throughout the ages. Haeckel, in his *Shopfungsgeschichte*, shows a double drawing representing two embryos – that of a dog six weeks old, and that of a man, eight weeks. The two, except the slight difference in the head, larger and wider about the brain in the man, are undistinguishable. "In fact, we may say that every human being passes through the stage of fish and reptile before arriving at that of mammal and finally of man. If we take him up at the more advanced stage where the embryo has already passed the reptilian form . . . for a considerable time, the line of development remains the same as that of other mammalia. The rudimentary limbs are exactly similar, the five fingers and toes develop in the same way, and the resemblance after the first four weeks' growth between the embryo of a man and a dog is such that it is scarcely possible to distinguish them. Even at the age of eight weeks the embryo man is an animal with a tail hardly to be distinguished from an embryo puppy" ("*Modern Science*," etc., p. 171).

Why, then, not make man and dog evolve from a common ancestor, or from a reptile – a *Naga*, instead of coupling man with the *quadrumana*? This would be just as logical as the other, and more so. The shape and the stages of the human embryo have not changed since historical times, and these metamorphoses were known to Aesculapius and Hippocrates as well as to Mr. Huxley. Therefore, since the Kabalists had remarked it since prehistoric times, it is no new discovery. In "*Isis*," Vol. I, 389, it is noticed and half explained.

As the embryo of man has no more of the ape in it than of any other mammal, but contains in itself the totality of the kingdoms of nature, and since it seems to be "a persistent type" of life, far more so than even the *Foraminifera*, it seems as illogical to make him evolve from the ape as it would be to trace his origin to the frog or the dog. Both Occult and Eastern philosophies believe in evolution, which Manu and Kapila[*] give with far more clearness than any scientist does at present. No need to repeat that which was fully debated in *Isis Unveiled*, as the reader may find all these arguments and the description of the basis on which all the Eastern doctrines of Evolution rested, in our earlier books.[†] But no Occultist can accept the unreasonable proposition that all the now existing forms, "from the structureless Amoeba to man," are the direct lineal descendants of organisms which lived millions and millions of years before the birth of man, in the pre-Silurian epochs, in the sea or land mud. The Occultists believe in an inherent law of progressive development.[‡] Mr. Darwin never did, and says so himself.

On page 145 of the "*Origin of Species*" we find him stating that, since there can be no advantage "to the infusorian *animalcule* or an intestinal worm . . . to become highly organized," therefore, "natural selection," not including necessarily progressive development – leaves the *animalcule* and the worm (the "persistent types") quiet.

There does not appear much uniform law in such behaviour of Nature, and it looks more like the discriminative action of some Super-Natural selection; perhaps, that aspect of Karma, which Eastern Occultists would call the "Law of Retardation," may have something to do with it.

---

* Hence the philosophy in the allegory of the 7, 10, and finally 21 *Prajâpati, Rishis, Munis*, etc., who all are made the *fathers* of various things and beings. The order of the seven classes or orders of plants, animals, and even inanimate things, given at random in the *Purânas*, is found in several commentaries in the correct rotation. Thus, Prithu is the father of the Earth. He *milks her*, and makes her bear every kind of grain and vegetable, all enumerated and specified. Kasyapa is the father of all the reptiles, snakes, demons, etc., etc.

† See Vol. I. 152, et seq., about the tree of evolution — The "Mundane Tree."

‡ Checked and modified, however, by the Law of Retardation, which imposes a restriction on the advance of all species when a Higher Type makes its appearance.

But there is every reason to doubt whether Mr. Darwin himself ever gave such an importance to his law – as is given to it now by his atheistic followers. The knowledge of the various living forms in the geological periods that have gone by is very meagre. The reasons given for this by Dr. Bastian are very suggestive: (1) On account of the imperfect manner in which the several forms may be represented in the strata pertaining to the period; (2) on account of the extremely limited nature of the explorations which have been made in these imperfectly representative strata; and (3) because so many parts of the record are absolutely inaccessible to us – nearly all beneath the Silurian system having been blotted out by time, whilst those two-thirds of the earth's surface in which the remaining strata are to be found are now covered over by seas. Hence Mr. Darwin says himself,

> For my part, following out Lyell's metaphor, I look at the geological record as a history of the world imperfectly kept, and written in a changing dialect; of this history we possess the last volume alone, relating only to two or three countries. Of this volume, only here and there a short chapter has been preserved, and of each page only here and there a few lines.

It is not on such meagre data, certainly, that the last word of Science can be said. Nor is it on any ground of human pride or unreasonable belief in man's representing even here on earth – (in our period, perhaps) – the highest type of life, that Occultism denies that all the preceding forms of human life belonged to types lower than our own, for it is not so. But simply because the "missing link," such as to prove the existing theory undeniably, will never be found by palaeontologists. Believing as we do that man has evolved from, and passed through, (during the preceding Rounds) the lowest forms of every life, vegetable and animal, on earth, there is nothing very degrading in the idea of having the orangoutang as an ancestor of our physical form. Quite the reverse, as it would forward the Occult doctrine with regard to the final evolution of everything in terrestrial nature into man, most irresistibly. One may even enquire how it is that biologists and anthropologists, having once firmly accepted the theory of the descent of man from the ape – how it is that they have hitherto left untouched the future evolution of the existing apes into man? This is only a logical sequence of the first theory, unless Science would make of man a privileged being, and his evolution a non-precedent in nature, quite a special and unique case. And that is what all this leads physical Science to. The reason, however, why the Occultists reject the Darwinian, and especially the Haeckelian, hypothesis is because it is the ape which is, in sober truth, a special and unique instance, not man. The pithecoid is an accidental creation, a forced growth, the result of an unnatural process.

The occult doctrine, is, we think, more logical. It teaches a cyclic, never varying law in nature, the latter having no personal, "special design," but acting on a uniform plan that prevails through the whole manvantaric period and deals with the land worm as it deals with man. Neither the one nor the other have sought to come into being, hence both are under the same evolutionary law, and both have to progress according to Karmic law. Both have started from the same neutral centre of Life and both have to re-merge into it at the consummation of the cycle.

It is not denied that in the preceding Round man was a gigantic apelike creature, and when we say "man" we ought perhaps to say, the rough mould that was developing for the use of man in this Round only – the middle, or the transition point of which we have hardly reached. Nor was man what he is now during the first two and a half Root Races. That point he reached, as said before, only 18,000,000 years ago, during the secondary period, as we claim.

Till then he was, according to tradition and Occult teaching, "a god on earth who had fallen into matter," or generation. This may or may not be accepted, since the Secret Doctrine does not impose itself as an infallible dogma; and since, whether its prehistoric records are accepted or rejected, it has nothing to do with the question of the actual man and his inner nature, the Fall mentioned above having left no original sin on Humanity. But all this has been sufficiently dealt with.

Furthermore, we are taught that the transformations through which man passed on the descending arc – which is centrifugal for spirit and centripetal for matter – and those he prepares to go through, henceforward, on his ascending path, which will reverse the direction of the two forces – viz., matter will become centrifugal and spirit centripetal – that all such transformations are next in store for the anthropoid ape also, all those, at any rate, who have reached the remove next to man in this Round – and these will all be men in the Fifth Round, as present men inhabited ape-like forms in the Third, the preceding Round.

Behold, then, in the modern denizens of the great forests of Sumatra the degraded and dwarfed examples – "blurred copies," as Mr. Huxley has it – of ourselves, as we (the majority of mankind) were in the earliest sub-races of the Fourth Root Race during the period of what is called the "Fall into generation." The ape we know is not the product of natural evolution but an accident, a cross breed between an animal being, or form, and man. As has been shown in the present volume (anthropogenesis), it is the speechless animal that first started sexual connection, having been the first to separate into males and females. Nor was it intended by Nature that man should follow the bestial example – as shown by the comparatively painless procreation of their species by the animals, and the terrible suffering and danger of the same in the woman. The Ape is, indeed, as remarked in *Isis Unveiled* (Vol. II, 278) "a transformation of species most directly connected with that of the human family – a hybrid branch engrafted on their own stock before the final perfection of the latter" – or man. The apes are millions of years later than the speaking human being, and are the latest contemporaries of our Fifth Race. Thus, it is most important to remember that the Egos of the apes are entities compelled by their Karma to incarnate in the animal forms, which resulted from the bestiality of the latest Third and the earliest Fourth Race men. They are entities who had already reached the "human stage" before this Round. Consequently, they form an exception to the general rule. The numberless traditions about Satyrs are no fables, but represent an extinct race of animal men. The animal "Eves" were their foremothers, and the human "Adams" their forefathers; hence the Kabalistic allegory of Lilith or Lilatu, Adam's first wife, whom the Talmud describes as a charming woman, with long wavy hair, i.e.– a female hairy animal of a character now unknown, still a female animal, who in the Kabalistic and Talmudic allegories is called the female reflection of Samael,

Samael-Lilith, or man-animal united, a being called Hayo Bischat, the Beast or Evil Beast (*Zohar*). It is from this unnatural union that the present apes descended. The latter are truly "speechless men," and will become speaking animals (or men of a lower order) in the Fifth Round, while the adepts of a certain school hope that some of the Egos of the apes of a higher intelligence will reappear at the close of the Sixth Root Race. What their form will be is of secondary consideration. The form means nothing. Species and genera of the flora, fauna, and the highest animal, its crown – man, change and vary according to the environments and climatic variations, not only with every Round, but every Root Race likewise, as well as after every geological cataclysm that puts an end to, or produces a turning point in the latter. In the Sixth Root Race the fossils of the Orang, the Gorilla and the Chimpanzee will be those of extinct quadrumanous mammals; and new forms – though fewer and ever wider apart as ages pass on and the close of the *Manvantara* approaches – will develop from the "cast off" types of the human races as they revert once again to astral, out of the mire of physical, life. There were none before man, and they will be extinct before the Seventh Race develops. Karma will lead on the monads of the unprogressed men of our race and lodge them in the newly evolved human frames of the thus physiologically regenerated baboon. (But see Part III, *Addenda*.)

This will take place, of course, millions of years hence. But the picture of this cyclic precession of all that lives and breathes now on earth, of each species in its turn, is a true one, and needs no "special creation" or miraculous formation of man, beast, and plant *ex nihilo*.

This is how Occult Science explains the absence of any link between ape and man, and shows the former evolving from the latter.

SD, ii 258–263

THE NATURAL FALL

The THIRD RACE FELL – and created no longer: it begot its progeny. Being still mindless at the period of separation it begot, moreover, anomalous offspring, until its physiological nature had adjusted its instincts in the right direction. Like the "lords the gods" of the *Bible* the "Sons of Wisdom," the *Dhyan-Chohans*, had warned them to leave alone the fruit forbidden by Nature, but the warning proved of no value. Men realized the unfitness – we must not say sin – of what they had done, only when too late: after the angelic monads from higher spheres had incarnated in, and endowed them with understanding. To that day they had remained simply physical, like the animals generated from them. For what is the distinction? The doctrine teaches that the only difference between animate and inanimate objects on earth, between an animal and a human frame, is that in some the various "fires" are latent, and in others they are active. The vital fires are in all things and not an atom is devoid of them. But no animal has the three higher principles awakened in him; they are simply potential, latent, and thus non-existing. And so would the animal frames of men be to this day, had they been left as they came out from the bodies of their Progenitors, whose shadows they were, to grow, unfolded only by the powers and forces immanent in matter. But as said in *Pymander*:

> This is a Mystery that to this day was sealed and hidden. Nature being mingled with Man brought forth a wondrous miracle; the harmonious commingling of the essence of the Seven (*Pitris*, governors) and her own; the Fire and the Spirit and Nature (the noumenon of matter); which (commingling) forthwith brought forth seven men of opposite sexes (negative and positive) according to the essences of the seven governors. (*Divine Pymander*, Chap. I., Sect. 16.)

Thus saith Hermes, the thrice great Initiate, "the Power of the Thought Divine." St. Paul, another Initiate, called our world "the enigmatical mirror of pure truth," and St. Gregory, of Nazianzen, corroborated Hermes by stating that "things visible are but the shadow and delineation of things that we cannot see." It is an eternal combination, and images are repeated from the higher rung of the ladder of being down to the lower. The "Fall of the Angels," and the "War in Heaven" are repeated on every plane, the lower "mirror" disfiguring the image of the superior mirror, and each repeating it in its own way. Thus the Christian dogmas are but the reminiscences of the paradigms of Plato, who spoke of these things cautiously, as every Initiate would. But it is all as expressed in these few sentences of the Desatir:

> All that is on Earth, saith the Lord (Ormazd), is the shadow of something that is in the superior spheres. This luminous object (light, fire, etc.) is the shadow of that which is still more luminous than itself, and so on till it reaches ME, who am the light of lights.

In the Kabalistic books, and in the *Zohar* pre-eminently, the idea that everything objective on earth or in this Universe is the Shadow – Dyooknah – of the eternal Light or Deity, is very strong.

The Third Race was pre-eminently the bright shadow, at first, of the gods, whom tradition exiles on Earth after the allegorical war in Heaven, which became still more allegorical on Earth, for it was the war between spirit and matter. This war will last till the inner and divine man adjusts his outer terrestrial self to his own spiritual nature. Till then the dark and fierce passions of the former will be at eternal feud with his master, the Divine Man. But the animal will be tamed one day, because its nature will be changed, and harmony will reign once more between the two as before the "Fall," when even mortal man was created by the Elements and was not born.

The above is made clear in all the great theogonies, principally in the Grecian (see Hesiod and *Theogony*). The mutilation of Uranos by his son *Kronos*, who thus condemns him to impotency, has never been understood by the modern Mythographers. Yet, it is very plain, and having been universal (*Vide* footnote *infra*), it must have contained a great abstract and philosophical idea, now lost to our modern sages. This punishment in the allegory marks, indeed "a new period, a second phase in the development of creation," as justly remarked by Decharme (*Mythologie de la Grece Antique*, p. 7), who, however, renounces the attempt to explain it. Uranos has tried to oppose an impediment to that development, or natural evolution, by destroying all his children as soon as born. Uranos, who personifies all the creative powers of, and in, Chaos (Space, or the unmanifested Deity) is thus made to pay the penalty, for it is those powers which cause the *Pitris* to evolve primordial men from themselves – as, later on, these men evolve their progeny – without any sense or desire for procreation. The work of generation, suspended during a moment, passes into the hands of *Kronos*,* time, who unites himself with Rhea (the earth in esotericism – matter in general), and thus produces, after celestial – terrestrial Titans. The whole of this symbolism relates to the mysteries of Evolution.

This allegory is the exoteric version of the esoteric doctrine given in this part of our work. For in KRONOS we see the same story repeated again. As Uranos destroyed his children from Gaia (one, in the world of manifestation, with Aditi or the Great Cosmic Deep) by confining them in the bosom of the Earth, Tythea, so *Kronos* at this second stage of creation destroyed his children from Rhea – by devouring them. This is an allusion to the fruitless efforts of Earth or Nature alone to create real human men. (See our Stanzas III – X, *et seq*, and also Berosus' account of primeval creation.) Time swallows its own fruitless work. Then comes Zeus – Jupiter, who dethrones his father in his turn. Jupiter the Titan, is Prometheus, in one sense, and varies from Zeus, the Great "Father of the Gods." He is the "disrespectful son" in Hesiod. Hermes calls him the "Heavenly man" (*Pymander*), and even in the *Bible* he is found again under the name of Adam, and, later on – by transmutation – under that of Ham. Yet these are all personifications of the "sons of Wisdom." The necessary corroboration that Jupiter belongs to the purely human Atlantean cycle – if Uranus and *Kronos* who precede him are found insufficient – may be found in Hesiod, who tells us that the Immortals have made men and created the Golden and the Silver age (First and Second Races), while Jupiter created the generations

---

* KRONOS is not only Χρόνος *Cronos*, 'time', but also, as Bréal showed in his *Hercule et Cacus* (p. 57), comes from the root *Kar*, "to make, to create." Whether Bréal and Decharme, who quotes him, are as right in saying that in the *Vedas*, *Kronan* is a creative god, we have our doubts. Bréal probably meant Karma, or rather Visva-Karma, the creative god, the "Omnificent" and the "great Architect of the world."

of Bronze (an admixture of two elements), of Heroes, and the men of the age of Iron. After this he sends his fatal present, by Pandora, to Epimetheus, which present Hesiod calls "a fatal gift," or the first woman. It was a punishment, he explains, sent to man "for the theft of divine creative fire." Her apparition on earth is the signal of every kind of evil. Before her appearance, the human races lived happy, exempt from sickness and suffering – as the same races are made to live under Yima's rule, in the Mazdean *Vendidad*.

Thus, the four races being found mentioned by the oldest Greek poets, though very much confused anachronistically, our doctrines are once more corroborated by the classics. But this is all "Mythology" and poetry. What can modern science have to say to such an euhemerization of old fictions? The verdict is not difficult to foresee. Therefore an attempt must be made to answer by anticipation, and prove that fictions and empirical speculations are so much of the domain of that same science, that none of the men of learning have the slightest right, with such a heavy beam in their own eye, to point to the speck in the eye of the Occultist, even if that speck be not a figment of our opponents' imagination."

SD, ii 267–271

THE GOLDEN AGE

40. THEN THE THIRD AND FOURTH (*races*) BECAME TALL WITH PRIDE. WE ARE THE KINGS, WE ARE THE GODS (*a*).

41. THEY TOOK WIVES FAIR TO LOOK AT. WIVES FROM THE "MINDLESS," THE NARROW-HEADED. THEY BRED MONSTERS, WICKED DEMONS, MALE AND FEMALE. ALSO KHADO (*Dakini*) WITH LITTLE MINDS (*b*).

42. THEY BUILT TEMPLES FOR HUMAN BODY. MALE AND FEMALE THEY WORSHIPPED (*c*). THEN THE THIRD EYE ACTED NO LONGER (*d*).

(*a*) Such were the first truly physical men, whose first characteristic was – pride! It is the Third Race and the gigantic Atlanteans, the memory of whom lingered from one generation and race to another generation and race down to the days of Moses, and which found an objective form in those ante-diluvian giants, those terrible sorcerers and magicians, of whom the Roman Church has preserved such vivid and at the same time distorted legends. One who has read and studied the Commentaries on the archaic doctrine, will easily recognise in some Atlanteans, the prototypes of the Nimrods, the Builders of the Tower of Babel, the Hamites, and all these *tutti quanti* of "accursed memory," as theological literature expresses it: of those, in short, who have furnished posterity with the orthodox types of Satan. And this leads us naturally to inquire into the religious ethics of these early races, mythical as these may be.

What was the religion of the Third and Fourth Races? In the common acceptation of the term, neither the Lemurians, nor yet their progeny, the Lemuro-Atlanteans, had any, as they knew no dogma, nor had they to believe on faith. No sooner had the mental eye of man been opened to understanding, than the Third Race felt itself one with the ever-present as the ever to be unknown and invisible ALL, the One Universal Deity. Endowed with divine powers, and feeling in himself his inner God, each felt he was a Man-God in his nature, though an animal in his physical Self. The struggle between the two began from the very day they tasted of the fruit of the Tree of Wisdom, a struggle for life between the spiritual and the psychic, the psychic and the physical. Those who conquered the lower principles by obtaining mastery over the body, joined the "Sons of Light." Those who fell victims to their lower natures, became the slaves of Matter. From "Sons of Light and Wisdom" they ended by becoming the "Sons of Darkness." They had fallen in the battle of mortal life with Life immortal, and all those so fallen became the seed of the future generations of Atlanteans. *

At the dawn of his consciousness, the man of the Third Root Race had thus no beliefs that could be called religion. That is to say, he was equally as ignorant of "gay religions, full of pomp and gold" as of any system of faith or outward worship. But if the term is to be defined as the binding together of the masses in one form of reverence paid to those we feel higher than ourselves, of piety – as a feeling expressed by a child toward a loved parent – then even the earliest Lemurians had a religion – and a most beautiful one – from the very beginning of their intellectual life. Had they not their bright gods of the elements around them, and even within themselves? † Was not their childhood passed with, nursed and tendered by those who had given them life and called them forth to intelligent, conscious life? We are assured it was so, and we believe it. For the evolution of Spirit into matter could never have been achieved, nor would it have received its first impulse, had not the bright Spirits sacrificed their own respective super-ethereal essences to animate the man of clay, by endowing each of his inner principles with a portion, or rather, a reflection of that essence. The *Dhyanis* of the Seven Heavens (the seven planes of Being)

---

* The name is used here in the sense of, and as a synonym of "sorcerers." The Atlantean races were many, and lasted in their evolution for millions of years: all were not bad. They became so toward their end, as we (the fifth) are fast becoming now.

† The "Gods of the Elements" are by no means the Elementals. The latter are at best used by them as vehicles and materials in which to clothe themselves. . .

are the NOUMENOI of the actual and the future Elements, just as the Angels of the Seven Powers of nature – the grosser effects of which are perceived by us in what Science is pleased to call the "modes of motion" – the imponderable forces and what not – are the still higher *noumenoi* of still higher Hierarchies.

It was the "Golden Age" in those days of old, the age when the "gods walked the earth, and mixed freely with the mortals." Since then, the gods departed (i.e., became invisible), and later generations ended by worshipping their kingdoms – the Elements.

It was the Atlanteans, the first progeny of semi-divine man after his separation into sexes – hence the first-begotten and humanly-born mortals – who became the first "Sacrificers" to the god of matter. They stand in the far-away dim past, in ages more than prehistoric, as the prototype on which the great symbol of Cain was built, ‡ as the first anthropomorphists who worshipped form and matter. That worship degenerated very soon into self-worship, thence led to phallicism, or that which reigns supreme to this day in the symbolisms of every exoteric religion of ritual, dogma, and form. Adam and Eve became matter, or furnished the soil, Cain and Abel – the latter the life-bearing soil, the former "the tiller of that ground or field."

Thus the first Atlantean races, born on the Lemurian Continent, separated from their earliest tribes into the righteous and the unrighteous, into those who worshipped the one unseen Spirit of Nature, the ray of which man feels within himself – or the Pantheists, and those who offered fanatical worship to the Spirits of the Earth, the dark Cosmic, anthropomorphic Powers, with whom they made alliance. These were the earliest Gibborim, "the mighty men of renown in those days" (*Gen.* vi.), who become with the Fifth Race the *Kabirim*: *Kabiri* with the Egyptians and the Phœnicians, Titans with the Greeks, and *Râkshasas* and Daityas with the Indian races.

---

‡ Cain was the sacrificer, as shown at first in chap. iv. of *Genesis*, of "the fruit of the ground," of which he was first tiller, while Abel "brought of the firstlings of his flock" to the Lord. Cain is the symbol of the first male, Abel of the first female humanity, Adam and Eve being the types of the third race. (See "*The Mystery of Cain and Abel*".) The "murdering" is blood-shedding, but not taking life.

Such was the secret and mysterious origin of all the subsequent and modern religions, especially of the worship of the later Hebrews for their tribal god. At the same time this sexual religion was closely allied to, based upon and blended, so to say, with astronomical phenomena. The Lemurians gravitated toward the North Pole, or the Heaven of their Progenitors (the Hyperborean Continent); the Atlanteans, toward the Southern Pole, the pit, cosmically and terrestrially – whence breathe the hot passions blown into hurricanes by the cosmic Elementals, whose abode it is. The two poles were denominated, by the ancients, Dragons and Serpents – hence good and bad Dragons and Serpents, and also the names given to the "Sons of God" (Sons of Spirit and Matter): the good and bad Magicians. This is the origin of this dual and triple nature in man. The legend of the "Fallen Angels" in its esoteric signification, contains the key to the manifold contradictions of human character; it points to the secret of man's self-consciousness; it is the angle iron on which hinges his entire lifecycle – the history of his evolution and growth.

On a firm grasp of this doctrine depends the correct understanding of esoteric anthropogenesis. It gives a clue to the vexed question of the Origin of Evil, and shows how man himself is the separator of the ONE into various contrasted aspects.

The reader, therefore, will not be surprised if so considerable space is devoted in each case to an attempt to elucidate this difficult and obscure subject. A good deal must necessarily be said on its symbological aspect, because, by so doing, hints are given to the thoughtful student for his own investigations, and more light can thus be suggested than it is possible to convey in the technical phrases of a more formal, philosophical exposition. The "Fallen Angels," so-called, are Humanity itself. The Demon of Pride, Lust, Rebellion, and Hatred, has never had any being before the appearance of physical conscious man. It is man who has begotten, nurtured, and allowed the fiend to develop in his heart; he, again, who has contaminated the indwelling god in himself, by linking the pure spirit with the impure demon of matter. And, if the Kabalistic saying, *"Demon est Deus inversus"* finds its metaphysical and theoretical corroboration in dual manifested nature, its practical application is found in Mankind alone.

Thus it has now become self-evident that postulating as we do (*a*) the appearance of man before that of other mammalia, and even before the ages of the huge reptiles; (*b*) periodical deluges and glacial periods owing to the karmic disturbance of the axis; and chiefly (*c*) the birth of man from a Superior Being, or what materialism would call a supernatural Being, though it is only super-human – it is evident that our teachings have very few chances of an impartial hearing. Add to it the claim that a portion of the Mankind in the Third Race – all those Monads of men who had reached the highest point of Merit and Karma in the preceding *Manvantara* – owed their psychic and rational natures to divine Beings hypostasizing into their fifth principles, and the Secret Doctrine must lose caste in the eyes of not only Materialism but even of dogmatic Christianity. For, no sooner will the latter have learned that those angels are identical with their "Fallen" Spirits, than the esoteric tenet will be proclaimed most terribly heretical and pernicious.* The divine man dwelt in the animal, and, therefore, when the physiological separation took place in the natural course of evolution – when also "all the animal creation was untied," and males were attracted to females – that race fell, not because they had eaten of the fruit of Knowledge and knew good from evil, but because they knew no better. Propelled by the sexless creative instinct, the early sub-races had evolved an intermediate race in which, as hinted in the Stanzas, the higher *Dhyan-Chohans* had incarnated. † "When we have ascertained the extent of the Universe and learnt to know all that there is in it, we will multiply our race," answer the Sons of Will and Yoga

---

* It is, perhaps, with an eye to this degradation of the highest and purest Spirits, who broke through the intermediate planes of lower consciousness (the "Seven circles of fire" of Pymander), that St. James is made to say that "this Wisdom (*psüche* in the original) descended not from above, but is earthly, sensual, devilish"; and *Psüche* is *Manas*, the "human soul," the Spiritual Wisdom or Soul being *Buddhi*. Yet *Buddhi* per se, being so near the Absolute, is only latent consciousness.

† This is the "undying race" as it is called in Esotericism, and exoterically the fruitless generation of the first progeny of *Daksha*, who curses Narada, the divine *Rishi*, alleged to have dissuaded the Haryaswas and the Sabalâswas, the sons of *Daksha*, from procreating their species, by saying "Be born in the womb; there shall not be a resting place for thee in all these regions"; after this Narada, the representative of that race of fruitless ascetics, is said, as soon as he dies in one body, to be reborn in another.

to their brethren of the same race, who invite them to do as they do. This means that the great Adepts and Initiated ascetics will "multiply," i.e., once more produce Mind-born immaculate Sons – in the Seventh Root Race.

It is so stated in the *Purânas*, in *Adi Parvan* (p. 115) and *Brahmâ Purâna*, etc. In one portion of the *Pushkara Mahatmya*, moreover, the separation of the sexes is allegorized by *Daksha*, who, seeing that his will-born progeny (the "Sons of passive Yoga"), will not create men, "converts half himself into a female by whom he begets daughters," the future females of the Third Race which begat the giants of Atlantis, the Fourth Race, so called. In the *Vishnu Purâna* it is simply said that *Daksha*, the father of mankind, established sexual intercourse as the means of peopling the world.

Happily for the human race the "Elect Race" had already become the vehicle of incarnation of the (intellectually and spiritually) highest *Dhyanis* before Humanity had become quite material. When the last sub-races – save some lowest – of the Third Race had perished with the great Lemurian Continent, "the seeds of the Trinity of Wisdom" had already acquired the secret of immortality on Earth, that gift which allows the same great personality to step *ad libitum* from one worn-out body into another."

SD, ii 271–276

VISION AND KARMA

In the beginning, every class and family of living species was hermaphrodite and objectively one eyed. In the animal, whose form was as ethereal (astrally) as that of man, before the bodies of both began to evolve their coats of skin, viz., to evolve from within without the thick coating of physical substance or matter with its internal physiological mechanism – the third eye was primarily, as in man, the only seeing organ. The two physical front eyes developed * later on in both brute and man, whose organ of physical sight was, at the commencement of the Third Race, in the same position as that of some of the blind vertebrata, in our day, i.e., beneath an opaque skin. † Only the stages of the odd, or primeval eye, in man and brute, are now inverted, as the former has already passed that animal non-rational stage in the Third Round, and is ahead of mere brute creation by a whole plane of consciousness. Therefore, while the "Cyclopean" eye was, and still is, in

---

* But in a very different manner to that pictured by Hâckel as an "evolution by natural selection in the struggle for existence" ("*Pedigree of Man*", "Sense Organs," p. 335). The mere "thermal sensibility of the skin," to hypothetical light-waves, is absurdly incompetent to account for the beautiful combination of adaptations present in the eye. It has, moreover, been previously shown that "natural Selection" is a pure myth when credited with the origination of variations (*Vide infra*, Part III, on Darwinian mechanical causation); as the "survival of the fittest" can only take place after useful variations have sprung up, together with improved organisms. Whence came the "useful variations," which developed the eye? Only from "blind forces . . . without aim, without design?" The argument is puerile. The true solution of the mystery is to be found in the impersonal Divine Wisdom, in its IDEATION - reflected through matter.

† Palaeontology has ascertained that in the animals of the Cenozoic age - the Saurians especially, such as the ante-diluvian Labyrinthodon, whose fossil skull exhibits a perforation otherwise inexplicable - the third, or odd eye must have been much developed. Several naturalists, among others E. Korscheldt, feel convinced that whereas, notwithstanding the opaque skin covering it, such an eye in the reptiles of the present period can only distinguish light from darkness (as the human eyes do when bound with a handkerchief, or even tightly closed), in the now extinct animals that eye functioned and was a real organ of vision.

man the organ of spiritual sight, in the animal it was that of objective vision. And this eye, having performed its function, was replaced, in the course of physical evolution from the simple to the complex, by two eyes, and thus was stored and laid aside by nature for further use in Aeons to come.

This explains why the pineal gland reached its highest development proportionately with the lowest physical development. It is the *vertebrata* in which it is the most prominent and objective, and in man it is most carefully hidden and inaccessible, except to the anatomist. No less light is thrown thereby on the future physical, spiritual, and intellectual state of mankind, in periods corresponding on parallel lines with other past periods, and always on the lines of ascending and descending cyclic evolution and development. Thus, a few centuries before the *Kali Yuga* – the black age which began nearly 5,000 years ago – it was said (paraphrased into comprehensible sentences):

> We (the Fifth Root Race) in our first half (of duration) onward (on the now ASCENDING arc of the cycle) are on the mid point of (or between) the First and the Second Races – falling downward (i.e., the races were then on the descending arc of the cycle). . . . . Calculate for thyself, Lanoo, and see. (*Commentary* xx)

Calculating as advised, we find that during that transitional period – namely, in the second half of the First Spiritual ethero-astral race – nascent mankind was devoid of the intellectual brain element. As it was on its descending line, and as we are parallel to it, on the ascending, we are, therefore devoid of the Spiritual element, which is now replaced by the intellectual. For, remember well, as we are in the *manasa* period of our cycle of races, or in the Fifth, we have, therefore, crossed the meridian point of the perfect adjustment of Spirit and Matter – or that equilibrium between brain intellect and Spiritual perception. One important point has, however, to be borne in mind.

We are only in the Fourth Round, and it is in the Fifth that the full development of *Manas*, as a direct ray from the Universal MAHAT – a ray unimpeded by matter – will be finally reached. Nevertheless, as every sub-race and nation have their cycles and stages of developmental evolution repeated on a smaller scale, it must be the more so in the case of a Root Race. Our race then has, as a Root Race, crossed the equatorial line and is cycling onward on the Spiritual side, but some of our sub-races still find themselves on the shadowy descending arc of their respective national cycles, while others again – the oldest – having crossed their crucial point, which alone decides whether a race, a nation, or a tribe will live or perish, are at the apex of spiritual development as sub-races.

It becomes comprehensible now why the "odd eye" has been gradually transformed into a simple gland, after the physical Fall of those we have agreed to call the "Lemurians."

It is a curious fact that it is especially in human beings that the cerebral hemispheres and the lateral ventricles have been developed, and that the *optic thalami, corpora quadrigemina,* and *corpora striata* are the principal parts which are developed in the mammalian brain. Moreover it is asserted that the intellect of any man may to some extent be gauged by the development of the central convolutions and the fore part of the cerebral hemispheres. It would seem a natural corollary that if the development and increased size of the pineal gland may be considered to be an index of the astral capacities and spiritual proclivities of any man, there will be a corresponding development of that part of the cranium, or an increase in the size of the pineal gland at the expense of the hinder part of the cerebral hemispheres. It is a curious speculation which would receive a confirmation in this case. We should see, below and behind, the cerebellum which has been held to be the seat of all the animal proclivities of a human being, and which is allowed by science to be the great centre for all the physiologically co-ordinated movements of the body, such as walking, eating, etc., etc.; in front, the fore-part of the brain – the cerebral hemispheres – the part especially connected with the development of the intellectual powers in man; and in the middle, dominating them both, and especially the animal functions, the developed pineal gland, in connection with the more highly evolved, or spiritual man.

It must be remembered that these are only physical correspondences, just as the ordinary human brain is the registering organ of memory, but not memory itself.

This is, then, the organ which gave rise to so many legends and traditions, among others to that of man with one head but two faces. These may be found in several Chinese works, besides being referred to in the Chaldean fragments. Apart from the work already cited – the Shan Hai King, compiled by King Chia from engravings on nine urns made 2,255 B.C., by the Emperor Yu, they may be found in another work, called the "*Bamboo Books*," and in a third one, the "Rh Ya" – "initiated according to tradition by Chow Kung, uncle of Wu Wang, the first Emperor of the Chow Dynasty, B.C., 1,122" – says Mr. Ch. Gould in his "*Mythical Monsters*." The *Bamboo Books* contain the ancient annals of China, found A.D. 279 at the opening of the grave of King Seang of Wai, who died B.C. 295. Both these works mention men with two faces on one head – one in front and one behind (p. 27).

Now that which the students of Occultism ought to know is that THE "THIRD EYE" IS INDISSOLUBLY CONNECTED WITH KARMA. The tenet is so mysterious that very few have heard of it.

The "eye of Siva" did not become entirely atrophied before the close of the Fourth Race. When spirituality and all the divine powers and attributes of the *deva*-man of the Third had been made the hand-maidens of the newly-awakened physiological and psychic passions of the physical man, instead of the reverse, the eye lost its powers. But such was the law of Evolution, and it was, in strict accuracy, no FALL. The sin was not in using those newly-developed powers, but in misusing them, in making of the tabernacle, designed to contain a god, the fane of every spiritual iniquity. And if we say "sin" it is merely that everyone should understand our meaning, as the term Karma *
would be the right one to use in this case, while the reader who would feel perplexed at the use of the term "spiritual" instead of "physical" iniquity, is reminded of the fact that there can be no physical iniquity. The body is simply the irresponsible organ, the tool of the psychic, if

---

* Karma is a word of many meanings, and has a special term for almost every one of its aspects. It means, as a synonym of sin, the performance of some action for the attainment of an object of worldly, hence selfish, desire, which cannot fail to be hurtful to somebody else. Karman is action, the Cause; and Karma again is "the law of ethical causation"; the effect of an act produced egotistically, when the great law of harmony depends on altruism.

not of the "Spiritual man." While in the case of the Atlanteans, it was precisely the Spiritual being which sinned, the Spirit element being still the "Master" principle in man, in those days. Thus it is in those days that the heaviest Karma of the Fifth Race was generated by our Monads.

As this sentence may again be found puzzling, it is better that it should be explained for the benefit of those who are ignorant of the theosophical teachings.

Questions with regard to Karma and rebirths are constantly offered, and a great confusion seems to exist upon this subject. Those who are born and bred in the Christian faith, and have been trained in the idea that a new soul is created by God for every newly-born infant, are among the most perplexed. They ask whether in such case the number of incarnating Monads on earth is limited, to which they are answered in the affirmative. For, however countless, in our conceptions, the number of the incarnating monads – even if we take into account the fact that ever since the Second Race, when their respective seven groups were furnished with bodies, several births and deaths may be allowed for every second of time in the aeons already passed – still, there must be a limit. It was stated that Karma-Nemesis, whose bond-maid is Nature, adjusted everything in the most harmonious manner, and that, therefore, the fresh pouring-in, or arrival of new Monads, had ceased as soon as Humanity had reached its full physical development. No fresh Monads have incarnated since the middle point of the Atlanteans. Hence, remembering that, save in the case of young children, and of individuals whose lives were violently cut off by some accident, no Spiritual Entity can reincarnate before a period of many centuries has elapsed, such gaps alone must show that the number of Monads is necessarily finite and limited. Moreover, a reasonable time must be given to other animals for their evolutionary progress.

Hence the assertion that many of us are now working off the effects of the evil Karmic causes produced by us in Atlantean bodies. The Law of KARMA is inextricably interwoven with that of Reincarnation."

SD, ii 299–303

THE CRUCIFIXION OF PROMETHEUS

The foregoing teachings of the SECRET DOCTRINE, supplemented by universal traditions, must now have demonstrated that the *Brâhmanas* and *Purânas*, the *Yâthâs* and other Mazdean Scriptures, down to the Egyptian, Greek, and Roman, and finally to the Jewish Sacred records, all have the same origin. None are meaningless and baseless stories, invented to entrap the unwary profane: all are allegories intended to convey, under a more or less fantastic veil, the great truths gathered in the same field of pre-historic tradition. Space forbids us from entering, in these two volumes, into further and more minute details with respect to the four Races which preceded our own. But before offering to the student the history of the psychic and spiritual evolution of the direct ante-diluvian fathers of our Fifth (Aryan) humanity, and before demonstrating its bearing upon all the other side branches grown from the same trunk, we have to elucidate a few more facts. It has been shown, on the evidence of the whole ancient literary world, and the intuitional speculations of more than one philosopher and scientist of the later ages, that the tenets of our Esoteric Doctrine are corroborated by inferential as well as by direct proof in almost every case. That neither the "legendary" giants, nor the lost continents, nor yet the evolution of the preceding races, are quite baseless tales. In the Addenda which close this volume, science will find itself more than once unable to reply; they will, it is hoped, finally dispose of every sceptical remark with regard to the sacred number in nature, and our figures in general. (*Vide* §§ on the Septenaries.)

Meanwhile, one task is left incomplete: that of disposing of that most pernicious of all the theological dogmas – the CURSE under which mankind is alleged to have suffered ever since the supposed disobedience of Adam and Eve in the bower of Eden.

Creative powers in man were the gift of divine wisdom, not the result of sin. This is clearly instanced in the paradoxical behaviour of Jehovah, who first curses Adam and Eve (or Humanity) for the supposed committed crime, and then blesses his "chosen people" by saying "Be fruitful and multiply, and replenish the earth" (*Gen.* ix. 1). The curse was not brought on mankind by the Fourth Race, for the comparatively sinless Third Race, the still more gigantic ante-diluvians, had perished in the same way; hence the Deluge was no punishment, but simply a result of a periodical and geological law. Nor was the curse of KARMA called down upon them for seeking natural union, as all the mindless animal world does in its proper seasons, but, for abusing the creative power, for desecrating the divine gift, and wasting the life essence for no purpose except bestial personal gratification. When understood, the third chapter of *Genesis* will be found to refer to the Adam and Eve of the closing Third and the commencing Fourth Races. In the beginning, conception was as easy for woman as it was for all animal creation. Nature had never intended that woman should bring forth her young ones "in sorrow." Since that period, however, during the evolution of the Fourth Race, there came enmity between its seed, and the "Serpent's" seed, the seed or product of Karma and divine wisdom. For the seed of woman or lust, bruised the head of the seed of the fruit of wisdom and knowledge, by turning the holy mystery of procreation into animal gratification; hence the law of Karma "bruised the heel" of the Atlantean race, by gradually changing physiologically, morally, physically, and mentally, the whole nature of the Fourth Race of mankind, * until, from the healthy King of animal creation of the Third Race, man became in the Fifth, our

---

* How wise and grand, how far-seeing and morally beneficent are the laws of *Manu* on connubial life, when compared with the licence tacitly allowed to man in civilized countries. That those laws have been neglected for the last two millenniums does not prevent us from admiring their forethought. The Brahmin was a *grihasta*, a family man, till a certain period of his life, when, after begetting a son, he broke with married life and became a chaste Yogi. His very connubial life was regulated by his Brahmin astrologer in accordance with his nature. Therefore, in such countries as the Punjab, for instance, where the lethal influence of Mussulman, and later on of European, licentiousness, has hardly touched the orthodox Aryan castes, one still finds the finest men – so far as stature and physical strength go – on the whole globe; whereas the mighty men of old have found themselves replaced in the Deccan, and especially in Bengal, by men whose generation becomes with every century (and almost with every year) dwarfed and weakened.

race, a helpless, scrofulous being, and has now become the wealthiest heir on the globe to constitutional and hereditary diseases, the most consciously and intelligently bestial of all animals! *

This is the real CURSE from the physiological standpoint, almost the only one touched upon in the Kabalistic esotericism. Viewed from this aspect, the curse is undeniable, for it is evident. The intellectual evolution, in its progress hand-in-hand with the physical, has certainly been a curse instead of a blessing – a gift quickened by the "Lords of Wisdom," who have poured on the human *manas* the fresh dew of their own spirit and essence. The divine Titan has then suffered in vain, and one feels inclined to regret his benefaction to mankind, and sigh for those days so graphically depicted by Aeschylus, in his "*Prometheus Bound*," when, at the close of the first Titanic age (the age that followed that of ethereal man, of the pious Kandu and Pramlocha), nascent, physical mankind, still mindless and (physiologically) senseless, is described as –

> Seeing, they saw in vain;
> Hearing, they heard not; but like shapes in dreams,
> Through the long time all things at random mixed.

Our Saviours, the *Agnishwatta* and other divine "Sons of the Flame of Wisdom" (personified by the Greeks in Prometheus †), may well, in

---

* Diseases and over-population are facts that can never be denied.

† In Mrs. Anna Swanwick's volumes, "*The Dramas of Aeschylus*," it is said of "*Prometheus Bound*" (Vol. II, pp. 146, 147), that Prometheus truly appears in it "as the champion and benefactor of mankind, whose condition . . . . is depicted as weak and miserable in the extreme. . . . Zeus, it is said, proposed to annihilate these puny ephemerals, and to plant upon the earth a new race in their stead." We see the Lords of Being doing likewise, and exterminating the first product of nature and the sea, in the Stanzas (V, *et seq.*). . . . Prometheus represents himself as having frustrated this design, and as being consequently subjected, for the sake of mortals, to the most agonising pain, inflicted by the remorseless cruelty of Zeus. We have, thus, the Titan, the symbol of finite reason and free will (of intellectual humanity, or the higher aspect of *Manas*), depicted as the sublime philanthropist, while Zeus, the supreme deity of Hellas, is portrayed as the cruel and obdurate despot, a character peculiarly revolting to Athenian sentiment." The reason for it is explained further on. The "Supreme Deity" bears, in every ancient Pantheon – including that of the Jews – a dual character, composed of light and shadow.

the injustice of the human heart, be left unrecognized and unthanked. They may, in our ignorance of the truth, be indirectly cursed for Pandora's gift: but to find themselves proclaimed and declared by the mouth of the clergy, the EVIL ONES, is too heavy a Karma for "Him" "who dared alone " – when Zeus "ardently desired" to quench the entire human race – to save "that mortal race" from perdition, or, as the suffering Titan is made to say:

> From sinking blasted down to Hades' gloom.
> For this by the dire tortures I am bent,
> Grievous to suffer, piteous to behold,
> I who did mortals pity! . . . .

The chorus remarking very pertinently:

> Vast boon was this thou gavest unto mortals . . . .

Prometheus answers:

> Yea, and besides 'twas I that gave them fire.
> CHORUS: Have now these short-lived creatures flame-eyed fire?
> PROM.: Ay, and by it full many arts will learn. . . . .

But, with the arts, the fire received has turned into the greatest curse: the animal element, and consciousness of its possession, has changed periodical instinct into chronic animalism and sensuality. ‡ It is this which hangs over humanity like a heavy funereal pall. Thus arises the responsibility of free will; the Titanic passions which represent humanity in its darkest aspect; "the restless insatiability of the lower passions and desires, when, with self-asserting insolence, they bid defiance to the restraints of law." §

Prometheus having endowed man, according to Plato's "*Protagoras*," with that "wisdom which ministers to physical well being," but the lower aspect of *manas* of the animal (*Kama*) having remained unchanged, instead of "an untainted mind, heaven's first gift" (Aeschylus), there was

---

‡ The animal world, having simple instinct to guide it, has its seasons of procreation, and the sexes become neutralized during the rest of the year. Therefore, the free animal knows sickness but once in its life – before it dies.

§ Introduction to "*Prometheus Bound*," p. 152.

created the eternal vulture of the ever unsatisfied desire, of regret and despair coupled with "the dreamlike feebleness that fetters the blind race of mortals" (p. 556), unto the day when Prometheus is released by his heaven-appointed deliverer, Herakles.

Now Christians – Roman Catholics especially – have tried to prophetically connect this drama with the coming of Christ. No greater mistake could be made. The true theosophist, the pursuer of divine wisdom and worshipper of ABSOLUTE perfection – the unknown deity which is neither Zeus nor Jehovah – will demur to such an idea. Pointing to antiquity he will prove that there never was an original sin, but only an abuse of physical intelligence – the psychic being guided by the animal, and both putting out the light of the spiritual. He will say, "All ye who can read between the lines, study ancient wisdom in the old dramas – the Indian and the Greek; read carefully the one just mentioned, one enacted on the theatres of Athens 2,400 years ago, namely 'Prometheus Bound'." The myth belongs to neither Hesiod nor Aeschylus, but, as Bunsen says, it "is older than the Hellenes themselves," for it belongs, in truth, to the dawn of human consciousness. The Crucified Titan is the personified symbol of the collective Logos, the "Host," and of the "Lords of Wisdom" or the HEAVENLY MAN, who incarnated in Humanity. Moreover, as his name Pro-me-theus, meaning "he who sees before him" or futurity, shows* – in the arts he devised

---

* From πρὸ μῆτις, "forethought." "Professor Kuhn," we are told in the above-named volumes of "The Dramas of Aeschylus," "considers the name of the Titan to be derived from the Sanskrit word Pramantha, the instrument used for kindling fire. The root mand or manth, implies rotatory motion, and the word manthami (used to denote the process of fire kindling) acquired the secondary sense of snatching away; hence we find another word of the same stock, pramatha, signifying theft." This is very ingenious, but perhaps not altogether correct; besides, there is a very prosaic element in it. No doubt in physical nature, the higher forms may develop from the lower ones, but it is hardly so in the world of thought. And as we are told that the word manthami passed into the Greek language and became the word manthano, to learn; that is to say, to appropriate knowledge; whence prometheia, fore-knowledge, fore-thought; we may find, in searching, a more poetical origin for the "fire-bringer" than that displayed in its Sanskrit origin. The Svastica, the sacred sign and the instrument for kindling sacred fire, may explain it better. "Prometheus, the fire-bringer, is the Pramantha personified," goes on the author; "he finds his prototype in the Aryan Matarisvan, a divine . . . . personage, closely associated with the fire god of the Veda, Agni. . . ." Mati, in Sanskrit, is "understanding," and a

and taught to humanity, psychological insight was not the least. For as
he complains to the daughters of Oceanos:

> Of prophecies the various modes I fixed,
> And among dreams did first discriminate
> The truthful vision . . . and mortals guided
> To a mysterious art. . . . .
> All arts to mortals from Prometheus came. . .

Leaving for a few pages the main subject, let us pause and see what
may be the hidden meaning of this, the most ancient as it is the most
suggestive of traditional allegories. As it relates directly to the early
races, this will be no real digression.

The subject of Aeschylus' drama (the trilogy is lost) is known to all
cultured readers. The demi-god robs the gods (the *Elohim*) of their secret
– the mystery of the creative fire. For this sacrilegious attempt he is
struck down by KRONOS † and delivered unto Zeus, the FATHER and
creator of a mankind which he would wish to have blind intellectually,
and animal-like, a personal deity, which will not see MAN "like one of
us." Hence Prometheus, "the fire and light-giver," is chained on Mount
Caucasus and condemned to suffer torture. But the triform Fates
(Karma), whose decrees, as the Titan says, even Zeus:

> E'en he the fore-ordained cannot escape. . .

– ordain that those sufferings will last only to that day when a son of
Zeus –

> Ay, a son bearing stronger than his sire (787)
> One of thine (Io's) own descendants it must be. . (791)

– is born. This "Son" will deliver Prometheus (the suffering Humanity)
from his own fatal gift. His name is, "He who has to come. . "

On the authority, then, of these few lines, which, like any other
allegorical sentence, may be twisted into almost any meaning;

---

synonym of MAHAT and *manas*, and must be of some account in the origin of the
name: *Promati* is the son of *Fohat*, and has his story also.

† *Kronos* is "time," and thus the allegory becomes very suggestive. (See closing
pages of this Sub-section.)

namely, on the words pronounced by Prometheus and addressed to Io, the daughter of Inachos, persecuted by Zeus – a whole prophecy is constructed by some Catholic writers. Says the crucified Titan:

> And, portent past belief, the speaking oaks
> By which full clearly, in no riddling phrase
> Wast hailed as the illustrious spouse of Zeus
> . . . . (v. 853).
> . . . . stroking thee
> With touch alone of unalarming hand;
> Then thou dark Epaphos shalt bear, whose name
> Records his sacred gendering . . . . (870)

This was construed by several fanatics – des Mousseaux and de Mirville amongst others – into a clear prophecy. Io "is the mother of God," we are told; and "dark Epaphos" – Christ. But, the latter has not dethroned his father, except metaphorically, if one has to regard Jehovah as that "Father"; nor has the Christian Saviour hurled his Father down into Hades. Prometheus says, in verse 930, that Zeus will be humbled yet, as for himself:

> . . . . such marriage he prepares
> Which from his throne of power to nothingness
> Shall hurl him down; so shall be all fulfilled
> His father KRONOS' curse . . . .
> . . . . Then let him sit
> Confiding in his lofty thunder-peals,
> And wielding with both hands the fiery bolt;
> For these shall not avail, but fail he shall, A fall disgraceful, not to be endured . . . . " (v. 980).

"Dark Epaphos" was the Dionysos-Sabazius, the son of Zeus and of Demeter in the Sabasian Mysteries, during which the "father of the gods," assuming the shape of a Serpent, begot on Demeter, Dionysos, or the solar Bacchus. Io is the moon, and at the same time the EVE of a new race, and so is Demeter – in the present case. The Promethean myth is a prophecy indeed, but it does not relate to any of the cyclic Saviours who have appeared periodically in various countries and among various nations, in their transitionary conditions of evolution. It points to the last of the mysteries of cyclic transformations, in the series of which mankind, having passed from the ethereal to the solid physical state, from spiritual to physiological procreation, is now carried onward on the opposite arc of the cycle, toward that second phase of its primitive state, when woman knew no man, and human progeny was created, not begotten.

That state will return to it and to the world at large, when the latter shall discover and really appreciate the truths which underlie this vast problem of sex. It will be like "the light that never shone on sea or land," and has to come to men through the Theosophical Society. That light will lead on and up to the true spiritual intuition. Then (as expressed once in a letter to a theosophist), "the world will have a race of Buddhas and Christs, for the world will have discovered that individuals have it in their own powers to procreate Buddha-like children – or demons." "When that knowledge comes, all dogmatic religions, and with these the demons, will die out."

SD, ii 410–415

ONE OF THE FUNCTIONS OF ZEUS

There is one eternal Law in nature, one that always tends to adjust contraries and to produce final harmony. It is owing to this law of spiritual development superseding the physical and purely intellectual, that mankind will become freed from its false gods, and find itself finally — SELF-REDEEMED.

In its final revelation, the old myth of Prometheus — his proto- and anti-types being found in every ancient theogony — stands in each of them at the very origin of physical evil, because at the threshold of human physical life. KRONOS is "Time," whose first law is that the order of the successive and harmonious phases in the process of evolution during cyclic development should be strictly preserved — under the severe penalty of abnormal growth with all its ensuing results. It was not in the programme of natural development that man — higher animal though he may be — should become at once — intellectually, spiritually, and psychically — the demi-god he is on earth, while his physical frame remains weaker and more helpless and ephemeral than that of almost any huge mammal. The contrast is too grotesque and violent; the tabernacle much too unworthy of its indwelling god. The gift of Prometheus thus became a CURSE — though foreknown and foreseen by the HOST personified in that personage, as his name well shows.* It is in this that rests, at one and the same time, its sin and its

---

* *Vide supra*, a foot-note concerning the etymology of promh'tiß or forethought. Prometheus confesses it in the drama when saying:

"Oh! holy Ether, swiftly-winged gales . . . .
Behold what I, a god, from gods endure . . . .
And yet what say I? Clearly I foreknew
All that must happen . . . .
. . . . The Destined it behoves,
As best I may, to bear, for well I wot
How incontestable the strength of Fate . . . . (105)

"Fate" stands here for KARMA, or Nemesis.

redemption. For the Host that incarnated in a portion of humanity, though led to it by Karma or Nemesis, preferred free-will to passive slavery, intellectual self-conscious pain and even torture "while myriad time shall flow" — to inane, imbecile, instinctual beatitude. Knowing such an incarnation was premature and not in the programme of nature, the heavenly host, "Prometheus," still sacrificed itself to benefit thereby, at least, one portion of mankind.[†] But while saving man from mental darkness, they inflicted upon him the tortures of the self-consciousness of his responsibility — the result of his free will — besides every ill to which mortal man and flesh are heir to. This torture Prometheus accepted for himself, since the Host became henceforward blended with the tabernacle prepared for them, which was still unachieved at that period of formation.

Spiritual evolution being incapable of keeping pace with the physical, once its homogeneity was broken by the admixture, the gift thus became the chief cause, if not the sole origin of Evil. [‡] The allegory which shows KRONOS cursing Zeus for dethroning him (in the primitive "golden" age of Saturn, when all men were demi-gods), and for creating a physical race of men weak and helpless in comparison; and then as delivering to his (Zeus') revenge the culprit, who despoiled the gods of their prerogative of creation and who thereby raised man to their level, intellectually and spiritually — is highly philosophical. In the case of Prometheus, Zeus represents the Host of the primeval progenitors, of the PITAR, the "Fathers" who created man senseless

---

† Mankind is obviously divided into god-informed men and lower human creatures. The intellectual difference between the Aryan and other civilized nations and such savages as the South Sea Islanders, is inexplicable on any other grounds. No amount of culture, nor generations of training amid civilization, could raise such human specimens as the Bushmen, the Veddhas of Ceylon, and some African tribes, to the same intellectual level as the Aryans, the Semites, and the Turanians so called. The "sacred spark" is missing in them and it is they who are the only inferior races on the globe, now happily — owing to the wise adjustment of nature which ever works in that direction — fast dying out. Verily mankind is "of one blood," but not of the same essence. We are the hot-house, artificially quickened plants in nature, having in us a spark, which in them is latent.

‡ The philosophical view of Indian metaphysics places the Root of Evil in the differentiation of the Homogeneous into the Heterogeneous, of the unit into plurality.

and without any mind; while the divine Titan stands for the Spiritual creators, the devas who "fell" into generation. The former are spiritually lower, but physically stronger, than the "Prometheans": therefore, the latter are shown conquered. "The lower Host, whose work the Titan spoiled and thus defeated the plans of Zeus," was on this earth in its own sphere and plane of action; whereas, the superior Host was an exile from Heaven, who had got entangled in the meshes of matter. They (the inferior "Host") were masters of all the Cosmic and lower titanic forces; the higher Titan possessed only the intellectual and spiritual fire. This drama of the struggle of Prometheus with the Olympic tyrant and despot, sensual Zeus, one sees enacted daily within our actual mankind: the lower passions chain the higher aspirations to the rock of matter, to generate in many a case the vulture of sorrow, pain, and repentance. In every such case one sees once more —

"A god . . . in fetters, anguish fraught;
The foe of Zeus, in hatred held by all. . . . "
A god, bereft even of that supreme consolation of Prometheus, who suffered in self-sacrifice —
"For that to men he bare too fond a mind. . ."

as the divine Titan is moved by altruism, but the mortal man by Selfishness and Egoism in every instance.

The modern Prometheus has now become Epi-metheus, "he who sees only after the event"; because the universal philanthropy of the former has long ago degenerated into selfishness and self-adoration. Man will rebecome the free Titan of old, but not before cyclic evolution has re-established the broken harmony between the two natures — the terrestrial and the divine; after which he becomes impermeable to the lower titanic forces, invulnerable in his personality, and immortal in his individuality, which cannot happen before every animal element is eliminated from his nature. When man understands that "Deus non fecit mortem" (Sap. I., 13), but that man has created it himself, he will re-become the Prometheus before his Fall.

For the full symbolism of Prometheus and the origin of this mythos in Greece, the reader is referred to Part II. of this Volume, chapter "A

Second Key to Prometheus," etc. In the said Part — a kind of supplement to the present portion — every additional information is given upon those tenets that will be the most controverted and questioned. This work is so heterodox, when confronted with the acknowledged standards of theology and modern science, that no proof which tends to show that these standards often usurp an illegal authority should be neglected.

SD, ii 420-422

THE FATHER OF MORTALS

In our modern day there does not exist the slightest doubt in the minds of the best European symbologists that the name Prometheus possessed the greatest and most mysterious significance in antiquity. While giving the history of Deukalion, whom the Bœotians regarded as the ancestor of the human races, and who was the Son of Prometheus, according to the significant legend, the author of the *Mythologie de la Grece Antique* remarks: "Thus Prometheus is something more than the archetype of humanity; he is its generator. In the same way that we saw Hephaestus moulding the first woman (Pandora) and endowing her with life, so Prometheus kneads the moist clay, of which he fashions the body of the first man whom he will endow with the soul spark" (Apollodorus, I., 7, 1). After the Flood of Deukalion, Zeus, it was taught, had commanded Prometheus and Athena to call forth a new race of men from the mire left by the waters of the deluge (Ovid, *Metam.* 1, 81. *Etym. M. v. Προμηθεύς*); and in the day of Pausanias the slime which the hero had used for this purpose was still shown in Phocea (*Paus.* x, 4, 4). "On several archaic monuments one still sees Prometheus modelling a human body, either alone or with Athena's help" (*Myth. Grèce Ant.* 246).

The same authors remind the world of another equally mysterious personage, though one less generally known than Prometheus, whose legend offers remarkable analogies with that of the Titan. The name of this second ancestor and generator is Phoroneus, the hero of an ancient poem, now unfortunately no longer extant – the *Phoronidae*. His legend was localized in Argolis, where a perpetual flame was preserved on his altar as a reminder that he was the bringer of fire upon earth (*Pausanias*, 11, 19, 5; Cf. 20, 3.) A benefactor of men as Prometheus was, he had made them participators of every bliss on earth. Plato (*Timæus*, p. 22), and Clemens Alexandrinus (*Strom.* 1, p. 380) say that Phoroneus was the first man, or "the father of mortals." His genealogy, which assigns to him as his father Inachos, the river, reminds one of that of

Prometheus, which makes that Titan the son of the *Oceanid* Clymene. But the mother of Phoroneus was the nymph Melia, a significant descent which distinguishes him from Prometheus.

Melia, Decharme thinks, is the personification of the ash tree, whence, according to Hesiod, issued the race of the age of Bronze *
(*Opera et Dies*, 142–145); and which with the Greeks is the celestial tree common to every Aryan mythology. This ash is the *Yggdrasil* of the Norse antiquity, which the Norns sprinkle daily with the waters from the fountain of Urd, that it may not wither. It remains verdant till the last days of the Golden Age. Then the Norns – the three sisters who gaze respectively into the Past, the Present, and the Future – make known the decree of Fate (Karma, Orlog), but men are conscious only of the Present. But when Gultweig comes (the golden ore) "the bewitching enchantress who, thrice cast into the fire, arises each time more beautiful, and fills the souls of gods and men with unapproachable longing, then the Norns . . . enter into being, and the blessed peace of childhood's dreams passes away, and Sin comes into existence with all its evil consequences . . ." and KARMA (See *"Asgard and the Gods,"* p. 10–12). The thrice purified Gold is – *Manas*, the Conscious Soul.

With the Greeks, the "ash tree" represented the same idea. Its luxuriant boughs are the sidereal heaven, golden by day and studded with stars by night – the fruits of Melia and *Yggdrasil*, under whose protecting shadow humanity lived during the Golden Age without desire as without any fear . . . "That tree had a fruit, or an inflamed bough, which was lightning," Decharme guesses.

And here steps in the killing materialism of the age, that peculiar twist in the modern mind, which, like a Northern blast, bends all on its way, and freezes every intuition, allowing it no hand in the physical speculations of the day. After having seen in Prometheus no better than fire by friction, the learned author of the *"Mythologie de la Grece Antique"*

---

* According to the Occult teaching, three *yugas* passed away during the time of the Third Root Race, i.e., the *Satya*, the *Treta*, and the *Dvâpara yuga*, answering to the golden age of its early innocence: to the silver, when it reached its maturity: and to the Bronze age, when, separating into sexes, they became the mighty demi-gods of old.

perceives in this "fruit" a trifle more than an allusion to terrestrial fire and its discovery. It is no longer fire, owing to the fall of lightning setting some dry fuel in a blaze, and thus revealing all its priceless benefits to Palaeolithic men – but something more mysterious this time, though still as earthly. . . . "A divine bird, nestled in the boughs of the celestial ash tree, stole that bough (or the fruit) and carried it down on the earth in its bill. Now the Greek word φορώνευς is the rigid equivalent of the Sanskrit word *bhuranyu* ('the rapid') an epithet of Agni, considered as the carrier of the divine spark. Phoroneus, son of Melia or of the celestial ash, thus corresponds to a conception far more ancient, probably, than that one which transformed the *pramântha* (of the old Aryan Hindus) into the Greek Prometheus. Phoroneus is the (personified) bird, that brings the heavenly lightning to the Earth. Traditions relating to the birth and origin of the race of Bronze, and those which made of Phoroneus the father of the Argians, are an evidence to us that this thunderbolt (or lightning), as in the legends of Hephaestus or Prometheus, was the origin of the human race" (266).

This still affords us no more than the external meaning of the symbols and the allegory. It is now supposed that the name of Prometheus has been unriddled, and the modern mythologists and Orientalists see in it no longer what their fathers saw on the authority of the whole of classical antiquity. They only find therein something far more appropriate to the spirit of the age, namely, a phallic element. But the name of Phoroneus, as well as that of Prometheus, bears not one, nor even two, but a series of esoteric meanings. Both relate to the seven celestial fires: to Agni Abhimânin, his three sons, and their forty-five sons, constituting the forty-nine fires. Do all these numbers relate only to the terrestrial mode of fire and to the flame of sexual passion? Did the Hindu Aryan mind never soar above such purely sensual conceptions? that mind which is declared by Prof. Max Muller to be the most spiritual and mystically inclined on the whole globe? The number of those fires alone ought to have suggested an inkling of the truth.

We are told that one is no longer permitted, in this age of rational thought, to explain the name of Prometheus as the old Greeks did. The latter, it seems, "basing themselves on the false analogy of προμηθεύς with the verb προμανθάνειν, saw in him the type of the 'foreseeing' man, to whom, for the sake of symmetry, a brother was added – Epimetheus, or 'he who takes counsel after the event.' " But now the Orientalists have decided otherwise. They know the real meaning of the two names better than those who invented them.

The legend is based upon an event of universal importance. It was built "to commemorate a great event which must have strongly impressed itself upon the imagination of the first witnesses to it, and its remembrance has never since faded out from popular memory." What is it? Laying aside every poetical fiction, all those dreams of the golden age, let us imagine – argue the modern scholars – in all its gross realism, the first miserable state of humanity, the striking picture of which was traced for us after Aeschylus by Lucretius, and the exact truth of which is now confirmed by science, and then one may understand better that a new life really began for man, on that day when he saw the first spark produced by the friction of two pieces of wood, or from the veins of a flint. How could man help feeling gratitude to that mysterious and marvellous being which they were henceforth enabled to create at their will, and which was no sooner born, than it grew and expanded, developing with singular power. "This terrestrial flame, was it not analogous in nature to that one which they received from above, or that other which frightened them in the thunderbolt?"

"Was it not derived from the same source? And if its origin was in heaven, it must have been brought down some day on earth. If so, who was the powerful being, the beneficent being, god or man, who had conquered it? Such are the questions which the curiosity of the Aryans offered in the early days of their existence, and which found their answer in the myth of Prometheus" (*Mythologie de la Grece Antique*, p. 258).

The philosophy of Occult Science finds two weak points in the above reflections, and points them out. The miserable state of Humanity described by Aeschylus and Prometheus was no more wretched then, in the early days of the Aryans, than it is now. That "state" was limited to the savage tribes, and the now-existing savages are not a whit more happy or unhappy than their forefathers were a million years ago.

It is an accepted fact in Science that "rude implements, exactly resembling those in use among existing savages," are found in river gravels and caves geologically "implying an enormous antiquity." So great is that resemblance that, as the author of "*The Modern Zoroastrian*" tells us: "If the collection in the Colonial Exhibition of stone celts and arrowheads used now by the Bushmen of South Africa were placed side by side with one from the British Museum of similar objects from Kent's Cavern or the Caves of Dordogne, no one but an expert could distinguish between them" (p. 145). And if there are Bushmen existing now, in our age of the highest civilization, who are no higher intellectually than the race of men which inhabited Devonshire and Southern France during the Palaeolithic age, why could not the latter have lived simultaneously with, and have been the contemporary of, other races as highly civilized for their day as we are for ours? That the sum of knowledge increases daily in mankind, "but that intellectual capacity does not increase with it," is shown when the intellect, if not the physical knowledge, of the Euclids, Pythagorases, Pâninis, Kapilas, Platos, and Socrates, is compared with that of the Newtons, Kants, and the modern Huxleys and Haeckels. On comparing the results obtained by Dr. J. Barnard Davis, the Craniologist, worked out in 1868 (*Trans. of the Royal Society of London*), with regard to the internal capacity of the skull – its volume being taken as the standard and test for judging of the intellectual capacities – Dr. Pfaff finds that this capacity among the French (certainly in the highest rank of mankind) is 88.4 cubic inches, being thus "perceptibly smaller than that of the Polynesians generally, which, even among many Papuans and Alfuras of the lowest grade, amounts to 89 and 89.7 cubic inches", which shows that it is the quality and not the quantity of the brain that is the cause of intellectual capacity. The average index of skulls among various races having been now recognized to be "one of the most characteristic marks of difference between different races," the following comparison is suggestive: "The index of breadth among the Scandinavians (is) at 75: among the English at 76; among Holsteiners at 77; in Bresgau at 80; Schiller's skull shows an index of breadth even of 82 . . . the Madurese also 82!" Finally, the same comparison between the oldest skulls known and the European, brings to light the startling fact "that most of these old skulls, belonging to the stone period, are above rather than below the average of the brain of the now living man in volume." Calculating the measures for the height, breadth, and length in inches from the average measurements of several skulls, the following sums are obtained:

1. Old Northern skulls of the stone age . . . . 18.877 ins.
2. Average of 48 skulls of the same period from England . . 18.858 "
3. Average of 7 skulls of the same period from Wales . . . . . 18.649 "
4. Average of 36 skulls of the stone age from France .. . . . . .18.220 "

The average of the now living Europeans is 18.579 inches; of Hottentots, 17.795 inches!

Which figures show plainly "that the size of the brain of the oldest populations known to us is not such as to place them on a lower level than that of the now living inhabitants of the Earth" (*The Age and Origin of Man*"). Besides which, they show the "missing link" vanishing into thin air. Of these, however, more anon: we must return to our direct subject.

The race which Jupiter so ardently desired "to quench, and plant a new one in its stead" (Aeschulus, * 241), suffered mental, not physical misery. The first boon Prometheus gave to mortals, as he tells the "Chorus," was to hinder them "from foreseeing death" (256); he "saved the mortal race from sinking blasted down to Hades' gloom" (244); and then only, "besides" that, he gave them fire (260). This shows plainly the dual character, at any rate of the Promethean myth, if Orientalists will not accept the existence of the seven keys taught in Occultism. This relates to the first opening of man's spiritual perceptions, not to his first seeing or discovering fire. For fire was never "discovered," but existed on earth since its beginning. It existed in the seismic activity of the early ages, volcanic eruptions being as frequent and constant in those periods as fog is in England now. And if we are told that men appeared so late on Earth that nearly all the volcanoes, with the exception of a few, were already extinct, and that geological disturbances had made room for a more settled state of things, we answer: Let a new race of men – whether evolved from angel or gorilla – appear now

---

* *Prometheus Vinctus.*

on any uninhabited spot of the globe, with the exception perhaps of the Sahara, and a thousand to one it would not be a year or two old before discovering fire, through the fall of lightning setting in flames grass or something else. This assumption, that primitive man lived ages on earth before he was made acquainted with fire, is one of the most painfully illogical of all. But old Aeschylus was an initiate, and knew well what he was giving out. *

No occultist acquainted with symbology and the fact that Wisdom came to us from the East, will deny for a moment that the myth of Prometheus has reached Europe from Aryavarta. Nor is he likely to deny that in one sense Prometheus represents fire by friction. Therefore, he admires the sagacity of M. F. Baudry, who shows in his *Les Mythes du feu et breuvage celeste* (*Revue Germanique*, 1861, p. 356) † one of the aspects of Prometheus and his origin from India. He shows the reader the supposed primitive process to obtain fire, still in use today in India to light the sacrificial flame. This is what he says:

> This process, such as it is minutely described in the Vedic *Sutras*, consists in rapidly turning a stick in a socket made in the centre of a piece of wood. The friction develops intense heat and ends by setting on fire the particles of wood in contact. The motion of the stick is not a continuous rotation, but a series of motions in contrary senses, by means of a cord fixed to the stick in its middle: the operator holds one of the ends in each hand and pulls them alternately. . . . The full process is designated in Sanskrit by the verb *manthâmi, mathnâni,* which means 'to rub, agitate, shake and obtain by rubbing,' and is especially applied to rotatory friction, as proved by its derivation from *mandala,* which signifies a circle. . . . The pieces of wood serving for the production of fire have each their name in Sanskrit. The stick which turns is called *pramantha;* the discus which receives it is called

---

* The modern attempt of some Greek scholars (poor and pseudo scholars, they would have appeared in the day of the old Greek writers!) to explain the real meaning of the ideas of Aeschylus, which, being an ignorant ancient Greek, he could not express so well himself, is absurdly ludicrous!

† See also his *Memoires de la Societe de la Linguistique* following the "*Fire Myths,*" (Vol. I, p. 337, *et seq.*)

arani and *aranî,* two *aranis* designating the ensemble of the instrument
(p. 358 *et seq.*). ‡

It remains to be seen what the Brahmins will say to this. But
supposing Prometheus has been conceived in one of the aspects of his
myth as the producer of fire by means of *pramantha,* or as an animate and
divine *pramantha,* would this imply that the symbolism had no other
than the phallic meaning attributed to it by the modern symbologists?
Decharme, at any rate, seems to have a correct glimmering of the truth,
for he unconsciously corroborates by his remarks all that the Occult
sciences teach with regard to the *Manasa Devas,* who have endowed
man with the consciousness of his immortal soul: that consciousness
which hinders man "from foreseeing death," and makes him know
he is immortal.§ "How has Prometheus got into the possession of the
(divine) spark?" he asks. "Fire having its abode in heaven, it is there he
must have gone to find it before he could carry it down to men, and, to
approach the gods, he must have been a god himself." The Greeks held
that he was of the divine race; the Hindus, that he was a *Deva.* Hence
"with the Greeks he was the son of the Titan Iapetos," Ἰαπετονίδες
(*Theog.* 528) . . . . "But celestial fire belonged in the beginning to the
gods alone; it was a treasure they reserved for themselves . . . over
which they jealously watched . . . 'The prudent son of Iapetus,' says
Hesiod, 'deceived Jupiter by stealing and concealing in the cavity of
a narthex, the indefatigable fire of the resplendent glow' (*Theog.* 565)
. . . Thus the gift made by Prometheus to men was a conquest made
from heaven. . . " "Now according to Greek ideas," (identical in this

---

‡ There is the upper and nether piece of timber used to produce this sacred fire by
attrition at sacrifices, and it is the *aranî* which contains the socket. This is proven
by an allegory in the *Vâyu Purâna* and others, which tell us that Nemi, the son
of Ikshwaku, had left no successor, and that the *Rishis,* fearing to leave the earth
without a ruler, introduced the king's body into the socket of an *aranî* – like an
upper *aranî* – and produced from it a prince named Janaka. "It was by reason of
the peculiar way in which he was engendered that he was called Janaka." (But see
Goldstucker's *Sanskrit Dictionary* at the word *Arani.*) Devaki, Krishna's mother, in
prayer addressed to her, is called "the *aranî* whose attrition engenders fire."

§ The monad of the animal is as immortal as that of man, yet the brute knows
nothing of this; it lives an animal life of sensation just as the first human would
have lived, when attaining physical development in the Third Race, had it not been
for the *Agnishwatta* and the *Manasa Pitris.*

with those of the Occultists) "this possession forced from Jupiter, this human trespassing upon the property of the gods, had to be followed by an expiation. . . . Prometheus, moreover, belongs to that race of Titans who had rebelled* against the gods, and whom the master of Olympus had hurled down into Tartarus; like them, he is the genius of Evil, doomed to cruel suffering, etc., etc."

That which is revolting in the explanations that follow, is the one-sided view taken of this grandest of all the myths. The most intuitional among modern writers cannot or will not rise in their conceptions above the level of the Earth and Cosmic phenomena. It is not denied that the moral idea in the myth, as presented in the Theogony of Hesiod, plays a certain part in the primitive Greek conception. The Titan is more than a thief of the celestial fire. He is the representation of humanity – active, industrious, intelligent, but at the same time ambitious, which aims at equalling divine powers. Therefore it is humanity punished in the person of Prometheus, but it is only so with the Greeks. With the latter, Prometheus is not a criminal, save in the eyes of the gods. In his relation with the Earth, he is, on the contrary, a god himself, a friend of mankind (φιλάνθρεπος), which he has raised to civilization and initiated into the knowledge of all the arts, a conception which found its most poetical expounder in Aeschylus. But with all other nations Prometheus is – what? The fallen Angel, Satan, as the Church would have it? Not at all. He is simply the image of the pernicious and dreaded effects of lightning. He is the "evil fire" (*mal feu*) and the symbol of the divine reproductive male organ. "Reduced to its simple expression, the myth we are trying to explain is then simply a (Cosmic) genius of fire" (p. 261). It is the former idea (the phallic) which was pre-eminently Aryan, if we believe Ad. Kuhn (in his *Herabkunft des Feuers und des Gottertranks*) and Baudry. For –

> The fire used by man being the result of the action of *pramantha* in the *aranî*, the Aryas must have ascribed (?) the same origin to celestial fire, and they must [†] have imagined (?) that a god armed with *pramantha*, or a divine *pramantha*, exercised in the bosom of

---

* The fallen angels, therefore; the *Asuras* of the Indian Pantheon.

† The italics are ours; they show how assumptions are raised to laws in our day.

the clouds a violent friction, which gave birth to lightning and thunderbolts. . . . . This idea is supported by the fact that, according to Plutarch's testimony (*Philosoph. Plant.*, iii 3), the Stoics thought that thunder was the result of the struggle of storm clouds and lightning – a conflagration due to friction, while Aristotle saw in the thunderbolt only the action of clouds which clashed with each other. What was this theory, if not the scientific translation of the production of fire by friction? . . . . . . Everything leads us to think that, from the highest antiquity, and before the dispersion of the Aryans, it was believed that the *pramantha* lighted fire in the storm cloud as well as in the *aranîs*. (*Revue Germanique*, p. 368.)

Thus, suppositions and idle hypotheses are made to stand for discovered truths. Defenders of the *Bible* dead letter could never help the writers of missionary tracts more effectually, than do materialistic Symbologists in thus taking for granted that the ancient Aryans based their religious conceptions on no higher thought than the physiological.

But it is not so, and the very spirit of Vedic philosophy is against such an interpretation. And if, as Decharme himself confesses, "this idea of the creative power of fire is explained at once by the ancient assimilation of the human soul to a celestial spark," as shown by the imagery often made use of in the *Vedas* when speaking of *Aranî*, it would mean something higher than simply a gross sexual conception. A hymn to Agni in the *Veda* is cited as example: "Here is the *pramantha*, the generator is ready. Bring the mistress of the race (the female *Aranî*). Let us produce Agni by attrition, according to ancient custom" – which means no worse than an abstract idea expressed in the tongue of mortals. The "female *Aranî*," the mistress of the race, is Aditi, the mother of the gods, or Shekinah, eternal light – in the world of Spirit, the "Great Deep" and CHAOS, or primordial Substance in its first remove from the UNKNOWN, in the manifested Kosmos. If, ages later, the same epithet is applied to Devaki, the mother of Krishna, or the incarnated LOGOS; and if the symbol, owing to the gradual and irrepressible spread of exoteric religions, may already be regarded as having a sexual significance, this in no way mars the original purity of the image. The subjective had been transformed into the objective;

Spirit had fallen into matter. The universal kosmic polarity of Spirit-Substance had become, in human thought, the mystic, but still sexual union of Spirit and Matter, and had thus acquired an anthropomorphic colouring which it had never had in the beginning. Between the *Vedas* and the *Purânas* there is an abyss of which both are the poles, like the seventh (atmic) and the first or lowest principle (the physical body) in the Septenary constitution of man. The primitive, purely spiritual language of the *Vedas*, conceived many decades of millenniums earlier, had found its purely human expression for the purpose of describing events taking place 5,000 years ago, the date of Krishna's death (from which day the *Kali Yuga*, or Black Age, began for mankind).

As Aditi is called Surârani (the matrix or "mother" of the *sura* gods), so Kunti, the mother of the Pandavas, is called in *Mahabhârata* Pandavârani – which term is already physiologized. But Devaki, the antetype of the Roman Catholic Madonna, is a later anthropomorphized form of Aditi. The latter is the goddess mother, the *"Deva-matri"* of Seven Sons (the six and the seven *Adityas* of early Vedic times); the mother of Krishna, Devaki, has six embryos conveyed into her womb by Jagaddhâtri (the "nurse of the world"), the seventh (Krishna, the *Logos*,) being transferred to that Rohini. Mary, the mother of Jesus, is the mother of seven children, of five sons and two daughters, (a later transformation of sex) in Matthew's Gospel (xiii 55–56). No one of the worshippers of the Roman Catholic Virgin would object to reciting in her honour the prayer addressed by the gods to Devaki. Let the reader judge.

> Thou art that *Prakriti* (essence), infinite and subtile, which bore Brahmâ in its womb. Thou eternal being, comprising in thy substance the essence of all created things, wast identical with creation; thou wast the parent of the triform sacrifice, becoming the germ of all. . . . Thou art sacrifice, whence all fruit proceeds; thou art the *aranî* whose attrition engenders fire" . . . . ("Womb of Light," "holy Vessel," are the epithets of the Virgin). "As Aditi, thou art the parent of the gods. . . . Thou art *Jyotsna* (the morning twilight)." The Virgin is often addressed as the "morning Star" and the "star of Salvation" – the light whence day is begotten. "Thou art Samnati (humility, a daughter of *Daksha*), the mother of Wisdom; thou art Niti, the parent of harmony

(*Naya*); thou art modesty, the progenitrix of affection (*Prasraya* or *vinaya*); thou art desire, of whom love is born. . . . Thou art the mother of knowledge (*Avabodha*); patience (*Dhriti*), the parent of fortitude (*Dhairya*) . . . . etc., etc.

Thus *aranî* is shown here as the Roman Catholic "vase of election" and no worse. As to its primitive meaning, it was purely metaphysical. No unclean thought traversed these conceptions in the ancient mind. Even in the *Zohar* – far less metaphysical than any other symbolism – the idea is an abstraction and nothing more. Thus, when the *Zohar* (iii, 290) says: "All that which exists, all that which has been formed by the ancient, whose name is holy, can only exist through a male and female principle," it means no more than this: "The divine Spirit of Life is ever coalescing with matter." It is the WILL of the Deity that acts, and the idea is purely Schopenhauerian. "When *Atteekah Kaddosha*, the ancient and the concealed of the concealed, desired to form all things, it formed all things like male and female. This wisdom comprises ALL when it goeth forth." Hence *Chochmah* (male wisdom) and *Binah* (female consciousness or Intellect) are said to create all between the two – the active and the passive principles. As the eye of the expert jeweller discerns under the rough and uncouth oyster shell the pure immaculate pearl, enshrined within its bosom, his hand dealing with the former but to get at its contents, so the eye of the true philosopher reads between the lines of the *Purânas* the sublime Vedic truths, and corrects the form with the help of the Vedantic wisdom. Our Orientalists, however, never perceive the pearl under the thick coating of the shell, and – act accordingly.

From all that has been said in this section, one sees clearly that, between the Serpent of Eden and the Devil of Christianity, there is an abyss. Alone the sledge hammer of ancient philosophy can kill this dogma.

SD, ii 519–528

MAN, THE PARENT OF
ALL THE MAMMALS

But the able author of the "*Book of the Beginnings*" and of "*The Natural Genesis*" does – very fortunately, for us – quite the reverse. He demonstrates most triumphantly our Esoteric (Buddhist) teachings, by showing them identical with those of Egypt. Let the reader judge from his learned lecture on "*The Seven Souls of Man*." * Says the author:

> The first form of the mystical SEVEN was seen to be figured in heaven by the Seven large stars of the great Bear, the constellation assigned by the Egyptians to the Mother of Time, and of the Seven Elemental Powers.

Just so, for the Hindus place in the great Bear their seven primitive *Rishis* and call this constellation the abode of the *Saptarishi*, *Riksha* and *Chitra-Sikhandinas*. But whether it is only an astronomical myth or a primordial mystery, having a deeper meaning than it bears on its surface, is what their adepts claim to know. We are also told that "the Egyptians divided the face of the sky by night into seven parts. The primary Heaven was seven-fold." So it was with the Aryans. One has but read the *Purânas* about the beginnings of Brahmâ, and his "Egg" to see it. Have the Aryans taken the idea from the Egyptians? – "The earliest forces," proceeds the lecturer, "recognized in nature were reckoned as seven in number. These became seven elementals, devils (?) or later, divinities. Seven properties were assigned to nature, as matter, cohesion, fluxion, coagulation, accumulation, station, and

---

* The fact that this learned Egyptologist does not recognise in the doctrine of the "Seven Souls," as he terms our principles, or "metaphysical concepts," but "the primitive biology or physiology of the Soul," does not invalidate our argument. The lecturer touches on only two keys, those that unlock the astronomical and the physiological mysteries of esotericism, and leaves out the other five. Otherwise he would have promptly understood that what he calls the physiological divisions of the living Soul of man, are regarded by theosophists as also psychological and spiritual.

246

division and seven elements or souls to man."

All this was taught in the esoteric doctrine, but it was interpreted and its mysteries unlocked, as already stated, with seven, not two, or at the utmost, three keys; hence the causes and their effects worked in invisible or mystic as well as psychic nature, and were made referable to metaphysics and psychology as much as to physiology. "The principle of sevening" – as the author says – "was introduced, and the number seven supplied a sacred type that could be used for manifold purposes", and it was so used. For "the seven Souls of the Pharaoh are often mentioned in the Egyptian texts. . . . Seven Souls or principles in man were identified by our British Druids. . . . . The Rabbins also ran the number of souls up to seven; so, likewise, do the Karens of India."

And then, the author tabulates the two teachings – the Esoteric and the Egyptian – and shows that the latter had the same series and in the same order.

Table 1. Esoteric and Egyptian Seven-fold Divisions

(Esoteric) Indian †	Egyptian
I. *Rupa*, body or element of form.	I. *Kha*, body.
2. *Prana*, the breath of life.	2. *Ba*, the Soul of Breath.
3. Astral body.	3. *Khaba*, the shade.
4. *Manas* – or Intelligence.	4. *Akhu*, Intelligence or Perception.
5. *Kama* – *rupa*, or animal soul.	5. *Seb*, ancestral Soul.
6. *Buddhi*, Spiritual Soul.	6. *Putah*, the first intellectual father.
7. *Atma*, pure spirit. . . .	7. *Atmu*, a divine or eternal soul.

Further on, the lecturer formulates these seven (Egyptian) souls, as (1) The Soul of Blood – the formative; (2) The Soul of Breath – "that breathes"; (3) The Shade or Covering Soul – "that envelopes"; (4) The

---

† This is a great mistake made in the Esoteric enumeration. *Manas* (#4 above) is the fifth, not the fourth; and *Manas* corresponds precisely with *Seb*, the Egyptian fifth principle, for that portion of *Manas*, which follows the two higher principles, is the ancestral soul, indeed, the bright, immortal thread of the higher Ego, to which clings the Spiritual aroma of all the lives or births.

Soul of Perception – "that perceives;" (5) The Soul of Pubescence "that procreates"; (6) The Intellectual Soul – "that reproduces intellectually"; and (7) The Spiritual Soul – "that is perpetuated permanently."

From the exoteric and physiological standpoint this may be very correct; it becomes less so from the esoteric point of view. To maintain this, does not at all mean that the "Esoteric Buddhists" resolve men into a number of elementary Spirits, as Mr. G. Massey, in the same lecture, accuses them of maintaining. No "Esoteric Buddhist" has ever been guilty of any such absurdity. Nor has it been ever imagined that these shadows "become spiritual beings in another world," or "seven potential spirits or elementaries of another life." What is maintained is simply that every time the immortal Ego incarnates it becomes, as a total, a compound unit of Matter and Spirit, which together act on seven different planes of being and consciousness. Elsewhere, Mr. G. Massey adds, "The seven souls (our "Principles") are often mentioned in the Egyptian texts. The moon god, *Taht-Esmun*, or the later sun god, expressed the seven nature powers that were prior to himself, and were summed up in him as his seven souls (we say "principles") . . . . The seven stars in the hand of Christ in the Revelation, have the same significance," etc.

And a still greater one, as these stars represent also the seven keys of the Seven Churches or the SODALIAN MYSTERIES, cabalistically. However, we will not stop to discuss, but add that other Egyptologists have also found out that the septenary constitution of man was a cardinal doctrine with the old Egyptians. In a series of remarkable articles in the "Sphinx" (Munich) Herr Franz Lambert gives incontrovertible proof of his conclusions from the "*Book of the Dead*" and other Egyptian records. For details the reader must be referred to the articles themselves, but the following diagram, summing up the author's conclusions, is demonstrative evidence of the identity of Egyptian psychology with the septenary division in "*Esoteric Buddhism.*"

On the left hand side the Kabalistic names of the corresponding

---

is the fifth, not the fourth; and *Manas* corresponds precisely with Seb, the Egyptian fifth principle, for that portion of *Manas*, which follows the two higher principles, is the ancestral soul, indeed, the bright, immortal thread of the higher Ego, to which clings the Spiritual aroma of all the lives or births.

human principles are placed, and on the right the hieroglyphic names with their renderings as in the diagram of F. Lambert.

Table 2. Identity of Egyptian Psychology with the Septenary Division.*

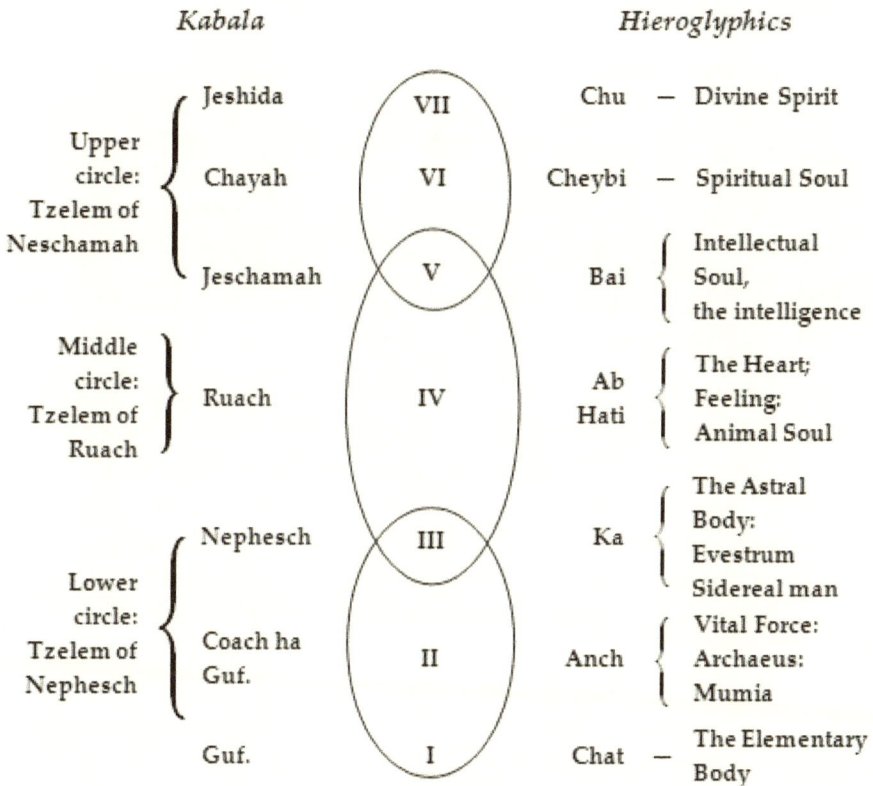

Kabala		*Hieroglyphics*	
Upper circle: Tzelem of Neschamah	Jeshida — VII	Chu	— Divine Spirit
	Chayah — VI	Cheybi	— Spiritual Soul
	Jeschamah — V	Bai	{ Intellectual Soul, the intelligence
Middle circle: Tzelem of Ruach	Ruach — IV	Ab Hati	{ The Heart; Feeling; Animal Soul
Lower circle: Tzelem of Nephesch	Nephesch — III	Ka	{ The Astral Body: Evestrum Sidereal man
	Coach ha Guf. — II	Anch	{ Vital Force: Archaeus: Mumia
	Guf. — I	Chat	— The Elementary Body

This is a very fair representation of the number of the "principles" of Occultism, but much confused; and this is what we call the 7 principles in man, and what Mr. Massey calls "Souls," giving the same name to the Ego or the Monad which reincarnates and resurrects, so to speak, at each rebirth, as the Egyptians did, namely – "the Renewed." But how can *Ruach* (Spirit) be lodged in *Kama rupa*? What does Böhme, the Prince of all the mediaeval Seers, say?

---

* There seems a confusion – lasting for many centuries – in the minds of Western Kabalists. They call *Ruach* (Spirit) what we call *Kama-rupa*; whereas, with us *Ruach* would be the "Spiritual Soul" *Buddhi*, and *Nephesh* the 4th principle, the Vital, Animal Soul. Eliphas Levi falls into the same error.

We find Seven especial properties in nature whereby this only Mother works all things" (which he calls – fire, light, sound (the upper three) and desire, bitterness, anguish, and substantiality, thus analysing the lower in his own mystic way) . . . "whatever the six forms are spiritually, that the seventh, the body (or substantiality), is essentially." These are the seven forms of the Mother of all Beings from whence all that is in this world is generated,* and again in *Aurora* xxiv. p. 27 (quoted in *Natural Genesis*) – "The Creator hath in the body of this world generated himself as it were creaturely in his qualifying Fountain Spirits, and all the stars are . . . God's powers, and the whole body of the world consisteth in the seven qualifying or Fountain Spirits.

This is rendering in mystical language our theosophical doctrine. . . But how can we agree with Mr. G. Massey when he states that:

The Seven Races of men that have been sublimated and made Planetary (?) by *Esoteric Buddhism*,† may be met with in the *Bundahish* as (1) the earth-men; (2) water-men; (3) breast-eared men; (4) breast-eyed men; (5) one-legged men; (6) bat-winged men; (7) men with tails." . . . Each of these descriptions, allegorical and even perverted in their later form – is, nevertheless, an echo of the Secret Doctrine teaching. They all refer to the pre-Human evolution of the water-men "terrible and bad" by unaided Nature through millions of years, as previously described. But we deny point blank the assertion made that "these were never real races," and point to the Archaic *Stanzas* for our answer. It is easy to infer and to say that our "instructors have mistaken these shadows of the Past, for things human and spiritual", but that "they are neither, and never were either," it is less easy to prove. The assertion must ever remain on a par with the Darwinian claim that man and the ape had a common pithecoid ancestor. What the Lecturer takes for a "mode of expression" and nothing more, in the Egyptian Ritual, we take as having quite another and an important meaning. Here is one instance. Says the Ritual, the *"Book of the Dead"* – "I am the mouse." "I

---

* *Signatura rerum* xiv. ps. 10, 15 *et seq.*

† This is indeed news! It makes us fear that the Lecturer had never read *"Esoteric Buddhism"* before criticising it, as there are too many such misconceptions in his notices of it.

am the hawk." "I am the ape." . . . "I am the crocodile whose Soul Comes FROM MEN." "I am the Soul of the Gods." Of these last two sentences, one: "whose soul comes from men" – is explained by the Lecturer, who says parenthetically, "that is, as a type of intelligence," and the other: "I am the Soul of the Gods," as meaning, "the Horus, or Christ, as the outcome of all.

The occult teaching answers: "It means far more." . . .

It gives first of all a corroboration of the teaching that, while the human monad has passed on globe A and others, in the First Round, through all the three kingdoms – the mineral, the vegetable, and the animal – in this our Fourth Round, every mammal has sprung from Man if the semi-ethereal, many-shaped creature with the human Monad in it, of the first two races, can be regarded as Man. But it must be so called; for, in the esoteric language, it is not the form of flesh, blood, and bones, now referred to as Man, which is in any way the MAN, but the inner divine MONAD with its manifold principles or aspects.

The lecture referred to, however, much as it opposes *"Esoteric Buddhism"* and its teachings, is an eloquent answer to those who have tried to represent the whole as a newfangled doctrine. And there are many such, in Europe, America, and even India. Yet, between the esotericism of the old *Arhats*, and that which has now survived in India among the few Brahmins who have seriously studied their Secret Philosophy, the difference does not appear so very great. It seems centred in, and limited to, the question of the order of the evolution of cosmic and other principles, more than anything else. At all events it is no greater divergence than the everlasting question of the filioque dogma, which since the XIIth. century has separated the Roman Catholic from the older Greek Eastern Church. Yet, whatever the differences in the forms in which the septenary dogma is presented, the substance is there, and its presence and importance in the Brahminical system may be judged by what one of India's learned metaphysicians and Vedantic scholars says of it:

> The real esoteric seven-fold classification is one of the most important, if not the most important classification, which has

received its arrangement from the mysterious constitution of this eternal type. I may also mention in this connection that the four-fold classification claims the same origin. The light of life, as it were, seems to be refracted by the treble-faced prism of *Prakriti*, having the three *Gunams* for its three faces, and divided into seven rays, which develop in course of time the seven principles of this classification. The progress of development presents some points of similarity to the gradual development of the rays of the spectrum. While the four-fold classification is amply sufficient for all practical purposes, this real seven-fold classification is of great theoretical and scientific importance. It will be necessary to adopt it to explain certain classes of phenomena noticed by occultists, and it is perhaps better fitted to be the basis of a perfect system of psychology. It is not the peculiar property of 'the trans-Himalayan esoteric doctrine.' In fact, it has a closer connection with the Brahminical *Logos* than with the Buddhist *Logos*. In order to make my meaning clear I may point out here that the *Logos* has seven forms. In other words, there are seven kinds of *Logoi* in the Cosmos. Each of these has become the central figure of one of the seven main branches of the ancient Wisdom religion. This classification is not the seven-fold classification we have adopted. I make this assertion without the slightest fear of contradiction. The real classification has all the requisites of a scientific classification. It has seven distinct principles, which correspond with seven distinct states of *Pragna* or consciousness. It bridges the gulf between the objective and subjective, and indicates the mysterious circuit through which ideation passes. The seven principles are allied to seven states of matter, and to seven forms of force. These principles are harmoniously arranged between two poles, which define the limits of human consciousness. *

The above is perfectly correct, save, perhaps, one point. The "seven-fold classification" in the esoteric system has never been claimed (to the writer's knowledge) by any one belonging to it, as "the peculiar property of the Trans-Himalayan esoteric doctrine", but only as having survived in that old school alone. It is no more the property of the trans, than it is of the cis-Himalayan esoteric doctrine, but is simply the common inheritance of all such schools, left to the sages of the Fifth

---

* *The Theosophist*, 1887 (Madras).

Root Race by the great *Siddhas* † of the Fourth. Let us remember that the Atlanteans became the terrible sorcerers, now celebrated in so many of the oldest MSS. of India, only toward their fall, the submersion of their continent having been brought on by it. What is claimed is simply the fact that the wisdom imparted by the "Divine Ones" – born through the *Kriyasakti* powers of the Third Race before its Fall and Separation into sexes – to the adepts of the early Fourth Race, has remained in all its pristine purity in a certain Brotherhood. The said School or Fraternity being closely connected with a certain island of an inland sea, believed in by both Hindus and Buddhists, but called "mythical" by geographers and Orientalists, the less one talks of it, the wiser he will be. Nor can one accept the said "seven-fold classification" as having "a closer connection with the Brahminical *Logos* than with the Buddhist *Logos*," since both are identical, whether the one *"Logos"* is called *Eswara* or *Avalôkitêswara*, Brahmâ or *Padmapani*. These are, however, very small differences, more fanciful than real, in fact. Brahmanism and Buddhism, both viewed from their orthodox aspects, are as inimical and as irreconcilable as water and oil. Each of these great bodies, however, has a vulnerable place in its constitution. While even in their esoteric interpretation both can agree but to disagree, once that their respective vulnerable points are confronted, every disagreement must fall, for the two will find themselves on common ground. The "heel of Achilles" of orthodox Brahmanism is the *Advaita* philosophy, whose followers are called by the pious "Buddhists in disguise", as that of orthodox Buddhism is Northern mysticism, as represented by the disciples of the philosophies of Aryâsanga (the *Yogâchârya* School) and *Mahâyana*, who are twitted in their turn by their correligionists as "Vedantins in disguise." The esoteric philosophy of both these can be but one if carefully analysed and compared, as Gautama Buddha and Sankarachârya are most closely connected, if one believes tradition

---

† According to *Svetâsvatara-Upanishad* (357) the *Siddhas* are those who are possessed from birth of superhuman powers, as also of "knowledge and indifference to the world." According to the Occult teachings, however, *Siddhas* are the *Nirmanakayas* or the "spirits" (in the sense of an individual, or conscious spirit) of great sages from spheres on a higher plane than our own, who voluntarily incarnate in mortal bodies in order to help the human race in its upward progress. Hence their innate knowledge, wisdom and powers.

and certain esoteric teachings. Thus every difference between the two will be found one of form rather than of substance.

A most mystic discourse, full of septenary symbology, may be found in the *Anugîtâ*.* There the Brâhmana narrates the bliss of having crossed beyond the regions of illusion, "in which fancies are the gadflies and mosquitoes, in which grief and joy are cold and heat, in which delusion is the blinding darkness, avarice, the beasts of prey and reptiles, and desire and anger are the obstructors." . . . . The sage describes the entrance into and exit from the forest (a symbol for man's lifetime) and also that forest itself: †

> In that forest are seven large trees (the Senses, Mind and Understanding, or *Manas* and *Buddhi* included), seven fruits and seven guests, seven hermitages, seven (forms of) concentration, and seven (forms of) initiation. This is the description of the forest. That forest is filled with trees producing splendid flowers and fruits of five colours.

"The senses," says the commentator, "are called trees, as being producers of the fruits . . . . pleasures and pains; the guests are the powers of each sense personified – they receive the fruits above described; the hermitages are the trees, in which the guests take shelter. The seven forms of concentration are the exclusion from the self of the seven functions of the seven senses, etc., already referred to; the seven forms of initiation refer to the initiation into the higher life . . . by repudiating as not one's own the actions of each member out of the group of seven." (See *Khândagya*, p. 219, and *Com.*)

The explanation is harmless, if unsatisfactory.

Says the Brâhmana continuing his description:

> That forest is filled with trees producing flowers and fruits of four

---

* "*The Sacred Books of the East,*" vol. viii, *Anugîtâ*, p. 284, *et seq.*

† I propose to follow here the text and the editor's commentaries, who accepts Arjuna Misra and Nilakantha's dead-letter explanations. Our Orientalists never trouble to think that if a native commentator is a non-initiate, he could not explain correctly, and if an Initiate, would not.

colours. That forest is filled with trees producing flowers and fruits of three colours, and mixed. That forest is filled with trees producing flowers and fruits of two colours, and of beautiful colours. That forest is filled with trees producing flowers and fruits of one colour and fragrant. That forest is filled (instead of seven) with two large trees producing numerous flowers and fruits of undistinguished colours (mind and understanding – the two higher senses, or theosophically, '*Manas-Buddhi*'). Here is one Fire (Self) here connected with the Brahman ‡ and having a good mind (or true knowledge, according to Arjuna Misra). And there is fuel here, namely, the five senses (or human passions). The Seven (forms of) emancipation from them are the Seven (forms of) initiation. The qualities are the fruits. . . . There, the great Sages receive hospitality. And when they have been worshipped and have disappeared, another forest shines forth, in which intelligence is the tree, and emancipation the fruit, and which possesses shade (in the form of) tranquillity, which depends on Knowledge, which has contentment for its water, and the *KSHETRAGNA* (the "Supreme SELF," says Krishna, in the *Bhagavad Gîtâ*, p. 102 *et seq.*) within for the Sun.

Now, all the above is very plain, and no theosophist, even among the least learned, could fail to understand the allegory. And yet, we see great Orientalists making a perfect mess of it in their explanations. The "great sages" who "receive hospitality" are explained as meaning the senses, "which, having worked as unconnected with the self are finally absorbed into it." But one fails to understand, if the senses are "unconnected" with the "Higher Self," in what manner can they be "absorbed into it." One would think, on the contrary, that just because the personal senses gravitate and strive to be connected with the impersonal Self, that the latter, which is FIRE, burns the lower five and purifies thereby the higher two, "mind and understanding" or the higher aspects of *Manas* § and *Buddhi*. This is quite apparent from

---

‡ The English editor explains here, saying, "I presume devoted to the Brâhman." This would be a very poor devotion, indeed, in the accomplishment of the gradually emancipating process of Yoga. We venture to say that the "Fire" or Self is the higher real SELF "connected with," that is to say one with Brahma, the One Deity. The "Self" separates itself no longer from the universal Spirit.

§ As *Mahat* (universal intelligence) is first born, or manifests, as Vishnu, and then, when it falls into matter and develops self-consciousness, it becomes Egoism,

the text. The "great sages" disappear after having "been worshipped."
Worshipped by whom if they (the presumed senses) are "unconnected
with the self"? By MIND, of course, by *Manas* (in this case merged
in the sixth sense) which is not, and cannot be, the Brahman, the
SELF, or *Kshetragna* – the soul's spiritual sun. Into the latter, in time,
Manas itself must be absorbed. It has worshipped "great sages" and
given hospitality to terrestrial wisdom: but once that "another forest
shone forth" upon it, it is Intelligence (*Buddhi*, the 7th sense, but 6th
principle) which is transformed into the tree – that tree whose fruit is
emancipation – which finally destroys the very roots of the *Aswattha*
tree, the symbol of life and of its illusive joys and pleasures. And
therefore, those who attain to that state of emancipation have, in the
words of the above-cited sage, "no fear afterwards." In this state "the
end cannot be perceived because it extends on all sides."

"There always dwell seven females there," he goes on to say, carrying
out the imagery. These females, who, according to Arjuna Misra, are
the *Mahat*, *Ahamkara* and five *Tanmâtras*, have always their faces turned
downwards, as they are obstacles in the way of spiritual ascension.

" . . . . In that same (Brahman, the 'Self') the Seven perfect Sages,
together with their chiefs, abide and again emerge from the same.
Glory, brilliance and greatness, enlightenment, victory, perfection
and power – these seven rays follow after this same Sun (*Kshetragna*,
the Higher Self). . . . Those whose wishes are reduced (unselfish). . . .
whose sins (passions) are burnt up by restraint, merging the Self in the
Self * devote themselves to Brahman. Those people who understand
the forest of Knowledge (Brahman, or SELF) praise tranquillity. And
aspiring to that forest, they are (re-) born so as not to lose courage.

Selfishness, so *Manas* is of a dual nature. It is respectively under the sun and moon,
for as Sankarachârya says "The moon is the mind, and the sun the understanding."
The sun and moon are the deities of our planetary Macrocosmos, and therefore
Sankara adds that "the mind and the understanding are the respective deities of the
(human) organs" (*Vide Brihadâranyaka*, pp. 521, *et seq.*) This is perhaps why Arjuna
Misra says that the moon and the Fire (the self, the sun) constitute the universe.

* "The body in the Soul," as Arjuna Misra is credited with saying, or rather the
"Soul in the Spirit," and on a still higher plane of development: "the SELF or *Atman*
in the Universal Self."

Such indeed, is this holy forest . . . . and understanding it, they (the Sages) act accordingly, being directed by the *KSHETRAGNA*. . . . "

No translator among the Western Orientalists has yet perceived in the foregoing allegory anything higher than mysteries connected with sacrificial ritualism, penance, or ascetic ceremonies, and Hatha Yoga. But he who understands symbolical imagery, and hears the voice of SELF WITHIN SELF, will see in this something far higher than mere ritualism, however often he may err in minor details of the philosophy.

And here, we must be allowed a last remark. No true theosophist, from the most ignorant up to the most learned, ought to claim infallibility for anything he may say or write upon occult matters. The chief point is to admit that, in many a way, in the classification of either cosmic or human principles, in addition to mistakes in the order of evolution, and especially on metaphysical questions, those of us who pretend to teach others more ignorant than ourselves – are all liable to err. Thus mistakes have been made in *"Isis Unveiled,"* in *"Esoteric Buddhism,"* in *"Man,"* in *"Magic: White and Black,"* etc., etc., and more than one mistake is likely to be found in the present work. This cannot be helped. For a large or even a small work on such abstruse subjects to be entirely exempt from error and blunder, it would have to be written from its first to its last page by a great adept, if not by an Avatar. Then only should we say, "This is verily a work without sin or blemish in it!" But, so long as the artist is imperfect, how can his work be perfect? "Endless is the search for truth!" Let us love it and aspire to it for its own sake, and not for the glory or benefit a minute portion of its revelation may confer on us. For who of us can presume to have the whole truth at his fingers' ends, even upon one minor teaching of Occultism?

Our chief point in the present subject, however, was to show that the Septenary doctrine, or division of the constitution of man, was a very ancient one, and was not invented by us. This has been successfully done, for we are supported in this, consciously and unconsciously, by a number of ancient, mediaeval, and modern writers. What the former said, was well said; what the latter repeated, was generally distorted. An instance: read the "*Pythagorean Fragments*," and compare the Septenary man as given by the Rev. G. Oliver, the learned mason, in his "*Pythagorean Triangle*" (ch. on "*Science of Numbers*," p. 179).

He speaks as follows:

The Theosophic Philosophy counted SEVEN properties (or principles), in Man, viz.:

(1.) The divine golden Man;

(2.) The inward holy body from fire and light, like pure silver;

(3.) The elemental man;

(4.) The mercurial paradisiacal man;

(5.) The martial Soul-like man;

(6.) The passionate man of desires;

(7.) The Solar man; a witness to and inspector of the wonders of the Universe. They had also seven fountain Spirits, or Powers of Nature.

Compare this jumbled account and distribution of Western theosophic philosophy with the latest theosophic explanations by the Eastern School of Theosophy, and then decide which is the more correct. Verily:

Wisdom hath builded her house,
She hath hewn out her seven pillars. (*Prov.* ix, 1.)

As to the charge that our School has not adopted the Seven-fold classification of the Brahmins, but has confused it, it is quite unjust. To begin with, the "School" is one thing, its exponents (to Europeans) quite another. The latter have first to learn the A B C of practical Eastern Occultism, before they can be made to understand correctly the tremendously abstruse classification based on the seven distinct states of *Pragna* (consciousness), and, above all, to realize thoroughly what *Pragna* is, in the Eastern metaphysics. To give a Western student that classification is to try to make him suppose that he can account for the origin of consciousness, by accounting for the process by which a certain knowledge, through only one of the states of that consciousness, came to him; in other words, it is to make him account for something he knows on this plane, by something he knows nothing about on the other planes, i.e., to lead him from the spiritual and the psychological, direct to the ontological. This is why the primary, old, classification was adopted by the Theosophists, of which classifications there are many.

To busy oneself, after such a tremendous number of independent witnesses and proofs have been brought before the public, with an additional enumeration from theological sources, would be quite useless. The seven capital sins and seven virtues of the Christian scheme are far less philosophical than even the Seven Liberal and the Seven Accursed Sciences – or the Seven Arts of enchantment of the Gnostics. For one of the latter is now before the public, pregnant with danger in the present as for the future. The modern name for it is HYPNOTISM. In the ignorance of the seven principles, and used by scientific and ignorant materialists, it will soon become SATANISM in the full acceptation of the term."

SD, ii 631–641

THE DARWINISTS AND
THEIR OPPONENTS

". . . the absurdity of such an unnatural descent of man is so palpable in the face of all the proofs and evidence of the skull of the pithecoid as compared to that of man, that even de Quatrefages resorted unconsciously to our esoteric theory by saying that it is rather the apes that can claim descent from man than vice versa. As proven by Gratiolet, with regard to the cavities of the brain of the anthropoids, in which species that organ develops in an inverse ratio to what would be the case were the corresponding organs in man really the product of the development of the said organs in the apes — the size of the human skull and its brain, as well as the cavities, increase with the individual development of man. His intellect develops and increases with age, while his facial bones and jaws diminish and straighten, thus being more and more spiritualized: whereas with the ape it is the reverse. In its youth the anthropoid is far more intelligent and good-natured, while with age it becomes duller; and, as its skull recedes and seems to diminish as it grows, its facial bones and jaws develop, the brain being finally crushed, and thrown entirely back, to make with every day more room for the animal type. The organ of thought — the brain — recedes and diminishes, entirely conquered and replaced by that of the wild beast — the jaw apparatus.

Thus, as wittily remarked in the French work, a gorilla would have a perfect right to address an Evolutionist, claiming its right of descent from himself. It would say to him, "We, anthropoid apes, form a retrogressive departure from the human type, and therefore our development and evolution are expressed by a transition from a human-like to an animal-like structure of organism; but in what way could you, men, descend from us — how can you form a continuation of our genus? For, to make this possible, your organization would have to differ still more than ours does from the human structure, it would have to approach still closer to that of the beast than ours does; and in such a case justice demands that you should give up to us your place in nature. You are lower than we are, once that you insist on tracing your genealogy from our kind; for the structure of our organization and its development are such that we are unable to generate forms of a higher organization than our own."

This is where the Occult Sciences agree entirely with de Quatrefages. Owing to the very type of his development man cannot descend from either an ape or an ancestor common to both, but shows his origin from a type far superior to himself. And this type is the "Heavenly man" — the Dhyan Chohans, or the *Pitris* so-called, as shown in the first Part of this volume. On the other hand, the pithecoids, the orang-outang, the gorilla, and the chimpanzee can, and, as the Occult Sciences teach, do, descend from the animalized Fourth human Root-Race, being the product of man and an extinct species of mammal — whose remote ancestors were themselves the product of Lemurian bestiality — which lived in the Miocene age. The ancestry of this semi-human monster is explained in the Stanzas as originating in the sin of the "Mind-less" races of the middle Third Race period.

When it is borne in mind that all forms which now people the earth, are so many variations on basic types originally thrown off by the MAN of the Third and Fourth Round, such an evolutionist argument as that insisting on the "unity of structural plan" characterising all vertebrates, loses its edge. The basic types referred to were very few in number in comparison with the multitude of organisms to which they ultimately gave rise; but a general unity of type has, nevertheless, been preserved throughout the ages. The economy of Nature does not sanction the co-existence of several utterly opposed "ground plans" of organic evolution on one planet. Once, however, that the general drift of the occult explanation is formulated, inference as to detail may well be left to the intuitive reader.

Similarly with the important question of the "rudimentary" organs discovered by anatomists in the human organism. Doubtless this line of argument, when wielded by Darwin and Haeckel against their European adversaries, proved of great weight. Anthropologists, who ventured to dispute the derivation of man from an animal ancestry, were sorely puzzled how to deal with the presence of gill-clefts, with the "tail" problem, and so on. Here again Occultism comes to our assistance with the necessary data.

The fact is that, as previously stated, the human type is the repertory of all potential organic forms, and the central point from which these latter radiate. In this postulate we find a true "Evolution" or "Unfolding" — a sense which cannot be said to belong to the mechanical theory of natural selection. Criticising Darwin's inference from "rudiments," an able writer remarks: "Why is it not just as probably a true hypothesis to suppose that Man was created with the rudimentary sketches in his organization, and that they became useful appendages in the lower animals into which man degenerated, as to suppose that these parts existed in full development in the lower animals out of which man was generated?" (*"Creation or Evolution?"* Geo. T. Curtis, p. 76.)

Read for "into which Man degenerated," "the prototypes which man *shed* in the course of his astral developments," and an aspect of the true esoteric solution is before us. But a wider generalization is now to be formulated.

So far as our present *Fourth Round* terrestrial period is concerned, the mammalian fauna are alone to be regarded as traceable to prototypes shed by Man. The amphibia, birds, reptiles, fishes, etc., are the resultants of the Third Round, astral fossil forms stored up in the auric envelope of the Earth and projected into physical objectivity subsequent to the deposition of the first Laurentian rocks. "Evolution" has to deal with the progressive modifications, which palæontology shows to have affected the lower animal and vegetable kingdoms in the course of geological time. It does not, and from the nature of things cannot, touch on the subject of the pre-physical types which served as the basis for future differentiation. Tabulate the general laws controlling the development of physical organisms it certainly may, and to a certain extent it has acquitted itself ably of the task.

SD, ii 682-684

THEOSOPHICAL GLOSSARY

Origins of Self-Consciousness in
The Secret Doctrine
by H. P. BLAVATSKY

A.

Absoluteness. When predicated of the UNIVERSAL PRINCIPLE, it denotes an abstract noun, which is more correct and logical than to apply the adjective "absolute " to that which has neither attributes nor limitations, nor can IT have any.

Adam (Heb.). In the *Kabalah* Adam is the "only-begotten", and means also "red earth". (See "Adam-Adami" in the *S.D.* II p. 452.) It is almost identical with *Athamas* or *Thomas*, and is rendered into Greek by *Didumos*, the "twin"– Adam, "the first", in chap. 1 of *Genesis*, being shown, "male-female."

Adam Kadmon *(Heb)*. Archetypal Man; Humanity. The "Heavenly Man" not fallen into sin; Kabalists refer it to the Ten Sephiroth on the plane of human perception. [w.w.w.]

In the *Kabalah* Adam Kadmon is the manifested Logos corresponding to our *Third* Logos; the Unmanifested being the first paradigmic ideal Man, and symbolizing the Universe in *abscondito*, or in its "privation" in the Aristotelean sense. The First Logos is the "Light of the World", the Second and the Third – its gradually deepening shadows.

Adept *(Lat.)*. *Adeptus*, "He who has obtained." In Occultism one who has reached the stage of Initiation, and become a Master in the science of Esoteric philosophy.

Âditi *(Sk.)*. The Vedic name for the *Mûlaprakriti* of the Vedantists; the abstract aspect of Parabrahman, though both unmanifested and unknowable. In the *Vedas* Âditi is the "Mother-Goddess", her terrestrial symbol being infinite and shoreless space.

Adwaita *(Sk.)*. A Vedânta sect. The non-dualistic (A-dwaita) school of Vedântic philosophy founded by Sankarâchârya, the greatest of the historical Brahmin sages. The two other schools are the Dwaita (dualistic) and the Visishtadwaita; all the three call themselves Vedântic.

Adwaitin (*Sk.*). A follower of the said school.

Æther (*Gr.*). With the ancients the divine luminiferous substance which pervades the whole universe, the "garment" of the Supreme Deity, Zeus, or Jupiter. With the moderns, Ether, for the meaning of which in physics and chemistry see Webster's *Dictionary* or any other. In esotericism Æther is the third principle of the Kosmic Septenary; the Earth being the lowest, then the Astral light, Ether and *Âkâsa* (phonetically *Âkâsha*) the highest.

Agathodæmon (*Gr.*). The beneficent, good Spirit as contrasted with the bad one, Kakodæmon. The "Brazen Serpent" of the Bible is the former; the flying serpents of fire are an aspect of Kakodæmon. The Ophites called Agathodæmon the Logos and Divine Wisdom, which in the Bacchanalian Mysteries was represented by a serpent erect on a pole.

Agni (*Sk.*). The God of Fire in the Veda; the oldest and the most revered of Gods in India. He is one of the three great deities: Agni, Vâyu and Sûrya, and also all the three, as he is the triple aspect of fire; in heaven as the Sun; in the atmosphere or air (Vâyu), as Lightning; on. earth, as ordinary Fire. Agni belonged to the earlier Vedic *Trimûrti* before Vishnu was given a place of honour and before Brahmâ and Siva were invented.

Agnishwattas (*Sk.*). A class of Pitris, the creators of the first ethereal race of men. Our solar ancestors as contrasted with the *Barhishads,* the "lunar" Pitris or ancestors, though otherwise explained in the *Purânas.*

Aham (*Sk.*). "I" – the basis of *Ahankâra*, Self-hood.

Ahankâra (*Sk.*). The conception of "I", Self-consciousness or Self- identity; the "I", the egotistical and *mâyâvic* principle in man, due to our ignorance which separates our "I" from the Universal ONE-SELF Personality, Egoism.

Ahura (*Zend.*). The same as *Asura*, the holy, the Breath-like. Ahura Mazda, the Ormuzd of the Zoroastrians or Parsis, is the Lord who bestows light and intelligence, whose symbol is the Sun (See "Ahura Mazda"), and of whom Ahriman, a European form of "Angra Mainyu" (q.v.), is the dark aspect.

Ahura Mazda (*Zend*). The personified deity, the Principle of Universal Divine Light of the Parsis. From Ahura or *Asura*, breath, "spiritual, divine" in the oldest *Rig Veda,* degraded by the orthodox Brahmans into *A -sura*, "no gods", just as the Mazdeans have degraded the Hindu Devas (Gods) into Dæva (Devils).

Ain Soph (*Heb.*). The "Boundless" or Limitless; Deity emanating and extending. [w.w.w.]

Ain Soph is also written *En Soph* and *Ain Suph*, no one, not even Rabbis, being sure of their vowels. In the religious metaphysics of the old Hebrew philosophers, the ONE Principle was an abstraction, like Parabrahmam, though modern Kabbalists have succeeded now, by dint of mere sophistry and paradoxes, in making a "Supreme God" of it and nothing higher. But with the early Chaldean Kabbalists Ain Soph is "without form or being", having "no likeness with anything else" (Franck, *Die Kabbala,* p. 126). That Ain Soph has never been considered as the "Creator" is proved by even such an orthodox Jew as Philo calling the "Creator" the *Logos,* who stands next the "Limitless One", and the "Second God". "The Second God is its (Ain Soph's) wisdom", says Philo *(Quaest. et Solut.).* Deity is NO-THING; it is nameless, and therefore called Ain Soph; the word *Ain* meaning NOTHING. (See Franck's *Kabbala,* p. 153 ff.)

Aitareya *(Sk.).* The name of an Aranyaka (Brâhmana) and a Upanishad of the *Rig Veda.* Some of its portions are purely Vedântic.

Akâsa *(Sk.).* The subtle, supersensuous spiritual essence which pervades all space; the primordial substance erroneously identified with Ether. But it is to Ether what Spirit is to Matter, or *Âtmâ* to *Kâma-rûpa.* It is, in fact, the Universal Space in which lies inherent the eternal Ideation of the Universe in its ever-changing aspects on the planes of matter and objectivity, and from which radiates the *First Logos,* or expressed thought. This is why it is stated in the *Purânas* that Âkâsa has but one attribute, namely sound, for sound is but the translated symbol of Logos – "Speech" in its mystic sense. In the same sacrifice *(the Jyotishtoma Agnishtoma)* it is called the "God Âkâsa". In these sacrificial mysteries Âkâsa is the all-directing 'and omnipotent Deva who plays the part of Sadasya, the superintendent over the magical effects of the religious performance, and it had its own appointed Hotri (priest) in days of old, who took its name. The Âkâsa is the indispensable agent of every *Krityâ* (magical performance) religious or profane. The expression "to stir up the Brahmâ", means to stir up the power which lies latent at the bottom of every magical operation, Vedic sacrifices being in fact nothing if not ceremonial magic. This power is the Âkâsa – in another aspect, *Kundalini* – occult electricity, the alkahest of the alchemists in one sense, or the universal solvent, the same *anima mundi* on the higher plane as the *astral light* is on the lower. "At the moment of the sacrifice the priest becomes imbued with the spirit of Brahmâ, is, for the time being, Brahmâ himself". *(Isis Unveiled).*

Alaya *(Sk.).* The Universal Soul (See *Secret Doctrine* Vol. I. pp. 47 *et seq.).* The name belongs to the Tibetan system of the contemplative *Mahâyâna* School. Identical with *Âkâsa* in its mystic sense, and with *Mulâprâkriti,* in its essence, as it is the basis or root of all things.

Amânasa *(Sk.).* The " Mindless", the early races of this planet; also certain Hindu gods.

Ambhâmsi *(Sk.).* A name of the chief of the Kumâras Sanat-Sujâta, signifying the "waters". This epithet will become more comprehensible when we remember that the later type of Sanat-Sujâta was Michael, the Archangel, who is called in the Talmud "the Prince of *Waters*", and in the Roman Catholic

Church is regarded as the patron of gulfs and promontories. Sanat-Sujâta is the immaculate son of the immaculate mother (Ambâ or Aditi, chaos and space) or the "waters" of limitless space. (See *Secret Doctrine-*, Vol. I., p. 460.)

Amesha Spentas (*Zend*). Amshaspends. The six angels or divine Forces personified as gods who attend upon Ahura Mazda, of which he is the synthesis and the seventh. They are one of the prototypes of the Roman Catholic "Seven Spirits" or Angels with Michael as chief, or the "Celestial Host"; the " Seven Angels of the Presence". They are the Builders, Cosmocratores, of the Gnostics and identical with the Seven Prajâpatis, the Sephiroth, etc. (q.v.).

Ananta-Sesha (*Sk.*). The Serpent of Eternity – the couch of Vishnu during Pralaya (lit., endless remain).

Anaxagoras (*Gr.*) A famous Ionian philosopher who lived 500 B.C., studied philosophy under Anaximenes of Miletus, and settled in the days of Pericles at Athens. Socrates, Euripides, Archelaus and other distinguished men and philosophers were among his disciples and pupils. He was a most learned astronomer and was one of the first to explain openly that which was taught by Pythagoras secretly, namely, the movements of the planets, the eclipses of the sun and moon, etc. It was he who taught the theory of Chaos, on the principle that "nothing comes from nothing"; and of atoms, as the underlying essence and substance of all bodies, "of the same nature as the bodies which they formed".

These atoms, he taught, were primarily put in motion by Nous (Universal Intelligence, the Mahat of the Hindus), which Nous is an immaterial, eternal, spiritual entity; by this combination the world was formed, the material gross bodies sinking down, and the ethereal atoms (or fiery ether) rising and spreading in the upper celestial regions. Antedating modern science by over 2000 years, he taught that the stars were of the same material as our earth, and the sun a glowing mass; that the moon was a dark, uninhabitable body, receiving its light from the sun; the comets, wandering stars or bodies ; and over and above the said science, he confessed himself thoroughly convinced that the real existence of things, perceived by our senses, could not be demonstrably proved. He died in exile at Lampsacus at the age of seventy-two.

Androgyne Ray (*Esot.*). The first differentiated ray; the Second Logos; Adam Kadmon in the *Kabalah;* the "male and female created he them", of the first chapter of *Genesis.*

AnimaMundi (*Lat.*). The"Soul of the World", the same as the *Alaya* of the Northern Buddhists; the divine essence which permeates, animates and informs all, from the smallest atom of matter to man and god. It is in a sense the "seven-skinned mother" of the stanzas in the *Secret Doctrine*, the essence of seven planes of sentience, consciousness and differentiation, moral and physical. In its highest aspect it is *Nirvâna*, in its lowest Astral Light. It was feminine with the Gnostics, the early Christians and the Nazarenes; bisexual with other sects, who considered it only in its four lower planes. Of igneous, ethereal nature in the objective world of form (and then ether), and divine and spiritual in its three higher planes. When it is said that every human soul was born by detaching itself from the *Anima Mundi*, it means, esoterically, that our higher Egos are of an essence identical with It, which is a radiation of the ever unknown Universal ABSOLUTE.

Anthropomorphism (*Gr.*). From "anthropos" meaning man. The act of endowing god or gods with a human form and human attributes or qualities.

Anugîtâ (*Sk.*). One of the *Upanishads*. A very occult treatise. (*See The sacred Books of the East.*)

Anupâdaka (*Sk.*). Anupapâdaka, also Aupapâduka; means parentless", "self-existing", born without any parents or progenitors. A term applied to certain self-created gods, and the Dhyâni Buddhas.

Archæus (*Gr.*). "The Ancient." Used of the oldest manifested deity; a term employed in the *Kabalah* ; "archaic ", old, ancient.

Archangel (*Gr.*). Highest supreme angel. From the Greek *arch*, "chief" or "primordial", and *angelos,* "messenger ".

Archæus (*Gr.*). "The Ancient." Used of the oldest manifested deity; a term employed in the *Kabalah* ; "archaic ", old, ancient.

Archetypal Universe (*Kab.*). The ideal universe upon which the objective world was built. [w.w.w.]

Arûpa (*Sk.*). "Bodiless", formless, as opposed to *rûpa*, "body", or form.

Arvâksrotas (*Sk.*). The *seventh* creation, that of man, in the *Vishnu Purâna.*

Âryasangha (*Sk.*) The Founder of the *first* Yogâchârya School. This Arhat, a direct disciple of Gautama, the Buddha, is most unaccountably mixed up and confounded with a personage of the same name, who is said to have lived in Ayôdhya (Oude) about the fifth or sixth century of our era, and taught Tântrika worship in addition to the Yogâchârya system. Those who sought to make it popular, claimed that he was the same Âryasangha, that had been a follower of Sâkyamuni, and that he was 1,000 years old. Internal evidence alone is sufficient to show that the works written by him and translated about the year 600 of our era, works full of Tantra worship, ritualism, and tenets followed now considerably by the "red-cap" sects in Sikhim, Bhutan, and Little Tibet, cannot be the same as the lofty system of the early Yogâcharya school of pure Buddhism, which is neither northern nor southern, but absolutely esoteric. Though none of the genunine Yogâchârya books (the *Narjol chodpa*) have ever been made public or marketable, yet one finds in the *Yogâchârya Bhûmi Shâstra* of the *pseudo*-Âryasangha a great deal from the older system, into the tenets of which he may have been initiated. It is, however, so mixed up with Sivaism and Tantrika magic and superstitions, that the work defeats its own end, notwithstanding its remarkable dialectical subtilty. (See the *Theosophical Glossary*)

Astral Body, or Astral "Double". The ethereal counterpart or shadow of man or animal. The **Linga Sharira**, the "Doppelgäinger". The reader must not confuse it with the ASTRAL SOUL, another name for the lower Manas, or Kama-Manas so-called, the reflection of the HIGHER EGO.

Astral Light (*Occult*) The invisible region that surrounds our globe, as it does every other, and corresponding as the second Principle of Kosmos (the third being Life, of which it is the vehicle) to the *Linga Sharira* or the Astral Double in man. A subtle Essence visible only to a clairvoyant eye, and the lowest but one (*viz.*, the earth), of the Seven Akâsic or Kosmic Principles. Eliphas Levi calls it the great Serpent and the Dragon from which radiates on Humanity every evil influence. This is so; but why not add that the Astral Light gives out nothing but what it has received; that it is the great terrestrial crucible, in which the vile emanations of the earth (moral and physical) upon which the Astral Light is fed, are all converted into their subtlest essence, and radiated back intensified, thus becoming epidemics – moral, psychic and physical. Finally, the Astral Light is the same as the *Sidereal Light* of Paracelsus and other Hermetic philosophers. "Physically, it is the ether of modern science. Metaphysically, and in its spiritual, or occult sense, ether is a great deal more than is often imagined. In occult physics, and alchemy, it is well demonstrated to enclose within its shoreless waves not only Mr. Tyndall's *'promise* and potency of every quality of life'*, but also the *realization* of the potency of every quality of spirit. Alchemists and Hermetists believe that their *astral*, or sidereal ether, besides the above properties of sulphur, and white and red magnesia, or *magnes*, is the *anima mundi*, the workshop of Nature and of all the Kosmos, spiritually, as well as physically. The 'grand magisterium' asserts itself in the phenomenon of mesmerism, in the 'levitation' of human and inert objects; and may be called the ether from its spiritual aspect. The designation *astral* is ancient, and was used by some of the Neo-platonists, although it is claimed by some that the word was coined by the Martinists. Porphyry describes the celestial body which is always joined with the soul as 'immortal, luminous, and star-like'. The root of this word may be found, perhaps, in the Scythic *Aist-aer* – which means star, or the Assyrian *Istar*, which, according to Burnouf has the same sense." (*Isis Unveiled.*)

Asuras (*Sk.*). Exoterically, elementals and evil, gods – considered maleficent; demons, and *no* gods. But esoterically – the reverse. For in the most ancient portions of the *Rig Veda*, the term is used for the Supreme Spirit, and therefore the Asuras are spiritual and divine It is only in the last book of the *Rig Veda*, its latest part, and in the *Atharva Veda*, and the *Brâhmanas*, that the epithet, which had been given to Agni, the greatest Vedic Deity, to Indra and Varuna, has come to signify the reverse of gods. *Asu* means breath, and it is with his breath that Prajâpati (Brahmâ) creates the Asuras. When ritualism and dogma got the better of the Wisdom religion, the initial letter **a** was adopted as a negative prefix, and the term ended by signifying "not a god", and Sura only a deity. But in the Vedas the Suras have ever been connected with *Surya*, the sun, and regarded as *inferior* deities, devas.

Aswattha (*Sk.*) The *Bo-tree*, the tree of knowledge, *ficus religiosa*.

Avalokiteswara (*Sk.*) "The on-looking Lord" In the exoteric interpretation, he is Padmapâni (the lotus bearer and the lotus-born) in Tibet, the first divine ancestor of the Tibetans, the complete incarnation or Avatar of Avalokiteswara; but in esoteric philosophy Avaloki, the "on-looker", is the Higher Self, while Padmapâni is the Higher Ego or Manas. The mystic formula "Om mani padme hum" is specially used to invoke their joint help. While popular fancy claims for Avalokiteswara many incarnations on earth, and sees in him, not very wrongly, the spiritual guide of every believer, the esoteric interpretation sees in him the Logos, both celestial and human. Therefore, when the Yogâchârya School has declared Avalokiteswara as Padmâpani "to be the Dhyâni Bodhisattva of Amitâbha Buddha", it is indeed, because the former is *the spiritual reflex in the world of forms* of the latter, both being one – one in heaven, the other on earth.

Avatâra (*Sk.*) Divine incarnation. The descent of a god or some exalted Being, who has progressed beyond the necessity of Rebirths, into the body of a simple mortal. Krishna was an avatar of Vishnu. The Dalai Lama is regarded as an avatar of Avalokiteswara, and the Teschu Lama as one of Tson-kha-pa, or Amitâbha. There are two kinds of avatars: those born from woman, and the parentless, the *anupapâdaka*.

B.

Barhishad (*Sk.*). A class of the "lunar" Pitris or "Ancestors", Fathers, who are believed in popular superstition to have kept up in their past incarnations the household sacred flame and made fire-offerings. Esoterically the Pitris who evolved their shadows or *chhayas* to make there-with the first man. (See *Secret Doctrine*, Vol. II.)

Bhûta-sarga (*Sk.*). Elemental or incipient Creation, i.e., when matter was several degrees less material than it is now.

Bhûts (Sk.). *Bhûta*.: Ghosts, phantoms. To call them "demons", as do the Orientalists, is incorrect. For, if on the one hand, a Bhûta is "a malignant spirit which haunts cemeteries, lurks in trees, animates dead bodies, and deludes and devours human beings", in popular fancy, in India in Tibet and China, by Bhûtas are also meant "heretics" who besmear their bodies with ashes, or Shaiva ascetics (Siva being held in India for the King of Bhûtas).

Binah (*Heb.*). Understanding. The third of the 10 Sephiroth, the third of the Supernal Triad; a female potency, corresponding to the letter *hé* of the Tetragrammaton IHVH. Binah is called AIMA, the Supernal Mother, and "the great Sea". [w.w.w.]

Book of the Dead. An ancient Egyptian ritualistic and occult work attributed to Thot-Hermes. Found in the coffins of ancient mummies.

Brahma (*Sk.*). The student must distinguish between Brahma the neuter, and Brahmâ, the male creator of the Indian Pantheon. The former, Brahma or Brahman, is the impersonal, supreme and uncognizable Principle of the Universe from the essence of which all emanates, and into which all returns, which is incorporeal, immaterial, unborn, eternal, beginningless and endless. It is all-pervading, animating the highest god as well as the smallest mineral atom. Brahmâ on the other hand, the male and the alleged Creator, exists periodically in his manifestation only, and then again goes into pralaya, i.e., disappears and is annihilated.

Brahmâ's Day. A period of 2,160,000,000 years during which Brahmâ having emerged out of his golden egg (*Hiranyagarbha*), creates and fashions the material world (being simply the fertilizing and creative force in Nature). After this period, the worlds being destroyed in turn, by fire and water, he vanishes with objective nature, and then comes Brahmâ's Night.

Brahmâ's Night. A period of equal duration, during which Brahmâ. is said to be asleep. Upon awakening he recommences the process, and this goes on for an AGE of Brahmâ composed of alternate "Days", and "Nights", and lasting 100 years (of 2,160,000,000 years each). It requires fifteen figures to express the duration of such an age; after the expiration of which the *Mahapralaya* or the Great Dissolution sets in, and lasts in its turn for the same space of fifteen figures.

Brahmâ Vâch (*Sk.*) Male and female Brahmâ. Vâch is also some-times called the female logos; for Vâch means Speech, literally. (See *Manu* Book I., and *Vishnu Purâna.*)

Brahma Vidyâ (*Sk.*) The knowledge, the esoteric science, about the two Brahmas and their true nature.

Brahmâ Virâj. (*Sk.*) The same: Brahmâ separating his body into two halves, male and female, creates in them Vâch and Virâj. In plainer terms and *esotericlly* Brahmâ the Universe, differentiating, produced thereby material nature, Virâj, and spiritual intelligent Nature, Vâch – which is the *Logos* of Deity or the manifested expression of the eternal divine Ideation.

Brâhman (*Sk.*) The highest of the four castes in India, one supposed or rather fancying himself, as high among men, as Brahman, the ABSOLUTE of the Vedantins, is high among, or above the gods.

Brahmâputrâs (*Sk.*) The Sons of Brahmâ.

Buddha (*Sk.*). Lit., "The Enlightened". The highest degree of knowledge. To become a Buddha one has to break through the bondage of sense and personality; to acquire a complete perception of the REAL SELF and learn not to separate it from all otherselves; to learn by experience the utter unreality of all phenomena of the visible Kosmos foremost of all; to reach a complete detachment from all that is evanescent and finite, and live while yet on Earth in the immortal and the everlasting alone, in a supreme state of holiness.

Buddhi (*Sk.*). Universal Soul or Mind. *Mahâbuddhi* is a name of Mahat (see "Alaya"); also the spiritual Soul in man (the sixth principle), the vehicle of Atmâ exoterically the seventh.

Buddhism. Buddhism is now split into two distinct Churches : the Southern and the Northern Church. The former is said to be the purer form, as having preserved more religiously the original teachings of the Lord Buddha. It is the religion of Ceylon, Siam, Burmah and other places, while Northern Buddhism is confined to Tibet, China and Nepaul. Such a distinction, however, is incorrect. If the Southern Church is nearer, in that it has not departed, except perhaps in some trifling dogmas due to the many councils held after the death of the Master, from the public or *exoteric* teachings of Sâkyamuni – the Northern Church is the outcome of Siddhârta Buddha's esoteric teachings which he confined to his elect Bhikshus and Arhats. In fact, Buddhism in the present age, cannot he justly judged either by one or the other of its exoteric popular forms. Real Buddhism can be appreciated only by blending the philosophy of the Southern Church and the metaphysics of the Northern Schools. If one seems too iconoclastic and stero:, and the other too metaphysical and transcendental, even to being overgrown with the weeds of Indian exotericism – many of the gods of its Pantheon having been transplanted under new names to Tibetan soil – it is entirely due to the popular expression of Buddhism in both Churches. Correspondentially they stand in their relation to each other as Protestantism to Roman Catholicism. Both err by an excess of zeal and erroneous interpretations, though neither the Southern nor the Northern Buddhist clergy have ever departed from truth consciously, still less have they acted under the dictates of *priestocracy*, ambition, or with an eye to personal gain and power, as the two Christian Churches have.

C

Cain or Kayn (*Heb.*) In Esoteric symbology he is said to be identical with Jehovah or the "Lord God" of the fourth chapter of *Genesis*. It is held, moreover, that Abel is not his brother, but his female aspect. (See *Sec.Doct.*, *sub voce*.)

Capricornus (*Lat.*) The 10th sign of the Zodiac (*Makâra* in Sanskrit), considered, on account of its hidden meaning, the most important among the constellations of the mysterious Zodiac. it is fully described in the *Secret Doctrine*, and therefore needs but a few words more. Whether, agreeably with exoteric statements, Capricornus was related in any way to the wet-nurse Amalthæa who fed Jupiter with her milk, or whether it was the god Pan who changed himself into a goat and left his impress upon the sidereal records, matters little. Each of the fables has its significance. Everything in Nature is intimately correlated to the rest, and therefore the students of ancient lore will not be too much surprised when told that even the seven steps taken in the direction of every one of the four points of the compass, or – 28 steps – taken by the new-born infant Buddha, are closely related to the 28 stars of the constellation of Capricornus.

Causal Body. This "body", which is no body either objective or subjective, but *Buddhi*, the Spiritual Soul, is so called because it is the direct cause of the Sushupti condition, leading to the *Turya* state, the highest state of *Samadhi*. It is called *Karanopadhi*, "the basis of the Cause", by the Târaka Raja Yogis; and in the Vedânta system it corresponds to both the *Vignânamaya* and *Anandamaya Kosha*, the latter coming next to Atma, and therefore being the vehicle of the universal Spirit. Buddhi alone could not be called a "Causal Body ", but becomes so in conjunction with Manas, the incarnating Entity or EGO.

Chakra (*Sk.*) A wheel, a disk, or the circle of Vishnu generally. Used also of a cycle of time, and with other meanings.

Chaldeans, or *Kasdim*. At first a tribe, then a caste of learned Kabbalists. They were the *savants*, the magians of Babylonia, astrologers and diviners. The famous Hillel, the precursor of Jesus in philosophy and in ethics, was a Chaldean. Franck in his *Kabbala* points to the close resemblance of the "secret doctrine" found in the *Avesta* and the religious metaphysics of the Chaldees.

Chaos (*Gr.*) The Abyss, the "Great Deep". It was personified in Egypt by the Goddess Neïth, anterior to all gods. As Deveria says, "the only God, without form and sex, who gave birth to itself, and without fecundation, is adored under the form of a Virgin Mother". She is the vulture-headed Goddess found in the oldest period of Abydos, who belongs, accordingly to Mariette Bey, to the first Dynasty, which would make her, even on the confession of the time-dwarfing Orientalists, about 7,000 years old. As Mr. Bonwick tells us in his excellent work on Egyptian belief – "Neïth, Nut, Nepte, Nuk (her names as variously read !) is a philosophical conception worthy of the nineteenth century after the Christian era, rather than the thirty-ninth before it or earlier than that". And he adds: " Neith or Nout is neither more nor less than the *Great Mother*, a yet the *Immaculate Virgin*, or female God from whom all things proceeded".

Neïth is the "Father-mother" of the *Stanzas* of the *Secret Doctrine*, the Swabhavat of the Northern Buddhists, the *immaculate* Mother indeed, the prototype of the latest "Virgin" of all; for, as Sharpe says, "the Feast of Candlemas – in honour of the goddess Neïth – is yet marked in our Almanacs as Candlemas day, or the Purification of the Virgin Mary"; and Beauregard tells us of "the Immaculate Conception of the Virgin, who can henceforth, as well as the Egyptian Minerva, the mysterious Neïth, boast of having come from herself, and of having given birth to God". He who would deny the working of cycles and the recurrence of events, let him read what Neïth was years ago, in the conception of the Egyptian Initiates, trying to popularize a philosophy too abstract for the masses; and then remember the subjects of dispute at the Council of Ephesus in 431, when Mary was declared Mother of God; and her Immaculate Conception forced on the World as by command of God, by Pope and Council in 1858. Neïth is *Swabhdvat* and also the Vedic *Aditi* and the Purânic *Akâsa*, for "she is not only the celestial vault, or ether, but is made to appear in a tree, from which she gives the fruit of the Tree of Life (like another Eve) or pours upon her worshippers some of the divine water of life". Hence she gained the favourite appellation of "Lady of the Sycamore", an epithet applied to another Virgin (Bonwick). (See *The Theosophical Glossary*.)

Chelâ (*Sk.*) A disciple, the pupil of a Guru or Sage, the follower of some adept of a school of philosophy *(lit.,* child).

Cherubim (*Heb.*) According to the Kabbalists, a group of angels, which they specially associated with the Sephira Jesod. in Christian teaching, an order of angels who are "watchers". *Genesis* places Cherubim to guard the lost Eden, and the O.T. frequently refers to them as guardians of the divine glory. Two winged representations in gold were placed over the Ark of the Covenant; colossal figures of the same were also placed in the Sanctum Sanctorum of the Temple of Solomon. Ezekiel describes them in poetic language. Each Cherub appears to have been a compound figure with four faces – of a man, eagle, lion, and ox, and was certainly winged. (See *The Theosophical Glossary*.)

Chhâyâ (*Sk.*) "Shade" or " Shadow". The name of a creature produced by Sanjnâ, the wife of Surya, from herself (astral body). Unable to endure the ardour of her husband, Sanjnâ left Chhâyâ in her place as a wife, going herself away to perform austerities. Chhâyâ is the astral image of a person in esoteric philosophy.

Chhaya loka (*Sk.*) The world of Shades; like Hades, the world of the *Eidola* and *Umbræ*. We call it *Kâmaloka*.

Chohan (*Tib.*) "Lord" or "Master" ; a chief; thus **Dhyan-Chohan** would answer to "Chief of the Dhyanis", or celestial Lights – which in English would he translated Archangels.

Chokmah (Heb) Wisdom; the second of the ten Sephiroth, and the second of the supernal Triad. A masculine potency corresponding to the Yod (I) of the Tetragrammaton IHVH, and to **Ab**, the Father. [w.w.w.]

Chréstos (*Gr.*) The early Gnostic form of Christ. It was used in the fifth century B.C. by Æschylus, Herodotus, and others. The *Manteumata pythochresta*, or the "oracles delivered by a Pythian god" "through a pythoness, are mentioned by the former (*Choeph*.901). *Chréstian* is not only "the seat of an oracle", but an offering to, or for, the oracle.

Chréstés is one who explains oracles, "a prophet and soothsayer", and Chrésterios one who serves an oracle or a god. The earliest Christian writer, Justin Martyr, in his first *Apology* calls his co-religionists Chréstians. It is only through ignorance that men call themselves Christians instead of Chréstians," says Lactantius (lib. iv., cap. vii.). The terms Christ and Christians, spelt originally Chrést and Chréstians, were borrowed from the Temple vocabulary of the Pagans. Chréstos meant in that vocabulary a disciple on probation, a candidate for hierophantship. When he had attained to this through initiation, long trials, and suffering, and had been *"anointed"* (i.e., "rubbed with oil", as were Initiates and even idols of the gods, as the last touch of ritualistic observance), his name was changed into Christos, the "purified", in esoteric or mystery language. In mystic symbology, indeed, *Christés*, or *Christos*, meant that the "Way", the Path, was already trodden and the goal reached ; when the fruits of the arduous labour, uniting the personality of evanescent clay with the indestructible INDIVIDUALITY, transformed it thereby into the immortal EGO. "At the end of the Way stands the *Chréstes"*, the *Purifier*, and the union once accomplished, the *Chrestos*, the "man of sorrow", became *Christos* himself. Paul, the Initiate, knew this, and meant this precisely, when he is made to say, in bad translation : "I travail in birth again until Christ be formed in you" (Gal. iv.19), the true rendering of which is . . . "until ye form the Christos within yourselves" But the profane who knew only that Chréstés was in some way connected with priest and prophet, and knew nothing about the hidden meaning of Christos, insisted, as did Lactantius and Justin Martyr, on being called *Chréstians* instead of Christians. Every good individual, therefore, may find Christ in his "inner man" as Paul expresses it (Ephes. iii. 16,17), whether he be Jew, Mussulman, Hindu, or Christian. Kenneth Mackenzie seemed to think that the word *Chréstos* was a synonym of Soter, "an appellation assigned to deities, great kings and heroes," indicating "Saviour," – and he was right. For, as he adds:"It has been applied redundantly to Jesus Christ, whose name Jesus or Joshua bears the same interpretation. The name Jesus, in fact, is rather a title of honour than a name – the true name of the Soter of Christianity being Emmanuel, or God with us (*Matt*.i, 23.).Great divinities among all nations, who are represented as expiatory or self-sacrificing, have been designated by the same title." (*R. M. Cyclop.*) The Asklepios (or Æsculapius) of the Greeks had the title of *Soter.*

Codex Nazaraeus (Lat.) The "Book of Adam" – the latter name meaning *anthropos*, Man or Humanity. The Nazarene faith is called sometimes the Bardesanian system, though Bardesanes (B.C. 155 to 228) does not seem to have had any connection with it. True, he was born at Edessa in Syria, and was a famous astrologer and Sabian before his alleged conversion. But he was a well-educated man of noble family, and would not have used the almost incomprehensible Chaldeo dialect mixed with the mystery language of the Gnostics, in which the Codex is written. The sect of the Nazarenes was pre-Christian. Pliny and Josephus speak of the Nazarites as settled on the banks of the Jordan 150 years B.C. (*Ant.Jud.* xiii. p. 9); and Munk says that the "Naziareate was an institution established before the laws of Musah" or Moses. (Munk p. 169.) Their modern name is in Arabic – *El Mogtasila*; in European languages – the Mendæans or "Christians of St. John". (See "Baptism".) But if the term Baptists may well be applied to them, it is not with the Christian meaning: for while they were, and still are Sabians, or pure astrolaters, the Mendæans of Syria, called the Galileans, are pure polytheists, as every traveller in Syria and on the Euphrates can ascertain, once he acquaints himself with their mysterious rites and ceremonies. (*See Isis Unv. ii. 290, et seq.*) So secretly did they preserve their beliefs from the very beginning, that Epiphanius who wrote against the Heresies in the14th century confesses himself unable to say what they believed in (i. 122); he simply states that they never mention the name of Jesus, nor do they call themselves Christians (*loc. cit.* 190. Yet it is undeniable that some of the alleged philosophical views and doctrines of Bardesanes are found in the codex of the Nazarenes. (See Norberg's *Codex Nazaræous* or the "Book of Adam", and also "Mendæans ".)

Cosmic Gods. Inferior gods, those connected with the formation of matter.

Cosmic ideation (*Occult.*) Eternal thought, impressed on substance or spirit-matter, in the eternity ; thought which becomes active at the beginning of every new life-cycle.

Cosmocratores (*Gr.*). "Builders of the Universe", the "world architects", or the Creative Forces personified.

Crocodile. "The great reptile of Typhon." The seat of its "worship" was Crocodilopolis and it was sacred to Set and Sebak – its alleged creators. The primitive Rishis in India, the *Manus*, and Sons of Brahmâ, are each the progenitors of some animal species, of which he is the alleged "father"; in Egypt, each god was credited with the formation or creation of certain animals which were sacred to him. Crocodiles must have been numerous in Egypt during the early dynasties, if one has to judge by the almost incalculable number of their mummies. Thousands upon thousands have been excavated from the grottoes of Moabdeh, and many a vast *necropolis* of that Typhonic animal is still left untouched. But the Crocodile was only worshipped where his god and "father" received honours. Typhon (*q.v.*) had once received such honours and, as Bunsen shows, had been considered a great god. His words are, " Down to the time of Ramses B.C. 1300, Typhon was one of the most venerated and powerful gods, a god who pours blessings and life on the rulers of Egypt." As explained elsewhere, Typhon is the material aspect of Osiris. When Typhon, the Quaternary, *kills* Osiris, the triad or divine Light, and cuts it metaphorically into 14 pieces, and separates himself from the "god", he incurs the execration of the masses; he becomes the evil god, the storm and hurricane god, the burning sand of the Desert, the constant enemy of the Nile, and the "slayer of the evening beneficent dew", because Osiris is the ideal Universe, Siva the great Regenerative Force, and Typhon the material portion of it, the evil side of the god, or the Destroying Siva. This is why the crocodile is also partly venerated and partly execrated. The appearance of the crocodile in the Desert, far from the water, prognosticated the happy event of the coming inundation – hence its adoration at Thebes and Ombos. But he destroyed thousands of human and animal beings yearly – hence also the hatred and persecution of the Crocodile at Elephantine and Tentyra.

Cycle. From the Greek *Kuklos*. The ancients divided time into end less cycles, wheels within wheels, all such periods being of various durations, and each marking the beginning or the end of some event either cosmic, mundane, physical or metaphysical. There were cycles of only a few years, and cycles of immense duration, the great Orphic cycle, referring to the ethnological change of races, lasting 120,000 years, and the cycle of Cassandrus of 136,000, which brought about a complete change in planetary influences and their correlations between men and gods – a fact entirely lost sight of by modern astrologers.

D

Dæmon (*Gr.*) In the original Hermetic works and ancient classics it has a meaning identical with that of "god", "angel" or "genius". The Dæmon of Socrates is the incorruptible part of the man, or rather the real inner man which we call Nous or the rational divine Ego. At all events the Dæmon (or Daimon of the great Sage was surely not the demon of the Christian Hell or of Christian orthodox theology. The name was given by ancient peoples, and especially the philosophers of the Alexandrian school, to all kinds of spirits, whether good or bad, human or otherwise. The appellation is often synonymous with that of gods or angels. But some philosophers tried, with good reason, to make a just distinction between the many classes.

Daitya Guru (*Sk.*) The instructor of the giants, called *Daityas* (*q.v.*) Allegorically, it is the title given to the planet Venus-Lucifer, or rather to its indwelling Ruler, *Sukra,* a male deity (See *Sec. Doct..* ii. p. 30).

Daityas *(Sk.)* Giants, Titans, and exoterically demons, but in truth identical with certain Asuras, the intellectual gods, the opponents of the useless gods of ritualism and the enemies of *puja* sacrifices.

Dâkinî *(Sk.)* Female demons, vampires and blood-drinkers *(asra-pas)*. In the *Purânas* they attend upon the goddess Kâli and feed on human flesh. A species of evil "Elementals" *(q.v.)*.

Daksha *(Sk.)* A form of Brahmâ and his son in the Purânas But the *Rig Veda* states that "Daksha sprang from Aditi, and Aditi from Daksha", which proves him to be a personified correlating Creative Force acting on *all the planes*. The Orientalists seem very much perplexed what to make of him; but Roth is nearer the truth than any, when saying that Daksha is the spiritual power, and at the same time the male energy that generates the gods in eternity, which is represented by Aditi. The Purânas as a matter of course, anthropomorphize the idea, and show Daksha instituting "sexual intercourse on this earth", after trying every other means of procreation. The generative Force, spiritual at the commencement, becomes of course at the most material end of its evolution a procreative Force on the physical plane ; and so far the Purânic allegory is correct, as the Secret Science teaches that our present mode of procreation began towards the end of the third Root-Race.

Dangma *(Sk.)* In Esotericism a purified Soul. A Seer and an Initiate; one who has attained full wisdom.

Day of Brahmâ. See "Brahmâ's Day" etc.

Demeter The Hellenic name for the Latin Ceres, the goddess of corn and tillage. The astronomical sign, Virgo. The Eleusinian Mysteries were celebrated in her honour.

Demiurgic Mind.The same as "Universal Mind". Mahat, the first "product" of Brahmâ, or himself.

Demiurgos *(Gr)* The Demiurge or Artificer; the Supernal Power which built the universe. Freemasons derive from this word their phrase of "Supreme Architect ". With the Occultists it is the third manifested Logos, or Plato's "second god", the second logos being represented by him as the "Father", the only Deity that he dared mention as an Initiate into the Mysteries.

Demons. According to the Kabbalah, the demons dwell in the world of Assiah, the world of matter and of the "shells"' of the dead. They are the Klippoth. There are Seven Hells, whose demon dwellers represent the vices personified. Their prince is Samael, his female companion is Isheth Zenunim – the woman of prostitution: united in aspect, they are named "The Beast", Chiva. [w.w.w.]

Demon est Deus inversus *(Lat)* A Kabbalistic axiom; lit., "the devil is god reversed"; which means that there is neither evil nor good, but that the forces which create the one create the other, according to the nature of the materials they find to work upon.

Deva (*Sk.*). A god, a "resplendent" deity. Deva-Deus, from the root *div* "to shine". A Deva is a celestial being – whether good, bad, or indifferent. Devas inhabit "the three worlds", which are the *three planes* above us. There are 33 groups or 330 millions of them.

Deva Sarga (*Sk.*). Creation: the origin of the principles, said to be Intelligence born of the qualities or the attributes of nature.

Devachan (*Sk.*). The "dwelling of the gods". A state intermediate between two earth-lives, into which the EGO (Atmâ-Buddhi-Manas, or the Trinity made One) enters, after its separation from Kâma Rupa, and the disintegration of the lower principles on earth.

Devajnânas (*Sk.*). or *Daivajna*. The higher classes of celestial beings, those who possess divine knowledge.

Devaki (*Sk.*). The mother of Krishna. She was shut up in a dungeon by her brother, King Kansa, for fear of the fulfilment of a prophecy which stated that a son of his sister should dethrone and kill him. Notwithstanding the strict watch kept, Devaki was overshadowed by Vishnu, the holy Spirit, and thus gave birth to that god's *avatara*, Krishna. (See "Kansa".)

Deva-lôkas (*Sk.*). The abodes of the Gods or Devas in superior spheres. The seven celestial worlds above Meru.

Devamâtri (*Sk.*). Lit., "the mother of the gods". A title of Aditi, Mystic Space.

Dhyan Chohans (*Sk*). Lit., "The Lords of Light". The highest gods, answering to the Roman Catholic Archangels. The divine Intelligences charged with the supervision of Kosmos.

Dhyâna (*Sk.*). In Buddhism one of the six Paramitas of perfection, a state of abstraction which carries the ascetic practising it far above this plane of sensuous perception and out of the world of matter. Lit., "contemplation". The six stages of Dhyan differ only in the degrees of abstraction of the personal Ego from sensuous life.

Dhyani Bodhisattyas (*Sk.*). In Buddhism, the five sons of the Dhyani-Buddhas. They have a mystic meaning in Esoteric Philosophy.

Dhyani Buddhas (*Sk.*). They "of the Merciful Heart"; worshipped especially in Nepaul. These have again a secret meaning.

Dianoia (*Gr.*). The same as the Logos. The eternal source of thought, "divine ideation", which is the root of all thought. (See "Ennoia.")

Drakôn (*Gr.*) or Dragon. Now considered a "mythical" monster, perpetuated in the West only on seals,. &c., as a heraldic griffin, and the Devil slain by St. George, &c. In fact an extinct antediluvian monster In Babylonian antiquities it is referred to as the "scaly one" and connected on many gems with Tiamat the sea. "The Dragon of the Sea" is repeatedly mentioned. In Egypt, it is the star of the Dragon (then the North Pole Star), the origin of the connection of almost all the gods with the Dragon. Bel and the Dragon, Apollo and Python, Osiris and Typhon, Sigur and Fafnir, and finally St. George and the Dragon, are the same. They were all solar gods, and wherever we find the Sun there also is the Dragon, the symbol of Wisdom – Thoth-Hermes. The Hierophants of Egypt and of Babylon styled themselves "Sons of the Serpent-God" and "Sons of the Dragon". "I am a Serpent, I am a Druid", said the Druid of the Celto-Britannic regions, for the Serpent and the Dragon were both types of Wisdom, Immortality and Rebirth. As the serpent casts its old skin only to reappear in a new one, so does the immortal Ego cast off one personality but to assume another.

Druids. A sacerdotal caste which flourished in Britain and Gaul. They were Initiates who admitted females into their sacred order, and initiated them into the mysteries of their religion. They never entrusted their sacred verses and scriptures to writing, but, like the Brahmans of old, committed them to memory; a feat which, according to the statement of Cæsar took twenty years to accomplish. Like the Parsis they had no images or statues of their gods. The Celtic religion considered it blasphemy to represent any god, even of a minor character, under a human figure. It would have been well if the Greek and Roman Christians had learnt this lesson from the "pagan" Druids. The three chief commandments of their religion were: – "Obedience to divine laws; concern for the welfare of mankind; suffering with fortitude all the evils of life".

Dwapara Yuga (*Sk.*). The third of the "Four Ages" in Hindu Philosophy ; or the second age counted from below.

Dynasties. In India there are two, the Lunar and the Solar, or the *Somavansa* and the *Suryavansa*. In Chaldea and Egypt there were also two distinct kinds of dynasties, the *divine* and the *human.* In both countries people were ruled in the beginning of time by Dynasties of Gods. In Chaldea they reigned one hundred and twenty Sari, or in all 432,000 years; which amounts to the same figures as a Hindu Mahayuga 4,320,000 years. The chronology prefacing the *Book of Genesis* (English translation) is given "Before Christ, 4004". But the figures are a rendering by solar years. In the original Hebrew, which preserved a lunar calculation, the figures are 4,320 years. This "coincidence" is well explained in Occultism.

Dzyn or Dzyan (*Tib.*). Written also *Dzen*. A corruption of the Sanskrit Dhyan and *jnâna* (or *gnyâna* phonetically) – Wisdom, divine knowledge. In Tibetan, learning is called *dzin*.

E

Eden (*Heb.*). "Delight", pleasure. In *Genesis* the "Garden of Delight" built by God ; in the Kabbala the "Garden of Delight", a place of Initiation into the mysteries. Orientalists identify it with a place which was situated in Babylonia in the district of Karduniyas, called also Gan-dunu, which is almost like the Gan-eden of the Jews. (See the works of Sir H. Rawlinson, and G. Smith.) That district has four rivers, Euphrates, Tigris, Surappi, Ukni. The two first have been adopted without any change by the Jews; the other two they have probably transformed into "Gihon and Pison", so as to have something original. The following are some of the reasons for the identification of Eden, given by Assyriologists. The cities of Babylon, Larancha and Sippara, were founded before the flood, according to the chronology of the Jews.

"Surippak was the city of the ark, the mountain east of the Tigris was the resting place of the ark, Babylon was the site of the tower, and Ur of the Chaldees the birthplace of Abraham." And, as Abraham, "the first leader of the Hebrew race, migrated from Ur to Harran in Syria and from thence to Palestine", the best Assyriologists think that it is "so much evidence in favour of the hypothesis that Chaldea was the original home of these stories (in the Bible) and that the Jews received them originally from the Babylonians".

Ego (*Lat.*). "Self" ; the consciousness in man "I am I" – or the feeling of "I-am-ship". Esoteric philosophy teaches the existence of two Egos in man, the mortal or personal, and the Higher, the Divine and the Impersonal, calling the former "personality" and the latter "Individuality Egoity. From the word "Ego". Egoity means "individuality", never "personality", and is the opposite of egoism or "selfishness", the characteristic par excellence of the latter.

Elementals. Spirits of the Elements. The creatures evolved in the four Kingdoms or Elements – earth, air, fire, and water. They are called by the Kabbalists, Gnomes (of the earth), Sylphs (of the air), Salamanders (of the fire), and Undines (of the water). Except a few of the higher kinds, and their rulers, they are rather forces of nature than ethereal men and women. These forces, as the servile agents of the Occultists, may produce various effects; but if employed by" Elementaries" (*q.v.*) – in which case they enslave the mediums – they will deceive the credulous. All the lower invisible beings generated on the 5th 6th, and 7th planes of our terrestrial atmosphere, are called Elementals, Peris, Devs, Djins, Sylvans, Satyrs, Fauns, Elves, Dwarfs, Trolls, Kobolds, Brownies, Nixies, Goblins, Pinkies, Banshees, Moss People, White Ladies, Spooks, Fairies, etc., etc., etc.

Elementaries. Properly, the disembodied souls of the depraved; these souls having at some time prior to death separated from themselves their divine spirits, and so lost their chance for immortality; but at the present stage of learning it has been thought best to apply the term to the spooks or phantoms of disembodied persons, in general, to those whose temporary habitation is the Kâma Loka. Eliphas Lévi and some other Kabbalists make little distinction between elementary spirits who have been men, and those beings which people the elements, and are the blind forces of nature. Once divorced from their higher triads and their bodies, these souls remain in their *Kâma-rupic* envelopes, and are irresistibly drawn to the earth amid elements congenial to their gross natures. Their stay in the Kâma Loka varies as to its duration; but ends invariably in disintegration, dissolving like a column of mist, atom by atom, in the surrounding elements.

Elohîm (*Heb.*). Also *Alhim*, the word being variously spelled. Godfrey Higgins, who has written much upon its meaning, always spells it *Aleim*. The Hebrew letters are *aleph, lamed, hé,yod, mem*, and are numerically 1, 30, 5, 10, 40 = 86. It seems to be the plural of the feminine noun *Eloah*, ALH, formed by adding the common plural form IM, a masculine ending; and hence the whole seems to imply the emitted active and passive essences. As a title it is referred to "Binah" the Supernal Mother, as is also the fuller title IHVH ALHIM, Jehovah Elohim. As Binah leads on to seven succeedent Emanations, so " Elohim" has been said to represent a sevenfold power of godhead. [w.w. w.]

Emanation *The Doctrine of*. In its metaphysical meaning, it is opposed to Evolution, yet one with it. Science teaches that evolution is physiologically a mode of generation in which the germ that develops the foetus pre-exists already in the parent, the development and final form and characteristics of that germ being accomplished in nature; and that in cosmology the process takes place blindly through the correlation of the elements, and their various compounds. Occultism answers that this is only the *apparent* mode, the real process being Emanation, guided by intelligent Forces under an immutable LAW. Therefore, while the Occultists and Theosophists believe thoroughly in the doctrine of Evolution as given out by Kapila and Manu, they are *Emanationists* rather than *Evolutionists*. The doctrine of Emanation was at one time universal. It was taught by the Alexandrian as well as by the Indian philosophers, by the Egyptian, the Chaldean and Hellenic Hierophants, and also by the Hebrews (in their Kabbala, and even in *Genesis*). For it is only owing to deliberate mistranslation that the Hebrew word asdt has been translated "angels" from the Septuagint, when it means *Emanations, Æons*, precisely as with the Gnostics. Indeed, in Deuteronomy (xxxiii., 2) the word *asdt* or *ashdt* is translated as" fiery law", whilst the correct rendering of the passage should be "from his right hand went [not a fiery law, but a fire according to law "; viz., that the fire of one flame is imparted to, and caught up by another like as in a trail of inflammable substance. This is precisely emanation. As shown in Isis Unveiled : "In Evolution, as it is now beginning to he understood, there is supposed to be in all matter an impulse to take on a higher form – a supposition clearly expressed by Manu and other Hindu philosophers of the highest antiquity. The philosopher's tree illustrates it in the case of the zinc solution. The controversy between the followers of this school and the Emanationists may he briefly stated thus The Evolutionist stops all inquiry at the borders of ' the Unknowable "; the Emanationist believes that nothing can be evolved – or, as the word means, unwombed or born – except it has first been involved, thus indicating that life is from a spiritual potency above the whole."

En (or **Ain**) **Soph** (*Heb.*). The endless, limitless and boundless. The absolute deific Principle, impersonal and unknowable. It means literally "no-thing" i.e., nothing that could be classed with anything else. The word and ideas are equivalent to the Vedantic conceptions of Parabrahmn. [w.w.w.]

Some Western Kabbalists, however, contrive to make of IT, a personal "He", a male deity instead of an impersonal deity.

Epimetheus (*Gr.*). Lit., "He who takes counsel *after*" the event. A brother of Prometheus in Greek Mythology.

Epinoia (*Gr.*). Thought, invention, design. A name adopted by the Gnostics for the first passive Æon.

Eros (*Gr.*). Hesiod makes of the god Eros the third personage of the Hellenic primordial Trinity composed of Ouranos, Gæa and Eros. It is the personified procreative Force in nature in its abstract sense, the propeller to "creation" and procreation. Exoterically, mythology makes of Eros the god of lustful, animal desire, whence the term *erotic* esoterically, it is different. (See " Kâma".)

Esoteric (*Gr.*). Hidden, secret. From the Greek *esotericos*, "inner" concealed.

Esoteric Bodhism. Secret wisdom or intelligence from the Greek *esotericos* "inner", and the Sanskrit *Bodhi*, "knowledge", intelligence – in contradistinction to *Buddhi,* "the *faculty* of knowledge or intelligence" and *Buddhism*, the philosophy or Law of Buddha (the Enlightened). Also written " Budhism", from *Budha* (Intelligence and Wisdom) the Son of Soma.

Ether. Students are but too apt to confuse this with Akâsa and with Astral Light. It is neither, in the sense in which ether is described by physical Science. Ether is a material agent, though hitherto undetected by any physical apparatus; whereas Akâsa is a distinctly spiritual agent, identical, in one sense, with the Anima Mundi, while the Astral Light is only the seventh and highest principle of the terrestrial atmosphere, as undetectable as Akâsa and real Ether, because it is something quite on another plane. The seventh principle of the earth's atmosphere, as said, the Astral Light, is only the second on the Cosmic scale. The scale of Cosmic Forces, Principles and Planes, of Emanations – on the metaphysical – and Evolutions – on the physical plane – is the Cosmic Serpent biting its own tail, the Serpent reflecting the Higher, and reflected in its turn by the lower Serpent. The Caduceus explains the mystery, and the four-fold Dodecahedron on the model of which the universe is said by Plato to have been built by the manifested Logos – synthesized by the unmanifested First-Born – yields geometrically the key to Cosmogony and its microcosmic reflection – our Earth.

Evolution. The development of higher orders of animals from lower. As said in *Isis Unveiled:* "Modern Science holds but to a one-sided physical evolution, prudently avoiding and ignoring the higher or spiritual evolution, which would force our contemporaries to confess the superiority of the ancient philosophers and psychologists over themselves. The ancient sages, ascending to the UNKNOWABLE, made their starting- point from the first manifestation of the unseen, the unavoidable, and, from a strictly logical reasoning, the absolutely necessary creative Being, the Demiurgos of the universe. Evolution began with them from pure spirit, which descending lower and lower down, assumed at last a visible and comprehensible form, and became matter. Arrived at this point, they speculated in the Darwinian method, but on a far more large and comprehensive basis." (See "Emanation".)

Exoteric. Outward, public; the opposite of esoteric or hidden.

F

First Point. Metaphysically the first point of manifestation, the germ of primeval differentiation, or the point in the infinite Circle "whose centre is everywhere, and circumference nowhere". The Point is the Logos.

Fire *(Living)*. A figure of speech to denote deity, the "One" life. A theurgic term, used later by the Rosicrucians. The symbol of the *living fire* is the sun, *certain of whose rays develope the fire of life in a diseased body, impart the knowledge of the future* to the sluggish mind, and stimulate to active function a certain psychic and generally dormant faculty in man. The meaning is very occult.

Fohat *(Tib.)*. A term used to represent the active (male) potency of the Sakti (female reproductive power) in nature. The essence of cosmic electricity. An occult Tibetan term for *Daiviprakriti* primordial light: and in the universe of manifestation the ever-present electrical energy and ceaseless destructive and formative power. Esoterically, it is the same, Fohat being the universal propelling Vital Force, at once the propeller and the resultant.

G

Gabriel. According to the Gnostics, the "Spirit" or Christos, the "messenger of life", and Gabriel are one. The former "is called some-times the Angel Gabriel Hebrew 'the mighty one of God'," and took with the Gnostics the place of the Logos, while the Holy Spirit was considered one with the Æon Life, (see *Irenæus* I., xii.). Therefore we find Theodoret saying (in *Hævet. Fab.*, II vii.) : " The heretics agree with us (Christians) respecting the beginning of all things. But they say there is not one Christ (God), *but one above* and *the other below*. And this last *formerly dwelt in many;* but the Jesus, they at one time say is *from* God, at another they call him a Spirit;" The key to this is given in the esoteric philosophy. The "spirit" with the Gnostics was a female potency exoterically, it was the ray proceeding from the Higher Manas, the Ego, and that which the Esotericists refer to as the *Kâma Manas* or the lower personal Ego, which is radiated in every human entity by the Higher Ego or Christos, the god within us. Therefore, they were right in saying: "there is not one Christ, but one above and the other below". Every student of Occultism will understand this, and also that Gabriel – or "the mighty one of God" – is one with the Higher Ego. (See *Isis Unveiled*.)

Gæa (*Gr.*). Primordial Matter, in the Cosmogony of Hesiod; Earth, as some think; the wife of Ouranos, the sky or heavens. The female personage of the primeval Trinity, composed of Ouranos, Gæa and Eros.

Genesis. The whole of the Book of Genesis down to the death of Joseph, is found to he a hardly altered version of the Cosmogony of the Chaldeans, as is now repeatedly proven from the Assyrian tiles. The first three chapters are transcribed from the allegorical narratives of the beginnings common to all nations. Chapters four and five are a new allegorical adaptation of the same narration in the secret *Book of Numbers*; chapter six is an astronomical narrative of the Solar year and the seven *cosmocratores* from the Egyptian original of the Pymander and the symbolical visions of a series of *Enoichioi* (Seers) – from whom came also the Book of Enoch. The beginning of Exodus, and the story of Moses is that of the Babylonian Sargon, who having flourished (as even that unwilling authority Dr. Sayce tells us) 3750 B.C. preceded the Jewish lawgiver by almost 2300 years. (See *Secret Doctrine*, vol. II., pp. 691 et seq.) Nevertheless, *Genesis* is an undeniably esoteric work. It has not borrowed, nor has it disfigured the universal symbols and teachings on the lines of which it was written, but simply adapted the eternal truths to its own national spirit and clothed them in cunning allegories comprehensible only to its Kabbalists and Initiates. The Gnostics have done the same, each sect in its own way, as thousands of years before, India, Egypt, Chaldea and Greece, had also dressed the same incommunicable truths each in its own national garb. The key and solution to all such narratives can be found *only in the esoteric teachings*.

Genii (*Lat.*) A name for Æons, or angels, with the Gnostics. The names of their hierarchies and classes are simply legion.

Gnâna (*Sk.*) Knowledge as applied to the esoteric sciences.

Gnân Devas (*Sk.*) Lit., "the gods of knowledge". The higher classes of gods or devas; the "mind-born" sons of Brahmâ, and others including the Manasa-putras (the Sons of Intellect). Esoterically, our reincarnating Egos.

Gnânasakti (Sk.) The power of true knowledge, one of the seven great forces in Nature (*six,* exoterically).

Gnôsis (*Gr.*) Lit., "knowledge". The technical term used by the schools of religious philosophy, both before and during the first centuries of so-called Christianity, to denote the object of their enquiry. This Spiritual and Sacred Knowledge, the *Gupta Vidya* of the Hindus, could only be obtained by Initiation into Spiritual Mysteries of which the ceremonial "Mysteries" were a type.

Gnostics (*Gr.*) The philosophers who formulated and taught the Gnôsis or Knowledge (*q.v.*). They flourished in the first three centuries of the Christian era: the following were eminent, Valentinus, Basilides, Marcion, Simon Magus, etc. [w.w. w.]

Golden Age. The ancients divided the life cycle into the Golden, Silver, Bronze and Iron Ages. The Golden was an age of primeval purity, simplicity and general happiness.

Great Age. There were several "great ages" mentioned by the ancients. In India it embraced the whole Maha-manvantara, the "age of Brahmâ", each "Day" of which represents the life cycle of a chain – i.e. it embraces a period of seven Rounds. (See *Esoteric Buddhism,* by A. P. Sinnett.) Thus while a "Day" and a "Night" represent, as Manvantara and Pralaya, 8,640,000,000 years, an "age" lasts through a period of 311,040,000,000,000 years; after which the Pralaya, or dissolution of the universe, becomes universal. With the Egyptians and Greeks the "great age" referred only to the tropical or sidereal year, the duration of which is 25,868 solar years. Of the complete age – that of the gods – they say nothing, as it was a matter to he discussed and divulged only in the Mysteries, during the initiating ceremonies. The "great age" of the Chaldees was the same in figures as that of the Hindus.

Grihastha (*Sk.*) Lit., "a householder", "one who lives in a house with his family". A Brahman " family priest" in popular rendering, and the sarcerdotal hierarchy of the Hindus.

Gupta Vidyâ (*Sk.*) The same as Guhya Vidyâ; Esoteric or Secret Science; knowledge.

Guru (*Sk.*) Spiritual Teacher; a master in metaphysical and ethical doctrines; used also for a teacher of any science.

H

Hades (*Gr.*), or *Aïdes*. The "invisible", i.e., the land of the shadows, one of whose regions was Tartarus, a place of complete darkness, like the region of profound dreamless sleep in the Egyptian Amenti. Judging by the allegorical description of the various punishments inflicted therein, the place was purely Karmic. Neither Hades nor Amenti were the hell still preached by some retrograde priests and clergymen; but whether represented by the Elysian Fields or by Tartarus, Hades was a place of retributive justice and no more. This could only be reached by crossing the river to the "other shore", i.e. by crossing the river Death, and being once more reborn, for weal or for woe. As well expressed in Egyptian Belief: "The story of Charon, the ferryman (of the, Styx) is to be found not only in Homer, but in the poetry of many lands. The River must be crossed before gaining the Isles of the Blest. The Ritual of Egypt described a Charon and his boat long ages before Homer. He is Khu-en-ua, the hawk-headed steersman." (See "Amenti", "Hel" and "Happy Fields".)

Hanuman (Sk.) The monkey god of the *Ramayana*; the *generalissimo* of Rama's army; the son of Vayu, the god of the wind, and of a virtuous she-demon. Hanuman was the faithful ally of Rama and by his unparalleled audacity and wit, helped the Avatar of Vishnu to finally conquer the demon-king of Lanka, Ravana, who had carried off the beautiful Sita, Rama's wife, an outrage which led to the celebrated war described in the Hindu epic poem.

Heavenly Adam. The synthesis of the Sephirothal Tree, or of all the Forces in Nature and their informing deific essence. In the diagrams, the Seventh of the lower Sephiroth, Sephira *Malkhooth* – the Kingdom of Harmony – represents the feet of the ideal Macrocosm, whose head reaches to the first manifested Head. This Heavenly Adam is the *natura naturans*, the abstract world, while the Adam of Earth (Humanity) is the *natura naturata* or the material universe. The former is the presence of Deity in its universal essence; the latter the manifestation of the intelligence of that essence. In the *real Zohar* not the fantastic and anthropomorphic caricature which we often find in the writings of Western Kabbalists – there is not a particle of the personal deity which we find so prominent in the dark cloaking of the Secret Wisdom known as the Mosaic Pentateuch.

Hell. A term with the Anglo-Saxons, evidently derived from the name of the goddess *Hela* (*q.v.*), and by the Sclavonians from the Greek Hades: hell being in Russian and other Sclavonian tongues – *ad*, the only difference between the Scandinavian cold hell and the hot hell of the Christians, being found in their respective temperatures. But even the idea of those overheated regions is not original with the Europeans, many peoples having entertained the conception of an underworld climate; as well may we if we localise our Hell in the centre of the earth. All exoteric religions – the creeds of the Brahmans, Buddhists,

Zoroastrians, Mahommedans, Jews, and the rest, make their hells hot and dark, though many are more attractive than frightful. The idea of a hot hell is an afterthought, the distortion of an astronomical allegory. With the Egyptians, Hell became a place of punishment by fire not earlier than the seventeenth or eighteenth dynasty, when Typhon was transformed from a god into a devil. But at whatever time this dread superstition was implanted in the minds of the poor ignorant masses, the scheme of a burning hell and souls tormented therein is purely Egyptian. Ra (the Sun) became the Lord of the Furnace in Karr, the hell of the Pharaohs, and the sinner was threatened with misery "in the heat of infernal fires". "A lion was there" says Dr. Birch "and was called the roaring monster". Another describes the place as "the bottomless pit and lake of fire, into which the victims are thrown" (compare *Revelation*). The Hebrew word *gaï-hinnom* (Gehenna) never really had the significance given to it in Christian orthodoxy.

Hermaphrodite (*Gr.*). Dual-sexed; a male and female Being, whether man or animal.

Hermes Trismegistus (*Gr.*). The "thrice great Hermes", the Egyptian. The mythical personage after whom the Hermetic philosophy was named. In Egypt the God Thoth or Thot. A generic name of many ancient Greek writers on philosophy and Alchemy. Hermes Trismegistus is the name of Hermes or Thoth in his human aspect, as a god he is far more than this. As *Hermes-Thoth-Aah*, he is Thoth, the moon, i.e., his symbol is the bright side of the moon, supposed to contain the essence of creative Wisdom, "the elixir of Hermes ". As such he is associated with the Cynocephalus, the dog-headed monkey, for the same reason as was Anubis, one of the aspects of Thoth. (See " Hermanubis".) The same idea underlies the form of the Hindu God of Wisdom, the elephant-headed Ganesa, or Ganpat, the son of Parvati and Siva. (See "Ganesa".) When he has the head of an *ibis,* he is the sacred scribe of the gods; but even then he wears the crown *atef* and the lunar disk. He is the most mysterious of gods. As a serpent, Hermes Thoth is the divine creative 'Wisdom. The Church Fathers speak at length of Thoth-Hermes. (See "Hermetic".)

Hermetic. Any doctrine or writing connected with the esoteric teachings of Hermes, who, whether as the Egyptian Thoth or the Greek Hermes, was the God of Wisdom with the Ancients, and, according to Plato, "discovered numbers, geometry, astronomy and letters". Though mostly considered as spurious, nevertheless the Hermetic writings were highly prized by St. Augustine, Lactantius, Cyril and others. In the words of Mr. J. Bonwick, " They are more or less touched up by the Platonic philosophers among the early Christians (such as Origen and Clemens Alexandrinus) who sought to substantiate their Christian arguments by appeals to these heathen and revered writings, though they could not resist the temptation of making them say a little too much. Though represented by some clever and interested writers as teaching pure monotheism, the Hermetic or Trismegistic books are, nevertheless, purely pantheistic. The Deity referred to in them is defined by Paul as that in *which* "we live, and move and have our being" – notwithstanding the "in Him" of the translators.

Higher Self. The Supreme Divine Spirit overshadowing man. The crown of the upper spiritual Triad in man – Atmân.

Hochmah (*Heb.*). See "Chochmah".

Humanity. Occultly and Kabbalistically, the whole of mankind is symbolised, by Manu in India; by Vajrasattva or Dorjesempa, the head of the Seven Dhyani, in Northern Buddhism; and by Adam Kadmon in the Kabbala. All these represent the totality of mankind whose beginning is in this androgynic protoplast, and whose end is in the Absolute, beyond all these symbols and myths of human origin. Humanity is a great Brotherhood by virtue of the sameness of the material from which it is formed physically and morally. Unless, however, it becomes a Brotherhood also intellectually, it is no better than a superior genus of animals.

I

Incarnations (*Divine*) or *Avatars*. The Immaculate Conception is as pre-eminently Egyptian as it is Indian. As the author of *Egyptian Belief* has it: "It is not the vulgar, coarse and sensual story as in Greek mythology, but refined, moral and spiritual "; and again the incarnation idea was found revealed on the wall of a Theban temple by Samuel Sharpe, who thus analyzes it: "First the god Thoth . . . as the messenger of the gods, like the Mercury of the Greeks (or the Gabriel of the first Gospel), tells the *maiden* queen Mautmes, that she is to give birth to a son, who is to be king Amunotaph III. Secondly, the god Kneph, the Spirit . . . . and the goddess Hathor (Nature) both take hold of the queen by the hands and put into her mouth the character for life, a cross, which is to be the life of the coming child", etc., etc. Truly divine incarnation, or the *avatar* doctrine, constituted the grandest mystery of every old religious system!

Individuality. One of the names given in Theosophy and Occultism to the Human Higher EGO. We make a distinction between the immortal and divine Ego, and the mortal human Ego which perishes. The latter, or "personality" (personal Ego) survives the dead body only for a time in the Kama Loka; the Individuality prevails forever.

Initiate. From the Latin *Initiatus*. The designation of anyone who was received into and had revealed to him the mysteries and secrets of either Masonry or Occultism. In times of antiquity, those who had been initiated into the arcane knowledge taught by the Hierophants of the Mysteries; and in our modern days those who have been initiated by the adepts of mystic lore into the mysterious knowledge, which, notwithstanding the lapse of ages, has yet a few real votaries on earth.

Initiation. From the same root as the Latin *initia,* which means the basic or first principles of any Science. The practice of initiation or admission into the sacred Mysteries, taught by the Hierophants and learned priests of the Temples, is one of the most ancient customs. This was practised in every old national religion. In Europe it was abolished with the fall of the last pagan temple. There exists at present but one kind of initiation known to the public, namely that into the Masonic rites. Masonry, however, has no more secrets to give out or conceal. In the palmy days of old, the Mysteries, according to the greatest Greek and Roman philosophers, were the most sacred of all solemnities as well as the most beneficent, and greatly promoted virtue. The Mysteries represented the passage from mortal life into finite death, and the experiences of the disembodied Spirit and Soul in the world of subjectivity. In our own day, as the secret is lost, the candidate passes through sundry meaningless ceremonies and is initiated into the solar allegory of Hiram Abiff, the "Widow's Son".

Inner Man. An occult term, used to designate the true and immortal Entity in us, not the outward and mortal form of clay that we call our body. The term applies, strictly speaking, only to the Higher Ego, the "astral man" being the appellation of the Double and of Kâma Rupa (*q.v.*) or the surviving *eidolon*.

Isis. In Egyptian *Issa,* the goddess Virgin-Mother; personified nature. In Egyptian or Koptic *Uasari,* the female reflection of *Uasar* or Osiris. She is the "woman clothed with the sun" of the land of Chemi. Isis Latona is the Roman Isis.

Iswara (*Sk.*). The "Lord" or the personal god – *divine Spirit in man. Lit.,* sovereign (independent) existence. A title given to Siva and other gods in India. Siva is also called Iswaradeva, or sovereign deva.

J

Jadoo (*Hind.*). Sorcery, black magic, enchantment.

Jadoogar (*Hind.*). A Sorcerer, or Wizard.

Jehovah (*Heb.*). The Jewish "Deity name J'hovah, is a compound of two words, *viz* of *Jah* (y, i, or j, *Yôdh,* the tenth letter of the alphabet) and *hovah* (Hâvah, or Eve)," says a Kabalistic authority, Mr. J. Ralston Skinner of Cincinnati, U.S.A. And again, "The word Jehovah, or *Jah-Eve,* has the primary meaning of existence or being as male female". It means Kabalistically the latter, indeed, and nothing more; and as repeatedly shown is entirely phallic. Thus, verse 26 in the IVth chapter of *Genesis,* reads in its disfigured translation . . . . "then began men to call upon the name of the Lord", whereas it ought to read correctly . .

. . "then began men to call themselves by the name of *Jah-hovah*" or males and females, which they had become after the separation of sexes. In fact the latter is described in the same chapter, when Cain (the male or *Jah*) "rose up against Abel, his (*sister*, not) brother and slew him"(*spilt his blood*, in the original). Chapter IV of Genesis contains in truth, the allegorical narrative of that period of anthropological and physiological evolution which is described in the *Secret Doctrine* when treating of the third Root race of mankind. It is followed by Chapter V *as a blind*; but ought to be succeeded by Chapter VI, where the Sons of God took as their wives the daughters of men or of the giants. For this is an allegory hinting at the mystery of the Divine Egos incarnating in mankind, after which the hitherto senseless races "became mighty men, . . . men of renown" (v. 4), having acquired minds (*manas*) which they had not before.

Jhâna (*Sk.*) or *Jnana.* Knowledge; Occult Wisdom.

Jiva (*Sk.*). Life, as the Absolute; the Monad also or "Atma-Buddhi".

Jivanmukta (*Sk.*). An adept or yogi who has reached the ultimate state of holiness, and separated himself from matter; a Mahatma, or *Nirvânee*, a "dweller in bliss" and emancipation. Virtually one who has reached Nirvâna during life.

Jivatma (*Sk.*). The ONE universal life, generally; but also the divine Spirit in Man.

Jnânam (*Sk.*). The same as "Gnâna", etc., the same as "Jhâna" (*q.v.*).

Jnâna Sakti (*Sk.*). The power of intellect.

Jupiter (*Lat.*). From the same root as the Greek Zeus, the greatest god of the ancient Greeks and Romans, adopted also by other nations. His names are among others: (1) Jupiter-Aërios; (2) Jupiter-Ammon of Egypt ; (3) Jupiter Bel-Moloch, the Chaldean; (4) Jupiter-Mundus, Deus Mundus, "God of the World"; (5) Jupiter-Fulgur, "the Fulgurant", etc.,etc.

K

Kabalah (*Heb.*). The hidden wisdom of the Hebrew Rabbis of the middle ages derived from the older secret doctrines concerning divine things and cosmogony, which were combined into a theology after the time of the captivity of the Jews in Babylon. All the works that fall under the esoteric category are termed Kabalistic.

Kabalist. From Q B L H, KABALA, an unwritten or oral tradition. The kabalist is a student of "secret science", one who interprets the hidden meaning of the Scriptures with the help of the symbolical Kabala, and explains the real one by these means. The Tanaim were the first kabalists among the Jews; they appeared at Jerusalem about the beginning of the third century before the Christian era. The books of *Ezekiel, Daniel, Henoch,* and the *Revelation* of St. John, are purely kabalistical. This secret doctrine is identical with that of Chaldeans, and includes at the same time much of the Persian wisdom, or "magic". History catches glimpses of famous kabalists ever since the eleventh century. The Mediæval ages, and even our own times, have had an enormous number of the most learned and intellectual men who were students of the Kabala (or Qabbalah, as some spell it). The most famous among the former were Paracelsus, Henry Khunrath, Jacob Böhmen, Robert Fludd, the two Van Helmonts, the Abbot John Trithemius, Cornelius Agrippa, Cardinal Nicolao Cusani, Jerome Carden, Pope Sixtus IV., and such Christian scholars as Raymond Lully, Giovanni Pico de la Mirandola, Guillaume Postel, the great John Reuchlin, Dr. Henry More, Eugenius Philalethes (Thomas Vaughan), the erudite Jesuit Athanasius Kircher, Christian Knorr (Baron) von Rosenroth; then Sir Isaac Newton., Leibniz, Lord Bacon, Spinosa, etc., etc., the list being almost inexhaustible. As remarked by Mr. Isaac Myer, in his Qabbalah, the ideas of the Kabalists have largely influenced European literature.

Kabiri (*Phœn.*) or the *Kabirim.* Deities and very mysterious gods with the ancient nations, including the Israelites, some of whom – as Terah, Abram's father – worshipped them under the name of *Teraphim.* With the Christians, however, they are now devils, although the modern Archangels are the direct transformation of these same Kabiri. In Hebrew the latter name means "the mighty ones", Gibborim. At one time all the deities connected with fire – whether they were divine, infernal or volcanic – were called Kabirian.

Kadmon (*Heb.*). Archetypal man. See."Adam Kadmon".

Kaliyuga (*Sk.*). The fourth, the black or iron age, our present period, the duration of which us 432,000 years. The last of the ages into which the evolutionary period of man is divided by a series of such ages. It began 3,102 years B.C. at the moment of Krishna's death, and the first cycle of 5,ooo years will end between the years 1897 and 1898.

Kalpa (*Sk.*). The period of a mundane revolution, generally a cycle of time, but usually, it represents a "day" and "night" of Brahmâ, a period of 4,320,000,000 years.

Kama (*Sk.*) Evil desire, lust, volition; the cleaving to existence. Kama is generally identified with *Mara* the tempter.

Kamadeva (*Sk.*). In the popular notions the god of love, a Visva-deva, in the Hindu Pantheon. As the *Eros* of Hesiod, degraded into Cupid by exoteric law, and still more degraded by a later popular sense attributed to the term, so is Kama a most mysterious and metaphysical subject. The earlier Vedic description of Kama alone gives the key-note to what he emblematizes. Kama is the first conscious, *all embracing desire* for universal good, love, and for all that lives and feels, needs help and kindness, the first feeling of infinite tender compassion and mercy that arose in the consciousness of the creative ONE Force, as soon as it came into life and being as a ray from the ABSOLUTE. Says the *Rig Veda*, "Desire first arose in IT, which was the primal germ of mind, and which Sages, searching with their intellect, have discovered in their heart to be the bond which connects Entity with non-Entity", or *Manas* with pure *Atma-Buddhi*. There is no idea of sexual love in the conception. Kama is pre-eminently the divine desire of creating happiness and love; and it is only ages later, as mankind began to materialize by anthropomorphization its grandest ideals into cut and dried dogmas, that Kama became the power that gratifies desire on the animal plane. This is shown by what every *Veda* and some *Brahmanas* say. In the *Atharva Veda*, Kama is represented as the Supreme Deity and Creator. In the Taitarîya Brahmana, he is the child of Dharma, the god of Law and Justice, of Sraddha and faith. In another account he springs from the heart of Brahmâ. Others show him born from water, i.e., from primordial chaos, or the "Deep". Hence one of his many names, *Irâ-ja*, "the water-born"; and *Aja*, "unborn" ; and *Atmabhu* or "Self-existent". Because of the sign of *Makara* (Capricornus) on his banner, he is also called " Makara Ketu". The allegory about Siva, the "Great Yogin ", reducing Kama to ashes by the fire from his *central* (or third) *Eye*, for inspiring the Mahadeva with thoughts of his wife, while he was at his devotions – is very suggestive, as it is said that he thereby reduced Kama to his primeval spiritual form.

Kamaloka (*Sk.*). The *semi*-material plane, to us subjective and invisible, where the disembodied "personalities", the astral forms, called *Kamarupa* remain, until they fade out from it by the complete exhaustion of the effects of the mental impulses that created these eidolons of human and animal passions and desires; (See "Kamarupa".) It is the Hades of the ancient Greeks and the Amenti of the Egyptians, the land of Silent Shadows; a division of the first group of the *Trailôkya*. (See "Kamadhâtu".)

Kamarupa (*Sk.*). Metaphysically, and in our esoteric philosophy, it is the subjective form created through the mental and physical desires and thoughts in connection with things of matter, by all sentient beings, a form which survives the death of their bodies. After that death three of the seven "principles" – or let us say planes of senses and consciousness on which the human instincts and ideation act in turn – viz., the body, its astral prototype and physical vitality, – being of no further use, remain on earth; the three higher principles, grouped into one, merge into the state of Devachan (*q.v.*), in which state the Higher Ego will remain until the hour for a new reincarnation arrives; and the *eidolon* of the ex-Personality is left alone in its new abode. Here, the pale copy of the man that was, vegetates for a period of time, the duration of which is variable and according to the element of materiality which is left in it, and which is determined by the past life of the defunct. Bereft as it is of its higher mind, spirit and physical senses, if left alone to its own senseless devices, it will gradually fade out and disintegrate. But, if forcibly drawn back into the terrestrial sphere whether by the passionate desires and appeals of the surviving friends or by regular necromantic practices – one of the most pernicious of which is mediumship – the "spook" may prevail for a period greatly exceeding the span of the natural life of its body. Once the Kamarupa has learnt the way back to living human bodies, it becomes a vampire, feeding on the vitality of those who are so anxious for its company. In India these *eidolons* are called *Pisâchas,* and are much dreaded, as already explained elsewhere.

Karabtanos (*Gr.*). The spirit of blind or animal desire; the symbol of Kamarupa. The Spirit "without sense or judgment" in the Codex of the Nazarenes. He is the symbol of matter and stands for the father of the seven spirits of concupiscence begotten by him on his mother, the "Spiritus" or the Astral Light.

Kârana (*Sk.*). Cause (metaphysically).

Kârana Sarîra (*Sk.*). The "Causal body". It is dual in its meaning. Exoterically, it is Avidya, ignorance, or that which is the cause of the evolution of a human ego and its reincarnation ; hence the lower Manas esoterically – the causal body or Kâranopadhi stands in the Taraka Raja yoga as corresponding to Buddhi and the Higher " Manas," or Spiritual Soul.

Kâranopadhi (*Sk.*). The basis or *upadhi* of Karana, the "causal soul". In Taraka Rajayoga, it corresponds with both *Manas* and *Buddhi*. See Table in the *Secret Doctrine*, Vol. I, p. 157.

Karma (*Sk.*). Physically, action: metaphysically, the LAW OF RETRIBUTION, the Law of cause and effect or Ethical Causation. Nemesis, only in one sense, that of bad Karma. It is the eleventh *Nidana* in the concatenation of causes and effects in orthodox Buddhism ; yet it is the power that controls all things, the resultant of moral action, the meta physical *Samskâra*, or the moral effect of an act committed for the attainment of something which gratifies a personal desire. There is the Karma of merit and the Karma of demerit. Karma neither punishes nor rewards, it is simply *the one* Universal LAW which guides unerringly, and, so to say, blindly, all other laws productive of certain effects along the grooves of their respective causations. When Buddhism teaches that "Karma is that moral kernel (of any being) which alone survives death and continues in transmigration ' or reincarnation, it simply means that there remains nought after each Personality but the causes produced by it ; causes which are undying, i.e., which cannot be eliminated from the Universe until replaced by their legitimate effects, and wiped out by them, so to speak, and such causes – unless compensated during the life of the person who produced them with adequate effects, will follow the reincarnated Ego, and reach it in its subsequent reincarnation until a harmony between effects and causes is fully reestablished. No "personality" – a mere bundle of material atoms and of instinctual and mental characteristics – can of course continue, as such, in the world of pure Spirit. Only that which is immortal in its very nature and divine in its essence, namely, the Ego, can exist for ever. And as it is that Ego which chooses the personality it will inform, after each Devachan, and which receives through these personalities the effects of the Karmic causes produced, it is therefore the Ego, that *self* which is the "moral kernel" referred to and embodied karma, "which alone survives death."

Kartikeya *(Sk)*, or *Kartika.* The Indian God of War, son of Siva, born of his seed fallen into the Ganges. He is also the personification of the power of the Logos. The planet Mars. Kartika is a very occult personage, a nursling of the Pleiades, and a Kumâra. (See *Secret Doctrine.*)

Kether *(Heb.)*. The Crown, the highest of the ten Sephiroth; the first of the Supernal Triad. It corresponds to the Macroprosopus, vast countenance, or Arikh Anpin, which differentiates into Chokmah and Binah. [w.w.w.]

Khem *(Eg.)*. The same as Horus. "The God Khem will avenge his father Osiris"; says a text in a papyrus.

Kosmos *(Gr.)*. The Universe, as distinguished from the world, which may mean our globe or earth.

Krishna *(Sk.)*.. The most celebrated avatar of Vishnu, the "Saviour" of the Hindus and their most popular god. He is the- eighth Avatar, the son of Devaki, and the nephew of Kansa, the Indian King Herod, who while seeking for him among the shepherds and cow-herds who concealed him, slew thousands of their newly-born babes. The story of Krishna's conception, birth, and childhood are the exact prototype of the New Testament story. The missionaries, of course, try to show that the Hindus stole the story of the Nativity from the early Christians who came to India.

Krita-Yuga *(Sk.)*. The first of the four Yugas or Ages of the Brahmans; also called *Satya-Yuga,* a period lasting 1,728,000 years.

Kriyasakti *(Gk.)*. The power of thought; one of the seven forces of Nature. Creative potency of the *Siddhis* (powers) of the full Yogis.

Kronos *(Gr.)*. Saturn. The God of Boundless Time and of the Cycles.

Kshetrajna or *Kshetrajneswara* *(Sk.)*. Embodied spirit, the Conscious Ego in its highest manifestations; the reincarnating Principle; the "Lord" in us.

Kumâra *(Sk.)*. A virgin boy, or young celibate. The first Kumâras are the seven sons of Brahmâ born out of the limbs of the god, in the so-called ninth creation. It is stated that the name was given to them owing to their formal refusal to "procreate their species", and so they "remained Yogis", as the legend says.

L

Lanoo (*Sk.*). A disciple, the same as "chela".

Laya or *Layam* (*Sk.*). From the root *Li* "to dissolve, to disintegrate" a point of equilibrium (*zero-point*) in physics and chemistry. In occultism, that point where substance becomes homogeneous and is unable to act or differentiate.

Lemuria. A modern term first used by some naturalists, and now adopted by Theosophists, to indicate a continent that, according to the *Secret Doctrine* of the East, preceded Atlantis. Its Eastern name would not reveal much to European ears.

Lha (*Tib.*). Spirits of the highest spheres, whence the name of Lhassa, the residence of the Dalaï-Lama. The title of Lha is often given in Tibet to some *Narjols* (Saints and Yogi adepts) who have attained great occult powers.

Lhamayin (*Tib.*). Elemental sprites of the lower terrestrial plane. Popular fancy makes of them demons and devils.

Linga or *Lingam* (*Sk.*). A sign or a symbol of abstract creation. Force becomes the organ of procreation only on this earth. In India there are 12 great Lingams of Siva, some of which are on mountains and rocks, and also in temples. Such is the *Kedâresa* in the Himalaya, a huge and shapeless mass of rock. In its origin the Lingam had never the gross meaning connected with the phallus, an idea which is altogether of a later date. The symbol in India has the same meaning which it had in Egypt, which is simply that the creative or procreative Force is divine. It also denotes who was the dual Creator – male and female, Siva and his Sakti. The gross and immodest idea connected with the phallus is not Indian but Greek and pre-eminently Jewish. The Biblical *Bethels* were real priapic stones, the " Beth-el" (phallus) wherein God dwells. The same symbol was concealed within the ark of the Covenant, the "Holy of Holies". Therefore the "Lingam" even as a phallus is not "a symbol of Siva" only, but that of every "Creator" or creative god in every nation, including the Israelites and their "God of Abraham and Jacob".

Linga Purâna (*Sk.*). A scripture of the Saivas or worshippers of Siva. Therein *Maheswara*, "the great Lord", concealed in the Agni Linga explains the ethics of life – duty, virtue, self-sacrifice and finally liberation by and through ascetic life at the end of the *Agni Kalpa* (the Seventh Round). As Professor Wilson justly observed "the Spirit of the worship (phallic) is as little influenced by the character of the type as can well be imagined. *There is nothing like the phallic orgies of antiquity; it is all mystical and spiritual.*"

Linga Sharîra (*Sk.*). The "body", i.e., the aerial symbol of the body. This term designates the *döppelganger* or the "astral body" of man or animal. It is the *eidolon* of the Greeks, the vital and *prototypal* body; the reflection of the men of flesh. It is born *before* and dies or fades out, with the disappearance of the last atom of the body.

Lipikas (*Sk.*). The celestial recorders, the "Scribes", those who record every word and deed, said or done by man while on this earth. As Occultism teaches, they are the agents of KARMA – the retributive Law.

Logos (*Gr.*). The manifested deity with every nation and people; the outward expression, or the effect of the cause which is ever concealed. Thus, speech is the Logos of thought; hence it is aptly translated by the "Verbum" and "Word" in its metaphysical sense.

Loka (*Sk.*). A region or circumscribed place. In metaphysics, a world or sphere or plane. The Purânas in India speak incessantly of seven and fourteen Lokas, above, and below our earth; of heavens and hells,

Lotus (*Gr.*). A most occult plant, sacred in Egypt, India and else where; called "the child of the Universe bearing the likeness of its mother in its bosom". There was a time "when the world was a golden lotus" (*padma*) says the allegory. A great variety of these plants, from the majestic Indian lotus, down to the marsh-lotus (bird's foot trefoil) and the Grecian "Dioscoridis", is eaten at Crete and other islands. It is a species of nymphala, first introduced from India to Egypt to which it was-not indigenous. See the text of *Archaic Symbolism* in the Appendix Viii. "The Lotus, as a Universal Symbol".

Lucifer (*Lat.*). The planet Venus, as the bright "Morning Star". Before Milton, Lucifer had never been a name of the Devil. Quite the reverse, since the Christian Saviour is made to say of himself in *Revelations* (xvi. 22.) "I am . . . the bright morning star" or Lucifer. One of the early Popes of Rome bore that name; and there was even a Christian sect in the fourth century which was called the *Luciferians*.

Lunar Gods. Called in India the Fathers, "Pitris" or the lunar ancestors. They are subdivided, like the rest, into seven classes or Hierarchies, In Egypt although the moon received less worship than in Chaldea or India, still Isis stands as the representative of Luna-Lunus, "the celestial Hermaphrodite". Strange enough while the modern connect the moon only with lunacy and generation, the ancient nations, who knew better, have, individually and collectively, connected their "wisdom gods" with it. Thus in Egypt the lunar gods are Thoth-Hermes and Chons; in India it is Budha, the Son of *Soma*, the moon; in Chaldea Nebo is the lunar god of Secret Wisdom, etc., etc. The wife of Thoth, *Sifix*, the lunar goddess, holds a pole with five rays or the five-pointed star, symbol of man, the Microcosm, in distinction from the Septenary Macrocosm. As in all theogonies a goddess precedes a god, on the principle most likely that the chick can hardly precede its egg, in Chaldea the moon was held as older and more venerable than the Sun, because, as they said, darkness precedes light at every periodical rebirth (or "creation") of the universe. Osiris although connected with the Sun and a Solar god is, nevertheless, born on Mount *Sinai*, because *Sin* is the Chaldeo-Assyrian word for the moon; so was Dio-Nysos, god of Nyssi or *Nisi*, which latter appelation was that of Sinai in Egypt, where it was called Mount Nissa. The *crescent* is not – as proven by many writers – an ensign of the Turks, but was adopted by Christians for their symbol before the Mahommedans. For ages the crescent was the emblem of the Chaldean Astarte, the Egyptian Isis, and the Greek Diana, all of them Queens of Heaven, and finally became the emblem of Mary the Virgin. "The Greek Christian Empire of Constantinople held it as their palladium. Upon the conquest by the Turks, the Sultan adopted it . . . and since that, the crescent has been made to oppose the idea of the *cross*".

M

Macrocosm (*Gr.*). The "Great Universe" literally, or Kosmos.

Macroprosopus (*Gr.*). A Kabalistic term, made of a compound Greek word: meaning the Vast or Great Countenance (See "Kabalistic Faces"); a title of Kether, the Crown, the highest Sephira. It is the name of the Universe, called *Arikh-Anpin*, the totality of that of which Microprosopus or *Zauir-Anpin* "the lesser countenance", is the part and antithesis. In its high or abstract metaphysical sense, Microprosopus is Adam Kadmon, the *vehicle of Ain-Suph*, and the crown of the Sephirothal Tree, though since Sephira and Adam Kadmon are in fact one under two aspects, it comes to the same thing. Interpretations are many, and they differ.

Mahâ Buddhi (*Sk.*). *Mahat.* The Intelligent Soul of the World. The seven *Prakritis* or seven "natures" or planes, are counted from Mahâbuddhi downwards.

Mahâ Manvantara (*Sk.*). Lit., the great interludes between the "Manus". The period of universal activity. Manvantara implying here simply a period of activity, as opposed to Pralaya, or rest – without reference to the length of the cycle.

Mahâ Mâyâ (*Sk.*). The great illusion of manifestation. This universe, and all in it in their mutual relation, is called the great Illusion or *Mahâmâyâ* It is also the usual title given to Gautama the Buddha's Immaculate Mother – Mayâdêvi, or the "Great Mystery", as she is called by the Mystics.

Mahâ Pralaya (*Sk.*). The opposite of Mahâmanvantara, literally "the great Dissolution", the "Night" following the "Day of Brahmâ". It is the great rest and sleep of all nature after a period of active manifestation; orthodox Christians would refer to it as the "Destruction of the World".

Mahâ Yuga (*Sk.*). The aggregate of four *Yugas* or ages, of 4,320,000 solar years; a "Day of Brahmâ", in the Brahmanical system ; lit., "the great age".

Mahat (*Sk.*). Lit., "The great one". The first principle of Universal Intelligence and Consciousness. In the Purânic philosophy the first product of root-nature or *Pradhâna* (the same as Mulaprakriti); the producer of *Manas* the thinking principle, and of *Ahankâra*, egotism or the feeling of "I am I" (in the lower Manas).

Mahâtma. Lit., "great soul". An adept of the highest order. Exalted beings who, having attained to the mastery over their lower principles are thus living unimpeded by the "man of flesh", and are in possession of knowledge and power commensurate with the stage they have reached in their spiritual evolution. Called in Pali Rahats and Arhats.

Maitreya Buddha (*Sk.*). The same as the *Kalki Avatar* of Vishnu (the "White Horse" Avatar), and of Sosiosh and other Messiahs. The only difference lies in the dates of their appearances. Thus, while Vishnu is expected to appear on his white horse at the end of the present *Kali Yuga* age "for the final destruction of the wicked, the renovation of creation and the restoration of purity", Maitreya is expected earlier. Exoteric or popular teaching making slight variations on the esoteric doctrine states that Sakyamuni (Gautama Buddha) visited him in Tushita (a celestial abode) and commissioned him to issue thence on earth as his successor at the expiration of five thousand years after his (Buddha's) death. This would be in less than 3,000 years hence. Esoteric philosophy teaches that the next Buddha will appear during the seventh (sub) race of this Round. The fact is that Maitreya was a follower of Buddha, a well-known Arhat, though not his direct disciple, and that he was the founder of an esoteric philosophical school. As shown by Eitel (*Sanskrit-Chinese Dict.*), "statues were erected in his honour as early as B.C. 350".

Makâra (*Sk.*). "The Crocodile." In Europe the same as Capricorn; the tenth sign of the Zodiac. Esoterically, a mystic class of devas. With the Hindus, the vehicle of Varuna, the water-god.

Manas (*Sk.*). Lit., "the mind", the mental faculty which makes of man an intelligent and moral being, and distinguishes him from the mere animal; a synonym of *Mahat. Esoterically,* however, it means, when unqualified, the Higher EGO, or the sentient reincarnating Principle in man. When qualified it is called by Theosophists *Buddhi-Manas* or the Spiritual Soul in contradistinction to its human reflection – *Kâma-Manas*.

Manas, Kâma (*Sk.*). Lit., "the mind of desire." With the Buddhists it is the *sixth* of the Chadâyatana (*q.v.*), or the six organs of knowledge, hence the highest of these, synthesized by the seventh called *Klichta*, the spiritual perception of that which defiles this (lower) Manas, or the "Human-animal

Soul", as the Occultists term it. While the Higher Manas or the Ego is directly related to *Vijnâna* (the 10th of the 12 Nidânas) – which is the perfect knowledge of all forms of knowledge, whether relating to object or subject in the nidânic concatenation of causes and effects; the lower, the Kâma Manas is but one of the *Indriya* or organs (roots) of Sense. Very little can be said of the dual Manas here, as the doctrine that treats of it, is correctly stated only in esoteric works. Its mention can thus be only very superficial.

Manas Taijasi (*Sk.*). Lit., the "radiant" Manas; a state of the Higher Ego, which only high metaphysicians are able to realize and comprehend.

Mânasa or *Manaswin* (*Sk.*). "The efflux of the *divine* mind," and explained as meaning that this efflux signifies the *manasa* or divine sons of Brahmâ-Virâj. Nilakantha who is the authority for this statement, further explains the term "manasa" by *manomâtrasarira*. These Manasa are the *Arupa* or incorporeal sons of the Prajâpati Virâj, in another version. But as Arjuna Misra identifies Virâj with Brahmâ, and as Brahmâ is Mahat, the universal mind, the exoteric blind becomes plain. The Pitris are identical with the Kumâra, the Vairaja, the Manasa-Putra (mind sons), and are finally identified with the human "Egos".

Mânasa Dhyânis (*Sk.*). The highest Pitris in the *Purânas*; the Agnishwatthas, or Solar Ancestors of Man, those who made of Man a rational being, by incarnating in the senseless forms of semi-ethereal flesh of the men of the third race. (See Vol. II. of *Secret Doctrine*.)

Mânasas (*Sk.*). Those who endowed humanity with *manas* or intelligence, the immortal EGOS in men. (See "Manas".)

Mânava Dharma Shâstra – is the ancient code of law of, or by Manu.

Manu (*Sk.*). The great Indian legislator. The name comes from the Sanskrit root *man* "to think" – mankind really, but stands for Swâyambhuva, the first of the Manus, who started from *Swâyambhu*, "the self-existent" hence the *Logos*, and the progenitor of mankind. Manu is the first Legislator, almost a Divine Being.

Manus (*Sk.*). The fourteen Manus are the patrons or guardians of the race cycles in a Manvantara, or Day of Brahmâ. The primeval Manus are seven, they become fourteen in the *Purânas*.

Manushi or *Manushi Buddhas* (*Sk.*). Human Buddhas, Bodhisattvas, or incarnated Dhyan Chohans.

Manvantara (*Sk.*). A period of manifestation, as opposed to Pralaya (dissolution, or rest), applied to various cycles, especially to a Day of Brahmâ, 4,320,000,000 Solar years – and to the reign of one Manu – 308,448,000. (See Vol. II. of the *Secret Doctrine*, p. 68 *et. seq.*) Lit., *Manuantara* – between Manus.

Mârttanda, (*Sk.*). The Vedic name of the Sun.

Mâyâ *(Sk.).* Illusion ; the cosmic power which renders phenomenal existence and the perceptions thereof possible. In Hindu philosophy that alone which is changeless and eternal is called *reality* ; all that which is subject to change through decay and differentiation and which has therefore a begining and an end is regarded as *mâyâ* – illusion.

Monad *(Gr.).* The Unity, the *one* ; but in Occultism it often means the unified triad, Atma-Buddhi-Manas, or the duad, Atma-Buddhi, that immortal part of man which reincarnates in the lower kingdoms, and gradually progresses through them to Man and then to the final goal – Nirvâna.

Monas *(Gr.).* The same as the term *Monad* ; "Alone", a unit. In the Pythagorean system the duad emanates from the higher and solitary Monas, which is thus the "First Cause".

Moon. The earth's satellite has figured very largely as an emblem in the religions of antiquity; and most commonly has been represented as Female, but this is not universal, for in the myths of the Teutons and Arabs, as well as in the conception of the Rajpoots of India (see Tod, *Hist.*), and in Tartary the moon was male. Latin authors speak of Luna. and also of Lunus, but with extreme rarity. The Greek name is Selene, the Hebrew Lebanah and also Yarcah. In Egypt the moon was associated with Isis, in Phenicia with Astarte and in Babylon with Ishtar. From certain points of view the ancients regarded the moon also as Androgyne. The astrologers allot an Influence to the moon over the several parts of a man, according to the several Zodiacal signs she traverses; as well as a special influence produced by the house she occupies in a figure.

The division of the Zodiac into the 28 mansions of the moon appears to be older than that into 12 signs: the Copts, Egyptians, Arabs, Persians and Hindoos used the division into 28 parts centuries ago, and the Chinese use it still.

The Hermetists said the moon gave man an astral form, while Theosophy teaches that the Lunar Pitris were the creators of our human bodies and lower principles. (See *Secret Doctrine* 1. 386.) [w.w.w.]

Mummy. The name for human bodies embalmed and preserved according to the ancient Egyptian method. The process of mummification is a rite of extreme antiquity in the land of the Pharaohs, and was considered as one of the most sacred ceremonies. It was, moreover, a process showing considerable learning in chemistry and surgery. Mummies 5,000 years old and more, reappear among us a preserved and fresh as when they first came from the hands of the *Parashistes*.

Munis *(Sk.).* Saints, or Sages.

Mysteries. Greek *teletai*, or finishings, celebrations of initiation or the Mysteries. They were observances, generally kept secret from the profane and uninitiated, in which were taught by dramatic representation and other methods, the origin of things, the nature of the human spirit, its relation to the body, and the method of its purification and restoration to higher life. Physical science, medicine, the laws of music, divination, were all taught in the same manner. The Hippocratic oath was but a mystic obligation. Hippocrates was a priest of Asklepios, some of whose writings chanced to become public. But the Asklepiades were initiates of the Æsculapian serpent-worship, as the Bacchantes were of the Dionysia; and both rites were eventually incorporated with the Eleusinia. The Sacred Mysteries were enacted in the ancient Temples by the initiated Hierophants for the benefit and instruction of the candidates. The most solemn and occult Mysteries were certainly those which were performed in Egypt by "the band of secret-keepers", as Mr. Bonwick calls the Hierophants. Maurice describes their nature very graphically in a few lines. Speaking of the Mysteries performed in Philæ (the Nile-island), he says that "it was in these gloomy caverns that the grand and mystic arcana of the goddess (Isis) were unfolded to the adoring aspirant, while the solemn hymn of initiation resounded through the long extent of these stony recesses". The word "mysteries" is derived from the Greek *muô*, "to close the mouth", and every symbol connected with them had, a hidden meaning. As Plato and many other sages of antiquity affirm, the Mysteries were highly religious, moral and beneficent as a school of ethics. The Grecian mysteries, those of Ceres and Bacchus, were only imitations of the Egyptian; and the author of *Egyptian Belief and Modern Thought*, informs us that our own "word *chapel* or *capella* is said to be the *Caph-El* or college of *El*, the Solar divinity". The well-known *Kabiri* are associated with the Mysteries. In short, the Mysteries were in every country a series of dramatic performances, in which the mysteries of cosmogony and nature, in general, were personified by the priests and neophytes, who enacted the part of various gods and goddesses, repeating supposed scenes (allegories) from their respective lives. These were explained in their hidden meaning to the candidates for initiation, and incorporated into philosophical doctrines.

N

Nâga (*Sk.*). Literally "Serpent". The name in the Indian Pantheon of the Serpent or Dragon Spirits, and of the inhabitants of Pâtâla, hell. But as Pâtâla means the *antipodes*, and was the name given to America by the ancients, who knew and visited that continent before Europe had ever heard of it, the term is probably akin to the Mexican Nagals the (now) sorcerers and medicine men. The Nagas are the Burmese *Nats*, serpent-gods, or "dragon demons". In Esotericism, however, and as already stated, this is a nick-name for the "wise men" or adepts in China and Tibet, the "Dragons." are regarded as the titulary deities of the world, and of various spots on the earth, and the word is explained as meaning adepts, yogis, and narjols. The term has simply reference to their great knowledge and wisdom. This is also proven in the ancient Sûtras and Buddha's biographies. The Nâga is ever a wise man, endowed with extraordinary magic powers, in South and Central America as in India, in Chaldea as also in ancient Egypt. In China the "worship" of the Nâgas was widespread, and it has become still more pronounced since Nâgarjuna (the "great Nâga", the "great adept" literally), the fourteenth Buddhist patriarch, visited China. The "Nâgas" are regarded by the Celestials as "the tutelary Spirits or gods of the five regions or the four points of the compass and the centre, as the guardians of the five lakes and four oceans" (**Eitel**). This, traced to its origin and translated esoterically, means that the five continents and their five root-races had always been under the guardianship of "terrestrial deities", i.e., Wise Adepts. The tradition that Nâgas washed Gautama Buddha at his birth, protected him and guarded the relics of his body when dead, points again to the Nâgas being only wise men, Arhats, and no monsters or Dragons. This is also corroborated by the innumerable stories of the conversion of Nâgas to Buddhism. The Nâga of a lake in a forest near Râjagriha and many other "Dragons" were thus converted by Buddha to the good Law.

Nârada (*Sk.*). One of the Seven great Rishis, a Son of Brahmâ This "Progenitor" is one of the most mysterious personages in the Brahmanical sacred symbology. Esoterically Nârada is the Ruler of events during various Karmic cycles, and the personification, in a certain sense, of the great human cycle; a Dhyan Chohan. He plays a great part in Brahmanism, which ascribes to him some of the most occult hymns in the *Rig Veda*, in which sacred work he is described as "of the Kanwa family". He is called Deva-Brahmâ, but as such has a distinct character from the one he assumes on earth – or Pâtâla. Daksha cursed him for his interference with his 5,000 and 10,000 sons, whom he persuaded to remain Yogins and *celibates*, to be reborn time after time on this earth (*Mahâbhârata*). But this is an allegory. He was the inventor of the Vina, a kind of lute, and a great "lawgiver". The story is too long to be given here.

Nârâyana (*Sk.*). The "mover on the Waters" of space: a title of Vishnu, in his aspect of the Holy Spirit, moving on the Waters of Creation. (See *Mânu*, Book II.) In esoteric symbology it stands for the primeval manifestation of the *life-principle,* spreading in infinite Space.

Nâstika (*Sk.*). Atheist, or rather he who does not worship or recognize the gods and idols.

Nephesh (*Heb.*). Breath of life. *Anima, Mens, Vita,* Appetites. This term is used very loosely in the Bible. It generally means *prana* "life"; in the Kabbalah it is the animal passions and the animal Soul. [w.w.w.]. Therefore, as maintained in theosophical teachings, *Nephesh* is the synonym of the Prâna-Kâmic Principle, or the vital animal Soul in man. [H. P. B.]

Nidâna (*Sk.*). The 12 causes of existence, or a chain of causation, "a concatenation of cause and effect in the whole range of existence through 12 links". This is the fundamental dogma of Buddhist thought, "the understanding of which solves the riddle of life, revealing the insanity of existence and preparing the mind for Nirvâna". (Eitel's *Sans. Chin. Dict.*) The 12 links stand thus in their enumeration. (1) Jail, or birth, according to one of the four modes of entering the stream of life and reincarnation – or *Chatur Yoni (q.v.)*, each mode placing the being born in one of the six *Gâti* (q.v.). (2) *Jarârnarana*, or decrepitude and death, following the maturity of the *Skandhas* (q.v.). (3) *Bhava*, the Karmic agent which leads every new sentient being to be born in this or another mode of existence in the *Trailokya* and Gâti. (4) *Upâdâna*, the creative cause of *Bhava* which thus becomes the cause of *Jati* which is the effect; and this creative cause is the *clinging to life.* (5) Trishnâ, love, whether pure or impure. (6) *Vêdâna*, or sensation; perception by the senses, it is the 5th Skandha. (7) Sparsa, the sense of touch. (8) *Chadâyatana*, the organs of sensation. (9) *Nâmarûpa*, personality, i.e., a form with a name to it, the symbol of the unreality of material phenomenal appearances. (10) *Vijnâna*, the perfect knowledge of every perceptible thing and of all objects in their concatenation and unity. (11) *Samskâra*, action on the plane of illusion. (12) *Avidyâ*, lack of true perception, or ignorance. The Nidânas belonging to the most subtle and abstruse doctrines of the Eastern metaphysical system, it is impossible to go into the subject at any greater length.

Nirguna (*Sk.*). Negative attribute; unbound, or without *Gunas* (attributes), i.e., that which is devoid of all qualities, the opposite of Saguna, that which has attributes (*Secret Doctrine*, II. 95), e.g., Parabrahmam is Nirguna; Brahmâ, Saguna. Nirguna is a term which shows the impersonality of the thing spoken of.

Nirmânakâya (*Sk.*). Something entirely different in esoteric philosophy from the popular meaning attached to it, and from the fancies of the Orientalists. Some call the *Nirmânakâya* body "Nirvana with remains" (Schlagintweit, etc.) on the supposition, probably, that it is a kind of Nirvânic condition during which consciousness and form are retained. Others say that it is one of the *Trikâya* (three bodies), with the "power of assuming any form of appearance in order to propagate Buddhism" (Eitel's idea); again, that "it is the incarnate avatâra of a deity" (*ibid.*), and so on. Occultism, on the other hand, says:that Nirmânakâya, although meaning literally a transformed "body", is a state. The form is that of the adept or yogi who enters, or chooses, that *post mortem* condition in preference to the Dharmakâya or *absolute* Nirvânic state. He does this because the latter *kâya* separates him for ever from the world of form, conferring upon him a state of *selfish* bliss, in which no other living being can participate, the adept being thus precluded from the possibility of helping humanity, or even *devas*. As a Nirmânakâya, however, the man leaves behind him only his physical body, and retains every other "principle" save the Kamic – for he has crushed this out for ever from his nature, during life, and it can never resurrect in his post mortem state. Thus, instead of going into selfish bliss, he chooses a life of self-sacrifice, an existence which ends only with the life-cycle, in order to be enabled to help mankind in an invisible yet most effective manner. (See *The Voice of the Silence*, third treatise, "The Seven Portals".) Thus a Nirmânakâya is not, as popularly believed, the body "in which a Buddha or a Bodhisattva appears on earth", but verily one, who whether a *Chutuktu* or a *Khubilkhan*, an adept or a yogi during life, has since become a member of that invisible Host which ever protects and watches over Humanity within Karmic limits. Mistaken often for a "Spirit", a Deva, God himself, &c., a Nirmânakâya is ever a protecting, compassionate, verily a *guardian* angel, to him who becomes worthy of his help. Whatever objection may be brought forward against this doctrine; however much it is denied, because, forsooth, it has never been hitherto made public in Europe and therefore since it is unknown to Orientalists, it must needs be "a myth of modern invention" – no one will be bold enough to say that this idea of helping suffering mankind at the price of one's own almost interminable self-sacrifice, is not one of the grandest and noblest that was ever evolved from human brain.

Nirvâna (*Sk.*). According to the Orientalists, the entire "blowing out", like the flame of a candle, the utter extinction of existence. But in the esoteric explanations it is the state of absolute existence and absolute consciousness, into which the Ego of a man who has reached the highest degree of perfection and holiness during life goes, after the body dies, and occasionally, as in the case of Gautama Buddha and others, during life. (See "Nirvânî".)

Nirvânî (ee) (Sk.). One who has attained Nirvana – an emancipated soul. That Nirvâna means nothing of the kind asserted by Orientalists every scholar who has visited China, India and Japan is well aware. It is "*escape* from misery" but only from that of matter, freedom from *Klêsha*, or *Kâma,* and the complete extinction of animal desires. If we are told that *Abidharma* defines Nirvâna "as a state of absolute annihilation", we concur, adding to the last word the qualification "of everything connected with matter or the physical world", and this simply because the latter (as also all in it) is illusion, *mâyâ*. Sâkya-mûni Buddha said in the last moments of his life that "the spiritual body is immortal" (See *Sans. Chin. Dict.*). As Mr. Eitel, the scholarly Sinologist, explains it: "The popular exoteric systems agree in defining Nirvâna *negatively* as a state of absolute exemption from the circle of transmigration; as a state of entire freedom from all forms of existence; to begin with, freedom from all passion and exertion; a state of indifference to all sensibility" and he might have added "death of all compassion for the world of suffering". And this is why the Bodhisattvas who prefer the Nirmânakâya to the Dharmakâya vesture, stand higher in the popular estimation than the Nirvânîs. But the same scholar adds that: "Positively (and esoterically) they define Nirvâna as the highest state of spiritual bliss, as absolute immortality through absorption of the soul (spirit rather) into itself, but *preserving individuality* so that, e.g., Buddhas, after entering Nirvâna, may reappear on earth" – i.e., in the future Manvantara.

Norns (*Scand.*). The three sister goddesses in the *Edda*, who make known to men the decrees of *Orlog* or Fate. They are shown as coming out of the unknown distances *enveloped in a dark veil* to the Ash Yggdrasil (*q.v.*), and "sprinkle it daily with water from the Fountain of Urd, that it may not wither but remain green and fresh and strong" (*Asgard and the Gods*). Their names are "Urd", the Past; "Werdandi", the Present; and "Skuld", the Future, "which is either rich in hope or dark with tears". Thus they reveal the decrees of Fate "for out of the past and present the events and actions of the future are born" (*loc. cit.*).

Nous. (*Gr.*). A Platonic term for the Higher Mind or Soul. It means Spirit as distinct from animal Soul – *psyche*; divine consciousness or mind in man: *Nous* was the designation given to the Supreme deity (third *logos*) by Anaxagoras. Taken from Egypt where it was called *Nout*, it was adopted by the Gnostics for their first conscious Æon which, with the Occultists, is the third *logos*, cosmically, and the third "principle" (from above) or *manas*, in man. (See "Nout".)

Nout. (*Gr.*). In the Pantheon of the Egyptians it meant the "One- only-One", because they did not proceed in their popular or exoteric religion higher than the third manifestation which radiates from the *Unknown* and the *Unknowable*, the first unmanifested and the second *logoi* in the esoteric philosophy of every nation. The Nous of Anaxagoras was the *Mahat* of the Hindu Brahmâ, *the first manifested* Deity – "the Mind or Spirit self-potent"; this creative Principle being of course the *primum mobile* of everything in the Universe – its Soul and Ideation. (See "Seven Principles" in man.)

O

Occult Sciences. The science of the secrets of nature – physical and psychic, mental and spiritual; called Hermetic and Esoteric Sciences. In the West, the Kabbalah may be named; in the East, mysticism, magic, and Yoga philosophy, which latter is often referred to by the Chelas in India as the *seventh* "Darshana" (school of philosophy), there being only *six* Darshanas in India known to the world of the profane. These sciences are, and have been for ages, hidden from the vulgar for the very good reason that they would never be appreciated by the selfish educated classes, nor understood by the uneducated; whilst the former might misuse them for their own profit, and thus turn the divine science into *black magic*. It is often brought forward as an accusation against the Esoteric philosophy and the Kabbalah that their literature is full of "a barbarous and meaningless jargon" unintelligible to the ordinary mind. But do not exact Sciences – medicine, physiology, chemistry, and the rest – do the same? Do not official Scientists equally veil their facts and discoveries with a newly coined and most barbarous Græco-Latin terminology? As justly remarked by our late brother,

Kenneth Mackenzie – "To juggle thus with words, when the facts are so simple, is the art of the Scientists of the present time, in striking contrast to those of the XVIIth century, who called spades spades, and not 'agricultural implements '." Moreover, whilst their facts would be as simple and as comprehensible if rendered in ordinary language, the facts of Occult Science are of so abstruse a nature, that in most cases no words exist in European languages to express them; in addition to which our "jargon" is a *double* necessity – (a) for the purpose of describing clearly these *facts* to him who is versed in the Occult terminology; and (b) to conceal them from the profane.

Occultist. One who studies the various branches of occult science. The term is used by the French Kabbalists (See Eliphas Lévi's works). Occultism embraces the whole range of psychological, physiological, cosmical, physical, and spiritual phenomena. From the word occultus hidden or secret. It therefore applies to the study of the **Kabbalah**, astrology, alchemy, and all arcane sciences.

Oeaohoo, or *Oeaihwu.* The manner of pronunciation depends on the accent. This is an esoteric term for the six in one or the mystic seven. The occult name for the "seven vowelled" ever-present manifestation of the Universal Principle.

Ophiomorphos (*Gr.*). The same, but in its material aspect, as the Ophis-Christos. With the Gnostics the Serpent represented "Wisdom in Eternity".

Orlog (*Scand.*). Fate, destiny, whose agents were the three Norns, the Norse *Parcæ*.

Osiris. (*Eg.*). The greatest God of Egypt, the Son of Seb (Saturn), celestial fire, and of Neith, primordial matter and infinite space. This shows him as the self-existent and self-created god, the first manifesting deity (our third Logos), identical with Ahura Mazda and other " First Causes". For as Ahura Mazda is one with, or the synthesis of, the Amshaspends, so Osiris, the collective unit, when differentiated and personified, becomes Typhon, his brother, Isis and Nephtys his sisters, Horus his son and his other aspects. He was born at Mount Sinai, the Nyssa of the 0. T. (See- *Exodus* xvii. 15), and buried at Abydos, after being killed by Typhon at the early age of twenty-eight, according to the allegory. According to Euripides he is the same as Zeus and Dionysos or *Dio-Nysos* "the god of Nysa", for Osiris is said by him to have been brought up in Nysa, in Arabia "the Happy". Query: how much did the latter tradition influence, or have anything in common with, the statement in the Bible, that "Moses built an altar and called the name Jehovah Nissi", or Kabbalistically – "Dio-Iao-Nyssi"? (See *Isis Unveiled* Vol. II. p. 165.) The four chief aspects of Osiris were – Osiris-Phtah (Light), the spiritual aspect; Osiris-Horus (Mind), the intellectual *manasic* aspect; Osiris-Lunus, the " Lunar" or psychic, astral aspect; Osiris-Typhon, Daïmonic, or physical, material, therefore passional turbulent aspect. In these four aspects he symbolizes the dual Ego – the divine and the human, the cosmico-spiritual and the terrestrial.

Of the many supreme gods, this Egyptian conception is the most suggestive and the grandest, as it embraces the whole range of physical and metaphysical thought. As a solar deity he had twelve minor gods under him – the twelve signs of the Zodiac. Though his name is the "Ineffable", his forty-two attributes bore each one of his names, and his seven dual aspects completed the forty-nine, or 7 X 7; the former symbolized by the fourteen members of his body, or twice seven. Thus the god is blended in man, and the man is deified into a god.

As to his human development, he is, as the author of the *Egyptian Belief* has it . . . "One of the Saviours or Deliverers of Humanity . . . . As such he is born in the world. He came as a benefactor, to relieve man of trouble . . . . In his efforts to do good he encounters evil . . . and he is temporarily overcome. He is killed . . Osiris is buried. His tomb was the object of pilgrimage for thousands of years. But he did not rest in his grave. At the end of three days, or forty, he rose again and ascended to Heaven. This is the story of his Humanity" (*Egypt. Belief*).

Ouranos (*Gr.*). The whole expanse of Heaven called the "Waters of Space", the Celestial Ocean, etc. The name very likely comes from the Vedic Varuna, personified as the water god and regarded as the chief Aditya among the seven planetary deities. In Hesiod's Theogony, Ouranos (or Uranus) is the same as Cœlus (Heaven) the oldest of all the gods and the father of the divine Titans.

P

Padma Kalpa (*Sk.*). The name of the last Kalpa or the preceding Manvantara, which was a year of Brahmâ.

Pagan (*Lat.*). Meaning at first no worse than a dweller in the country or the woods; one far removed from the city-temples, and therefore unacquainted with the state religion and ceremonies. The word "heathen" has a similar significance, meaning one who lives on the heaths and in the country. Now, however, both come to mean *idolaters.*

Pagan Gods. The term is erroneously understood to mean idols. The philosophical idea attached to them was never that of something objective or anthropomorphic, but in each case an abstract potency, a virtue, or quality in nature. There are gods who are divine planetary spirits (Dhyan Chohans) or Devas, among which are also our Egos. With this exception, and especially whenever represented by an idol or in anthropomorphic form, the gods represent symbolically in the Hindu, Egyptian, or Chaldean Pantheons – formless spiritual Potencies of the "Unseen Kosmos".

Palæolithic A newly-coined term meaning in geology "ancient stone" age, as a contrast to the term *neolithic,* the "newer" or later stone age.

Pandora (*Gr.*). A beautiful woman created by the gods under the orders of Zeus to be sent to Epimetheus, brother of Prometheus; she had charge of a casket in which all the evils, passions and plagues which torment humanity were locked up. This casket Pandora, led by curiosity, opened, and thus set free all the ills which prey on mankind.

Para (*Sk.*). "Infinite" and "supreme" in philosophy – the final limit.

Parabrahm (*Sk.*). "Beyond Brahmâ", literally. The Supreme Infinite Brahma, "Absolute" – the attributeless, the secondless reality. The impersonal and nameless universal Principle.

Paracelsus. The symbolical name adopted by the greatest Occultist of the middle ages – Philip Bombastes Aureolus Theophrastus von Hohenheim – born in the canton of Zurich in 1493. He was the cleverest physician of his age, and the most renowned for curing almost any illness by the power of talismans prepared by himself. He never had a friend, but was surrounded by enemies, the most bitter of whom were the Churchmen and their party. That he was accused of being in league with the devil stands to reason, nor is it to be wondered at that finally he was murdered by some unknown foe, at the early age of forty-eight. He died at Salzburg, leaving a number of works behind him, which are to this day greatly valued by the Kabbalists and Occultists. Many of his utterances have proved prophetic. He was a clairvoyant of great powers, one of the most learned and erudite philosophers and mystics, and a distinguished Alchemist. Physics is indebted to him for the discovery of nitrogen gas, or **Azote**.

Paramartha (*Sk*) Absolute existence.

Paranirvâna (*Sk.*). Absolute *Non-Being*, which is equivalent to absolute *Being* or "Be-ness", the state reached by the human Monad at the end of the great cycle (See *Secret Doctrine* I, 135). The same as *Paraniskpanna*.

Pentagon (*Gr.*), from *pente* "five", and *gonia* "angle" ; in geometry a plane figure with five angles.

Personality. In Occultism – which divides man into seven principles, considering him under the three aspects of the *divine*, the *thinking* or the *rational*, and the *animal* man – the lower *quaternary* or the purely astrophysical being; while by *Individuality* is meant the Higher Triad, considered as a Unity. Thus the *Personality* embraces all the characteristics and memories of one physical life, while the *Individuality* is the imperishable *Ego* which re-incarnates and clothes itself in one personality after another.

Phenomenon (*Gr.*). In reality "an appearance", something previously unseen, and puzzling when the cause of it is unknown. Leaving aside various kinds of phenomena, such as cosmic, electrical, chemical, etc., and holding merely to the phenomena of spiritism, let it be remembered that theosophically and esoterically every "miracle" – from the biblical to the theumaturgic – is simply a phenomenon, but that no phenomenon is ever a miracle, *i.e.*, something supernatural or outside of the laws of nature, as all such are impossibilities in nature.

Pitris (*Sk.*). The ancestors, or creators of mankind. They are of seven classes, three of which are incorporeal, *arupa*, and four corporeal. In popular theology they are said to be created from Brahmâ's side. They are variously genealogized, but in esoteric philosophy they are as given in the *Secret Doctrine*. In *Isis Unveiled* it is said of them "It is generally believed that the Hindu term means the spirits of our ancestors, of disembodied people, hence the argument of some Spiritualists that fakirs (and yogis) and other Eastern wonder-workers, are *mediums*. This is in more than one sense erroneous. The Pitris are not the ancestors of the present living men, but those of the human kind, or Adamic races; the spirits of human races, which on the great scale of descending evolution *preceded our races* of men, and they *were physically, as well as spiritually, far superior* to our modern pigmies. In *Mânava Dharma Shâstra* they are called the *Lunar Ancestors*." The *Secret Doctrine* has now explained that which was cautiously put forward in the earlier Theosophical volumes.

Planetary Spirits. Primarily the rulers or governors of the planets. As our earth has its hierarchy of terrestrial planetary spirits, from the highest to the lowest plane, so has every other heavenly body. In Occultism, however, the term "Planetary Spirit" is generally applied only to the seven highest hierarchies corresponding to the Christian archangels. These have all passed through a stage of evolution corresponding to the humanity of earth on other worlds, in long past cycles. Our earth, being as yet only in its fourth round, is far too young to have produced high planetary spirits. The highest planetary spirit ruling over any globe is in reality the "Personal God" of that planet and far more truly its "over-ruling providence" than the self-contradictory Infinite Personal Deity of modern Churchianity.

Plato. An Initiate into the Mysteries and the greatest Greek philosopher, whose writings are known the world over. He was the pupil of Socrates and the teacher of Aristotle. He flourished over 400 years before our era.

Popol Vuh. The Sacred Books of the Guatemalians. Quiché MSS., discovered by Brasseur de Bourbourg.

Pragna (*Sk.*) or *Prajna*. A synonym of *Mahat* the Universal Mind. The capacity for perception. (*S. D.*, I. 139) Consciousness.

Prajâpatis (*Sk.*). Progenitors; the givers of life to all on this Earth. They are seven and then ten – corresponding to the seven and ten Kabbalistic Sephiroth; to the Mazdean Amesha-Spentas, &c. Brahmâ the creator, is called Prajâpati as the synthesis of the Lords of Being.

Prakriti (*Sk.*). Nature in general, nature as opposed to Purusha – spiritual nature and Spirit, which together are the "two primeval aspects of the One Unknown Deity". (*Secret Doctrine*, I. 51.)

Pralaya (*Sk.*). A period of obscuration or repose – planetary, cosmic or universal – the opposite of Manvantara (*S. D.*, I. 370.).

Pramantha (*Sk.*). An accessory to producing the sacred fire by friction. The sticks used by Brahmins to kindle fire by friction.

Prâna (*Sk.*). Life-Principle ; the breath of Life.

Pranidhâna (*Sk.*). The fifth observance of the Yogis; ceaseless devotion. (See *Yoga Shâstras*, ii. 32.)

Pratyasarga (*Sk.*). In Sankhya philosophy the "intellectual evolution of the Universe" ; in the *Purânas* the 8th creation.

Prometheus (*Gr.*). The Greek *logos*; he, who by bringing on earth divine fire (intelligence and consciousness) endowed men with reason and mind. Prometheus is the Hellenic type of our Kumâras or *Egos,* those who, by incarnating in men, made of them latent gods instead of animals. The gods (or Elohim) were averse to men becoming "as one of us (*Genesis* iii., 22), and knowing "good and evil". Hence we see these gods in every religious legend punishing man for his desire to know. As the Greek myth has it, for stealing the fire he brought to men from Heaven, Prometheus was chained by the order of Zeus to a crag of the Caucasian Mountains.

Protogonos (*Gr.*). The "first-born"; used of all the manifested gods and of the Sun in our system.

Psyche (*Gr.*). The animal, terrestrial Soul; the lower *Manas.*

Purânas (*Sk.*). Lit., "ancient". A collection of symbolical and allegorical writings – eighteen in number now – supposed to have been composed by Vyâsa, the author of *Mahâbhârata.*

Purusha (*Sk.*). "Man", *heavenly man.* Spirit, the same as Nârâyana in another aspect. "The Spiritual Self."

Pymander (Gr.). The "Thought divine". The Egyptian Prometheus and the personified Nous or divine light, which appears to and instructs Hermes Trismegistus, in a hermetic work called "Pymander".

Q

Qabbalah (*Heb.*). The ancient Chaldean Secret Doctrine, abbreviated into Kabala. An occult system handed clown by oral transmission; but which, though accepting tradition, is not in itself composed of merely traditional teachings, as it was once a fundamental science, now disfigured by the additions of centuries, and by interpolation by the Western Occultists, especially by *Christian* Mystics.

It treats of hitherto esoteric interpretations of the Jewish Scriptures, and teaches several methods of interpreting Biblical allegories. Originally the doctrines were transmitted "from mouth to ear" only, says Dr. W. Wynn Westcott, "in an oral manner from teacher to pupil who received them; hence the name Kabbalah, Qabalah, or Cabbala from the Hebrew root QBL, to receive. Besides this Theoretic Kabbalah, there was created a Practical branch, which is concerned with the Hebrew letters, as types a like of Sounds, Numbers, and Ideas." (See "Gematria", "Notaricon", " Temura".) For the original book of the *Qabbalah* – the *Zohar* – see further on. But the *Zohar* we have now is not the *Zohar* left by Simeon Ben Jochai to his son and secretary as an heirloom. The author of the present *approximation* was one Moses de Leon, a Jew of the XIIIth century. (See "Kabalah" and "Zohar".)

Qadmon, Adam, or *Adam Kadmon (Heb.)*. The Heavenly or Celestial Man, the Microcosm *(q.v.)*, He is the manifested Logos; the *third* Logos according to Occultism, or the Paradigm of Humanity.

R

Ra *(Eg.)*. The divine Universal Soul in its manifested aspect – the ever-burning light; also the personified Sun.

Rajasâs *(Sk.)*. The elder *Agnishwattas* – the Fire-Pitris, "fire" standing as a symbol of enlightenment and intellect.

Râkshasas *(Sk.)*. *Lit.*, "raw eaters", and in the popular superstition evil spirits, demons. Esoterically, however, they are the *Gibborim* (giants) of the Bible, the Fourth Race or the Atlanteans. (See *Secret Doctrine*, II., 165.)

Reincarnation. The doctrine of rebirth, believed in by Jesus and the Apostles, as by all men in those days, but denied now by the Christians. All the Egyptian converts to Christianity, Church Fathers and others, believed in this doctrine, as shown by the writings of several. In the still existing symbols, the human-headed bird flying towards a mummy, a body, or "the soul uniting itself with its *sahou* (glorified body of the Ego, and also the *kâmalokic shell*) proves this belief. "The song of the Resurrection" chanted by Isis to recall her dead husband to life, might be translated "Song of Rebirth", as Osiris is collective Humanity. "Oh! Osiris [here follows the name of the Osirified mummy, or the departed], rise again in holy earth (matter), august mummy in the coffin, under thy corporeal substances", was the funeral prayer of the priest over the deceased. "Resurrection" with the Egyptians never meant the resurrection of the mutilated mummy, but of the *Soul* that informed it, the Ego in a new body. The putting on of flesh periodically by the Soul or the Ego, was a universal belief; nor can anything be more consonant with justice and Karmic law.

Rudras *(Sk.)*. The mighty ones; the lords of the three upper worlds. One of the classes of the "fallen" or incarnating spirits; they are all born of Brahmâ.

Rûpa (*Sk.*). Body; any form, applied even to the forms of the gods, which are subjective to us.

S

Sacred Science. The name given to the *inner* esoteric philosophy, the secrets taught in days of old to the initiated candidates, and divulged during the last and supreme Initiation by the Hierophants.

Samvritisatya (*Sk.*). Truth mixed with false conceptions (Samvriti); the reverse of absolute truth – or *Paramârthasatya,* self-consciousness in absolute truth or reality.

Sanat Kumâra (*Sk.*). The most prominent of the seven Kumâras, the Vaidhâtra the first of which are called Sanaka, Sananda, Sanâtana and Sanat Kumâra; which names are all significant qualifications of the degrees of human intellect.

Sânkhya (*Sk.*). The system of philosophy founded by Kapila Rishi, a system of analytical metaphysics, and one of the six *Darshanas* or schools of philosophy. It discourses on numerical categories and the meaning of the twenty-five *tatwas* (the forces of nature in various degrees). This "atomistic school", as some call it, explains nature by the interaction of twenty-four elements with *purusha* (spirit) modified by the three gunas (qualities), teaching the eternity of *pradhâna* (primordial, homogeneous matter), or the self-transformation of nature and the eternity of the human Egos.

Sanskrit (*Sk.*). The classical language of the Brahmans, never known *nor spoken in its true systematized form* (given later *approximately* by Pânini), except by the initiated Brahmans, as it was pre-eminently "a mystery language". It has now degenerated into the so-called Prâkrita.

Saptarshi (*Sk.*). The seven Rishis. As stars they are the constellation of 'the Great Bear, and called as such the *Riksha* and *Chitrasikhandinas,* bright-crested.

Satya Yuga (*Sk.*). The golden age, or the age of truth and purity; the first of the four Yugas, also called Krita Yuga.

Secret Doctrine. The general name given to the esoteric teachings of antiquity.

Sephira (*Heb.*) An emanation of Deity; the parent and synthesis of the ten Sephiroth when she stands at the head of the Sephirothal Tree; in the Kabbalah, Sephira,or the " Sacred Aged ", is the divine Intelligence (the same as Sophia or Metis), the first emanation from the "Endless" or Ain-Suph.

Sephiroth (*Heb.*). The ten emanations of Deity; the highest is formed by the concentration of the Ain Soph Aur, or the Limitless Light, and each: Sephira produces by emanation another Sephira. The names of the Ten Sephiroth are – 1. Kether – The Crown; 2. Chokmah – Wisdom; 3. Binah – Understanding; 4. Chesed- – Mercy; Geburah – Power; 6. Tiphereth – Beauty; 7. Netzach – Victory; 8. Hod – Splendour; 9. Jesod_Foundation; and 10. Malkuth – The Kingdom.

The conception of Deity embodied in the Ten Sephiroth is a very sublime one, and each Sephira is a picture to the Kabbalist of a group of exalted ideas, titles and attributes, which the name but faintly represents. Each Sephira is called either active or passive, though this attribution may lead to error; passive does not mean a return to negative existence; and the two words only express the relation between individual Sephiroth, and not any absolute quality. [w.w.w.]

Sesha (*Sk.*) *Ananta*, the great Serpent of Eternity, the couch of Vishnu; the symbol of infinite Time in Space. In the exoteric beliefs Sesha is represented as a *thousand*-headed and *seven*-headed cobra; the former the king of the nether world, called Pâtâla, the latter the carrier or support of Vishnu on the Ocean of Space.

Sharîra (Sarîra) (*Sk.*). Envelope or body.

Shekinah (*Heb.*). A title applied to Malkuth, the tenth Sephira, by the Kabbalists; but by the Jews to the cloud of glory which rested on the Mercy-seat in the Holy of Holies. As taught, however, by all the Rabbins of Asia Minor, its nature is of a more exalted kind, Shekinah being the veil of Ain-Soph, the Endless and the Absolute; hence a kind of Kabbalistic Mûlaprakriti. [w.w.w.]

Siddhas (*Sk.*). Saints and sages who have become almost divine also a hierarchy of Dhyan Chohans.

Sishta (*Sk.*). The great elect or Sages, left after every minor *Pralaya* (that which is called "obscuration" in Mr. Sinnett's *Esoteric Buddhism*), when the globe goes into its night or rest, to become, on its re-awakening, the seed of the next humanity. Lit. "remnant."

Siva (*Sk.*). The third person of the Hindu Trinity (the Trimûrti). He is a god of the first order, and in his character of Destroyer higher than Vishnu, the Preserver, as he destroys only to regenerate on a higher plane. He is born as Rudra, the Kumâra, and is the patron of all the Yogis, being called, as such, Mahâdeva the great ascetic, His titles are significant *Trilochana*, "the three-eyed", *Mahâdeva*, "the great god ", *Sankara*, etc., etc., etc.

Smaragdine Tablet of Hermes. As expressed by Eliphas Lévi,"this Tablet of Emerald is the whole of magic in a single page"; but India has a single word which, when understood, contains "the whole of magic ". This is a tablet, however, alleged to have been found by Sarai, Abraham's wife (!) *on the dead body of Hermes*. So say the Masons and Christian Kabbalists. But in Theosophy we call it an allegory. May it not mean that *Sarai-swati*, the wife of Brahmâ, or the goddess of secret wisdom and learning, finding still much of the ancient wisdom latent in the dead body of Humanity, revivified that wisdom? This led to the rebirth of the Occult Sciences, so long forgotten and neglected, the world over. The tablet itself, however, although containing the "whole of magic ", is too long to be reproduced here.

Soma (*Sk.*). The moon, and also the juice of the plant of that name used in the temples for trance purposes; a sacred beverage. Soma, the moon, is the symbol of the Secret Wisdom. In the *Upanishads* the word is used to denote gross matter (with an association of moisture) capable of producing life under the action of heat. (See " Soma-drink ".)

Soul. The **yuch**, or *nephesh* of the *Bible*; the vital principle, or the breath of life, which every animal, down to the infusoria, shares with man. In the translated Bible it stands indifferently for *life*, blood and soul. " Let us not kill his *nephesh* ", says the original text: "let us not kill *him* ", translate the Christians (*Genesis* xxxvii. 21), and so on.

Spirit. The lack of any mutual agreement between writers in the use of this word has resulted in dire confusion. It is commonly made synonymous with *soul*; and the lexicographers countenance the usage. In Theosophical teachings. the term "Spirit" is applied solely to that which *belongs directly to Universal Consciousness*, and which is its homogeneous and unadulterated emanation. Thus, the higher Mind in Man or his Ego (Manas) is, when linked indissolubly with Buddhi, a spirit; while the term "Soul", human or even animal (the lower Manas acting in animals as instinct), is applied only to Kâma-Manas, and qualified as the living soul. This is *nephesh*, in Hebrew, the "breath of life". Spirit is formless and *immaterial*, being, when individualised, of the highest spiritual substance – *Suddasatwa*, the divine essence, of which the body of the manifesting *highest* Dhyanis are formed. Therefore, the Theosophists reject the appellation " Spirits" for those phantoms which appear in the phenomenal manifestations of the Spiritualists, and call them "shells", and various other names. (See "Sukshma Sarîra".) Spirit, in short, is no entity in the sense of having form ; for, as Buddhist philosophy has it, where there is a form, there is a cause for pain and suffering. But each *individual* spirit – this individuality lasting only throughout the manvantaric life-cycle – may be described as a *centre of consciousness*, a self-sentient and self-conscious centre; a state, not a conditioned individual. This is why there is such a wealth of words in Sanskrit to express the different States of Being, Beings and Entities, each appellation showing the philosophical difference, the plane to which such *unit* belongs, and the degree of its spirituality or materiality. Unfortunately these terms are almost untranslatable into our Western tongues.

Sushupti Avasthâ (*Sk.*). Deep sleep; one of the four aspects of Prânava.

Sûtrâtman (*Sk.*). Lit., "the thread of spirit"; the immortal Ego, the Individuality which incarnates in men one life after the other, and upon which are strung, like beads on a string, his countless Personalities. The universal life-supporting air, *Samashti prau*; universal energy.

Svabhâvat (*Sk.*). Explained by the Orientalists as "plastic substance", which is an inadequate definition. Svabhâvat is the world-substance and stuff, or rather that which is behind it – the spirit and essence of substance. The name comes from *Subhâva* and is composed of three words – **su**, good, perfect, fair, handsome; **sva**, self; and **bkâva**, being, or *state of being*. From it all nature proceeds and into it all returns at the end of the life-cycles. In Esotericism it is called "Father-Mother". It is the plastic essence of matter.

Svasamvedanâ (*Sk.*). Lit., "the reflection which analyses itself "; a synonym of Paramârtha.

Svastika (Sk.). In popular notions, it is the Jaina cross, or the "four-footed" cross (*croix cramponnée*). In Masonic teachings, "the most ancient Order of the Brotherhood of the Mystic Cross" is said to have been founded by Fohi, 1,027 B.C., and introduced into China fifty-two years later, consisting of the three degrees. In Esoteric Philosophy, the most mystic and ancient diagram. It is "the originator of the fire by friction, and of the ' Forty-nine Fires'." Its symbol was stamped on Buddha's heart, and therefore called the " Heart's Seal". It is laid on the breasts of departed Initiates after their death ; and it is mentioned with the greatest respect in the *Râmâyana*. Engraved on every rock, temple and prehistoric building of India, and wherever Buddhists have left their landmarks; it is also found in China, Tibet and Siam, and among the ancient Germanic nations as Thor's Hammer. As described by Eitel in his *Hand-Book of Chinese Buddhism.* . (1) it is "found among Bonpas and Buddhists"; (2) it is "one of the sixty-five figures of the Sripâda" ; (it is "the symbol of esoteric Buddhism" ; (4) "the special mark of all deities worshipped by the Lotus School of China". Finally, and in Occultism, it is as sacred to us as the Pythagorean *Tetraktys*, of which it is indeed the double symbol.

T

Tanha (*Pali*). The thirst for life. Desire to live and clinging to life on this earth. This clinging is that which causes rebirth or reincarnation.

Tanmâtras (*Sk.*). The types or rudiments of the five Elements; the subtile essence of these, devoid of all qualities and identical with the properties of the five basic Elements – earth, water, fire, air and ether; i.e., the *tanmâtras* are, in one of their aspects, smell, taste, touch, sight, and hearing.

Tetragrammaton. The four-lettered name of God, its Greek title: the four letters are in Hebrew " yod, hé vau, hé " ,or in English capitals, IHVH. The true ancient pronunciation is now unknown; the sincere Hebrew considered this name too sacred for speech, and in reading the sacred writings he substituted the title " Adonai ", meaning Lord. In the *Kabbalah*, **I** is associated with Chokmah, **H** with Binah, **V** with Tiphereth, and **H** final with Malkuth. Christians in general call IHVH Jehovah, and many modern Biblical scholars write it Yahveh. In the *Secret Doctrine*, the name Jehovah is assigned to Sephira Binah alone, but this attribution is not recognised by the Rosicrucian school of Kabbalists, nor by Mathers in his translation of Knorr Von Rbsenroth's *Kabbalah Denudata*: certain Kabbalistic authorities have referred Binah alone to IHVH, but only in reference to the Jehovah of the exoteric Judaism. The IHVH of the *Kabbalah* has but a faint resemblance to the God of the Old Testament. [w.w.w.]

The *Kabbalah* of Knorr von Rosenroth is no authority to the Eastern Kabbalists; because it is well known that in writing his *Kabbalah Denudata* he followed the modern rather than the ancient (Chaldean) MSS.; and it is equally well known that those MSS. and writings of the *Zohar* that are classified as "ancient", mention, and some even use, the Hebrew vowel or Massoretic points. This alone would make these would-be Zoharic books spurious, as there are no direct traces of the Massorah scheme before the tenth century of our era, nor any remote trace of it before the seventh.

Theosophia (*Gr.*). Wisdom-religion, or "Divine Wisdom". The substratum and basis of all the world-religions and philosophies, taught and practised by a few elect ever since man became a thinking being. In its practical bearing, Theosophy is purely divine ethics; the definitions in dictionaries are pure nonsense, based on religious prejudice and ignorance of the true spirit of the early Rosicrucians and mediæval philosophers who called themselves Theosophists.

Theosophists. A name by which many mystics at various periods of history have called themselves. The Neo-Platonists of Alexandria were Theosophists; the Alchemists and Kabbalists during the mediæval ages were likewise so called, also the Martinists, the Quietists, and other kinds of mystics, whether acting independently or incorporated in a brotherhood or society. All real lovers of divine Wisdom and Truth had, and have, a right to the name, rather than those who, appropriating the qualification, live lives or perform actions opposed to the principles of Theosophy. As described by Brother Kenneth R. Mackenzie, the Theosophists of the past centuries – " entirely speculative, and founding no schools, have still exercised a silent influence upon philosophy; and, no doubt, when the time arrives, many ideas thus silently propounded may yet give new directions to human thought. One of the ways in which these doctrines have obtained not only authority, but power, has been among certain enthusiasts in the higher degrees of Masonry. This power has, however, to a great degree died with the founders, and modern Freemasonry contains few traces of theosophic influence. However accurate and beautiful some of the ideas of Swedenborg, Pernetty, Paschalis, Saint Martin, Marconis, Ragon, and Chastanier may have been, they have but little direct influence on society." This is true of the Theosophists of the last three centuries, but not of the later ones. For the Theosophists of the current century have already visibly impressed themselves on modern literature, and introduced the desire and craving for some philosophy in place of the blind dogmatic faith of yore, among the most intelligent portions of human-kind. Such is the difference between past and modern THEOSOPHY.

Titans (*Gr.*). Giants of divine origin in Greek mythology who made war against the gods. Prometheus was one of them.

To On (*Gr.*). The "Being", the "Ineffable All" of Plato. He" whom no person has seen except the Son".

Tretâ Yuga (*Sk.*). The second age of the world, a period of 1,296,000 years.

Triad, or *the Three*. The ten Sephiroth are contemplated as a group of three triads: Kether, Chochmah and Binah form the supernal triad; Chesed, Geburah and Tiphereth, the second; and Netzach, Hod and Yesod, the inferior triad. The tenth Sephira, Malkuth, is beyond the three triads. [w.w.w.]

The above is orthodox Western Kabalah. Eastern Occultists recognise but one triad – – the upper one (corresponding to Atmâ-Buddhi and the " Envelope" which reflects their light, the three in one) – and count seven lower Sephiroth, everyone of which stands for a " principle", beginning with the Higher Manas and ending with the Physical Body – of which Malkuth is the representative in the Microcosm and the Earth in the Macrocosm.

Typhon (*Eg.*). An aspect or shadow of Osiris. Typhon is not, as Plutarch asserts, the distinct " Evil Principle " or the Satan of the Jews; but rather the lower cosmic "principles " of the divine body of Osiris, the god in them – Osiris being the personified universe as an ideation, and Typhon as that same universe in its material realization. The two in one are Vishnu-Siva. The true meaning of the Egyptian myth is that Typhon is the terrestrial and material envelope of Osiris, who is the indwelling spirit thereof. In chapter 42 of the *Ritual* (" Book of the Dead"), Typhon is described as "Set, formerly called Thoth". Orientalists find themselves greatly perplexed by discovering Set-Typhon addressed in some papyri as "a great and good god ", and in others as the embodiment of evil. But is not Siva, one of the Hindu *Trimûrti*, described in some places as "the best and most bountiful of gods ", and at other times, "a dark, black, destroying, terrible " and " fierce god"? Did not Loki, the Scandinavian Typhon, after having been described in earlier times as a beneficent being, as the god of fire, the presiding genius of the peaceful domestic hearth, suddenly lose caste and become forthwith a power of evil, a cold-hell Satan and a demon of the worst kind? There is a good reason for such an invariable transformation. So long as these dual gods, symbols of good and necessary evil, of light and darkness, keep closely allied, i.e., stand for a combination of differentiated human qualities, or of the element they represent – they are simply an embodiment of the average *personal* god. No sooner, however, are they separated into two entities, each with its two characteristics, than they become respectively the two opposite poles of good and evil, of light and darkness ; they become in short, two independent and distinct entities or rather *personalities*. It is only by dint of sophistry that the Churches have succeeded to this day in preserving in the minds of the few the Jewish deity in his primeval integrity. Had they been logical they would have separated Christ from Jehovah, light and goodness from darkness and badness. And this was what happened to Osiris Typhon ;but no Orientalist has understood it, and thus their perplexity goes on increasing. (See the *Theosophical Glossary*)

U

Upâdhi (*Sk.*). Basis; the vehicle, carrier or bearer of something less material than itself: as the human body is the *upâdhi* of its spirit, ether the *upâdhi* of light, etc., etc.; a mould; a defining or limiting substance.

V

Vâch (Sk.). To call Vâch "speech" simply, is deficient in clearness. Vâch is the mystic personification of speech, and the female *Logos,* being one with Brahmâ, who created her out of one-half of his body, which he divided into two portions; she is also one with Virâj (called the "female" Virâj) who was created in her by Brahmâ. In one sense Vâch is "speech" by which knowledge was taught to man; in another she is the "mystic, secret speech" which descends upon and enters into the primeval Rishis, as the "tongues of fire" are said to have "sat upon" the apostles. For, she is called "the female creator ", the "mother of the Vedas ", etc., etc. Esoterically, she is the subjective Creative Force which, emanating from the Creative Deity (the subjective Universe, its "privation ", or *ideation*) becomes the manifested "world of speech ", i.e., the *concrete expression of ideation*, hence the "Word" or Logos. Vâch is "the male and female" Adam of the first chapter of *Genesis*, and thus called "Vâch-Virâj" by the sages. (See *Atharva Veda.*) She is also "the celestial Saraswatî produced from the heavens ", a "voice derived from *speechless* Brahmâ" (*Mahâbhârata*); the goddess of wisdom and eloquence. She is called *Sata-rûpa*, the goddess of *a hundred forms.*

Vâhan(a) (*Sk.*). A vehicle, the carrier of something immaterial and formless. All the gods and goddesses are, therefore, represented as using vâhanas to manifest themselves, which vehicles are ever symbolical. So, for instance, Vishnu has during Pralayas, *Ânanta* the infinite" (Space), symbolized by the serpent Sesha, and during the Manvantaras – *Garuda* the gigantic half-eagle, half-man, the symbol of the great cycle; Brahma appears as Brahmâ, descending into the planes of manifestations on *Kâlahamsa*, the "swan in time or finite eternity"; Siva (phonet, Shiva) appears as the bull *Nandi*; Osiris as the sacred bull *Apis*; Indra travels on an elephant; Kârttikeya, on a peacock; Kâmadeva on *Makâra*, at other times a parrot; Agni, the universal (and also solar) Fire-god, who is, as all of them are, "a consuming Fire", manifests itself as a ram and a lamb, *Ajâ*, "the unborn"; Varuna, as a fish; etc., etc., while the vehicle of MAN is his body.

Vaishnava (*Sk.*). A follower of any sect recognising and worshipping Vishnu as the one supreme God. The worshippers of Siva are called *Saivas*.

Vaivaswata (*Sk.*). The name of the Seventh Manu, the forefather of the post-diluvian race, or our own fifth humankind. A reputed son of Sûrya (the Sun), he became, after having been saved in an ark (built by the order of Vishnu) from the Deluge, the father of Ikshwâku, the founder of the solar race of kings. (See "*Sûryavansa*".)

Vâyu (*Sk.*). Air: the god and sovereign of the air; one of the five states of matter, namely the *gaseous*; one of the five elements, called, as wind, *Vâta*. The *Vishnu Purâna* makes Vâyu King of the Gandharvas. He is the father of Hanumân, in the *Râmâyana*. The trinity of the mystic gods in Kosmos closely related to each other, are " Agni (fire) whose place is on earth; Vâyu (air, or one of the forms of Indra), whose place is in the air ; and Sûrya (the sun) whose place is in the air (*Nirukta*.) In esoteric interpretation, these three cosmic principles, correspond with the three human principles, Kâma, Kâma-Manas and Manas, the sun of the intellect.

Vedânta (*Sk.*). A mystic system of philosophy which has developed from the efforts of generations of sages to interpret the secret meaning of the *Upanishads* (*q.v.*). It is called in the *Shad-Darshanas* (six schools or systems of demonstration), *Uttara Mîmânsâ*, attributed to *Vyâsa*, the compiler of the *Vedas*, who is thus referred to as the founder of the Vedânta. The orthodox Hindus call Vedânta_a term meaning literally the "end of all (Vedic) knowledge " – *Brahmâ-jnâna*, or pure and spiritual knowledge of Brahmâ. Even if we accept the late dates assigned to various Sanskrit schools and treatises by our Orientalists, the Vedânta must be 3,300 years old, as Vyâsa is said to have lived I,400 years B.C. If, as Elphinstone has it in his *History of India*, the *Brahmanas* are the *Talmud* of the Hindus, and the *Vedas* the Mosaic books, then the *Vedânta* may be correctly called the *Kabalah* of India. But how vastly more grand! Sankarâchârya, who was the popularizer of the Vedântic system, and the founder of the *Adwaita* philosophy, is sometimes called the founder of the modern schools of the Vedânta.

Vedas (*Sk.*). The "revelation". the scriptures of the Hindus, from the root *vid*, "to know ", or "divine knowledge". They are the most ancient as well as the most sacred of the Sanskrit works. The *Vedas* , on the date and antiquity of which no two Orientalists can agree, are claimed by the Hindus themselves, whose Brahmans and Pundits ought to know best about their own religious works, to have been first taught orally for thousands of years and then compiled on the shores of Lake Mânasa-Sarovara (phonetically, *Mansarovara*) beyond the Himalayas, in Tibet.

The Vedic writings are all classified in two great divisions, exoteric and esoteric, the former being called *Karma-Kânda*, "division of actions or works ", and the *Jnâna Kânda*, "division of (divine) knowledge", the Upanishads (q.v.) coming under this last classification. Both departments are regarded as *Sruti* or revelation. To each hymn of the *Rig -Veda*, the name of the Seer or Rishi to whom it was revealed is prefixed. It, thus, becomes evident on the authority of these very names (such as Vasishta, Viswâmitra, Nârada, etc.), all of which belong to men born in various manvantaras and even ages, that centuries, and perhaps millenniums, must have elapsed between the dates of their composition.

Vendîdâd (*Pahlavi*). The first book (*Nosk*) in the collection of Zend fragments usually known as the *Zend-Avesta*. The *Vendidâd* is a corruption of the compound-word "Vidaêvo-dâtern", meaning "the anti- demoniac law ", and is full of teachings how to avoid sin and defilement by purification, moral and physical – each of which teachings is based on Occult laws. It is a pre-eminently occult treatise, full of symbolism and often of meaning quite the reverse of that which is expressed in its dead-letter text. The *Vendîdâd*, as claimed by tradition, is the only one of the twenty-one Nosks (works) that has escaped the *auto-da-fé* at the hands of the drunken Iskander the Rûmi, he whom posterity calls Alexander the Great – though the epithet is justifiable only when applied to the brutality, vices and cruelty of this conqueror. It is through the vandalism of this Greek that literature and knowledge have lost much priceless lore in the Nosks burnt by him. Even the Vendidâd has reached us in only a fragmentary state. The first chapters are very mystical, and therefore called "mythical" in the renderings of European Orientalists. The two "creators" of "spirit-matter" or the world of differentiation – Ahura- Mazda and Angra-Mainyu (Ahriman) – are introduced in them, and also Yima (the first man, or mankind personified). The work is divided into *Fargards* or chapters, and a portion of these is devoted to the formation of our globe, or terrestrial evolution. (See *Zend-Avesta*.)

Vishnu (*Sk.*). The second person of the Hindu Trimûrti (trinity), composed of Brahmâ, Vishnu and Siva. From the root **vish**, "to pervade". in the *Rig -Veda*, Vishnu is no high god, but simply a manifestation of the solar energy, described as "striding through the seven regions of the Universe in *three* steps and enveloping all things with the dust (of his beams ".) Whatever may be the six other occult significances of the statement, this is related to the same class of types as the seven and ten Sephiroth, as the *seven* and *three* orifices of the perfect Adam Kadmon, as the seven "principles" and the higher triad in man, etc., etc. Later on this mystic type becomes a great god, the preserver and the renovator, he "of a thousand names – Sahasranâma ".

W

Wisdom. The " very essence of wisdom is contained in the Non- Being ". say the Kabbalists; but they also apply the term to the WORD or Logos, the Demiurge, by which the universe was called into existence. "The one Wisdom is in the Sound ", say the Occultists; the Logos again being meant by Sound, which is the substratum of Âkâsa. Says the *Zohar,* the " Book of Splendour" "It is the Principle of all the Principles, the mysterious Wisdom, the crown of all that which there is of the most High". (*Zohar*, iii., fol. 288, Myers *Qabbalah.*) And it is explained, "Above Kether is the Ayin, or Ens, i.e., Ain, the NOTHING". "It is so named because we do not know, and it is impossible to know, *that which there is in that Principle,* because . . . it is above Wisdom itself." (iii., fol. 288.) This shows that the real Kabbalists agree with the Occultists that the essence, or that which is in the principle of Wisdom, is still above that highest Wisdom.

Wisdom Religion. The one religion which underlies all the now-existing creeds. That "faith" which, being primordial, and revealed directly to human kind by their *progenitors* and informing EGOS (though the Church regards them as the "fallen angels"), required no "grace", nor *blind* faith to believe, for it was *knowledge.* (See "Gupta Vidyâ", Hidden Knowledge.) It is on this Wisdom Religion that *Theosophy is based.*

Y

Years of Brahmâ. The whole period of "Brahma's Age" (100 Years). Equals 311,040,000,000,000 years. (See "Yuga ".)

Yggdrasil (*Scand.*). The "World Tree of the Norse Cosmogony; the ash Yggdrasil ; the tree of the Universe, of time and of life". It has three roots, which reach down to cold Hel, and spread thence to Jotun heim, the land of the Hrimthurses, or " Frost Giants ", and to Midgard, the earth and dwelling of the children of men. Its upper boughs stretch out into heaven, and its highest branch overshadows Waihalla, the Devachan of the fallen heroes. The Yggdrasil is ever fresh and green, as it is daily sprinkled by the Norns, the three fateful sisters, the Past, the Present, and the Future, with the waters of life from the fountain of Urd that flows on our earth. It will wither and disappear only on the day when the last battle between good and evil is fought ; when, the former prevailing, life, time and space pass out of life and space and time. Every ancient people had their world-tree. The Babylonians had their "tree of life", which was the world-tree, whose roots penetrated into the great lower deep or Hades, whose trunk was on the earth, and whose upper boughs reached *Zikum*, the highest heaven above. Instead of in Walhalla, they placed its upper foliage in the holy house of Davkina, the "great mother" of Tammuz, the Saviour of the world – the Sun-god put to death by the enemies of light.

Yoga (*Sk.*). (1) One of the six Darshanas or schools of India; a school of philosophy founded by Patanjali, though the real Yoga doctrine, the one that is said to have helped to prepare the world for the preaching of Buddha, is attributed with good reasons to the more ancient sage Yâjnawalkya, the writer of the *Shatapatha Brâhmana*, of *Yajur Veda*, the *Brihad Âranyaka*, and other famous works. (2) The practice of meditation as a means of leading to spiritual liberation. Psycho-spiritual powers are obtained thereby, and induced ecstatic states lead to the clear and correct perception of the eternal truths, in both the visible and invisible universe.

Yogâchârya (*Sk.*). (1) A mystic school. (2) Lit., a teacher (*âchârya*) of Yoga, one who has mastered the doctrines and practices of ecstatic meditation – the culmination of which are the *Mahâsiddhis*. It is incorrect to confuse this school with the Tantra, or Mahâtantra school founded by Samantabhadra, for there are two Yogâchârya Schools, one esoteric, the other popular. The doctrines of the latter were compiled and glossed by Asamgha in the sixth century of our era, and his mystic tantras and mantras, his formularies, litanies, spells and mudrâ would certainly, if attempted without a Guru, serve rather purposes of sorcery and black magic than real Yoga. Those who undertake to write upon the subject are generally learned missionaries and haters of Eastern philosophy in general. From these no unbiassed views can be expected. Thus when we read in the *Sanskrit -Chinese Dictionary* of Eitel, that the reciting of mantras (which he calls " spells"!) " should he accompanied by music and distortions of the fingers (mudrâ), that a state of mental fixity (*Samâdhi*} might he reached ' – one acquainted, however slightly,. with the real practice of Yoga can only shrug his shoulders. These distortions of the fingers or ,mudrâ are necessary, the author thinks, for the reaching of Samâdhi, "characterized by there being neither thought nor annihilation of thought, and consisting of six-fold bodily (*sic*) and mental happiness *(yogi) whence would result endowment with supernatural miracle-working power*". Theosophists cannot be too much warned against such fantastic and prejudiced explanations.

Yuga (*Sk.*). A 1,000th part of a Kalpa. An age of the World of which there are four, and the series of which proceed in succession during the manvantaric cycle. Each Yuga is preceded by a period called in the *Purânas* Sandhyâ, twilight, or transition period, and is followed by another period of like duration called Sandhyânsa, "portion of twilight". Each is equal to one-tenth of the Yuga. The group of four Yugas is first computed by the *divine* years, or " years of the gods" – each such year being equal to 360 years of mortal men. Thus we have, in "divine" years :

	AGE	YEARS
1	Krita or Satya Yuga	4,000
	Sandhyâ	400
	Sandhyansa	400
		4,800

2	Tretâ Yuga	3,000
	Sandhyâ	300
	Sandhyânsa	300
		3,600

3	Dwâpara Yuga	2,000
	Sandhya	200
	Sandhyânsa	200
		2,400

4	Kali Yuga	1,000
	Sandhyâ	100
	Sandhyânsa	100
		1,200
	Total =	**12,000**

This rendered in years of mortals equals:

4,800	X	360	=	1,728,000
3,600	X	360	=	1,296,000
2,400	X	360	=	864,000
1,200	X	360	=	432,000
		Total	=	4,320,000

The above is called a Mahâyuga or Manvantara. 2,000 such Mahâyugas, or a period of 8,640,000 years, make a Kalpa the latter being only a "day and a night", or twenty-four hours, of Brahmâ. Thus an "age of Brahmâ", or one hundred of his divine years, must equal 311,040,000,000,000 of our mortal years. The old Mazdeans or Magi (the modern Parsis) had the same calculation, though the Orientalists do not seem to perceive it, for even the Parsi Moheds themselves have forgotten it. But their "Sovereign time of the Long Period" (*Zervan Dareghâ Hvadâta*) lasts 12,000 years, and these are the 12,000 *divine* years of a Mahâyuga as shown above, whereas the *Zervan Akarana* (Limitless Time), mentioned by Zarathustra, is the *Kâla*, out of space and time, of Parabrahm.

Z

Zend-Avesta (*Pahl.*). The general name for the sacred books of the Parsis, fire or sun worshippers, as they are ignorantly called. So little is understood of the grand doctrines which are still found in the various fragments that compose all that is now left of that collection of religious works, that Zoroastrianism is called indifferently Fire-worship, Mazdaism, or Magism, Dualism, Sun-worship, and what not. The *Avesta* has two parts as now collected together, the first portion containing the *Vendîdâd*, the *Vispêrad* and the *Yasna*; and the second portion, called the *Khorda Avesta* (Small Avesta), being composed of short prayers called Gâh, Nyâyish, etc. *Zend* means "a commentary or explanation", and *Avesta* (from the old Persian *âbashtâ*, "the law". (See Darmsteter.) As the translator of the Vendîdâd remarks in a foot note (see int. xxx.): "what it is customary to call 'the Zend language', ought to be named 'the Avesta language', the Zend being no language at all and if the word be used as the designation of one, it can be rightly applied only to the Pahlavi". But then, the Pahlavi itself is only the language into which certain original portions of the *Avesta* are translated. What name should be given to the old *Avesta* language, and particularly to the "special dialect, older than the general language of the *Avesta*" (Darmst.), in which the five Ghthas in the *Yasna* are written? To this day the Orientalists are mute upon the subject. Why should not the Zend be of the same family, if not identical with the Zen-sar, meaning also the speech explaining the abstract symbol, or the "mystery language," used by Initiates?

Zeus (*Gr.*). The "Father of the gods". *Zeus-Zen* is Æther, there fore Jupiter was called Pater Æther by some Latin races.

Zodiac (*Gr.*). From the word *zodion*, a diminutive of *zoon*, animal. This word is used in a dual meaning; it may refer to the fixed and intellectual Zodiac, or to the movable and natural Zodiac. "In astronomy", says Science, "it is an imaginary belt in the heavens 16° or 18° broad, through the middle of which passes the sun's path (the ecliptic) ."It contains the twelve constellations which constitute the twelve signs of the Zodiac, and from which they are named. As the nature of the *zodiacal light* – that elongated, luminous, triangular figure which, lying almost in the ecliptic, with its base on the horizon and its apex at greater and smaller altitudes, is to be seen only during the morning and evening twilights – is entirely unknown to science, the origin and real significance and occult meaning of the Zodiac were, and are still, a mystery, to all save the Initiates. The latter preserved their secrets well. Between the Chaldean star-gazer and the modern astrologer there lies to this day a wide gulf indeed; and they wander, in the words of Albumazar, "'twixt the poles, and heavenly hinges, 'mongst eccentricals, centres, concentricks, circles and epicycles", with vain pretence to more than *profane* human skill. Yet, some of the astrologers, from Tycho Braire and Kepler of astrological memory, down to the modern Zadkiels and Raphaels, have contrived to make a wonderful science from such scanty occult materials as they have had in hand from Ptolemy downwards. (See "Astrology".) To return to the astrological Zodiac proper, however, it is an imaginary circle passing round the earth in the plane of the equator, its first point being called Aries 0º. It is divided into twelve equal parts called "Signs of the Zodiac", each containing 30º of space, and on it is measured the right ascension of celestial bodies. The movable or natural Zodiac is a succession of constellations forming a belt of in width, lying north and south of the plane of the ecliptic. The precession of the Equinoxes is caused by the "motion" of the sun through space, which makes the constellations appear to move forward against the order of the signs at the rate of 501/3 seconds per year. A simple calculation will show that at this rate the constellation Taurus (Heb. *Aleph*) was in the first sign of the Zodiac at the beginning of the Kali Yuga, and consequently the Equinoctial point fell therein. At this time, also, Leo was in the summer solstice, Scorpio in the autumnal Equinox, and Aquarius in the winter solstice ; and these facts form the astronomical key to half the religious mysteries of the world- – the Christian scheme included. The Zodiac was known in India and Egypt for incalculable ages, and the knowledge of the sages (magi) of these countries, with regard to the occult influence of the stars and heavenly bodies on our earth, was far greater than profane astronomy can ever hope to reach to. If, even now, when most of the secrets of the Asuramayas and the Zoroasters are lost, it is still amply shown that horoscopes and judiciary astrology are far from being based on fiction, and if such men as Kepler and even Sir Isaac Newton believed that stars and constellations influenced the destiny of our globe and its humanities, it requires no great stretch of faith to believe that men who were initiated into all the mysteries of nature, as well as into astronomy and astrology, knew precisely in what way nations and mankind, whole races as well as individuals, would be affected by the so-called "signs of the Zodiac".

Zohar, or *Sohar*. A compendium of Kabbalistic Theosophy, which shares with the *Sepher Yetzirah* the reputation of being the oldest extant treatise on the Hebrew esoteric religious doctrines. Tradition assigns its authorship to Rabbi Simeon ben Jochai, AD. 80, but modern criticism is inclined to believe that a very large portion of the volume is no older than 1280, when it was certainly edited and published by Rabbi Moses de Leon, of Guadalaxara in Spain. The reader should consult the references to these two names. In *Lucifer* (Vol. I., p. 141) will be found also notes on this subject : further discussion will be attainable in the works of Zunz, Graetz, Jost, Steinschneider, Frankel and Ginsburg. The work of Franck (in French) upon the *Kabalah* may be referred to with advantage. The truth seems to lie in a middle path, viz., that while Moses de Leon was the first to produce the volume as a whole, yet a large part of some of its constituent tracts consists of traditional dogmas and illustrations, which have come down from the time of Simeon ben Jochai and the Second Temple. There are portions of the doctrines of the Zohar which bear the impress of Chaldee thought and civilization, to which the Jewish race had been exposed in the Babylonish captivity. Yet on the other hand, to condemn the theory that it is ancient in its entirety, it is noticed that the Crusades are mentioned; that a quotation is made from a hymn by Ibn Gebirol, A,D. 1050; that the asserted author, Simeon ben Jochai, is spoken of as more eminent than Moses; that it mentions the vowel-points, which did not come into use until Rabbi Mocha (AD. 570) introduced them to fix the pronunciation of words as a help to his pupils, and lastly, that it mentions -a comet which can be proved by the evidence of the context to have appeared in 1264. There is no English translation of the *Zohar* as a whole, nor even a Latin one.

Zoroaster. Greek form of Zarathustra (q.v.).

Zoroastrian. One who follows the religion of the Parsis, sun, or fire-worshippers.

For additional explanations of theosophical terminology, readers should consult *THE THEOSOPHICAL GLOSSARY* at http://www.theosophytrust.org/HPB_index.php.

Index

A

Absolute 4, 7, 8, 9, 23, 43, 134, 162, 209, 340
Absolute Consciousness 7
Adam 12, 13, 21, 43, 44, 45, 74, 75, 77, 82, 100, 101, 103, 108, 117, 119, 123, 133, 138, 149, 150, 152, 157, 158, 159, 162, 172, 186, 199, 203, 207, 216, 217, 257
Adam and Eve 117, 133, 207, 216, 217
Adam Kadmon 21, 43, 44, 45, 74, 75, 101, 103, 108
Adepts 35
Aditi 74, 87, 88, 144, 189, 203, 237, 238
Advaita 76, 247
Adwaitee 7
Aeschylus 218, 219, 220, 221, 231, 234, 236
Æther 12
Agathodaemon 115
Agni 130, 189, 220, 230, 237
Agnishwatta (s) 23, 118, 119, 120, 125, 126, 129, 218, 235, 257
Agnishwatta Pitris 23, 119
Aham 11, 79
Ahamkara 69, 70, 71, 250
Ahankâra 78, 79
Ahura-Mazdha 130
Ahura Mazda 136
Ain-Soph 43, 44, 71, 73
Aitareya Brahmana 10
Akâsa 12, 78, 85, 87
ALAYA 4
amanasa 128
Ambhamsi 84, 85, 87
Amshaspends 60, 74, 130
Ananta 9
Anaxagoras 6, 76
Ancient of Days 86
Androgyne(s) 45, 101, 166, 172
Angelic Host 53
Angels 47, 51, 55, 60, 71, 84, 85, 100, 103, 108, 110, 113, 114, 115, 122, 125, 131, 132, 133, 139, 140, 148, 149, 162, 176, 177, 178, 181, 183, 187, 188, 190, 202, 207, 208
Animal Man 58
Anima Mundi 4, 5, 6

B

C

G

L

M

N

O

P

For, on Path fourth, the lightest breeze of passion or desire will stir the steady light upon the pure white walls of Soul. The smallest wave of longing or regret for Maya's gifts illusive, along Antaskarana — the path that lies between thy Spirit and thy self, the highway of sensations, the rude arousers of Ahankara — a thought as fleeting as the lightning flash will make thee thy three prizes forfeit — the prizes thou hast won.

For know, that the ETERNAL knows no change.

"The eight dire miseries forsake for evermore. If not, to wisdom, sure, thou can'st not come, nor yet to liberation," saith the great Lord, the Tathagata of perfection, "he who has followed in the footsteps of his predecessors."

Stern and exacting is the virtue of Viraga. If thou its path would'st master, thou must keep thy mind and thy perceptions far freer than before from killing action.

Thou hast to saturate thyself with pure Alaya, become as one with Nature's Soul-Thought. At one with it thou art invincible; in separation, thou becomest the playground of Samvriti, origin of all the world's delusions.

All is impermanent in man except the pure bright essence of Alaya. Man is its crystal ray; a beam of light immaculate within, a form of clay material upon the lower surface. That beam is thy life-guide and thy true Self, the Watcher and the silent Thinker, the victim of thy lower Self. Thy Soul cannot be hurt but through thy erring body; control and master both, and thou art safe when crossing to the nearing "Gate of Balance."

Be of good cheer, O daring pilgrim "to the other shore." Heed not the whisperings of Mara's hosts; wave off the tempters, those ill-natured Sprites, the jealous Lhamayin in endless space.

Hold firm! Thou nearest now the middle portal, the gate of Woe, with its ten thousand snares.

Have mastery o'er thy thoughts, O striver for perfection, if thou would'st cross its threshold.

Have mastery o'er thy Soul, O seeker after truths undying, if thou would'st reach the goal.

Thy Soul-gaze centre on the One Pure Light, the Light that is free from affection, and use thy golden Key. .

The Seven Portals
H. P. Blavatsky

978-0-9793205-4-5

0-9793205-4-2

www.ingramcontent.com/pod-product-compliance
Lightning Source LLC
Chambersburg PA
CBHW021042090426
42738CB00006B/149

AND now, O Teacher of Compassion, point thou the way to other men. Behold, all those who knocking for admission, await in ignorance and darkness, to see the gate of the Sweet Law flung open!

The voice of the Candidates:

Shalt not thou, Master of thine own Mercy, reveal the Doctrine of the Heart? Shalt thou refuse to lead thy Servants unto the Path of Liberation?

Quoth the Teacher:

The Paths are two; the great Perfections three; six are the Virtues that transform the body into the Tree of Knowledge.

Who shall approach them?

Who shall first enter them?

Who shall first hear the doctrine of two Paths in one, the truth unveiled about the Secret Heart? The Law which, shunning learning, teaches Wisdom, reveals a tale of woe.

Alas, alas, that all men should possess Alaya, be one with the great Soul, and that possessing it, Alaya should so little avail them!

Behold how like the moon, reflected in the tranquil waves, Alaya is reflected by the small and by the great, is mirrored in the tiniest atoms, yet fails to reach the heart of all. Alas, that so few men should profit by the gift, the priceless boon of learning truth, the right perception of existing things, the Knowledge of the non-existent!

Saith the pupil:

O Teacher, what shall I do to reach to Wisdom?

O Wise one, what, to gain perfection?

Search for the Paths. But, O Lanoo, be of clean heart before thou startest on thy journey. Before thou takest thy first step learn to discern the real from the false, the ever-fleeting from the everlasting. Learn above all to separate Head-learning from Soul-Wisdom, the "Eye" from the "Heart" doctrine.

Yea, ignorance is like unto a closed and airless vessel; the soul a bird shut up within. It warbles not, nor can it stir a feather; but the songster mute and torpid sits, and of exhaustion dies.

But even ignorance is better than Head-learning with no Soul-wisdom to illuminate and guide it.

The Seven Portals
H. P. Blavatsky